THE EAST GERMAN NOVEL

THE EAST GERMAN NOVEL

Identity, Community, Continuity

Dennis Tate

St. Martin's Press
New York

© Bath University Press, 1984

All rights reserved. For information, write:
St. Martin's Press Inc.,
175 Fifth Avenue, New York, NY 10010

Printed in Great Britain

First published in the United States of America in 1984

ISBN 0-312-22487-7

Library of Congress Cataloging in Publication Data

Tate, Dennis.
  The East German novel.

  Bibliography: p.
  Includes index.
  1. German fiction—Germany (East)—History and
  criticism. I. Title.
  PT3723.T38 1984   833'.914'099431   84-18388
  ISBN 0-312-22487-7

CONTENTS

PREFACE

Only a decade ago, influential sectors of academic
opinion in this country still felt able to dismiss East
German creative writing in a phrase like 'Boy meets
Tractor literature'. Today, the study of the culture and
institutions of the German Democratic Republic is a major
growth area in German studies, supported in Western Europe
by specialist journals such as <u>Connaissance de la RDA</u>
(1976-), <u>GDR Monitor</u> (1979-) and the <u>Jahrbuch zur Literatur
in der DDR</u> (1980-). There are many reasons for this rapid
change of affairs - the most obvious include the fostering
of the spirit of unprejudiced inquiry into Eastern European
cultures by the process of detente in the 1970s; the increasing recognition of the value of studying literature
in its socio-political context, which is nowhere more
urgently needed than amidst the complexities of the post-
war German-speaking world; the special status of East
German literature as the most accessible in Eastern Europe,
both for reasons of the language in which it is written
and because it is rooted in the (relatively) familiar
culture of the 'Goethe era'; and the Western fascination
with a literature which has retained the social significance
which our own has long since surrendered to the mass media
and the social sciences. East German literature is the
most reliable source of critical information about the
GDR, and its authors are influential citizens, both
flattered and morally burdened by the awareness that their
writing is of such vital importance to their large domestic
readership.

The reception of East German literature in the West
has, in consequence, become more discriminating in recent
years, leading to a steady flow of publications, some devoted to the intricacies of 'Kulturpolitik', others acknowledging the European stature of authors such as Christa
Wolf and Johannes Bobrowski. This study is concerned
with the mainstream development of prose-writing, from its
theoretical origins - which actually predate the establishment of the GDR - in the exile debates of the 1930s, up
to the present day. It identifies five phases within this
development, each of which is marked by significant changes
in narrative structure and thematic focus. The contradictions of the period up to 1956, preoccupied with the
idea of establishing a prototype for a distinctively
German Socialist Realism, are exemplified in the work of
Johannes R. Becher, one of the GDR's founding fathers.
The four subsequent phases are each characterised by means
of a comparative analysis of a group of thematically related novels: the 'war novels' and the 'industrial novels'

of the 1956-65 period are viewed as the cautious endeavours of a new generation of authors to assert their creative independence; the 'contemporary biographies' and the historically based 'epic prose' published by the same generation of authors between 1965 and 1981 provide the evidence that East German literature has attained a new standard of authenticity in overcoming the constraints imposed by the cultural policy of the ruling Socialist Unity Party (SED).

Within each group of novels, the authors' presentation of the process of personality growth is significantly modified. At first, the achievement of identity appears to depend exclusively on the integration of the fictional protagonist into a rapidly evolving socialist 'Gemeinschaft'. Gradually, however, as the untenability of ideological preconceptions about the quality of communal experience available in the post-1945 era of German socialism becomes evident, the importance of the dimension of continuity in the protagonist's progress towards mature self-knowledge is acknowledged. At each stage of the development of East German fiction, the complex interplay between the demands of 'community' and 'continuity' produces a new perspective on the ultimate goal of self-realisation. The goal initially viewed as automatically attainable following the establishment of a socialist state is now shown to be depressingly remote from contemporary realities, although the authors continue to cling tenaciously to their conviction that it can still eventually be achieved.

My title, The East German Novel, represents something of an uneasy compromise. On the one hand, as the framework for the body of fiction I am concerned with was established before the creation of the German Democratic Republic in 1949, it could appear restrictive to refer simply to the novel "in the GDR". I have therefore opted for the politically vaguer adjective "East German", which has the modest virtue of taking us four years further back historically. On the other hand, I have retained the term "novel", even though this study necessarily includes works in which the demarcation line between biographical fiction and autobiography is deliberately blurred, and in which 'subjective authenticity' becomes a more important criterion than the pursuit of the more objective typicality of the traditional novel. "Prose" seems excessively comprehensive and colourless as an alternative. The other possibility, of a specifically cultural reference to "German Socialist Realism", is again too broad and might well prove misleading, given that a recurrent aspect of the development I shall be describing is the authors' struggle to extend the frontiers of what the SED's cultural politicians are prepared to acknowledge at any given time as Socialist Realism.

My focus on some twenty works of creative prose which exemplify this mainstream development within East German literature provides scope for a critical assessment of the individual progress of several important authors – J.R. Becher, Günter de Bruyn, Hermann Kant, Erik Neutsch, Brigitte Reimann and Christa Wolf – although it does mean, regrettably, that others who easily merit more detailed treatment, notably Franz Fühmann, Johannes Bobrowski and Volker Braun, have to be judged here primarily on the evidence of a single work. The comparative structure of each chapter also makes it impossible to consider inimitable achievements, such as Jurek Becker's <u>Jakob der Lügner</u>, Irmtraud Morgner's <u>Trobadora Beatriz</u> or Stefan Heym's <u>Fünf Tage im Juni</u>. The alternative would, however, have been a looser sequence of essays without the narrative and thematic coherence which is – for reasons more contradictory than the notion of a centrally controlled 'Kulturpolitik' implies – the dominant feature of the East German novel so far.

I wish to thank friends and colleagues at the University of Warwick, the New University of Ulster and the University of Bath for the support they have given me during the time I have been working on this subject. I owe special debts of gratitude to the late Roy Pascal, whose inspiring teaching laid the foundations for what has become this book, and to Richard Hinton Thomas, who guided its earlier progress with a wealth of helpful criticism and unfailing encouragement, and whose death during the final weeks of its production has been a great blow to me. I should also like to thank Geoffrey Butler for reading the text with such care and drawing my attention to many details which needed correction or clarification. Helga Yeates has produced this typescript with admirable efficiency and precision. My final word of thanks is to Sylvia, for bearing with me over the years.

Dennis Tate
University of Bath

INTRODUCTION

LUKÁCS AND THE CULTURAL HERITAGE

The blueprint for the East German novel was drawn up more than a decade before the German Democratic Republic came into existence; creative writers were prepared, for over twenty years thereafter, to deny the validity of their personal experience in conformity with it; and it was still being followed after the draughtsman himself had been publicly discredited. The dominant influence of Georg Lukács' literary criticism of the 1930s upon some thirty years of German socialist writing - from the end of the Weimar Republic, through the years of exile from Hitler's Germany and the post-war reconstruction in what was to become the GDR, and in the face of his unacceptable political involvement in the Hungarian uprising of 1956 - is characterised by such paradoxes. Although they can be explained partly by the authoritative coherence of Lukács' theory of literature (as evolved between 1931 and 1945) amidst a uniquely disorientating set of historical circumstances, they also derive from his strategic acuteness as a mediator between a Party bureaucracy seeking to reduce literature to an arm of propaganda and the creative independence of the author (or rather, those authors whom he regarded as true 'realists'). Those German socialist authors who, in the 1930s, adopted radically different perspectives on contemporary reality, found the gulf separating them from the cultural policy of the era of Stalin's purges unbridgeable. There was, in contrast, just enough common ground between Lukács and the administrators of Soviet Socialist Realism to allow him to pave the way for an East German literature of greater originality and authenticity than its mainstream Soviet counterpart. Nevertheless, the obsolescence of Lukács' ideological framework in terms of twentieth century experience was storing up difficulties of a different order for a future generation of writers.

The story might have been quite different if the vigorous public debate of the last years of the Weimar Republic on the form and the content of a distinctive German socialist culture had not been prematurely resolved in the aftermath of Hitler's rise to power in 1933. For although the debate was to continue after a whole generation of anti-fascist authors had been driven into exile - at their conference in Paris in 1935, or in the columns of newly established journals such as _Internationale Literatur_ or _Das Wort_ - the effective powers for determining the cultural policy of Germany's literary exiles were in the hands of the small group of leading Communist Party (KPD) exiles in the Soviet Union, whose intellectual mentor was Lukács.[1]

From the time that Lukács arrived in Berlin in the summer of 1931, he had been waging a "Kampf an zwei Fronten".[2] He had secured the support of the KPD's hierarchy to settle what they saw as sectarian conflict within the Bund proletarisch-revolutionärer Schriftsteller (BPRS) by discrediting its left wing (including Bertolt Brecht) and strengthening its leadership (under Johannes R. Becher). Quite independently, he was determined to counter the 'Proletkult' tendency, which was intent on aligning literature too rigidly with short-term propaganda needs, and thus threatening Lukács' plan for a cultural Popular Front to embrace established authors like Thomas Mann in the struggle against fascism. Lukács' essays of 1931-32 in the BPRS journal, Die Linkskurve, correspondingly marked the beginning of what - from today's perspective - was an indiscriminate assault on the broad spectrum of contemporary literature which threatened his pursuit of cultural unity, an assault conducted - or so it seems at first sight - on purely formal grounds. The overtly propagandist writing of working-class authors, exemplified by Willi Bredel's novels, was rejected as firmly as the innovations of a heterogeneous 'avant-garde', which included Brecht's didactic plays, the entire Expressionist movement and the wealth of new fictional techniques - inner monologue, montage, multi-perspective narration, free indirect speech, and so on - developed by 'decadent' authors such as Joyce, Dos Passos, Döblin and Kafka.

On closer inspection, however, it becomes clear that Lukács saw an indissoluble link between the author's choice of literary form and his view of the individual. Indeed, all the 'models' he was rejecting during the 1930s had one central feature in common: they had abandoned the organic conception of the human quest for identity, fundamental to classical European literature of the eighteenth and nineteenth centuries. Willi Bredel's characters are thus inauthentic because they show "keine Entwicklung" or, at best, "verwandeln ... sich mit einem Ruck"; the development of Ernst Ottwalt's hero ("Entwicklung" in inverted commas) in his reportage novel has been reduced to a "Rechenexempel", too schematic to leave scope for the unpredictable role of chance in normal experience; the characters of Expressionist drama (on the evidence of Hasenclever's Der Sohn) are "bloße Schattenrisse" displaying abstract emotions; and the "neuer Mensch" of the emerging Soviet Socialist Realism is no

more authentic - many recent novels being "statt mit Menschen mit einer Silhouettengalerie lebloser Schemata be-
völkert". For Lukács, the achievement of identity cannot
be separated from the notion of continuity of experience,
however much committed socialist authors may prefer to
dramatise a crucial moment of "Wandlung", of pseudo-
religious conversion, when their potential heroes see the
light of socialism:

> Der neue Mensch entsteht nicht fertig, nicht als
> ausschließender Gegensatz des alten, mit dem er
> dann gar nichts Gemeinsames hätte. Seine Existenz
> ist vielmehr von dem Kampf mit den Überresten des
> Kapitalismus überhaupt nicht zu trennen. Erst in
> diesem Kampfe entstehen und entfalten sich jene
> menschlichen Eigenschaften, die den neuen Menschen
> wirklich und konkret charakterisieren.

Similarly, the attempt to portray the emerging socialist
society as a spontaneous, harmonious community - "jene
abstrakte 'Gemeinschaft', die dem bürgerlichen Individual-
ismus gegenübergestellt wird" - is a completely misguided
recourse to bourgeois simplifications. The dichotomy between 'Gemeinschaft' and 'Gesellschaft' (as defined historically by Tönnies in his sociological study of 1887
and seized upon by the Expressionists for their idealised
visions of a future brotherhood of man) is, for Lukács,
an unacceptable shortcut for socialist writers to adopt,
since it means that the community depicted " [steht] in gar
keiner organischen Verbindung mit den großen Problemen
des sozialistischen Aufbaus". [3]
The dominant characteristic of these essays of the
1930s on contemporary literature is their negativity:
apart from his occasional praise, in passing, for authors
like Maxim Gorky and Thomas Mann, Lukács finds little
evidence that the organic nature of personal and social
development is either understood or convincingly portrayed.
He displays constructive intentions, however, in putting
these defects down to a basic misunderstanding of how
literature can contribute to radical social change, rather
than to lack of creative talent. He implies that, in
their endeavours to make an immediate political impact,
the revolutionary writers of his day had set their sights
too low, and could therefore not yet be considered as
genuine creative artists. The answer he provides to his
series of programmatic questions on whether socialist
literature should represent a fundamental break with bourgeois traditions - "Tendenz oder Parteilichkeit", "Reportage oder Gestaltung", "Erzählen oder Beschreiben" - is
that the function of the artist should not change signi-

ficantly in the era of socialism. The proletarian-
revolutionary writer is superior to his forbears because
of his command of dialectical materialism, which supplies
the correct perspective for a "Darstellung der objektiven
Wirklichkeit mit ihren wirklichen treibenden Kräften, mit
ihren wirklichen Entwicklungstendenzen". He should, however, remain, like them, an independent voice, whose
creative imagination is a more reliable guide to the objective understanding of his world than his politically
conscious intellect. [4] Partisanship is thus seen - in
direct contradiction to the views of the first generation
of Soviet cultural politicians, as exemplified by Zhdanov -
as the logical consequence of employing the organic
techniques of nineteenth century realism, since the historical "Prozeß" is leading inexorably towards the goal of
socialist society. For this reason, continuity - in terms
of building upon the common heritage of exemplary "Dichter"
and outstanding literary works - is just as crucial to
cultural development as it is on the personal and social
level.

In the Berlin of 1931-32, Lukács' expectations knew no
limits: the "höhere Aufgabe" he set out for his colleagues
in the BPRS was to create "das große proletarische Kunstwerk" - a novel achieving a Tolstoyan blend of insight into
personality growth and totality of social portrayal,
written from a perspective which shows the underlying
"Entwicklungstendenzen" to be those of revolutionary socialism. [5] Only a literature of such classical distinction
could make headway against the competition of the escapist
fiction deliberately mass-produced by a reactionary
establishment. With hindsight, it seems incredible that
this objective was the cornerstone of the BPRS policy
document drafted in 1932, during the last desperate months
of ideological struggle before the Nazis came to power.
The creation of such neo-Tolstoyan masterpieces would have
been the task of many tranquil years, while the relationship between quality and political impact might have seemed
a more dubious article of faith in the age of the electroni
media than in the lifetime of Dickens or Balzac or Tolstoy:

> Massenwirkung und Spitzenleistung sind in unserer
> Literatur keine Gegensätze, wie in der bürgerlichen
> Literatur der Gegenwart, im Gegenteil, sie bedingen
> sich wechselseitig. Nur durch die Erhöhung der
> künstlerischen Leistung ... können wir eine wirk-
> liche Massenbeeinflussung erreichen. [6]

Furthermore, the sense of cultural continuity Lukács was
seeking to cultivate was European rather than national,
believing no doubt that the internationalism of the post-

Russian-revolutionary era could compensate for the absence
of a distinctive German tradition of panoramic fictional
realism - a situation directly attributable to the political and economic backwardness of a fragmented nation, or
what Lukács was later to refer to simply as the "deutsche
Misere".[7]

The enforced exile which followed Hitler's rise to
power in 1933 brought about an important modification in
Lukács' strategy for German socialist culture. Amongst
the exiled writers there was a marked heightening of
patriotic sentiments, as they saw themselves engaged in a
desperate struggle (emotional as much as ideological) with
the fascists for the soul of the German nation, with each
claiming its noblest virtues and cultural achievements as
part of their own exclusive heritage. This situation encouraged a backward-looking yearning for the (imagined)
purity of the pre-capitalist, pre-fascist era, which they
sought to contrast in black-and-white terms with the
horror of the Third Reich, with the aid of emotive terms
such as 'Heimat' and 'Gemeinschaft'. As this coincided,
at least for German literary exiles in the Soviet Union,
with Zhdanov's exhortations - in the name of a patriotic
'revolutionary romanticism' - to writers to transform their
dreams of the socialist future into the contemporary
reality of their fiction, there was an obvious danger
that what Lukács saw as this abstract, bourgeois concept
of 'Gemeinschaft' would distort the literary portrayal of
Germany's past as well as of its potential for future
change.

It is in this context that Lukács' essay of 1936 on
Goethe's Wilhelm Meisters Lehrjahre should be seen.[8]
Following upon the negative tone of the bulk of Lukács'
own criticism since 1931 and the potentially disorientating
situation of exile, this essay establishes a model which
German authors might be more realistically expected to
emulate than the nebulous "großes proletarisches Kunstwerk". Lukács is now taking account of the uniqueness
of a German cultural heritage which finds its highest
expression in the line of 'Entwicklungsromane' stretching
from Goethe's Wilhelm Meister and Hölderlin's Hyperion
to Keller's Der grüne Heinrich and Thomas Mann's Der
Zauberberg. In doing so, he is also seeking to remind his
contemporaries that the 'deutsche Misere', which prevents
historically 'typical' figures such as Wilhelm Meister
from achieving the goal of identity through productive
social activity, is a deeply rooted phenomenon in a pre-
capitalist past which showed few of the features of
Tönnies' 'Gemeinschaft'. This focus on the classical
'Entwicklungsroman' also effectively leaves the issue of

the quality of a future German socialist society on the
horizon, while reopening the neglected prior issue of how
each individual can best develop the unique potential
which should form the basis of social progress. (It
might further have served to remind a 1930s readership
of the key passage in the Communist Manifesto, in which
"die freie Entwicklung eines jeden" is acknowledged to be
the condition for "die freie Entwicklung aller").[9]
   Goethe's supreme achievement in Wilhelm Meisters Lehrjahre is, according to Lukács, in illuminating the complicated process of how true individuality develops:

   [Er] stellt ... in diesem Roman mit einer Deutlich-
   keit und Prägnanz wie kaum ein Schriftsteller in
   irgendeinem anderen Werk der Weltliteratur den
   Menschen, die Verwirklichung und Entfaltung seiner
   Persönlichkeit in den Mittelpunkt.

The goal is "allseitige Entwicklung", to reverse the
disastrous effects of the division of labour,
and the process is unquestionably organic: "diese
schlummernden Kräfte in jedem einzelnen Menschen [sind]
zu erwecken, zur fruchtbaren Tätigkeit ... heranzubilden";
"die Menschen [sollen] kraft freier organischer Tätigkeit
gesellschaftlich werden". Education is an integral part
of this growth, although its effects cannot be easily
measured, and not at all in the short term. The group of
mature individuals - 'die Gesellschaft des Turms' - who
take it upon themselves to direct Wilhelm's progress are
not overtly successful, since unpredictable accidental
factors have such a major bearing upon its course. What
Goethe successfully demonstrates is "eine Einheit von
Planmäßigkeit und Zufall im menschlichen Leben, von be-
wußter Leitung und freier Spontaneität in allen Betätig-
ungen des Menschen". In the midst of a reactionary
society such an enlightened elite represents "die Keim-
zelle des Kommenden", an artificial island, but nevertheless one on which the utopian humanist dream of the self-
fulfilment of the individual comes historically closer to
attainment: "die Erfüllung der vollentfalteten Persönlichkeit" is presented as "ein reales Werden konkreter
Menschen unter konkreten Umständen". It is, of course,
still a considerable way from realisation, since real
identity - "Harmonie der Persönlichkeit und harmonische[s]
Zusammenwirken der freien Menschen" - will only become
possible under socialism.
   Lukács attaches great importance to structural features
of Wilhelm Meister: on the one hand, the omniscient,
ironical narrative perspective and the adoption of "dieses
bewußte erzieherische Prinzip", on the other, the movement

it indicates towards representative experience, away from
the narrow self-centred world of Goethe's first version,
Wilhelm Meisters Theatralische Sendung. This enables
Goethe to adopt a systematic, classical approach to
characterisation, achieving for each fictional figure a
blend of the 'typical' and the 'individual', and allowing
each to be located within a "Hierarchie der menschlichen
Bedeutsamkeit". Lukács also places Wilhelm Meister in a
revealing historical context, suggesting that its underlying optimism derives from the fact that it was written
during the "revolutionäre Übergangskrise" of 1793-95,
when it still seemed possible that the French Revolution
would pave the way towards the realisation of the dream of
identity - before the drift towards Napoleon's emperorship
finally dashed these hopes.

    He then emphasises that, when this historical tragedy
occurred, Goethe opted for a pragmatic accommodation with
the 'deutsche Misere', rather than falling prey to "die
blinde Revolte, die falsche Poesie der Romantik", as many
of his fellow-writers did. Wilhelm Meister's "Erziehung
... zum praktischen Verständnis der Wirklichkeit" consequently also involves learning how to compromise with
a highly imperfect reality, and not indulging in futile
self-sacrifice in the pursuit of absolute ideals. Lukács
had treated the same dilemma at greater length in his
slightly earlier essay on Hölderlin's Hyperion, which he
concluded with a clear contrast between these two examples
of what he always preferred to call the 'Erziehungsroman':

> Hölderlin stellt dem Goetheschen 'Erziehungsroman'
> zur Anpassung an die kapitalistische Wirklichkeit
> einen 'Erziehungsroman' zum heroischen Widerstand
> gegen diese Wirklichkeit entgegen.

The reason why he adjudged Goethe (and Hölderlin's
counterpart, Hegel) to be historically correct in their
compromise with a reactionary society was that it allowed
both of them to rescue and develop "das beste Erbe der
bürgerlichen Gedankenentwicklung, wenn auch in einer vielfach verbogenen und kleinlich gemachten Form", whereas
Hölderlin wasted his tremendous potential by driving himself into the "verzweifelte Sackgasse" of mental illness. [10]

    Neither Lukács' analysis of Wilhelm Meister nor his
account of Goethe's reactions to the "revolutionäre Übergangskrise" of the 1790s was purely historical. As well
as underlining the continuity of the individual's quest
for self-realisation over more than a century of German
history, Lukács also seemed to be hinting at a broad
parallelism between that turbulent era and his own day.

His final paragraph makes the point that Wilhelm Meister
is not only "ein unverlierbares Erbe für uns", but also
"ein sehr aktuelles Erbe". It comes as close as was
possible in Stalin's Soviet Union of 1936 to condemning
Socialist Realism, in its original conception, as a
vehicle for depicting the individual: "denn gerade die
ruhig-harmonische und doch sinnlich-einprägsame Gestaltung
der geistig und seelisch wichtigen Entwicklungen ist eine
der großen Aufgaben, die der sozialistische Realismus zu
lösen hat". There is also a message for the Party hierarchy - a modern 'Gesellschaft des Turms' - in his emphasis on the subtlety of Goethe's educational principle.

On the other hand, Lukács' positive view of the accommodation made by Goethe to 'post-Thermidorian' reality is
a means of justifying his own attitude to Stalinism after
emigrating to the Soviet Union in 1933. What Michael
Löwy, in his stimulating study of Lukács, has called his
"consistent attempt to 'reconcile' Stalinism with bourgeois democratic culture" [11] was based on the conviction
that the Soviet system had to be reformed from within,
and that short-term compromise was necessary if it allowed
him to survive and influence the longer-term progress of
communism into a genuinely democratic mass-movement. He
thus saw himself following Goethe's example in a new era
of post-revolutionary frustration - and was undoubtedly
prepared to risk a great deal more than Goethe in personal
terms in his strategic commitment to a better society.
In several key respects, therefore, Wilhelm Meister was the
obvious literary model for a German literature in exile
to emulate, in the 'Übergangszeit' of unpredictable duration
which would finally put an end to the 'deutsche Misere',
in order to lay a solid foundation for the German socialist
culture of the future.

Having insisted, through this analysis, on the absence
of genuine 'Gemeinschaft' in the German past, Lukács provided undoubted consolation for many of his fellow-
exiles when he turned his attentions to Der grüne Heinrich,
in the essay on Keller published in 1939. [12] For not
only did he bracket it together with Wilhelm Meister as
the only other "Erziehungsroman im engen und eigentlichen
Sinne", in which "Individuum und Gesellschaft noch nicht
unversöhnlich-feindlich aufeinanderprallen" - written
during another, lengthier era of transition, between the
1848 revolutions and the establishment of capitalism in
Swiss society. He also saw in the nineteenth century Swiss
society in which Heinrich Lee grows up - this "real-
existierende, noch vielfach urwüchsige Schweizer Demokratie" - a fundamental contrast to Wilhelm Meister's
Germany. Heinrich is brought up "in einer gewissen, wenn

auch oft problematischen Gemeinschaft" and later experiences
"die naturwüchsige Gemeinschaft der Künstler, später der
Handwerker und Arbeiter in München, die spontane Verbunden-
heit der echten Intellektuellen im Grafenschloß".
Capitalist alienation is still worlds away from this "Volk"
which "besteht ... aus lebendigen, individuell dargestellten
Persönlichkeiten", whose festivals are "organische, aus
dem Leben herausgewachsene natürliche Vereinigungen solcher
Individuen". Here a natural evolution into socialism
and the achievement of identity seem possible. Keller's
conviction that "individuelle Erfüllung der Persönlichkeit
und fruchtbare gesellschaftliche Wirksamkeit letzten Endes
harmonisch zusammenfallen müssen" is thwarted by the rise
of the Swiss bourgeoisie towards the end of his life. His
novel, however, proves to Lukács that "die Erfüllung der
Individualität in der sozialistischen Demokratie ist nicht
etwas radikal Neues, sondern eben die Erfüllung von jahr-
hunderte-, ja jahrtausendealten Bestrebungen der besten
Vertreter der menschlichen Gattung". In Der grüne Heinrich then, albeit under a combination of historical and
social circumstances unique within German-speaking culture,
identity and community come as close to harmonious realisation as is possible before the dawning of the socialist
era.
    Lukács thus blended his independent view of the nature
of individual and social development with a pragmatic
calculation of the 'art of the possible' under the most
difficult of political circumstances, in order to encourage the creation of a German socialist literature of
quality. As we know today, his ideas were subject to
widespread radical criticism, especially from German
writers in exile outside the Soviet Union. For Bertolt
Brecht and Walter Benjamin in Denmark, or Anna Seghers in
France, on the eve of the Second World War, Lukács was an
integral part of the "russische Literaturpolitik" they
regarded as fundamentally misguided and threateningly
authoritarian in its execution. They knew themselves to
be politically powerless to influence events in the Soviet
Union, however distinguished intellectually many of the
responses to Lukács and Soviet Socialist Realism might
have been during the cultural debate of the middle and
late 1930s. They were also in a position to acknowledge
the corrosive effects of existential fear on writing in the
Soviet Union: as Seghers commented to Lukács, "die so-
genannte 'Furcht vor der Abweichung' ... wirkt sehr ent-
realisierend". [13]
    The weakness of Lukács' conception of realism were
clearly identifiable at this distance. His choice of
the 'Entwicklungsroman' as the vehicle for portraying

a contemporary reality characterised by crisis rather
than continuity was seen as an anachronism. As early as
1934, Benjamin had expressed an unfounded confidence that
the coming German "Sowjetstaat" would have more important
tasks for its writers than exhorting them to display "den
längst verfälschten Reichtum der schöpferischen Persönlichkeit" in novels which would be grotesquely competing
with fascist fiction to become "der 'Wilhelm Meister',
der 'Grüne Heinrich' unserer Generation". [14]   He, like
Brecht, was also assuming that the advent of the electronic
mass-media would quickly do away with the elite of creative
writers and with the dominant cultural role of the novel -
an assumption which, from the perspective of today's GDR,
has proven equally unfounded.

Brecht was correspondingly scornful of the "anrüchige
Metaphysik des Organischen" and the "Kult des Individuums"
on the basis of which he saw Lukács clinging to a bourgeois
conception of identity, in the face of the transformed
understanding of the individual in twentieth century society stimulated, for example, by the new sciences of
psychoanalysis and sociology. Yet although Brecht had,
in his early work, tried to deny the uniqueness of personality entirely - suggesting, in **Mann ist Mann**, that any
man can be "wie ein Auto ummontiert" - he found himself
investigating identity in a more differentiated way in
his later 'epic' writing. His emphasis on man as "Gegen-
stand der Untersuchung", not "als bekannt vorausgesetzt",
whose development in an age of revolutionary upheavals
presupposes violent ruptures in continuity and the problem
of survival in alienating urban societies, was to assist
the evolution of East German literature, in the longer
term, beyond Lukács' organic view of experience. [15]

Furthermore, Lukács' use of the German cultural heritage
- and especially of Goethe and Hegel in the aftermath of
the French Revolution - as an indirect means of justifying
his own accommodation with Stalinism soon became trans-
parent to his critics. His emphasis on the classicism of
literary achievements such as **Wilhelm Meister**, following
upon an (understandable) personal compromise with a reactionary Germany, was countered by Anna Seghers' praise
for the incorruptibility of the German poets of the same
era (not to mention her own day) who, in some cases because
of the hostility of Goethe himself, had no opportunity to
create classical masterpieces and had become the tragic
victims of this post-revolutionary 'Übergangszeit' -
Kleist, Hölderlin, Lenz and Karoline von Günderrode. [16]

It was to be almost thirty years - the middle 1960s -
before the substance of these criticisms was made fully
available to a new generation of authors in the now fully

established GDR, and only after the growth of a new socialist literature had been seriously retarded. For Christa Wolf, Günter de Bruyn, Brigitte Reimann or Franz Fühmann this meant a belated opportunity to reconsider the nature of literary realism, the relationship between 'subjective' and 'typical' experience, in a state which was in many crucial respects a far cry from the organic entity of Lukács' dreams. Yet for German writers in the Soviet exile of the late 1930s, such as Johannes R. Becher, who saw themselves as laying the foundations for a new culture, Lukács' accounts of <u>Wilhelm Meister</u> and <u>Der grüne Heinrich</u> provided the most reliable guidance available for an immensely difficult creative and political task.

CHAPTER 1

AN EXEMPLARY FAILURE

Dies ist der größte Dichter, so redet und schreibt
                              man. Ich stimme
immer damit überein, er ist der größte, gewiß;
nämlich der größte tote Dichter bei Lebzeiten, einer,
den niemand hörte und las - aber er lebte und schrieb.

                                    Johannes Bobrowski

Als Dichter muß ich erst noch entdeckt werden, was das
Politische bis jetzt verhindert. Meine eigentliche
poetische Seele - wer kümmert sich darum.

                                    Johannes R. Becher[1]

Exile and the socialist 'Entwicklungsroman'

In the course of German socialist writing over the
past century, few authors can have undergone so contradictory a literary development as Johannes R. Becher, and
not least in the period between 1923-24, when he firmly
committed himself to the German communist party (KPD),
and the publication in 1940 of his novel Abschied, which
was intended to be an exemplary literary demonstration of
the depth of that commitment. When Becher took his far-
reaching political decision - after years of anguished
uncertainty - he was determined to obliterate all vestiges
of his privileged bourgeois past (as the son of a Munich
judge) and, in his creative writing, to sever all links
with bourgeois tradition. In his prose fragment of 1924,
"Quo Vadis", the bourgeois 'Wanderer' Hans Unfried has
to learn, at a meeting of militant factory workers, that
the concept of individuality - synonymous with 'Einsamkeit' - is obsolete in the era of merciless class-conflict:

> Die private Persönlichkeit ist für einen
> revolutionären Kämpfer ein für allemal aus-
> getilgt ... Diese Stunde, in der sich zwei
> Weltkräfte messen, erfordert als erstes Gebot
> von Euch: Disziplin! Disziplin, Genossen,
> Einordnung, unbedingten Gehorsam.

Surprisingly, though, the imagery used by Unfried to

describe his subsequent 'Entwicklungsweg' towards this socialist 'Gemeinschaft' is as traditional as it is dramatic: he sees it as a process of crucifixion and resurrection:

> ... der Mensch [muß] sich von der gegen-
> wärtigen Gesellschaft ablösen ... bis er
> eines Tages über die Einsamkeit, über sich
> selbst hinaus wieder die Gemeinschaft findet,
> die notgezwungenermaßen eine Kampfgemeinschaft
> ist. Dieser allen uns heute lebenden
> Menschen aufgedrungene Entwicklungsweg
> gleicht einer Passion, mit mehr als nur
> zwölf Stationen; die Einsamkeit ist die
> Kreuzigung, die Wiedererweckung des verein-
> samten Ichs zur Gemeinschaft: die Auf-
> erstehung ...[2]

There were in Becher's eyes no such identity crises and transformations to be weathered by the proletarian writers he began to foster as part of his new political role. These 'Arbeiterkorrespondenten', like Bredel, Grünberg and Marchwitza, were "ganze, tolle Kerle, die von Unruhe brodeln und ihre Sätze hinhauen, daß die Sprache platzt".[3]

He assumed that a radical new literature was needed to assist the transformation of society to which the KPD was dedicated, and felt that the crucial breakthrough in the pursuit of this cultural goal had been made by the Expressionist generation within which he had achieved his initial recognition. Expressionism had pointed the way to contemporary writing dedicated to the "rücksichtsloseste Entlarvung aller bürgerlichen Denk- und Seinsformen", stimulating a broad movement which was now combining the talents of the 'Arbeiterkorrespondenten' and middle-class intellectuals like Joyce, whose Ulysses was amongst the "Experimente in der Richtung des Lebens" he admired.[4]

There is always, however, a degree of ambivalence in Becher's own creative writing over what this determination to cut himself off entirely from his bourgeois roots actually meant. In 1926, in the poem "Aufgefordert, eine Biographie zu schreiben", he dismisses any thought of writing about his own past as a complete irrelevance. The depiction of the decisive step towards political commitment is all that matters:

> Das war mein Bestes:
> Daß Schulter an Schulter ich mitschritt
> Im Marschschritt kühner Erobererheere ...
> Daß mein irrnisblendendes Angesicht
> Ich von mir abtat,

> Wie man feurigen Staub abwischt ...
> Und daß das Auge ich mir ausriß,
> Das mich ärgerte,
> Und es zu Scherben warf ... [5]

In the same year, though, he published the novel Levisite [6], in which considerable attention is devoted to the childhood experience of a semi-autobiographical hero, Peter Friedjung, who comes to identify with the revolutionary cause in 1918-19, during the abortive attempt to set up a German 'Räterepublik' on the Soviet model. Here we find two distinct perspectives on Friedjung's personal development: an omniscient account by the narrator in Chapter I, and the uncommented presentation of the hero's 'Aufzeichnungen', discovered after his death in a May Day massacre which heralds the outbreak of the decisive class war at an unspecified time in Germany's future. These memoirs, forming Chapter VII of the novel, represent a 'subjective' attempt to explain the significance of Friedjung's liberation from bourgeois fatalism.

This is clearly a first attempt by Becher to give an exemplary slant to his own more protracted and erratic development, but it is also revealing that he preserves something of the tension between subjective and representative experience through this dual perspective. Furthermore, he introduces, at the analytical, objective level, personal motifs which he sees as having wider significance (and which are to become basic structural elements in Abschied): the dialectic of 'Abschiednehmen' and 'Anderswerden'; recognition that his father, as the agent of bourgeois justice, fulfils the role of executioner; and the instinctive, but powerless, awareness on his mother's part that the younger generation must make a decisive break with the past. Becher deliberately seeks to reduce the significance of these autobiographical elements by keeping his narrative framework ambitiously extensive, including other exemplary figures such as Friedjung's proletarian counterpart, Max Herse, and an American Rosa Luxemburg, Mary Green, and depicting a mining disaster, vicious class warfare on an international scale, and the imagined horrors of the ultimate war fought with poison gas. Nevertheless, Friedjung stands out as the most authentic character in Levisite, and, despite his absolute break with his parents in 1918, there appear to be some strands of continuity in his development - in the happy childhood which is the "Ankerkette seines Lebens" and the moral support his mother provides subsequently.

These inconsistencies in Becher's approach to his earlier life were exacerbated as he tried to respond loyally to the fluctuations in Soviet cultural policy

of the late 1920s (when he became president of the newly
founded BPRS in Berlin) and the early 1930s. Thus we
find him, a matter of months after praising Joyce, declaring that bourgeois literature as a whole, including
the "wahnwitzige, lebensunfähige Konstruktion" of Döblin's
Berlin Alexanderplatz, is finished, or criticising the
"Denkunfähigkeit und Verwirrung der Gefühle" of his whole
Expressionist generation, or - implicitly - denouncing the
excesses of his futuristic visions in Levisite.[7]
Although this was done in the name of an unsophisticated
proletarian literature intended to have an immediate propagandistic impact, he quickly had to shift his ground
again, after the arrival of Georg Lukács in Berlin in 1931
brought about a new emphasis on quality and the importance
of the cultural heritage of progressive bourgeois literature.

It is debatable whether Becher would have come round
to anything like the total reversal of priorities en-
tailed in Lukács' view of 'Gestaltung' - with such central
importance attached to the organic growth of personality -
had it not been for the profound psychological consequences
of exile. In the middle of 1932, he was still searching
for an alternative cultural heritage to Lukács' tradition
of great novels, in the "kleine Formen" of satire and
political pamphlets which considerably predate the rise
of the novel; by 1934, however, when he addressed the
Soviet Writers' Congress which was to codify Socialist
Realism, Becher's tone was quite different. In the face
of the Nazi exploitation of Germany's cultural heritage,
Becher's priority was, exactly like Lukács', to 'rescue'
and 'purify' it - "das große Erbe retten und reinigen
... von der faschistischen Beschmutzung" - and his list
of the great names coincided exactly with that of his
cultural mentor - Goethe, Lessing, Hegel, Hölderlin,
Schiller, Büchner and Heine.[8] This was to become, for
Becher, much more than the recognition of a continuity of
moral objectives sustained despite the 'deutsche Misere':
it developed into a profound desire to learn from Goethe,
in particular, how to overcome inner contradictions and
pursue wholeness of personality. He also began to show a
completely new interest in classical literary forms through
which this search for personal harmony was conveyed - the
sonnet (which he mastered as a vehicle for much of the
historically rooted, patriotic verse of his volume of
1938, Der Glücksucher und die sieben Lasten) and the
'Entwicklungsroman'.

What Becher actually absorbed of Goethe's conception
of individual growth is difficult to define. He seemed
to appreciate that Goethe's famous "Stirb und werde!"

meant something more complex than his own earlier desire
to cut himself off ruthlessly from his bourgeois past.
He carefully noted Goethe's description of how he
achieved a "lebendige Solidität" during his Italian
journey through the moral renewal of a "Wiedergeburt"
stimulated by a new openness to art and his surroundings
- and anticipated a similar renewal in the USSR.[9]   At
the same time, there was still little indication from
Becher of how this might relate to Goethe's other basic
metaphor of personality as an organic metamorphosis
brought about by the interaction of dynamic inner forces
and environmental influences - "geprägte Form, die lebend
sich entwickelt". And when he publicly announced his
determination to come to terms creatively with his own
past - in his speech to the congress of anti-fascist
writers in Paris in 1935 - the emphasis remained Becher's
older political one of self-transformation through a
decisive break in his development:

> Es ist ein neuer Wille da.   Es kommt eine
> neue Wertung. Nimm Abschied, heißt es,
> Abschied für immer, Abschied jede Stunde,
> eine ganze Zeit lang ... Abschied von vielem
> in dir selbst, ohne Umschaun und Tücherwinken,
> nicht durch Tränen zu erleichtern.   Streif
> die Larve ab, zynisches Sichbescheiden, daß
> sie nicht Deinem Wesen verwächst und du nicht
> gerinnst ... [10]

There is little doubt that Becher was already planning
his response to this challenge as a critical contribution
to the 'Entwicklungsroman' tradition.   Exile had provided
the necessary time for reflection after years of hectic
political activity, and the terms in which he introduces
his theme bear an uncanny resemblance to Thomas Mann's
description of the point of departure for his respectful
parody of the genre, Der Zauberberg, written a decade
earlier but dealing with the same middle-class generation's
pre-war crisis of values:

> ... es ist das Buch eines guten Willens und
> Entschlusses, ein Buch ideeller Absage an vieles
> Geliebte, an manche gefährliche Sympathie,
> Verzauberung und Verführung, zu der die
> europäische Seele sich neigte und neigt und
> welche alles in allem nur einen fromm-
> majestätischen Namen führt, - ein Buch des
> Abschiedes, sage ich, und pädagogischer
> Selbstdisziplinierung; sein Dienst ist
> Lebensdienst, sein Wille Gesundheit, sein
> Ziel die Zukunft. [11]

Although Mann preferred, in 1924, to see Hans Castorp's
transformation mainly in intellectual terms, and depicted
the problems of bourgeois society as metaphysical rather
than political and economic, it was vitally important to
Becher that his variant on the same crisis, written in the
aftermath of Hitler's rise to power, should take a more
comprehensive view of the malaise and suggest the inadequacy of purely moral responses to the earlier manifestations of the fascist threat.

He was nevertheless attempting to reconcile conflicting
impulses of his own in _Abschied_. Underlying the project,
if never actually acknowledged, was something of that
"inner necessity" which Roy Pascal described as the basis
of the best autobiographical writing - the consciousness
of a "weight of experience [which] is a burden that
cannot be borne until it is composed in the autobiography"[12] - and yet Becher's feelings towards the
'truth' of his past were highly ambivalent. It was
acutely embarrassing to him that his uncompromising involvement in revolutionary politics had only come many
anguished years after he had apparently signalled his
political conversion, in Expressionist poems such as
"Vorbereitung":

> Der Dichter meidet strahlende Akkorde.
> Er stößt durch Tuben, peitscht die Trommel schrill.
> Er reißt das Volk auf mit gehackten Sätzen. [13]

Even though he had also been the first German poet to pay
tribute to the achievement of the Russian revolution,
there was much else he would have preferred to forget:
his near-fatal involvement in a Kleistian joint suicide
pact; the long periods of drug-addiction and depressive
illnesses during the war years and afterwards; or the
recurrent yearning for the 'salvation' offered by religious mysticism or the reactionary aesthetics of a
Schopenhauer or a Nietzsche, as an alternative to his
tentative involvement in the Spartakus-Bund in 1916 or
the 1918 'November Revolution'. The middle-class Expressionist proclaiming the Brotherhood of Man had had to go
through an intellectual and physical hell before he had
felt able to accept a self-limiting role within the ruthless politics of the Weimar Republic.[14] But now, from
the distance of exile, with the German readership of a
better future in mind, and amidst the new existential
threats posed by Stalin's purges, the temptation to re-
write his past in a more exemplary manner, to suggest a
more clear-cut choice between totally different 'bourgeois'
and 'proletarian' ideologies, must have been overwhelming.

Becher's reluctance to dwell on the 'untypical'

personal difficulties which had persisted long after he
had gained his initial intellectual insights into the
nature of class conflict, would have been further
strengthened by the current understanding of cultural
politics within the German exile group in the USSR. He
had gradually come round to the view forcefully expressed
by Lukács that Expressionism was a dangerous bourgeois
aberration, to be overcome before political maturity
might be attained; [15] and he had reached an understanding
of the representative dimensions of his subjective experience which could confirm the correctness of Lukács'
insistence on the special importance of the 'Entwicklungsroman' for German socialist literature during the 'Übergangszeit' of exile. (This was not, of course, a direct
response to Lukács' essays of 1936 on Wilhelm Meister
and 1939 on Keller: not only was Abschied completed by
1938, but Lukács was evolving his ideas in consultation
with exiles like Becher for some time before they were
published.) As well as his new (if uncertain) interest
in Goethean concepts of personality development, Becher
certainly endorsed Lukács' view of Keller's importance.
According to Huppert's account of Becher's life in Moscow,
he kept Keller's novel at his side as he worked at
Abschied: "dem 'Grünen Heinrich' entsprangen bedeutsame
Impulse für die epische Pinselführung manches 'Abschied'-
kapitels". [16] As one of those exiles whose thoughts on
Germany were now overlaid with an emotional need for
'Heimat' and 'Gemeinschaft', Becher found Keller's portrayal of Heinrich's fortunes in the context of an existing
plebeian community particularly reassuring - no matter
how much Lukács might have stressed the exceptionality of
nineteenth century Switzerland within recent German history.
    It is not surprising, therefore, that Becher's idea of
the representative experience of his generation prevails
in certain key respects of his conception of Abschied. [17]
The novel is framed by two symbolical historical turning-
points: it opens with the New Year celebrations of the
year 1900 - the dawning of a new era - and ends with the
nationalistic fervour greeting the first German victory
in the World War begun in 1914 - the final proof of the
bankruptcy of bourgeois civilisation and thus the right
moment for his hero to make the definitive break with
his past. Although many cultural, social and political
events which made an impact on the Munich of these years
are carefully woven into Becher's plot, his main interest
lies in the general mood and its decisive polarising
effect on a wide range of fictional figures. The crucial
factor, to which everything else is subordinate, is the
division of society into two classes - totally distinct

not only in political-economic terms but in the whole
moral and ethical basis of their existence: on the one
hand, the bourgeois, intent on destroying themselves and
the rest of the world by their imperialistic ambitions and
concealing their inner emptiness behind a façade of
authoritarian discipline - 'das strammstehende Leben';
and on the other, 'das Volk', exploited and deprived
through their adherence to communal values and responsibilities, yet in harmony with nature and humane tradition
and still leading a fulfilling, many-sided life - 'das
standhafte Leben'.
Within the opening pages, the vague phrases used by
adults and child alike are established as central motifs:
"ich stand wie die anderen, das Glas erwartungsvoll er-
hoben, um von dem alten Jahrhundert Abschied zu nehmen"(8)
... "Die Großmutter flüsterte: Es soll anders werden"(11).
These motifs of 'Abschiednehmen' and 'Anderswerden',
clearly associated here as in Becher's preface -

> Es gilt Abschied zu nehmen, von Menschen und
> Zeiten. Von vielem, was uns verwandt und
> teuer war, nehmen wir Abschied, und das
> Scheiden tut weh ... Abschied. Und: es soll
> anders werden! Mach dich fertig!(6)

- define the structure of the novel. Out of the general
sense of discontent as regards the quality of individual
life and the state of society, there arise two utterly
irreconcilable views as to what is to be abandoned and
what form the change shall take. By 1914 the majority,
even the old Social Democrats, have succumbed to the
imperial dream of 'Anderswerden' - conquest and world
supremacy - while only the dedicated few have had the
courage to see the issue in terms of social justice and
morality.
Becher also reveals his 'exemplary' purpose in his
portrayal of his central figure, Hans Gastl. He makes
Gastl four or five years younger than himself, born around
1895 rather than 1891, a change which has a crucial bearing
on the later stages of the novel. It means that Gastl embarks on his literary career, as a sixth-former, shortly
before the war, and cannot therefore be in the vanguard
of Expressionism from around 1910, as Becher was. Consequently, there is nothing of Becher's Berlin experiences
(1911/12) in the novel, and a total contrast between his
historical role as a leader of opinion and the reflective
role of Gastl, who, on the fringe of activity in the Café
Stefanie in Munich, is caught up in the general mood of
anarchic decadence but is able to extricate himself easily
when the approach of war shocks him into serious political

awareness. Even though Gastl's surroundings and experiences
are otherwise broadly similar to Becher's own, the political message of the novel is that middle-class
intellectuals like Gastl allied themselves decisively by
1914 with the working-class movement against the war. It
is an unfortunately simplified argument, which runs
counter to historical fact, in the sense that the political resistance to the War, led by the Spartacists, was
scarcely organised before 1916, and that the intellectuals
were generally more committed to 'Geist' and the dream of
a pre-industrial, utopian 'Gemeinschaft' until the later
part of the war. [18] (Seen in this light, Becher's location of the conversion of his semi-autobiographical
hero in Levisite in 1918, after he has witnessed the
horrors of war, is much more credible, even though it
still greatly accelerates Becher's own progress.)
Futhermore, the fact that his years of creative development are, as Herzfelde said, "rücksichtslos zusammenge-
strichen", [19] means that Gastl's artistic leanings
materialise in a seemingly spontaneous way, and his ability to impress the clientele of Munich's Café Stefanie
with his poems is taken for granted. This unconvincing
negative portrayal of Gastl's artistic career leaves
him liberated, but in a total vacuum, at the end of the
novel.
    The narrative structure of Abschied comes as something
of a surprise, and seems to undermine Becher's didactic
intentions. It may be the only major exile novel consciously building on the historical structures of the 'Entwicklungsroman' and focusing on the neglected issue of individual growth, and as such clearly distinguishable from
the ponderous Socialist Realism of novels like Bredel's
Die Väter or Marchwitza's Die Kumiaks: but it is also
what Lukács described with some concern, in his sympathetic review of 1941, as "ein Ich-Roman in einem äußerst
radikalen Sinne". [20] First person narrative is rare in
exile prose, apart from in explicitly autobiographical
accounts of the path to socialism, such as Toller's
Eine Jugend in Deutschland and Uhse's Söldner und Soldat.
Finding it in Abschied, we might expect the confusions
and errors of Gastl's past to be presented from the secure
committed perspective of the present (as occurred, to some
degree, in Levisite). Becher's technique is, however, to
suggest that events in the novel are being presented
through Gastl's eyes, recording various stages in his
development in an apparently fragmentary way, without
explicit comment from an older and wiser Gastl, or
contrastive references to the time of writing. This may
well reflect a continuing artistic conviction that Joycean

stream of consciousness techniques, whose liberating
potential he had earlier recognised, might now be fruit-
fully allied to a Marxist view of recent history - and as
such would represent a courageous defiance of the post-
1934 Soviet taboo on 'decadent' bourgeois writing. It
also had one important consequence: it avoided the problem
of clarifying the narrator's perspective on the USSR of
the mid-1930s (which Becher resolved in his other work of
the period with the help of formulae like 'Heimat der
Heimat').

The modernist appearances prove deceptive in <u>Abschied</u>,
however ambiguous the strategic reasons for the stream of
consciousness veneer may have been. It quickly emerges
that Gastl's experiences are being carefully 'composed'
by a narrator who never betrays his presence, and that
there is consequently a serious credibility gap between
Gastl's powers of perception at any given point and the
lessons he learns from these experiences. [21] Virtually
every incident serves to illustrate a specific aspect of
his personality, a 'self' which he can isolate and evaluate
in terms of his subsequent growth. In the later stages of
the novel, he then reviews his past, with allegorical
certainty, in terms of the 'selves' which have upheld the
standards of 'das strammstehende Leben' and those which
have contributed to his liberation into 'das standhafte
Leben'. Each self is defined in a word which becomes an
important associative motif in the structure of the novel -
on the negative side he is 'der Kriegsspieler' or 'der
Henker', while during his transitional pursuit of meaning
and purpose in life he becomes 'der unentwegte Frager',
'der heimliche Leser' and so on, until he approaches integration with the underprivileged as 'der Andere'.

As Lukács pointed out in his review, this creates an
inauthentic sense of "Überdeutlichkeit" which betrays "ein
stellenweises Hineintragen der heutigen Wertungen Bechers
in die damalige Zeit". [22] It also, of course, conflicts
with the organic view of personality growth basic to
<u>Wilhelm Meister</u> or <u>Der grüne Heinrich</u>: Becher implies
that Gastl learns nothing positive from his bourgeois
surroundings. His errors have nothing of the longer term
value of sharpening his sensibilities or increasing his
insights that, for example, Wilhelm's pursuit of a career
in the theatre has. The interesting thing is that Lukács
passes over these formal heresies and inconsistencies, as
well as this dubious portrayal of Gastl's development,
relatively lightly. The ever-changing strategic imperatives
of the exile years probably played their part here: the
nightmarish period of the Soviet-German non-aggression
pact (1939-41) during which <u>Abschied</u> was published, and

which Lukács himself was fortunate to survive, was a time
for unprecedented solidarity in the Soviet Union amongst
the German exiles and their Hungarian mentor. [23] Becher
himself might not yet have been fully aware of the insur-
mountable creative problems he had stored up for himself
through the contradictions and over-simplifications in his
conception of Abschied: they were, however, to torment
him in a future he could not at this stage have even vague
ly envisaged.

Bourgeois society: 'das strammstehende Leben'

Becher's analysis of bourgeois life in Abschied is based
on the view that the rapid industrial expansion of Germany
following the creation of the Reich in 1871 destroyed the
humane basis of middle-class life and established ruthless
self-seeking attitudes in its place. The most destructive
aspect of this wide-ranging social transformation was clear
ly, in his eyes, the fact that large sections of the pre-
dominantly rural population had been either forced, for
economic reasons, or enticed, in the interests of social
ambition, into severing their links with their native
community and entering the alienating world of the city.
Through his characters, Becher reflects in an absolute
sense the general change from 'Gemeinschaft' to 'Gesellschaft' analysed by Tönnies. But whereas Becher adopts
Tönnies' point that the rise of capitalism is the direct
consequence of the loss of community and the whole range
of moral values - love, genuineness, mutual esteem, loyalty and so on - which it embodies, he takes a much more
extreme view of Gesellschaft: the Munich of 1900 presented in Abschied has nothing of the spirit of liberalism,
or the refinement of sensibility through culture, which
might indicate something of the positive moral basis of
urban society. [24] For the parents of Hans Gastl, social
life exerts unremitting pressures which have a corrosive
effect on personality, while injustice, repression and
moral decadence spread all round them.
   It is significant that both Gastl's parents have humble
country origins, and that there is always an atmosphere of
tension hanging over their household, indicating the
frustrations behind the façade of achievement. Through
his unflagging efforts, Heinrich Gastl has attained the
highly responsible office of public prosecutor and has all
the material comforts of a city residence. To the young
Hans, he emphasises that his success is a vindication of
a life based on hard work and self-reliance - "er [hatte]

es durch 'eigene Kraft' zu was gebracht"(45) - without
recourse to 'good connections' or nepotism. But for Gastl
there are harsh consequences to be reckoned with: his
affirmation of the harsh competitive spirit brings about
his own personal isolation. He may be "höherer Staatsbe-
amter und pensionsberechtigt", but his life is nothing
apart from the endless pressures of work, and his capacity for spontaneous feeling or creative activity has been
destroyed: even the weekly musical 'Trio' in which he
takes part is reduced to a mechanical gesture towards a
remote cultural tradition. For Gastl, the State is an
absolute moral force - "das Abbild der sittlichen Idee"
(119) - in the service of which all personal impulses have
to be eliminated, so that life becomes a process of
"Selbstüberwindung". The price of subservience is a high
one: Gastl becomes the arbiter of a biased class justice
which ensures that the underprivileged are always more
severely punished and the death penalty is widely used to
uphold the existing order. It is the realisation that his
father, prosecuting in a murder trial, has taken upon himself the role of "Henker", that first brings home to Hans
in a traumatic fashion the nature of his work.

On the domestic plane, Heinrich Gastl is a repressive
tyrant towards his son. For young Hans, life is a series
of "Verbotstafeln", of warnings against any form of un-
disciplined behaviour which conflicts with the undefined
notion of "Standesgefühl". The father reveals a constant
fear of "Skandal" and threatens terrifying consequences if
Hans' misbehaviour should continue - "auf dem Schafott
endet es"(66). Even though his mother is emotionally
opposed to this stifling regime, she initially proves too
weak to exert any effective opposition to it. In conversation she is always "dagegen", yet always yields in
the end to the demands of social propriety.

The generation differences between Hans' parents and
his grandmother emphasise how substantial the moral decline of the bourgeois has been. Her cultural sensibilities and tolerant, sympathetic attitudes recall the finer
days of the 'Bürgertum', when the spirit of Goethe still
prevailed. Although she is as powerless as Hans' mother
in instituting change, she does articulate her criticisms
in a manner which Hans gradually grows to understand, and
teaches him to paint and appreciate the fine arts. In her
final gesture of opting to be cremated, in line with the
heretical ideas of the Social Democrats, she is able to
reveal publicly her dissent against the bourgeois world.

It is scarcely surprising that, under these conditions,
with few signs of family affection or sympathetic interest,
Hans' moral growth is stunted. Although naturally lively
and highly curious, he receives no other stimulation from

his parents except through their gifts of toy soldiers and
books on martial themes. Their predictable, monotonous
existence compels him to search for illicit excitement as
"der Heimlichtuer", whether pilfering from his grandmother
or frustrating their attempts to insulate him from
corrupting influences "von unten", in the shape of his
affectionate nurse Christine and the bragging, irreverent
Xaver in the stables.
    Because of the terrifying image of authority presented
by his father, Hans soon learns that it is easier to lie
than to face dire threats and beatings. This process is
intensified as Hans begins school and discovers that the
educational system is based on exactly the same principles.
Goll, the class teacher, is another petty tyrant in the
Professor Unrat mould, indeed much more of a caricature
than Heinrich Mann's figure. Goll is just as much dedicated as the elder Gastl to the jaundiced view that working-
class children are by nature criminally inclined, and soon
helps to distort Hans' sense of morality to a more threatening extent, when he encourages Hans to let his proletarian
friend Franz Hartinger take the punishment for a day of
truancy together in the amusement-arcades of Munich, which
Hans had in fact planned and financed. The fundamental
'educational' principle brought home to Hans as he holds
down Hartinger and watches Goll beat him, is that it is
always less painful to relinquish moral responsibility:
a socially inferior scapegoat can always be found. Even
though this feeble act of betrayal earns Hans the nickname
"Henker" to share with his father, it is only the beginning
of a long period, not just of acquiescence, but of active
participation - in alliance with Feck and Freyschlag, the
budding tyrants within the class - in the preservation of
an iniquitous authority based on intimidation of the weak
and persecution of dissenters like Hartinger.
    There is much in these school-scenes which is reminis-
cent of Robert Musil's Die Verwirrungen des Zöglings
Törless: we are not just concerned with corrupt authority-
figures like Goll, but also with the psychology of children
in groups. Yet despite the echo of Musil's Reitling and
Basini in the craving for power and sadistic tendencies
revealed by Feck and Freyschlag, Becher's classroom
tyrants are too inherently depraved, for reasons of birth
rather than circumstance, to be more than flat clichés.
They do not change in any way over several years and throw
little light on the origins of Fascism, as they were presumably intended to do. Hans Gastl, however, in his bewildered involvement (at times the cruellest of all, then
tormented in his guilt-ridden dreams) in a degrading and
vicious process, is a narrator compelling in ways that the

more 'objective' Törless is not.

At the secondary level, the corrupting nature of what passes as education is most grotesquely illustrated during the year which Hans is forced to spend in the 'Erziehungsanstalt' in Öttingen as a punishment for his unsatisfactory progress at the local school, and particularly for further thefts of his grandmother's money. Förtsch, the principal, is not just a sadist who prides himself on his ability to get pupils to confess to anything, but also delights in titillating his salacious mind with details of adolescent sexual 'crimes'. The institutionalised existence contributes even more directly to the maintenance of State authority, through the greater scope it allows for glorification of military discipline and imperial ambitions.

Fortunately for the novel, there is a greater degree of differentiation in Becher's depiction of the Wilhelm-Gymnasium in Munich, to which Hans returns once his parents have forgiven him. Not only are there liberal voices, like that of the Jew Löwenstein, to be raised in class against the bullying practised by Hans, Feck and Freyschlag, but there also educationalists, like the mathematics teacher Waldvogel, who still uphold the humanistic values on which the school was founded. But even here, Becher's concept of the irreversible decline of the Bürger prevails, as Waldvogel is deliberately humiliated by the class tyrants in front of a school inspector and forced into premature retirement. Like Hans' grandmother, he can only make a gesture of dissent, in this case an improbable piece of rhetoric in which he attributes the destruction of values to the activities of a malevolent minority of "Barbaren" and "Hunnen"(195).

Only in the case of Heinrich Gastl does Becher attempt to include a problematical element, which shows some recognition of the complex psychological factors motivating even the most ruthless authority figures, and gives some credibility to an otherwise crude categorisation of the bourgeoisie. As the novel progresses, Heinrich Gastl occasionally shows that the publicly esteemed aspect of himself is nothing more than a distorted outer shell, a disintegrated fragment of his potential self, as the mirror reflections watched by Hans through a keyhole suggest:

> Ein mächtiger Vater stand da im Gang vor dem Spiegel, zwei Väter, einer vor dem Spiegel, einer im Spiegel. Ein Vater mit zwei Köpfen, und im Seitenflügel des Spiegels erschien ein dritter, überall Väter. Alle wie schwarz lackiert und mit dem gleichen aufgezwirbelten Schnurrbart.(37)

Although for long periods Hans sees in him only the roles
which society forces him to adopt - "der Frühaufsteher",
"der Strammsteher", "der Richter" and so on - Heinrich
Gastl still has an essential core of goodness and warmth
which he reveals on holiday in the Bavarian countryside,
when he is transformed into a loving father and a
connoisseur of nature. He has, however, lost his 'natural'
ability to communicate with ordinary countryfolk. When
he meets a childhood friend in the forest near Hohenschwan
gau, he tries in vain to regain command of the local dia-
lect. The social divide is unbridgeable:

> Der Holzfäller war daheim, aber der Vater
> hatte die Heimat verlassen und war in die
> Stadt gezogen, nützte ihm nichts, daß er die
> Stimme verstellte, der Holzfäller lebte weit
> weg von ihm ...(120)

As time passes, an ironic parallel is established:
Gastl - the uncompromising individualist - realises that
his scope for social betterment is just as rigidly limited
(on a higher plane) as that of the militant workers whom
he despises. Because of his lowly social origins, he has
no chance of gaining a State decoration or being elevated
to the nobility: the gradual realisation of this inescapable social law brings about a steady loss of his sense
of purpose. He lapses into reverie, talks disjointedly
to himself, and even - briefly - considers the possibility
of combating the evils of social discrimination, but it
is too late for protest or withdrawal.

In the end, Gastl discovers an aggressive outlet for
his frustrations in identifying himself with Germany's
bellicose imperial ambitions. He, like millions of
others, grasps eagerly at the myth that war is a means to
individual liberation, and endorses the high-sounding idea
of self-sacrifice in the national cause, glorifying it as
a dynamic alternative to the "sterbenslangweilig" routine
of his bureaucratic existence. Even then he continues to
dream of what might have been if he had placed greater
value on the enrichment of the community from which he
originated, rather than on his selfish aspirations in
urban society:

> Er spielte sich weg, weit weg. Er spielte
> den Landwirt, den er gerne geworden wäre.
> Während er im Wohnzimmer auf und ab schritt,
> besah er lächelnd den Teppich: schöne schwarze
> Erde, und Weinberge grünten aus den Tapeten ...
> (427)

The feeling that Gastl's insoluble inner conflict is to be seen as representative of the error of his whole generation is reinforced by the pronounced decline of the rest of the Gastl family - in the form of Hans' three uncles - into eccentricity and moral disarray. Only Hans' mother achieves a degree of liberation, becoming increasingly bolder in her desire to undermine the Gastl edifice, through barbs of irreverent criticism directed against convention and the Kaiser at social gatherings, and through her quiet encouragement of Hans' revolt.

For all the problems of the older Gastls, none of them reach the ultimate conclusion that there is no point in living on. But Hans, at every stage of his development, is compelled to come to terms with the reality of sudden, wasteful death. After the shock of seeing his father as society's executioner, he is twice confronted with suicide during his school years. A fellow pupil at the elementary school jumps to his death from the Groß-hesseloher Brücke: the causes are never discovered, mainly because the school authorities do their utmost to suppress the whole affair. Later, it is the neurotic young aristocrat known only as 'die Dusel', who falls prey to the socially ambitious Feck and soon drowns herself in despair. The effect of these experiences on Hans is to make it quite clear to him that the society which gives rise to such a range of intolerable sufferings and psychological disorders is one from which he must liberate himself. At his grandmother's cremation he makes a firm resolve to move out of the world of his parents and out of the clutches of Feck and Freyschlag:

> Nein, nochmals nein. Ich will nicht vor der
> Lüge mein Leben lang strammstehen ... Gibt
> es denn nur das: Strammstehen, Verrückt-
> werden oder die Großhesseloher Brücke ...
> Heilloses Durcheinander ...Keine andere
> Brücke, die über den Abgrund hinwegführt ...?
> Anders werden! Ja, anders werden ... Aber
> wie! Aber wie! ...

But the crucial problem remains of discovering a valid alternative in the midst of his adolescent confusion, with the taint of a bourgeois upbringing and its disintegrating effect on personality still strongly imprinted upon him:

> Nicht einer bin ich, nicht zwei, gleich ein
> ganzer Haufen. Welcher von allen denen soll
> ich nun eigentlich werden? (232)

The quest for identity: 'das Anderswerden'

Hans' inner determination to distance himself from his
bourgeois environment becomes increasingly manifest during
his middle years in the Gymnasium. At first he seeks fulfilment by striving for sporting success, and shows abilities - as part of the 'self' he later describes as both
"der Rekordschwimmer" and "der hartnäckige Blödian" -
which make him a potential national champion. Through a
period which is otherwise passed over quickly in the novel,
Hans is totally committed to his ambitions, until he becomes painfully aware that sport has had an essentially
escapist function for him. He is gripped by the powerful
moral and intellectual urge to examine "die so gefährliche
Frage nach dem großen 'Wofür' und 'Warum'"(208), which has
been stimulated by his encounters with a new scale of
values —   at school, in the figure of Löwenstein, and in
the world of the Hartingers and unspoilt country people
outside, as well as by the desire to 'know' which leads
him to literature. He becomes a voracious reader of
everything which, like the forbidden work of Haeckel on
his father's desk, might offer a solution to "die Welt-
rätsel", and begins to show creative abilities which at
first - in the tradition of the 'Entwicklungsroman' -
reflect only subjective preoccupations, in Hans' case in
poems obsessed with "das Absonderliche und Grauenhafte"(215)
    It is through a shattering emotional experience
that Hans is forced out of the constricting - but nonetheless insulating - world of his parents. In one of the
few sections in the later part of Abschied which correspond
closely to Becher's own experience, Hans has a remarkable
escape from death. He becomes involved with a shop-
assistant, Fanny Fuß, who also works as a part-time dancer
and prostitute, and experiences a remarkable intimacy
through his recognition of their common anguish as helpless captives of society. But because the world they know
offers no alternative, they decide to end it all, in misguided imitation of romantic legend, through a joint
suicide-pact. In the event, Hans only wounds himself
after fatally shooting her (and ironically, is absolved
from guilt in court through his father's bourgeois 'good
connections').
    Realising how pathetically disorientated he has become,
in his role as "der traurige Held", he resolves to find a
teacher to guide him into purposeful living:

> Ich brauchte einen, der ein standhaftes Leben
> mich lehrte. Vor dem Sterben für Großes ein
> Leben für Großes mich lehrte. Ich brauchte
> einen, der führte ...(262)

His thoughts move in two apparently complementary direc-
tions: on the one hand, he seeks enlightenment about
politics, and learns from Löwenstein - in the symbolical
fog of the English Garden - that there is a crucial responsibility resting on his own middle-class generation to
join the struggle for socialism:

> Es gibt eine Wahrheit. Ob sie dir nun paßt
> oder nicht. Diese geschichtliche Wahrheit
> spricht gegen uns. Wir müssen anders werden,
> als unsere Väter waren. Das bequeme,
> gesicherte Leben hat für uns aufgehört.
> Oder wir werden zusammen mit der großen Lüge
> untergehen, unsereins.(277-8)

On the other hand, he discovers through his reading a
literary hero in Richard Dehmel, the apparent advocate of
the rebellion of sons against their fathers. But when,
to Hans' delight, Dehmel responds to the poems he sends
him by arranging a meeting, the great "Dichter" turns out
to be as cautious as Hans' father, advising a period of
study and training for a "solider, anständiger Beruf"
before seeking recognition as an artist.(315) Hans is
quick to denounce him as a "Spießer" and rush headlong
into bohemian life.

It is in this aimless, spiteful mood that Hans comes
into contact with the world of Expressionism in the Café
Stefanie in Munich. In the scenes that follow, the whole
radical cultural movement is reduced to a decadent extension of the bourgeois world Hans is attempting to
leave behind. Instead of idealistic dedication towards
the realisation of 'der neue Mensch', Hans finds in the
majority of these 'artists' ruthless self-centred attitudes, a parasitic life-style and a childish desire to
shock. The prevailing ideology seems to be the half-
baked version of Freudian psycho-analysis embodied in Dr.
Hoch, with its obsessional concentration on the treatment
of individual 'complexes' rather than on the wider needs
of society. Related to this is a whole range of fads
and escapist activities, from snuff-taking and séances to
morphium and cocaine addiction - all of which doubtless
occurred as part of the anti-bourgeois rebellion, but
without implying, as Becher does here, that the whole
process was trivial and diversionary.

Hans' poetry is shown to derive essentially from the
desire to be incomprehensibly different:

> Keinerlei Regel mehr beachtend, gegen jedes
> irgendwie Gesetzmäßige kraß und bewußt ver-
> stoßend, schrieb ich in einer mir neu
> zurechtgemachten unleserlichen Schrift eine

'Stadt der Verdammnis' benannte Dichtung, in
der jeder, auch der sich zufällig einstellende
Reim durch eine knatternde Assonanz ersetzt
wurde, um nur ja nicht an Herkömmliches zu
erinnern ...(347)

Amongst the poets generally, the·iconoclastic urge is both
indiscriminate and directionless: Armageddon is proclaimed hysterically, and sinister pre-Fascist tendencies
lurk beneath the surface. Only Stefan Sack, who becomes
Hans' trusted poetic and moral counsellor in place of
Dehmel, has direct experience of deprivation, and sees
the artist's function in political terms. Together with
the attractive Magda, who remains a perceptive fringe-
observer, he helps to show Hans that the habitués of the
Café Stefanie are nothing more than "verrückt gewordene
Spießer".(363)   Magda goes as far as to suggest that
Hans' current poems are nothing compared to his "gut"
and "echt" earlier lyrics written in the simple folk-
styles of the Romantics.

When Hans, together with his newly-established friends
Löwenstein and Hartinger, sees how a group of these self-
 styled artists terrorise the editor of the <u>Münchner
Neueste Nachrichten</u> for writing a condemnatory article,
he realises that these 'bohemian' attitudes are no
different from those of Feck and Freyschlag at school and
that he must again think in terms of a decisive break.
As Löwenstein denounces the whole business as "eine
elende Feigheit ...überhaupt Café Stefanie", Hans is in
full agreement.(372) And if further confirmation were
needed,it is quickly provided by the widespread acclaim
with which these intellectuals greet the imperialist war
in 1914. As Dr. Hoch says, war is "der gewaltigste psy-
chische Befreiungsakt der Menschheit, die heilsamste
Massenentfesselung aller Komplexe".(384)

It is hardly coincidental that the caricature of Expressionism which emerges from these scenes reflects the
views developed by Lukács in "Größe und Verfall des Expressionismus". The whole movement is seen as developing
inexorably towards fascist elitism, and the route to political salvation for Gastl is to abandon all vestiges of
the artistic method along with the ideology. Becher evidently could only come to terms with Lukács' undifferentiated
critique by ensuring that his fictional 'Ich' remained on
the fringe and quickly relinquished his bourgeois artistic
ambitions as part of another expendable 'self'. Such an
attempt, in the interests of political expediency, to
show Gastl jettisoning whole spheres of experience in
order to support the proletarian cause in a totally undefined way, only serves to expose the superficiality of

the 'Anderswerden' motif and the underlying idea of depicting personality development in terms of a succession
of discrete selves.

Socialist utopia: 'das standhafte Leben'

The alternative to the bourgeois life-style which Hans
experiences at home, in school and in artistic circles is
always in evidence through the novel. At first the
differences are implicit in the personality of the 'plebeian' figures "von unten" with whom the young child comes
into contact, but as he grows more mature, they are articulated in moral and ideological terms. For the inquisi-
tive and adventurous child Hans, there is something immediately attractive and genuine about Christine, his nurse,
and Xaver, the orderly of Gastl's friend Major Bonnet.
Christine is tender and warm, with a capacity for deep
feeling that Hans' parents rarely reveal; the cradle song
he always associates with her is the lament of a generation
whose natural way of life is threatened by economic
necessity: "Muß i denn, muß i denn zum Städtele hinaus
... und du, mein Schatz, bleibst hier".(27) Christine's
own hopes of happiness have been destroyed by the death
of her beloved in the expansionist Franco-Prussian War.
Xaver stimulates Hans' sense of the illicit through his
coarse humour, his squalid surroundings and his disrespect
for authority - at least in private, whereas in uniform he
becomes for Hans the incarnation of the military hero.
But he shares with Christine the longing for his "Heimat",
which finds expression in his poignant accordion-playing.
Not only those who still have strong links with their
rural origins reveal this warmth and sense of vitality:
it is equally present in the domestic life of the crafts-
men who make up the urban proletariat, as Hans discovers
in the home of his schoolfriend Franz Hartinger, whose
father is an independent master-tailor:

> Aber es gab keinen Rohrstock, nichts im Zimmer
> sah nach Ohrfeigen aus. Nirgends Angst, die
> lähmte. Kein Gang, in dem ein Spiegel stand.
> Keine Bilder an den Wänden, die nachts über
> einen herfielen. Kein Teppich, der den Schritt
> des Vaters unhörbar machte. Das Klavier
> fehlte, zu dem man 'Deutschland, Deutschland
> über alles' singen mußte.(49)

In the Hartinger household, authority is not dependent

on violence and intimidation, and there is no concern for
appearances. In place of the stridency of nationalist
ambition there is an atmosphere of peace and mutual understanding. Hartinger's work is carried out under the eyes
of the family - it is an integral part of the humble
domestic situation. This is the only form of proletarian
life depicted by Becher in <u>Abschied</u>: there is nothing of
the misery of the anonymous factory worker or the dilution
of the craftsman's sense of pride through the division of
labour. It is this absence of a modern urban dimension
in his projection of the socialist future, which makes
for the insubstantial utopian nature of so many of the
scenes depicting "das standhafte Leben".

It is, however, through Franz Hartinger that Hans first
realises what this steadfastness entails: not only is
Franz's view of "Anderswerden" (they make the same New
Year's resolution in 1900) expressed clearly in socialist
terms(24), but he shows by his courage in school that he
has the strength of character to carry it through. He
offers a quality of friendship which Hans is incapable
of appreciating for many years and which is nowhere else
evident in the Munich of his childhood. Only later,
during a holiday in the Bavarian countryside, is Hans
brought into contact again with the same sense of
harmonious personal relationships he lost so dismally
through his classroom betrayal of Franz - "alle Menschen
schienen gut zueinander, lächelten und blickten verständ-
nisvoll".(112)

Now it means so much more to Hans, because it is part
of the new, intoxicating feeling of 'Heimat', gained
through the liberating experience of nature and the sudden
awareness of the 'roots' which bind him with the past:

> Wenn ich frühmorgens in den Tannenwald eintrat,
> der hinter dem Gasthaus 'Zum Alterschrofen'
> aufstieg, und, während der Wald wuchs und
> wuchs, ich zögernd dahinschritt, wie spurlos
> mir entschwindend - war ich da nicht wieder
> zurückgekehrt dorthin, wo ich einstmals
> gekommen war - ich wußte um mein Woher und
> kannte meine Herkunft - daher kam ich, das
> war die Heimat.(114)

In this sphere of idyllic peacefulness and beauty, Hans
falls in love for the first time - and hears the bewildering revolutionary news about the mutiny on the
Battleship Potemkin, which stimulates his imagination
so vividly that he sees Xaver and Franz amongst the
jubilant sailors singing "das Lied vom Anderswerden"(123)
and ignores his father's lectures about the evils of
socialism. Through this integration of the theme of

revolution - embodied in the novel in Hans' frequent recall of his excited vision of "ein Schiff, ein ganzes
Schiff" - with the highly emotional sense of 'Heimat',
Becher establishes the idea of continuity between the
communal past and the coming of socialism.

At times, this feeling comes close to sentimentality,
reflecting more than anything else the desperate loneli-
ness of exile for writers like Becher, which is particularly
striking when we remember the venom with which he de-
nounced all things German, in war-poems like "An Deutschland", in his Expressionist days:

> Deutschland, Reich der breigestampften Knechte!
> Reich Barbaren, stinkend Blut-Kot-Reich!
> Weh, aus Poren euerer Fluren wimmeln Schlächter.
> Eiterrinnsal gurgelnd Haut beschleicht ...

Writing in that vein, Becher's only sense of identity was
with "Europas Völkerbund" united against Germany. Not
only did he urge its destruction - "O Heimat klaff
entzwei!" - but he wanted to play an active part in it:

> Deutschland, wie ein tödliches Geschwür
> Ätz der Fluch des Dichters deinen Leib.

(The "Heimat" he envisaged in positive terms, in "Verfall"
and "Berlin", was both "fern" and "neu".)[25] Even in
the Weimar years, his repeated references to the emerging
socialist 'Gemeinschaft' (as in "Quo Vadis") excluded
this sense of history and continuity. The shock of
exile, however, brought with it a guilty admission of
his failings, as an intellectual out of touch with the
people who make up the 'Heimat', as the poems of <u>Der
Glücksucher</u> also show:

> Zu wenig haben wir geliebt, daher
> Kam vieles. Habe ich vielleicht gesprochen
> Mit jenem Bauern, der den Weinstock spritzte
> Dort bei Kreßbronn. Ich hab mich nicht
>   gekümmert
> Um seinen Weinstock. Darum muß ich jetzt
> Aus weiter Ferne die Gespräche führen,
> Die unterlassenen. Fremd ging ich vorbei
> Mit meinem Wissen, und an mir vorüber
> Ging wieder einer mit noch besserem Wissen ...

Thus the dominating note of these poems is the new feeling
- a keystone of Soviet cultural policy of the 1930s -
of the 'Volksverbundenheit', displayed humbly by the poet,
who

> Kehrt ... dort ein, wo er sich wiederfindet
> Und Eingang findet in des Volkes Mitte. [26]

This central concept of 'das Volk' is fully developed
during Hans' spell in the Franconian countryside, where
he gains brief respite from the misery of Förtsch's reformatory with 'Mops', his only friend there. Mops'
father, Herr Sieger, turns out to be an expert on local
history, with a particular interest in the organic
process by which the communal values of the past have
been preserved and developed by a dedicated minority.
Sieger's argument, which is close to that of Engels in
his study of the Peasants' Revolt, is that the people
involved in the resistance to feudalism in the 16th
century formed in effect the first communistic society,
through their opposition to private property and auto-
cratic authority. The suppression of their revolt led
directly to the devastation of the Thirty Years' War and
left Germany "verwüstet und verarmt, zerrissen in' seinem
Innern", fostering the "Kriegsgelüste" and "Herzensroheit"
which still afflict the country three hundred years later,
ill-contained by "eine heuchlerische Zivilisation".
Sieger believes that his generation has the capacity to
bring about a resurgence of the spirit of "das Volk"
under the leadership of the working-class movement:
"der neue Mensch" is to be created through "den deutschen
Arbeiter".(176-8)

For Hans, 'das Volk' takes on meaningful shape as he
thinks of Xaver, Hartinger, Christine and Herr Sieger
himself. His new insight becomes even more vivid as he
remembers that the Gastl 'Familienchronik' dates back
(as his father would prefer to forget) to 1546, when an
inn-keeping Gastl was tortured to death for his revolutionary activity - "in Ansehen seiner Unbotmäßigkeit gegen
geistliche und weltliche Herrschaft".(109) What previously puzzled the young Hans as "der dunkle Punkt" in
his family history now reveals itself as the vital force
capable of liberating the "Strammsteher".(184) And if
the fact needed emphasising, Hans then experiences, in
an Easter Sunday vision, the resurrection of the inn-
keeper, who appears as a new Messiah, the incarnation of
"das Anderswerden":

> Hochverehrter Erbe und Nachkomme! ... Der Weg
> war lang durch die Zeit her! Ich bin
> gekommen, die Zeit zu erfüllen. Ich bin das
> Anderswerden. Oder wie unser Herr, der Herr
> Jesus Christus sagt: 'Kommt alle her zu mir,
> die ihr mühselig und beladen seid ...'(181)

Despite the vividness of this encounter, Hans - through
lack of further contact with the 'Volk' in his elitist Gymnasium - remains a passive spectator upon life until after
his attempted suicide. What little knowledge he gathers
about socialism tends to be theoretical: the information he

gains from Löwenstein in the English Garden provides him
with a range of ideological catchphrases:

> Sozialismus. Die menschliche Gesellschaft.
> Klassen - Klassenkampf. Eine neue Zeit
> bricht an. Internationale. Proletarier
> aller Länder, vereinigt euch!(280-1)

It is another journey into the 'Heimat' - following his
renewal of friendship with Hartinger - which induces
deeper awareness of the past and encourages moral growth.
On a cycling trip round Lake Constance, accompanied by
Hartinger and Löwenstein, he visits places associated
with Jan Hus and the Peasants' Revolt and is introduced
by the others to the best humanistic traditions in literature through the works of Keller and Tolstoy. Once again,
mainly on the basis of the intoxicating emotional effect
of nature and the renewed associations of Easter Sunday,
Hans senses the intimate harmony between the spirit of
Jan Hus and the 'Potemkin' revolutionaries:

> Das alles, alles gehört zusammen. Das alles
> gehört zum Anderswerden und ist ein Ganzes,
> ein großes Ganzes. Eine ganz andere, neue
> Welt ist dies ...(326)

The feeling of 'Ganzheit' described here derives from
nothing more substantial than this self-immersion
in nature, significantly remote from the mass of mankind -
this very generalised sense of historical continuity, in
which revolution seems to mean a magical transformation
of life. Like other 'positive' concepts, this idea of
wholeness emerges from the assumption that there is always
a polar alternative in "das standhafte Leben" to what is
found repellent and unnatural in "das strammstehende
Leben". Once the latter has been shown to be inherently
destructive of inner harmony, through the insecure
"Scheinleben"(232) it forces upon men, then the alternative, based on the recreation of the organic community
disrupted by capitalism, will reflect 'natural' perfection.
   This dualistic style of argument is again reflected in
the vision of "der vollendete Mensch" which Hans has soon
afterwards. A certain distancing effect is introduced by
the fact that it is the newly 'converted' Hans who makes
the utopian proclamations rather than his friends; the
phlegmatic Hartinger restricts himself to a cautious
assertion that the 'Genossen' will seek each other out
when the time is ripe, while Löwenstein tends towards
sceptical dismissal of Hans' exuberant images as
"Träumerei".(332) Yet both of them later - at the outbreak of war - clearly assign a special role to Hans as a
"Dichter" through his capacity to bring about "eine Art

Umwandlung und Neuschöpfung der Welt ...ein Anderswerden".(388) The vision itself superficially recalls
the classical pattern of the 'Entwicklungsroman':

> Ich sah den 'Vollendeten Menschen'.
> Er wuchs in einer Umgebung auf, die alle seine
> guten Eigenschaften entwickelte und ihm schon
> von früh an ein reichhaltiges Wissen zugänglich
> machte. Der Vollendete Mensch war körperlich
> und geistig gleich vollendet. Lüge und
> Heuchlerei waren ihm fremd, denn keinerlei Grund
> war vorhanden, daß er sich irgendwie hätte
> herauslügen und irgendwem hätte etwas vor-
> heucheln müssen ...(332-3)

There is not, however, the slightest hint of the problematical aspects of growth, which Lukács stresses in his essay
on Wilhelm Meister: the inevitability of error, the paradox of learning more through 'accidental' experience than
through wise advice based on 'ein reichhaltiges Wissen',
and so on. The idea of inherent 'gute Eigenschaften' is
one which had been thoroughly questioned by the Expressionist generation, yet it is presented with incredible blandness here, just like the view that 'perfection' is easily attainable since all the forces
threatening identity have been magically eliminated. The
whole community is without contradictions and life has no
mysteries:

> Der vollendete Mensch kannte sich im Leben
> aus, das ganze unendliche Leben erschloß sich
> ihm, und keine Geheimnistuerei gab es, denn
> was wäre zu verbergen gewesen, da alles offen
> geschah und die Menschen frei miteinander
> lebten. Keiner konnte auf den anderen einen
> Zwang ausüben, und zu beherrschen war nur
> die Natur.(333)

This is paradise on earth, derived almost entirely from a
Rousseauesque conception of pre-industrial harmony in
nature. It suggests a future setting only in the sense
that "Hungersnöte" and "Kriegswirren" have been effectively eliminated, and that the beauty and fertility of the
earth are a result of man's rational mastering of its resources - "gemeinsame planvolle Anstrengungen" - rather
than God-given perfection.(333) What is again glaringly
lacking, particularly in view of Becher's narrative standpoint, twenty years removed from events in a technologically developing Soviet Union, is any sense of the industrialised context in which progress towards the new
'Gemeinschaft' would have to be made.

Becher in fact continues to rely on Christian symbolism throughout, to illustrate the psychological and historical changes involved in the transition from capitalism to socialism: it is difficult to see how metaphors illustrating a dualistic notion of Heaven and Hell can provide much insight into this complex process. Those who suffer at the hands of a cruel and repressive social system, from the inn-keeper in the 16th century to Hartinger in the 20th, are persecuted and tortured: the former suffers "Folterqualen und Feuertod"(180) while Hartinger's attitude "beim Foltern" at the hands of his socially superior classmates is "mit einem Märtyrer verglichen, mit dem heiligen Sebastian, der, am Marterpfahl stehend, von Pfeilen durchbohrt, seinen Gefährten im Jenseits zulächelte ...".(104) This recalls Becher's earlier poem on Rosa Luxemburg, in which her murder is seen as a crucifixion:

> Den geschundenen Leib
> Abnehmend vom Kreuz
> In weicheste Linnen ihn hüllend ...

and she is elevated to immaculate sainthood:

> Blanke unschuldsvolle
> Reine jungfrauweiße
> Taube ... Du Einzige! Du Heilige![27]

Life in urban capitalist society remains literally Hell throughout Becher's writing: Hans is "der Höllenwanderer" in the "Inferno des zwanzigsten Jahrhunderts", and what men seek is "Erlösung von ihrem Höllendasein".(308-10) For the chosen few amongst the bourgeois, "Sendboten" sent from "das standhafte Leben" appear, to indicate "den richtigen Weg" (405-6): these emissaries may be, like the inn-keeper and Hartinger, "auferstanden" from apparent death and thus take on Messianic qualities.(104, 180) Easter Sunday is the day when Hans has his illuminating visions of past martyrs and future paradise, and also when he seeks to transcend the miseries of life on earth through his suicide pact with Fanny Fuß.

This dualistic religious structure is embodied most comprehensively in the final grandiose, symbolical scene of the novel, in which all its characters - and all of Hans' earlier 'selves' - fight for his 'soul' on the steps outside his home. It is, of course, the dedicated minority of "die Gerechten" and "die Standhaften" who win the victory, and help Hans down the long flight of steps - "der Weg ins Freie oder der Glückspfad"(430) - so that he can at last become "Anders". We have already referred to the "Überdeutlichkeit" which this structural pattern imposes on the ostensible first-person narrative of the young

Gastl: it arises equally from Becher's failure to modify
his apocalyptic view of revolution and the 'neuer Mensch'
since his Expressionist days. Furthermore, his portrayal
of 'das standhafte Leben' has more to do with yearning
for the (imagined) perfection of pre-industrial 'Gemeinschaft' than with the potentialities of twentieth century
post-revolutionary society.

The continuation of 'Abschied' in the East German context

Near the end of the novel, as Hans extricates himself
from the decadent attractions of the Munich bohème, he
tells his life-story to his friend Stefan Sack, who
responds with great interest and insists that it should
form the basis for a novel. As Sack envisages it, the
novel should consist of two parts: the first, basically
autobiographical and "bekenntnishaft", but containing the
essential moral and social conflicts of the period, and
the second, in which "Selbstgestaltung" should give way
to a broad panorama of the lives of "die Standhaften" who
have assisted his development so far:

> Dem Standhaften Leben werden Sie ein Denkmal
> setzen. Die Standhaften werden fortleben in
> ihren Taten. Den Standhaften werden Sie das
> Wort geben, wenn sie einmal nicht mehr zu
> Wort kommen sollten ...(410)

The basis for this continuation is not to be mere surface
reality: Gastl, as a "Dichter", will create "Poesie ...
Menschliche Beziehungen, poetisch durchdacht. Poetisch
durchdachte Gestalten". Clearly, this scheme is much
closer to Lukács' idea of 'das große proletarische Kunstwerk' than what has been examined in Abschied, and there
is no doubt that the central intention here is the depiction in detail of the ordinary people who make up the
'Volk' - "Jeder Mensch, auch der geringste: ein Menschen-
wunder, eine Vielfalt menschlicher Lebewesen".(411)
   Abschied, as it exists today, corresponds exactly in
its structure to Sack's proposals for the first part of
Gastl's novel, indicating the extent to which Becher was
using Sack as his mouthpiece in this section of the novel.
The full title of the first edition of 1940, and of all
subsequent editions until 1954, Abschied. Einer deutscher
Tragödie erster Teil. 1900-14, leaves little doubt that,
over these years, Becher envisaged a Socialist Realist
continuation along the lines outlined by Sack.

Once the Second World War was over, it quickly became obvious how great an importance was placed upon the novel in Germany's Soviet Zone of Occupation. Just two months after the capitulation of the Third Reich, the 'Kultur-bund zur demokratischen Erneuerung Deutschlands' was established, with its own press, the Aufbau Verlag, and Becher as its first President. Amongst the first publications, late in 1945, of the Aufbau Verlag, was Abschied, in a substantial edition of 20,000. In a radio commentary marking the publication of Abschied, Hans Fallada emphasised the breakthrough it implied, as the first novel to appear "unter dem Zeichen der Pressefrei-heit, der erneuerten Demokratie", in Germany since 1933:

> Wenn der Zufall es zuwege gebracht hat, daß
> gerade Bechers Roman "Abschied" als Auftakt,
> als Herold einer neuen deutschen Epik auf-
> trat, so ist hier der Zufall klüger gewesen
> als alle Weisheit der Erfahrenen.

Fallada saw it as of particular value to young people in the chaos of Germany, in that it revealed "einen Weg aus dem Negativen" without suggesting any easy solutions - "der Held des Romans [geht] diesen Weg tastend, unter hundert Rückschlägen, durch viele Irrwege verführt" - and with the virtue of being "wirklich erlebt". The anonymous reviewer in Der Morgen was more astutely cautious: "man wird [den Roman] in seiner erziehungspolitischen Bedeutung erst ganz zu schätzen wissen, wenn der zweite Band er-schienen ist". [28]

For Becher, however, the post-war years were creatively arid. He admitted in a letter of 1947 to Hans Carossa how corrosive his twelve years of exile had been - "das Fege-feuer, wenn nicht die Hölle". [29] Abschied, for all the intractible creative dilemmas it caused, was the culmination of his exile writing: thereafter he had produced nothing better than a dutiful drama on the heroic Soviet defence of Stalingrad, Winterschlacht (1942), and a stream of conventional poems. The new German socialist state - an arbitrary segment of a divided nation - could not have been further removed from the comforting organic asso-ciations of 'Heimat' and 'Gemeinschaft' amidst the post-war chaos of homelessness, material deprivation and pro-found personal disorientation: and Becher himself was cut off politically from the Bavarian countryside with which he felt his strongest emotional ties. In 1947-48, he gave vent to profound feelings of melancholy and despair, in the poems which make up the volume Volk im Dunkel wandelnd (1948), like "Ruinen im Mond":

Ruinen, mondbeschienen ...
Es wächst aus dunkler Schicht
Hervor aus den Ruinen
Der Toten Angesicht,
Um in des Mondes Scheinen,
Von Menschen unbeweint,
Dem Licht sich zu vereinen,
Das weinend niederscheint.[30]

Only in the 'Goethe-Jahr' 1949 are there signs that
Becher was freeing himself from the depths of his depression, and, significantly, through renewed study of
the 'Vorbild', whom he had found such a stabilising force
during the exile years. In his speech at the anniversary
celebrations at Weimar, "Der Befreier", Becher showed how
Goethe's "geniale Selbstgestaltung" could become the basis
for the solution of mankind's most crucial problems:
Goethe was an outstanding "Menschheitserzieher" because
he came to incarnate "das neue Menschenbild", and not
through the dogmatic assertion of abstract truths. On detailed examination, this speech of Becher's reads as a
pitiless public self-examination, an attempt to overcome
the "Enttäuschung" and "Schrecken" of recent experience,
and to recognise that the freedom of the artist consists
in bringing himself "in Übereinstimmung ... mit den geschichtlichen Notwendigkeiten [des] Zeitalters". The
supreme task of the German poet is to come to terms with
present realities - "unsere deutsche Heimat uns zu einer
konkreten deutschen Heimat werden zu lassen" - but in doing
so to reject all utopian simplifications: Goethe was "all-
zusehr Realist, um nicht billige Wunschbilder sich vor-
gaukeln zu lassen".[31]

This speech marks a new determination in Becher to
overcome his artistic and personal crisis by a concrete
depiction of 'das standhafte Leben', in the state which
was about to establish its political identity as the
German Democratic Republic. Thanks to his new faith in
the Goethean process of 'Selbstgestaltung', he is more
aware of the pitfalls of the exemplary perspective of a
Hans Gastl, yet the coincidence that the founding of the
GDR, in October 1949, occurred just before the historical
'turning-point' of the half-century must have made thoughts
of a parallel situation to the opening of Abschied difficult to resist: if 1900 marked the beginning of the
critical era of 'Abschiednehmen', then, after all the
setbacks, 1950 might usher in the new era of 'Anderswerden'.
The form he chose for this long-delayed continuation of
Abschied was quite unorthodox, but one which might allow
for spontaneity with the least danger of schematism: the
keeping of a diary for 1950 which would, following Goethe's

example, harmonise private and historically significant experience.

In the opening sections of Becher's Diary, Auf andere Art so große Hoffnung [32], the parallels to Abschied are striking: it begins with the "Silvesterfeier", the sense of "Abschied" and the vague "Erwartung, daß noch irgend etwas geschehen müsse", but there is also a new awareness of "Langeweile" and of an unrelentingly harsh political climate.(11). The goal is still "Anderswerden"(21) but the way it might be achieved through the Tagebuch is not specified. He now hopes to solve the problem of perspective, of writing spontaneously about the immediate present, by opting for the diary-form and consciously moulding it into a 'Kunstform' for public consumption. He seeks on the one hand to present "ein 'Werden' ... in seiner ganzen Unmittelbarkeit und Widersprüchlichkeit"(21), and on the other to create "ein Denkmal des ersten Jahres der Republik".

Becher soon indicates why he cannot continue Abschied in the way he originally intended. He reveals that the writing of Abschied took five difficult years, most of which time was occupied with thoughts of abandoning the novel and writing a cycle of poems on the same theme, an admission of the anguish it caused him trying to strike an acceptable balance between ideological preconceptions and subjective experience:

> Wenn ich auch nur im geringsten geahnt hätte,
> was für Schwierigkeiten sich während des
> Schaffens für mich auftürmen würden, hätte
> ich fluchtartig mir einen anderen Beruf aus-
> gesucht und vor allem das Prosaschreiben für
> immer gelassen.(29)

There are, as Hans Mayer pointed out in his perceptive review of the Tagebuch, [33] fundamental differences between the diary and the novel, which expose the degree of wishful thinking behind Becher's view that the former might represent an adequate vehicle for the continuation of Abschied: in the diary, nothing is "wirklich durchgestaltet", problems are merely "angedeutet", and the novelist changing to the diary-form might easily be led into superficiality - "der Erzähler würde ... Stoffe bloß aphoristisch skizzieren, statt sie auszuführen und zu gestalten". While emphasising the real need for the continuation, Mayer makes it clear that the Tagebuch alone will not suffice:

> Wollte das Tagebuch 1950 die Fortsetzung
> bieten? Doch wohl kaum, denn die gewählte
> Form konnte niemals mehr als Materialien zu

einem nach wie vor fälligen Romanbericht
geben.

Becher's Tagebuch has indeed many highly unsatisfactory
aspects: his continual fluctuations of interest in the
project take him from vivid self-analysis and depictions
of encounters past and present, to ill-disguised padding
with speeches and didactic generalisations, which he freely admits afterwards to be "unverdauliche Brocken".(514)
It is, however, most significant for the light it casts on
two problematic aspects of Abschied: the depiction of the
Expressionist period and of everyday life in the new world
of socialism.

Becher's recollections of his Expressionist years in
the Tagebuch are sketchy and unrelated, but nonetheless
amount to a revision of his earlier ruthless attitude
towards his literary beginnings in Munich and Berlin.
The first reference shows how exciting and important it
all was to him, and gives the sense of rediscovery of a
vital part of himself:

> Die 'Weißen Blätter' und die 'Aktion' durch-
> blätternd, entdecke ich mich wieder selbst,
> Beiträge, die geradezu wie verschollen auf
> mich wirken, wie aus einem anderen Leben.(248)

For the first time since the 1920s, Becher suggests the
continuity of his personal development from bourgeois
rebellion to revolutionary commitment. Whether recalling
his feelings of delight at having a poem accepted by Franz
Pfemfert for Aktion (265), or admitting his "riesige
Schulden" to Emmy Hemmings (the Magda of Abschied) and
her friends, there is no sign of the guilt which had such
a distorting effect on his portrayal of the Café Stefanie
in the novel. The reason, however, is hardly the one put
forward by Weisbach in his study of the Tagebuch, that
Becher had depicted "alles Wesentliche und Prinzipielle
zum Expressionismus" in Abschied, and could therefore
allow himself the luxury of 'uncritical' reminiscence in
the Tagebuch! [34]   It is rather an integral part of his
stated purpose in compiling the Tagebuch - that of "Zu-
Gericht-Sitzen über sich selbst"(21) - that he should
begin a critical reappraisal of his Expressionist past at
this stage.

If these new 'heretical' insights into the past are
not plentiful, it is equally rare to discover evidence in
the Tagebuch of what is unique in 'der neue Mensch' in the
socialist Germany of 1950. For the most part, Becher's
only contact with the 'ordinary' working people is in his
official capacity as a State dignitary. He visits schools
where the pupils sing the new national anthem composed by

Hanns Eisler and himself (37); he inspects industrial
complexes like the Lauta mines and receives formal letters
of thanks from apprentices (483ff); he is fascinated by
the "Mitspielen der Zuschauer" at football matches.(447)
He appears surprisingly content with such remote exchanges
- the "rührende Zuschriften" he receives become his "täglich Brot" and help him to forget his moments of "Ver-
zweiflung".(37) Only occasionally is there indication of
a developing friendship outside his circle of cultured
friends: a young 'Aktivist' dares to inquire - "Und was
machst du?" - and thereby initiates a mutually enlightening
friendship, which allows Becher to feel that he understands
"den neuen Menschen ... in seiner greifbaren, sinnlichen
Körperlichkeit"(316-7), yet this living incarnation of the
ideal is never depicted in any individual detail. The
impression inevitably develops that Becher is at his
happiest in the tranquillity of his country retreat at
Saarow, and suffers frequently from boredom and depression
in his public duties.
    As Mayer suggests, the importance of the Tagebuch is
much more as a "Lebensdokument" than as a "kulturelles
Dokument für unser aller Leben", since "wesentliche Be-
reiche unseres Lebens kommen zu kurz, sind entweder nur
mit wenigen Hinweisen abgetan oder gar nicht erst ge-
staltet". He speculates pointedly whether the "Langeweile" which Becher attributed to everyday bureaucratic
routine was not more profoundly indicative of an inner
"Gefühl der Leere, der Entwirklichung des Lebens", resulting from a lack of meaningful contact with his fellow-
men. Mayer's summarising comments indicate why 'der neue
Mensch' remains as much an abstract concept here as in
Abschied: the political realities of 1950 are too often
viewed from this distance - "von außen, um nicht zu sagen:
von oben".
    This criticism clearly had a powerful effect on Becher,
because he refers to it in detail in the supplement of
1951 he later added to the Tagebuch: he feels unable to
accept that all his "menschliche Begegnungen" have been
"ohne tiefere Folge, ohne poetische Folgerung".(719)
But it had become obvious, as the year progressed, that
the Tagebuch was a "Fehlschlag"(718) above all as a
continuation of Abschied, and by Christmas 1950 he was
starting to sketch out the opening scene of a totally
distinct 'zweiter Teil' of his novel. He had also decided on a new name for his hero which would emphasise his
continuing search for a fulfilling role in life, which he
has Hans' friend and advisor Sack suggest to him: "ich
würde raten zu 'Wiederanders'. Dann brauchst du den Namen
nicht immer wieder zu ändern".(570)

The final reappraisal: 'Wiederanders'

After the <u>Tagebuch</u>, Becher's main contribution to
literary life in East Germany in the 1950s was through
the four volumes of his <u>Bemühungen</u>, which represent an
extension of the aesthetic deliberations and self-analysis
begun in the Diary, in a looser aphoristic form. [35]
Perhaps the most significant theme which emerges here is
that of growing disharmony within Becher between his private and public 'self', between the "Dichter" and the
"Funktionär". The impression given, with increasing
clarity, is that even Becher's previously unshakeable
loyalty to the Party was put under immense strain in this
harsh period of Cold War confrontation. He was nevertheless elevated to the post of Minister for Culture in 1954,
and dutifully continued to produce third-rate poems with
a half propagandistic, half emotional basis, in the manner
of "Schöne Deutsche Heimat":

> ... Schön sind die Menschen vor allem dadurch,
> Daß sie sich eine menschliche Ordnung geschaffen
> > haben,
> Eine schöne Menschengemeinschaft ...
>
> Darum ist die Heimat auch wahrhaft schön nur dort,
> Wo der Mensch sich eine menschliche Ordnung
> > geschaffen hat,
> Eine menschliche Schönheit.
> Die wahre Schönheit ist ganz.
> Singt das Lied der ganzen Schönheit! [36]

At the same time, he showed increasing opposition, in the
more 'private' <u>Bemühungen</u>, to the SED's ever tighter im-
position of the Soviet stereotype of Socialist Realism on
what he had hoped would become a distinctive literature
built on classical German foundations.
   Inevitably, these conflicts led to deliberations on the
inescapable pressures which, even under socialism, fragment
personality into various 'acceptable' roles - in glaring
contrast to his postulations of 'Ganzheit' in works like
<u>Abschied</u>. Indeed, he now suggests that inner harmony and
fulfilment are impossible in any modern society:

> Die Selbstentfremdung des Menschen zeigt sich
> vor allem in der Bewußtseinsspaltung. Sie ist
> nicht nur ein schwerer Krankheitsprozeß, der
> sich in zunehmendem Maße verbreitet und vertieft,
> sondern muß vor allem als ein gesellschaftliches
> Phänomen betrachtet werden. Dem modernen Menschen
> gegenüber erscheinen die Menschen früherer Zeiten
> als 'ganze' Menschen. Der heutige Mensch ist

> nicht mehr identisch mit dem Menschen, der er
> nach außen hin, und mit dem, der er nach innen
> hin ist. Der Privatmensch ist ein anderer als
> derjenige im Beruf ... Der Mensch ist nach allen
> Seiten hin gespalten ... [37]

Despite this, Becher still sees art as having the difficult task of recreating man in his original 'wholeness',
and it is in this context that he returns, with trepidation,
to his plans for Abschied, at different times through the
Bemühungen. On one occasion he feels he has received the
"Schöpfungsplan" for the continuation in a vision at
Saarow, akin to that of St. Paul on the road to Emmaeus,
and dares himself to resist the comfortable routine of
"die büromäßige Geschäftigkeit, das billige Sich-Bekannt-
machen und Geehrt-Werden", in order to describe his
passionate, explosive feelings at the beginnings of his
"Bewußtwerdung". He refers to it again as he laments his
"poetische Selbstverkümmerung": by writing poetry he has
taken the "Weg des geringsten Widerstandes" and avoided
the major work he feels he must write. As a warning to
himself, he recalls Engels' remarks on Platen:

> Er wußte wohl, daß ein solches großes Werk nötig
> sei, um seinem Ruhme Dauer zu verleihen; aber
> er fühlte auch, daß seine Kraft noch nicht dazu
> ausreiche, und hoffte von der Zukunft und seinen
> Vorarbeiten; indessen verfloß die Zeit, er kam
> aus den Vorarbeiten gar nicht heraus und starb
> endlich. [38]

The opportunity and the motivation for this arduous
task eventually came under circumstances which, ironically,
recall Becher's writing of Abschied, during the relief
from the burden of everyday political work that exile
brought after 1933. To the amazement of most intellectuals
in the GDR, who saw Becher as an incorrigible political
conformist (whose criticisms would always, as in his Bemühungen, be shrouded in the ambiguity of generalised
statements), he became the key figure behind the GDR's
brief cultural 'Thaw' of 1955-56. He used his political
power as Minister of Culture to facilitate a critical
debate on the disastrous effects of the rigid Stalinist
control of literature - a debate which demonstrated that
the exile generation of culturally significant figures
in the GDR, including Brecht, Seghers, Lukács and Becher
himself, despite their often radically differing views on
literature (and their personal antagonisms), were united
in their desire to liberate GDR literature from this
'Kulturpolitik'. [39]

Becher probably came closer than at any other time in
his career to complete agreement with Lukács, in the face
of the interchangeable 'Aufbauromane' which the SED had
attempted to establish as the dominant genre of the 1950s.
He reacted with unusual forcefulness to Hans Marchwitza's
Roheisen, the novel officially lauded as the model for
East German literature in 1955, as much as Abschied had
been a decade earlier, and which sought to portray the
industrial reconstruction of the GDR in the same terms of
harmonious 'Gemeinschaft' as Becher had used previously
for his utopian projections of the socialist future. In
what was much more than an objective criticism of
Marchwitza's failings, Becher finally showed himself
willing to recognise that proletarian individuals and
socialist society have to develop through conflict (just
as their bourgeois counterparts did historically), and
that positive heroes cannot be viewed as 'ganze Menschen'
unless their private lives are organically related to their
public achievements.[40]   His language echoes Lukács'
criticisms of Socialist Realism twenty years previously,
criticisms which Lukács himself was still repeating at
the Fourth Writers' Congress early in 1956, on one of his
rare visits to the GDR, when he took the Socialist Realism
of a new era to task for presenting "programmatische
Forderung" as contemporary reality, and insisted on respect
for the "Schlauheit der Wirklichkeit" in its erratic, and
slow, evolution towards socialism.[41]

Within months, these revived hopes of fostering an
authentic literature had apparently been dashed by political developments. Lukács was in disgrace following his
involvement with the Nagy government in Hungary and the
ruthless Soviet suppression of the insurrection; the
GDR's modest intellectual revolt had been easily crushed
and Becher had - unofficially at least - been relieved of
his responsibilities as Minister of Culture. However un-
pleasant life may have been for Becher in the immediate
aftermath of these events, before he reverted to his old
habits of ritual public conformism, is impossible to
assess: but one less unwelcome consequence of these upheavals was that he had time at last to devote himself to
the Wiederanders project. In the event, Becher had little
time left - he lived just two years longer (until October
1958) and was increasingly incapacitated by illness in
his last months - and nothing was known about this work
until after his death. Even the publication of revealing
excerpts from his unfinished manuscript in the special
number of Sinn und Form dedicated to Becher's work in
1959 failed to attract critical attention - perhaps
because he had long since been written off as a serious

creative artist. When the entire fragment of Wiederanders (almost 200 pages) was finally published in 1975 with Abschied in the eleventh volume of Becher's Gesammelte Werke, editorial efforts were made, with apparent success, to obscure the relationship between the two works.[42]

It is immediately obvious, however, that Wiederanders is not the long anticipated continuation of Abschied, but rather a fundamental reappraisal of the representative experience of Becher's generation, and especially of the importance of the Expressionist period. Furthermore, it has the narrative perspective on his past which he so transparently avoided offering in Abschied, a perspective which now gives him scope to record his views on the progress actually achieved towards 'das standhafte Leben' at the time of writing. Wiederanders - at least in its conception - is an autobiographical novel which could have had the depth, and the respect for the politically incalculable 'Schlauheit der Wirklichkeit', to become a worthy successor to those classical 'Entwicklungsromane' which are also 'revisions' of earlier versions, Wilhelm Meisters Lehrjahre and Der grüne Heinrich. The project was, of course, over-ambitious and doomed to failure, but there is enough evidence to make Becher's intentions, and his self-critical attitude to Abschied, perfectly clear.

The Wiederanders fragment is divided into three books: the first is devoted to the period when a 19 year-old Hans leaves home and enters bohemian circles in Munich, although there are still references to childhood experiences not included in Abschied; Book II covers his first experiences in the "Großstadtdschungel"(530) of Berlin, again in a recognisable Expressionist context; and Book III describes events in Munich following the outbreak of the First World War. This structure in itself reveals that Becher's primary interest was to depict his own experiences in the Expressionist era (roughly from 1910-15). It is true, as Becher's friend and publisher at this period, H.F. Bachmair, indicated in an assessment of Wiederanders,[43] that it is not directly autobiographical, but it is indubitably written in such a way that a far more authentic picture of the moral and intellectual climate emerges than in Abschied.

This is no longer the experience of the Hans Gastl, who was originally depicted as some four or five years younger than Becher, in order to reduce his possible contact with this 'bourgeois decadence' to a minimum. The names of most of the other characters have changed, even though some are still clearly recognisable: Sack is now Wagemühl, Hartinger has become Wedel, and Hans is now mainly referred to as "der Andere" (or occasionally

"Wiederanders"). Other historical figures, like van Hoddis
and Pfemfert, are depicted, not without irony, but more
accurately integrated into their historical setting.(550-7)
Hans' political involvement is presented as one fluctuating
element within a contradictory personality. He is at one
moment deeply engrossed in the study of Marx with
Wagemühl (509-10), then unflatteringly depicted wandering
in the morgue, trying to escape from his former self,
"in der Pose eines Hamlets mit der Zigarette im Mund".(547)
Similarly, in the few glimpses afforded into his life in
Munich in wartime, there are details of Hans' morphium
sessions with the beautiful Yvonne, as well as of his bold
reading of an anti-war poem in the Münchener Kammerspiele,
when he modifies Horace's "Dulce et decorum est ..." into

> Und darum ist es süß und ehrenvoll,
> Als Schlachtvieh auf dem Schlachtfeld zu
> verrecken.(596)

Overall, the process of 'Anderswerden' for the middle-
class intellectual of Becher's generation is now depicted,
much more plausibly, as tentative and confused.
　　The framework reflections of the third-person narrator
- "der Fünfundsechzigjährige", as Becher himself was in
1956 - throw more light on the reasons why Wiederanders
was not conceived as the continuation of Abschied, but
rather as the fresh presentation of his own development
up to the First World War, which was needed in order to
make a convincing continuation possible. In Wiederanders,
Hans' crucial break with the family comes at the end of
Book I, which, as Bachmair has pointed out, forms "eine
gedrängte Variante des 'Abschied' " in itself, when he embarks on an independent life as a poet and student in
Berlin. The narrator, unmistakably Becher, stresses the
implications of this important change of emphasis:

> Ich habe meine Jugend noch einmal geschrieben,
> umgeschrieben sozusagen. Man wird diese
> Beschreibung mit der vor zwanzig Jahren ver-
> gleichen und untersuchen, worin die beiden
> Beschreibungen sich voneinander unterscheiden.
> Man wird daraus Folgerungen ziehen. Das aber
> ist schon nicht mehr meine Sache ... Jetzt
> bin ich dort angelangt, wo Anders nach Berlin
> fährt. Er hat Abschied genommen. Das Anders-
> werden beginnt ...(512)

The opportunity to carry through this major re-structuring
of Abschied has come because the narrator has suddenly
been shorn of his official responsibilities and duties:

> Es tat .... sehr weh, als Staatsbürger ohne
> Amt und Würden sein Dasein einrichten zu
> müssen ... Eine Art Klaviatur schien unter
> ihm weggezogen zu sein.

He feels forced to make "Wiederbelebungsversuche", with
the hope "wieder ins Leben zurückzukehren", and discovers,
as he travels in the underground for the first time in
years, a new sense of liberation:

> Der Leutegeruch tat ihm wohl, und daß seine
> Hosen nicht mehr mit ihren Bügelfalten prahlen
> konnten, ließ ihn schmunzeln und, sie tröstend,
> sich auf die Schenkel klopfen.

He admits that the long years of political responsibility
have drained his 'human' sensitivities - "er war kein
Mensch mehr, sondern eine Instanz" - and made genuine,
fulfilling relationships impossible:

> So hatte sich auch die Beziehung zu den
> Menschen verändert. Die einen bemühten sich,
> den Umgang mit ihm nach Möglichkeit zu
> meiden, nachdem er in Amt und Würden geraten
> war, die anderen spürten ihn auf, wo sie nur
> konnten. Die einen sparten mit Worten ihm
> gegenüber und legten bewußt eine Distanz
> zwischen ihm und sich, die anderen ließen ihn
> überdeutlich den Respekt fühlen, den er ihnen
> einflößte ...(448-50)

The writing of <u>Wiederanders</u> is clearly an integral part
of his attempt to bring "Ordnung in sein Leben"(458),
which now allows him to reveal the real complexity -
"Wesensunendlichkeit" - of his personality and his completely unresolved problems of identity - "nicht zwei
Seelen wohnten in seiner Brust, sondern ein ganzer Seelen-
verein".(464)
The remarkable thing about <u>Wiederanders</u> - in relation
to <u>Abschied</u> - is the absence of visions of 'der vollendete
Mensch' or projections of 'das standhafte Leben'. The
process of "Rechenschaft, Rechtfertigung, Anklage und
Selbstbeschuldigung", which he sees as the eternal task
of old men (468), evidently left little scope for the
dreams of tomorrow. Just for one impressive moment, at
the end of Book II, Becher gives expression to an ex-
pansive personal sense of continuity which binds together
past, present and future. As he sits with his wife at
Saarow on 1st August 1957, captivated by the brightness
and tranquillity of the Scharmützelsee, he recalls the
same day over forty years previously, when the First World
War broke out. He remembers hearing the fateful news

whilst on a day's outing on the Müggelsee in the steamer
"Möwe", and seeing all its passengers drunk with patriotic
excitement at the thought of war. This in its turn revives
memories of Rimbaud's poem "Le bâteau ivre", which became
the "Marseillaise" of the Expressionist generation, and of
the Potemkin mutiny (evoking, as in <u>Abschied</u>, the motifs
"ein ganzes Schiff" and "das Lied vom Anderswerden" sung
by the sailors). Out of these memories and many-layered
associations emerges a new dream of future peace and freedom through the reunification of Germany - as Becher demonstrates his unwillingness to abandon another of his
heretical hopes of 1956:

> ... ein 'Glückhaftes Schiff' ist es, das jetzt
> dort unten an uns vorüberfährt, lachend,
> jubilierend - ein Lied von Freiheit und ,
> Frieden ... Es hat sich gelohnt, meinst du
> auch nicht [...] Aber man muß an Deutschland,
> an das ganze Deutschland denken - solche
> glückhaften Schiffe sollen auch auf dem Rhein,
> auf dem Bodensee fahren ...(582)

But this is nothing more than a single moment of utopian
vision in an otherwise highly reflective work, which shows
how tenuous the links had become between the artistic
priorities of Becher's generation of intellectuals and the
propandistic objectives of the SED by the middle 1950s.
The <u>Wiederanders</u> fragment offers impressive evidence
of how untenable the uneasy compromise of the 1930s with
Socialist Realism had become for Becher towards the end
of his life. Although <u>Wiederanders</u> is too incomplete to
stand as an alternative to Becher's earlier, 'exemplary'
novel, it demonstrates his recognition that he had made
a serious artistic error in distorting fundamental aspects
of his experience and anticipating the new socialist
Germany as a paradise, in which community is unthreatened,
continuity irrelevant in terms of personal development,
and identity instantly achievable.

CHAPTER 2

THE POST-WAR TRANSITION TO SOCIALISM

The fallible hero and the revival of
the 'Entwicklungsroman'

The brief 'Thaw' of 1955-56 did not make any enduring
impact on GDR literature: it did, however, provide an
invaluable temporary relief from the almost exclusive
cultural-political emphasis on the 'Aufbauroman' and the
industrial worker as positive hero. For the new generation
of writers too young to have had the option of political
exile from the Third Reich this meant a first opportunity
to come to terms creatively with their experience prior to
1945. For GDR literature generally there was a chance to correct
the impression of "Vergangenheitslosigkeit" brought about
by the ideological need to establish rigid demarcation
lines between the socialist 'Gemeinschaft' and the National
Socialist past.[1]
    The immediate outcome was a 'war literature' characterised
by such titles as Franz Fühmann's Kameraden (1955), Karl
Mundstock's Bis zum letzten Mann (1956) and Harry Thürk's
Die Stunde der toten Augen (1957), seeking to explore the
previously taboo issue of how the Third Reich won the
allegiance of so many idealistic, morally sensitive
members of the generation born in the 1920s. As a reaction to the pretentiousness of industrial novels claiming to portray the social totality of the 1950s in the
GDR, most of this literature was deliberately modest in
scope, concentrating on the severe psychological reper-
cussions of war experience without attempting to bridge
the gulf between those years and the present day in terms
of the continuity of personal development. The narrative
framework may be more comprehensive in Erwin Strittmatter's
Der Wundertäter (Part I, 1957), but even here a subversive
picaresque element is blended with the traditional moral
seriousness of the 'Entwicklungsroman', and the problems
of post-war development are left to a sequel which only
materialised in 1973.
    The fortunes of the sympathetic, but fallible, pro-
tagonists of these stories inevitably raised issues
challenging the ideological dualism which had hitherto
allowed no room for differentiation between the extremes
of alienation and 'Gemeinschaft', disorientation and
self-fulfilment (whether the contrast involved the Nazi
past or the current threat of the Federal Republic).

Fühmann's <u>Kameraden</u> depicts the crisis of a young soldier confronted with the corrupt reality behind the moral clichés to which National Socialism laid exclusive claim − 'Kameradschaft', the 'Volksgemeinschaft', 'Treue', 'Ehre' and so on − and has no omniscient socialist narrator to reassure the reader of this disconcertingly open-ended tale that the demoralising contradictions between ideology and expediency are a purely historical phenomenon. [2] The brutalising effects of war on sensitive individuals are so widely underlined elsewhere that the idea of a sudden post-war conversion to socialism as a dramatic 'Wandlung' is exposed as having been, at best, a tentative first step into the unknown. Although the protagonists of these stories have qualities worthy of admiration, they remain very limited in their capacity for independent reflection or taking a political initiative. The stories generally leave few illusions about the length of time any fundamental transference of allegiance might have required.

Quite apart from the implicit threats to ideological orthodoxy in the 'Menschenbild' emerging from this war fiction, it was too obviously tainted by Western stylistic influences (such as the 'naturalism' of Mailer or Hemingway) to be accorded creative respectability after 1957, once the SED had reasserted its authority over its dissident intellectuals. Preoccupation with the war had become a new and unwelcome factor threatening to draw the two German literatures closer together, and the popularity of the subject-matter in the GDR had at least as much to do with the search for vicarious exitement or the desire to relive past adventures as with the readership's readiness to draw radical conclusions from the horrors of the Third Reich. The protocols of the SED's carefully managed cultural conferences of the period 1957-59 reflect a widely held determination to suppress this war literature completely and revert to exhaustive examination of "unsere brennenden Gegenwartsprobleme" (in the build-up to the 'Bitterfelder Weg'). There was, however, some indication of a willingness to learn from the cultural-political mistakes of the earlier 1950s which had created the monotonously predictable 'Aufbauromane'. It was J.R. Becher's Stalinist successor as the key figure in the GDR's 'Kulturpolitik', Alfred Kurella, who recognised that the portrayal of unheroic individuals during the Third Reich could have positive educational potential − if the war itself were shown to be essentially anti-socialist and viewed from a mature contemporary perspective. This position was endorsed by younger critics such as Hermann Kant, who also acknowledged the need to cater for their readership's "Abenteuerbedürfnis", rather than pretending that it was somehow incompatible with socialist commitment. Kant, with his colleague Frank Wagner, enthusiastically anticipated a literature which would illuminate the character development of exemplary individuals, in an authentically complex way, beyond their early acceptance of fascism:

> Welch eine verlockende Vorstellung ist es für uns,
> ein Buch in unserer Hand halten zu können, das das
> Schicksal unserer Nation im Bereich und vom
> Standpunkt des Proletariats beleuchtet, das vor
> allem den Wurzeln der zeitweiligen faschistischen
> Erfolge nachspürt, dem Wirken der Demagogie und
> des Terrors, dann aber auch der einsetzenden Krise,
> dem langsamen Sichlösen, dem Wiederaufleben
> verschütteten Klassenbewußtseins, also dem Entstehen
> jener Menschen, die heute den sozialistischen Weg
> in Deutschland gehen.[4]

There was a grim irony in the fact that the SED's recognition of the value of 'Entwicklungsroman' structures was emerging as part of the wider campaign against the 'revisionism' of the 'Thaw'. Some of its intellectual leaders, like Brecht and Hans Mayer, by relating the failures of GDR literature to ignorance of the perceptions and techniques of twentieth century modernism, were felt to have opened the flood gates to the Western cultural influences which had allegedly marred the GDR's war fiction. Other figureheads, like Becher and Lukács, had, in contrast, sinned primarily through their broader political misjudgements. Rather inconveniently, it was the unmentionable Lukács who, just prior to his involvement with the provisional Hungarian government of 1956, had set out the central argument upon which this reorientation of the GDR's war-literature was being based, in his essay "Der kritische Realismus in der sozialistischen Gesellschaft".[5]
Lukács had emphasised the qualitative superiority of fiction which integrated the treatment of war into the broader totality of socialist progress - as Arnold Zweig had done - over the honest, but ideologically deficient anti-war novels of an E.M. Remarque or a Norman Mailer. He had gone on to stress the comparability of the dynamic changes in East European society since the war to the great upheavals - of 1789, 1848, and 1914-18 - which had given rise to all the major fictional studies of personality development since Wilhelm Meisters Lehrjahre. Around 1945 the receptive individual had again been faced with the historically decisive struggle to identify himself with the community preparing the way for a better future - and that now meant a new state based on socialist principles.

The superiority of the socialist 'Entwicklungsroman' lay
in its capacity to transcend the resignation and the in-
determinate open-endedness of its bourgeois counterpart
(and presumably now also the utopian expectations of a
work like <u>Abschied</u>). It alone could convey the insight
that in socialist society "der bürgerliche Individualis-
mus [...] vom Leben selbst zu einer bewußten Gesellschaft-
lichkeit umerzogen wird". At the same time, Lukács had
continued to stress the gradualness - "ungleichmäßige
Allmählichkeit" - of any individual's acquisition of socialist consciousness, and rejected the use of a narrative
standpoint which suggests that communism has been virtually achieved already - "die Perspektive des rapid nahenden
Kommunismus".[6]

Lukács was thus still endeavouring to create an ideological climate in which writers would feel able to trust
the apparent contradictoriness of their concrete experience. The GDR's cultural spokesmen of 1957 were
hoping that the structure of the 'Entwicklungsroman' could
be exploited for the narrower didactic purposes behind
their view of 'exemplary' experience. However ambiguous
the assignment being given to the GDR's young authors
might have been as a result, it did have unmistakable
literary consequences over the next five or six years.
On the one hand, there was little more of the open-ended
war-fiction published in 1955-57. On the other, a series
of semi-autobiographical novels with the desired structural
pattern and produced by previously little known figures,
such as Max Walter Schulz, Günter de Bruyn and Dieter
Noll, began to appear. Each of them sought to strike an
ideologically acceptable balance between personal and
'typical' experience, but each came to revealingly different
conclusions about how that balance was to be struck.
Furthermore, there was little evidence, amidst the confusion surrounding J.R. Becher's status between 1956 and
his death in 1958, that they were aware of his final, radical resolution of the same basic dilemma in his plans
for <u>Wiederanders</u>.

Dieter Noll was the first to publish after the ideological preferability of the 'Entwicklungsroman' to
straight war fiction had been made abundantly clear. The
emphasis he placed in the first part of <u>Die Abenteuer des
Werner Holt</u> (1960) on graphic depiction of adolescent adventures, bombing-raids, battle action and description of
Nazi atrocities suggested that he had retained substantial
affinities with 'naturalistic' writers such as Thürk and
Mundstock. Moreover, by opting for a straightforward
chronological approach, Noll restricted himself in the
first volume (as Strittmatter did in <u>Der Wundertäter</u>) to
the negative side of his protagonist's progress - from

Holt's last days in school as a rebellious sixteen-year-
old to his breakdown as war ends two years later. There
was only a vague indication of the moral growth to come
in the second volume. The outstanding popularity in the
GDR of this 'Roman einer Jugend' has evidently had as
much to do with the gripping documentary qualities of
Holt's war-time adventures as with his longer-term
exemplary status.

The works which followed, Max Walter Schulz's <u>Wir sind
nicht Staub im Wind</u> (1962) and Günter de Bruyn's
<u>Der Hohlweg</u> (1963), have a structure which consciously
contrasts with earlier war-literature and reflects the
rather schematic distinction made by Lukács between the
'Entwicklungsroman' in Critical and Socialist Realism.
Lukács had argued that the socialist 'Entwicklungsroman'
transcends the limitations of its bourgeois counterpart,
which tends to restrict itself to the period between
childhood and the "Krise der Mannbarkeit". In Socialist
Realism, the main focus should be placed upon "jene Krise
vom erwachsenen Menschen ... die die Entstehung des
Sozialismus in der bürgerlichen Intelligenz hervorruft",
and the subsequent process of integration into the
socialist community.[7] Both Schulz and de Bruyn
commence their narrative in the last months of war, with
the incident which provokes the fundamental identity-
crisis in their central figures, Rudi Hagedorn and
Wolfgang Weichmantel. In consequence, they are obliged
to motivate the crisis indirectly, through the economical
use of flashbacks, introspective analysis, meetings with
earlier friends, and similar devices. The description of
war-experience itself is thus reduced to a minimum, and
the emphasis laid upon the future course of development
for the hero.

The characterisation of Hagedorn and Weichmantel reflects each author's ponderous awareness of the literary
tradition within which he was working. Schulz in particular
has Hagedorn, as a naive adolescent, adopt the pseudonym
'Hyperion' and give expression to much of his most intimate
emotional and intellectual turmoil, both before and after
his years as a 'Frontschwein', in letters to the decidedly
ethereal Lea, a figure modelled closely on Hölderlin's
Diotima in <u>Hyperion</u>.[8] Furthermore, the post-war clash
of bourgeois and socialist mentalities is embodied in
representative figures who, in laboured imitation of
Thomas Mann's <u>Zauberberg</u>, engage in long philosophical
discussions remote from everyday realities. De Bruyn is
equally mindful of Hölderlin and the anguished references
in <u>Hyperion</u> to the "Zerrissenheit der Deutschen". He has
Weichmantel discover the novel as he recuperates from
wounds received in the last-ditch defence of the ravine

which gives the novel its title, and then identify with
Hyperion for much of the novel. De Bruyn also involves
Weichmantel in the nascent world of the theatre in post-
war Berlin, in an atmosphere broadly reminiscent of the
earlier sections of Wilhelm Meisters Lehrjahre. But, as
if to remind the reader that history also brings about
changes in experience, de Bruyn also provides a harsh
caricature of the enlightened aristocrats dear to Goethe
and Keller, through his depiction of the Oyst-Winterfeld
family, whose fortunes are linked with Weichmantel's from
the end of the war. Noll, when he came to write the second
volume of Werner Holt's adventures, the Roman einer Heimkehr, published in 1964, belatedly acknowledged his respect
for the GDR's more recent cultural heritage: at a crucial
moment, Holt is given Becher's Abschied and finds in it a
parallel to his ideological predicament. Analogies of
this kind run the risk of obscuring the historically distinctive aspects of growing up in the Third Reich, as does
their adherence to the practice of giving the hero a name
which emphasises a general aspect of personality: there
are suggestions of prickly individualism in Schulz's
'Hagedorn' and of the romantic dreamer shielding himself
from reality in de Bruyn's 'Weichmantel'.
    The only novel on this pattern in which the autobio-
graphical dimension seems to predominate over the 'exemplary'
is the one which marks Franz Fühmann's return to the theme
of the Third Reich, Das Judenauto (1962), with a first-
person narrator who is directly referred to as 'Fjumann'
by his Russian interrogators at one stage. This cycle of
stories, sub-titled 'Vierzehn Tage aus zwei Jahrzehnten',
provides an invaluable yardstick for assessing the schematic consequences of his colleagues' dependence on
literary models. Fühmann's stories appear very episodic,
but are in fact strongly unified through the consistency
of the narrative 'Ich', reflecting upon each station in
his development. Although the Sudeten German context is
Fühmann's own, he has made it clear that he shared the
endeavours of his contemporaries to concentrate upon the
historically significant aspects of their experience, and
not to offer irrelevant subjective detail.
    In the brief afterword to the subsequent Western edition
of Das Judenauto, Fühmann stated that the work was "keine
Selbstbiographie"; he had in any case indicated the representative quality of each episode by referring in its
title to an important contemporaneous event. This framework of progression - at times rather contrived - from
the Wall Street collapse of 1929 through events like the
Munich Agreement, the Battle for Stalingrad, the Nazi
capitulation and the formation of the SED, places the
fortunes of the narrator in the context of an inexorable

movement towards the achievement of socialism in Germany
after the war. He moves from vivid evocation of each
isolated incident to ironical self-analysis, emphasising
the contrasts between youthful naiveté and mature ideological insights. As his interest is mainly psychological,
to show how the values and prejudices of National Socialism
were absorbed naturally within a homogeneous environment,
Fühmann has not the same need to objectivise the 'reactionary' and 'progressive' tendencies of each period
within character-types, as the authors of the overt
'Entwicklungsromane' do in their quest for social breadth.
   As regards the portrayal of the protagonist himself,
however, all of these broadly autobiographical novels
reveal striking similarities. Their focus is concentrated
upon three main aspects of experience in a uniquely turbulent epoch. Firstly, they seek to analyse the values and
motives of their generation in contributing to the destructive power of the Third Reich, weighing up the relative importance of such factors as misguided idealism,
aggressive self-assertion and fearful compliance. Secondly, they depict the process of disillusionment, which
follows the realisation that war is meaninglessly wasteful
of human life and that they are on the side of the criminal
aggressor. This is seen to result in a major crisis of
identity and allegiance. Finally, they endeavour to show
how demoralised and sceptical young adults came to discover a new sense of purpose and commitment in aligning
themselves with the socialist regime established in East
Germany after 1945.
   Within this clearly defined tripartite structure, each
of these writers was still faced with the problem of maintaining psychological consistency in the development of
his central character. By offering a fairly complex analysis of the factors encouraging identification with
Hitler's Germany, and describing just how profound the
end-of-war alienation from authority and ideology was, he
would leave himself a task which was at once politically
hazardous and crucial to the credibility of literature in
the GDR: that of portraying the growth towards socialism
as a lengthy process, plagued with doubts and suspicions,
amidst the historically undeniable miseries of the post-
war years.[9]

'Bourgeois individualism':   growing up in the Third Reich

The notion of 'character' as something clearly divisible
into categories of relative good and evil is one which
these novels were evidently expected to endorse. Schulz
reflects this mentality at its crudest in the passage
marking the end of the review of Rudi Hagedorn's past in
Wir sind nicht Staub im Wind. Picking up a remark of one
of Hagedorn's comrades that he is a 'realist', Schulz
indicates his own acceptance of this designation by adding
that realists can be divided into those "mit und ohne
Charakter". Hagedorn, following the best traditions of
the genre, is at present only potentially good, revealing
"zwar ein leidlich guter ... aber kein starker Charakter".
The paragraph goes on to make it clear that what is required to fulfil such potential is a combination of such
factors as "Erkenntnis", the capacity for "Entweder-Oder-
Entscheidungen", "Geist", "Leben", the realisation of "den
schönen Reichtum menschlichen Wesens" and "praktische,
humane, charaktervolle Vernünftigkeit". (S 123-4)
     While the other authors are less abstractly didactic
in their conception of personality growth, there are many
common features in their depictions of the youthful weaknesses of their heroes. All of these figures are basically disorientated as they grow up in the Third Reich,
and much of the initial blame can be placed at the feet
of parents who have failed to offer any effective alternative to the prevailing ideology. Werner Holt's progress is
threatened by the break-up of his parents' marriage, caused
by a selfishly materialistic mother who is then mainly
responsible for his upbringing. The fathers of Hagedorn
and Weichmantel belong to the millions of Social Democrats who refused to continue the struggle against
Fascism after 1933, placing the retention of a lowly job
and family welfare first, but opting out of the task of
giving their sons moral and political guidance as a result. So even where social background should have helped
to create a sense of class-consciousness with which to
resist the call for a unified 'Volksgemeinschaft', Hagedorn
and Weichmantel find themselves adopting many of the
nebulous values exploited by the National Socialists.
Only the parents of Führmann's narrator, part of the
Sudeten German middle-class longing for the security which
integration into the Reich is expected to bring, support
Hitler enthusiastically, but only until it becomes clear
that killing and destruction are inevitable consequences
of his expansionist policies.
     Deprived of an effective parental example as to what
constitutes socially constructive behaviour, these figures
tend to direct their energies into a world of fantasy,

which never relates in more than a superficial way to the
threatened environment in which they live. Noll adopts
the unilluminating shorthand technique of indicating the
various elements which stimulate Holt's youthful imagination
through a list of his favourite books. The heroic Germanic
legends contained in the <u>Nibelungenlied</u>,the exotic exploits
of Karl May's heroes, the anarchic individualism of
Schiller's <u>Räuber</u> and the idealisation of love in the
romantic 'Märchen' are all interwoven with the recent
myth of war as the highest test of character, derived
from Ernst Jünger and Werner Beumelburg. From this hotch-
potch of disparate stimuli - "das Unvereinbare", as Noll
emphasises - Holt's generation has created its heroic
ideal, its "Heldentypus".(WH 21) The values especially
revered are the capacity for limitless loyalty and integrity in support of the supreme cause, which is fatally
undefined, and the proof of warrior-like toughness and
disregard for self whenever the 'Bewährungsprobe' is called
for. Holt and Fühmann's narrator are seen to be most
idealistically susceptible to such challenges, Holt endeavouring to assert himself amongst his new school-friends
and fellow-recruits by proving his aggressive superiority,
while his Sudeten counterpart needs to show his right to
inclusion amongst the 'true' Germans by a fanatical dedication to the nationalist cause. Fühmann evokes this
feeling by his vivid description of a huge gymnastic display in Breslau in 1938, which gave him his first glimpse
of the hallowed Führer.(J 37-8) The reference here to
Hitler as "ein Gott der Geschichte", as he salutes each
regional group during the march-past and enlists their
unwavering devotion,illustrates the concept of 'Schicksal'
with which Noll is centrally concerned in Book I of his
novel.[10] The dimension of moral choice and responsibility appears dispensable, whether one is in the hands
of a visible deity or the inscrutable destructive powers
which Holt imagines:

> Schicksal ... das ist jenes Große, Dunkle,
> Unbekannte, dem wir Menschen ausgeliefert
> sind ... Ist denn nicht auch unser Leben
> wie ein endloser, zielloser Weg, über dem
> die Vorsehung unser Schicksal wie ein
> Gewitter zusammenbraut?(WH 203)

The figures whose upbringing is more humble, Weichmantel
and Hagedorn, are less exposed to such broad sweeps of
imaginative fancy, which so usefully serve militaristic
ends. They tend to sustain themselves upon the more romantic and escapist aspects of the available models of
behaviour, perhaps as a reaction to the suppressed disaffection of their parents with the regime. From the

scanty information provided about Weichmantel's past, it
appears that he accepted something of the mythology of
"Vaterland" and "Fahneneid" (H 13), but tried to escape
whenever possible from the harsh world of the Hitler
Youth into sentimental daydreams. Hagedorn reflects in
greater detail upon his years as a charity pupil at the
Goethe-Schule in Reiffenberg. He was evidently so plagued
by feelings of inferiority amongst his middle-class companions that he found his chief consolation in identifying
with the ideals and passions of the Romantic hero in the
Hyperion mould, led on by a headmaster who was "jünglings-
haft verschwärmt" when it came to Hölderlin.(S 18)
     The greatest relief from such an oppressive environ-
ment comes in the isolation of nature. 'Weich'-mantel is
of course particularly sensitive to the elements:

> Wolfgang Weichmantel hatte Stille immer
> geliebt, draußen besonders, fern der Stadt.
> Er hatte auch die Nacht geliebt, die Sterne,
> flimmernd, weiß und rötlich, und die Erde
> hatte er geliebt, die schwarze, nasse
> Frühlingserde ...(H 11)

Hagedorn has an equally powerful awareness of nature and
the traditions developed over centuries in the small
mountain town in the Erzgebirge which he recognises as
his "Heimat". (S 35)   But neither of these more passive
figures has the pioneer's urge to reject civilisation and
survive in nature, which impels Holt and his intrepid
classmates to live out their dream of primitive heroism
for days in a mountain cave (even if their sustenance
comes at the expense of a poor farmer whose pig they steal).
     The development of genuine friendship in situations
where the dictates of fantasy far outweigh those of morality is fraught with hazards. Both Hagedorn and Holt find
themselves strongly influenced for the worse by older lads
who reveal reprehensible attitudes regarded as typical of
Hitler's Germany. Hagedorn's act of spontaneous courage
in saving Armin Saliger from drowning marks the start of
a relationship which for Saliger derives both from a
guilty sense of gratitude and a desire to dominate, whatever the oath of blood-brotherhood which they swear may
suggest to the idealistic Hagedorn. The class difference
between "Apothekersohn" and "Straßenkehrersohn" is emphasised from the outset, so that it comes as no surprise
when Saliger betrays the pledge of loyalty on the two
occasions when some moral probity or self-abnegation
would be required to uphold it. The sense of conflict
follows the arrival of Lea, the niece of their humanistic
headmaster Füßler, since her half-Jewish origins make her
persona non grata to respectable society, and yet both

lads are captivated by her charms. Saliger, as one of
the 'Scharführer' of the local Hitler Youth group, far
from defending Hagedorn when one of his 'Hyperion' love-
letters to Lea is discovered, plays a leading role in the
humiliation ritual conducted by the 'Geistergericht' in
the cellars under the school. Later, after Hagedorn has
resentfully left school and taken up an apprenticeship,
Saliger compounds the betrayal by seducing Lea and then
abandoning her as soon as the relationship becomes a
threat to his incipient career as an army officer.

Although Saliger reveals all the opportunism and
cowardice of the petit-bourgeois, spending the war-years
comfortably remote from the battlefront training recruits,
Holt's friend Wolzow provides ample evidence that the
military ethic is an equally strong driving-force in other
quarters of the middle-class. Wolzow, the latest offspring
of a long-established family of Prussian officers, directs
Holt's unspecific urge for 'Abenteuer' towards his own
monomaniac obsession with war as the only true adventure.
He leads Holt throughout their two years of rivalry into
excesses of inhumanity which distort the basically moral
response to life he shows elsewhere in taking up Karl
Moor's struggle for 'Gerechtigkeit'. Thus, while Holt
sets out to inflict retribution upon SS-officer Meißner,
who drove a peasant girl to suicide, Wolzow coldly ad-
ministers a vicious beating which goes beyond anything
Holt envisaged and leaves him bemused by "diese Mörder-
kaltblütigkeit mit gutem Gewissen".(WH 76) What makes
Wolzow a more sinister figure than the fanatical Nazis
encountered by Holt elsewhere is the calculated ruthlessness with which he dominates and destroys, whether it is
a matter of taking over control of a barracks from socially inferior recruits, or attacking Russian troops and
tanks along the Eastern front. Holt finally recognises,
as the war is undeniably lost, the perverse logic behind
Wolzow's exhortation to fight to the heroic end, and
realises that 'fate' is not a mysterious force but an
empty word used to delude the unwitting majority:

> Schicksal, dachte er, mein Schicksal heißt
> Wolzow ... ein Mensch, der sich Macht anmaßt
> über Leben und Tod ...Und er sah nun: Das
> Anonyme, das System, wohlgeordnet, mit Rang-
> abzeichen und Uniformen, eine Hierarchie der
> Gewalt ist unser aller Schicksal! Lüge,
> Betrug war alles, Verdummung war Gott und
> die Vorsehung nichts als Berechnung!(WH 529-30)

And yet, after he has made the decisive break with Wolzow,
Holt still risks his life in a vain attempt to save him

from the clutches of a marauding SS-group under the
leadership of Meißner, as if in a final attempt to assert
the validity of friendship and humanity across all the
ideological and moral barriers.

Fühmann and de Bruyn refrain from personalising the
corrupt and ruthless aspects of the Third Reich in this
way, evidently regarding it as an untenable simplification
to imply that the evils of the age were so readily identifiable. For similar reasons, the concrete representation
of the bourgeois delusion that salvation can be achieved
through love, regardless of the state of society, is
found not in Der Hohlweg or Das Judenauto, but in the
novels of Schulz and Noll.

Lea in Wir sind nicht Staub im Wind is a dubiously
ethereal creature - "die Schöne, Reine, Kluge, Unerreich-
bare, die Göttin".(S 10) Her mysterious origins - illegiti-
macy, an unknown but obviously distinguished father, a
theatrical mother, hints of Italian artistic ability in
earlier generations (S 13-14) - have a decidedly Goethean
flavour. This sense of derivativeness is reinforced by
Hagedorn's adoption of the Hyperion pseudonym and communication with Lea largely by means of letters, as if she
were a modern counterpart of Hölderlin's Diotima. Through
her Jewishness she is destined to a life of suffering and
isolation in the Third Reich: she is driven away from
the Goethe-Schule as her humanistic uncle is replaced as
headmaster by the thick-headed Nazi gym-teacher in 1938,
and is forced to carry out the most menial of hospital
jobs in the hope of avoiding persecution. She finally
falls into the hands of the Gestapo and is scarcely alive
when she is rescued by the Allies from a concentration
camp. Although Hagedorn has no contact with her, between
the time Saliger deserts her in 1939 and his return to
Reiffenberg at the end of the war, he still nourishes the
dream of serving and protecting her in any way possible.

During these years, Hagedorn's only other experience
of women has been at the level of fleeting sexual gratifi-
cation, which is symptomatic of the brutalisation of his
sensibilities, as his reflections after meeting Hilde
Panitzsch show:

> Wir haben alle schmutzige Hände. Wäre ich
> doch über sie hergefallen wie ein Stier. Wir
> sind doch alle Tiere. Das Menschliche ist
> nur noch eine raffinierte Tour.(S 51)

Werner Holt's development is marked by a similar dichotomy between romantic idealisation and the satisfaction
of basic sensual urges. He also discovers a "Göttin"(WH 69)
in the daughter of a Prussian officer, Uta Barnim, who
strives hard from the outset to disabuse Holt of many of

his illusions. But soon after they are separated through Holt's transfer to a training camp in the Ruhr area, he falls into the clutches of Frau Ziesche, the wife of a Nazi criminal involved in anti-Semitic atrocities. She tries cynically to 'educate' Holt into accepting that sensual pleasure is the only thing of value in life and that the all-powerful "Lustgewinnungstrieb" is part of man's inescapable "Schicksal". Holt, of course, soon escapes from this trap, only to find that Uta has disappeared following her father's murder, and is being hunted by the Gestapo (a situation only explained in Book II). Undeterred, he finds himself attracted to the young orphan Gundel, whom he meets during a brief holiday (in a painfully symbolical episode when the sun suddenly shines out of a cloud-covered sky). This more platonic relationship with an 'elfin' proletarian figure (WH 335), whose parents have been executed for communist activity, is a fresh twist of the emotional spiral, which, in an increasingly tedious fashion, marks Holt's erratic progress towards a solidly based socialist identity.

Love alone is, however, no adequate solace, and some of these authors were anxious to show that there were other liberating forces within the Third Reich, of which their disorientated protagonists were insufficiently aware. The two youngest, Noll and de Bruyn, go beyond the presentation of the problems of their autobiographical central figures by following the fortunes of the group of their peers with whom they are thrown together at the beginning of the novel - Holt's classmates in his new school, and Weichmantel's comrades in the impossible defence of the ravine. This provides an opportunity to depict characters who are more positive counterparts to their heroes than aggressive leaders in the Wolzow mould, such as Sepp Gomulka and Peter Wiese in Werner Holt, and Gert Eckert and Hans Springs in Der Hohlweg. The perceptive intellectual, the gifted musician and the straightforward country-lad all reject the German cause sooner and more decisively than the representative 'hero' rendered immobile by his delusions and bewilderment. Through their discussions, moreover, some of the post-war debate on ideologies and commitment is anticipated, and a thin line of socialist continuity is preserved, despite the efforts of National Socialism to destroy it completely. The older writers, Fühmann and Schulz, paint a much bleaker picture of their heroes at a comparable age. With several years of fighting and conflict in front of them, they are seen in the peculiar state of isolation that a tightly-knit community founded upon intolerance of individual deviation from the prevailing norm can induce. Schulz describes very effectively, in one of the last recollections of Hagedorn's

development before it is submerged amidst the dark anonymity of his years at the battlefront, the psychological
process by which his hero ends the nightmare of a period
of solitary confinement as an enthusiastic devotee of
Hitler.(S 522-7) Fühmann shows how intelligent awareness
of the distortions and sheer untruthfulness of propaganda
is no barrier to passionate acceptance of it for patriotic
reasons.(J 49) It is only in the aftermath of the Stalingrad campaign in 1943 that the façade of absolute uniformity begins to crumble. Both figures start groping
their way to a reconsideration of their loyalties, helped
by older soldiers with recollections of the pre-Hitler
days, like Hagedorn's friend Otto, or supposed 'Unter-
menschen' with alternative views of the world, like the
Ukrainian prisoners encountered by Fühmann's narrator.
    To summarise, it seems that two variants of what Lukács
calls 'bourgeois individualism' emerge in this series of
'Entwicklungsromane': the middle-class figure who willing-
ly accepts the language of 'Selbstbewährung', honour, and
struggle for victory as a logical extension of his cultural
experience, and the proletarian figure who finds in romantic dreams his main compensation for an environment in
which vitality and class identity have been suppressed.
The latter is involved reluctantly in the build-up to war
because he too is susceptible to appeals to higher values.
The undoubted authenticity of much of the depiction of
life in Hitler's Germany is, however, threatened where
the desire to encompass the spirit of the epoch within
fictional characters of the 'corrupt older friend' and
'perfect woman' variety becomes over-evident, as a result
of misguided conformity to literary models or ideological
expectations. On the whole, a convincing sense of delusion and disorientation, and the unavoidability of an
identity-crisis as the Third Reich collapses, is established
through these relatively detailed portrayals of childhood
and adolescence.

The experience of war

    These novels generally avoid direct description of
their heroes' exploits in war or any consideration of the
nature of war which might distract attention from the
broader analysis of personality development. Apart from
Dieter Noll's tendency to combine detailed accounts of
air-raids and battles with his pedagogic concern for
Werner Holt, it is regarded as sufficient to record reactions of disillusionment or horror in a phrase, like
Hagedorn's "stechendes Entsetzen vor der Sinnlosigkeit

des Sterbens"(S8) or Weichmantel's "Angst vor dem Tod, der
dort dröhnend heranrollte".(H 18) It is a dehumanising
nightmare which can do nothing to test character and
arrests the whole process of growth. The words of
Weichmantel's later friend Claudia sum up this recognition:

> Der Krieg macht keinen reifer, glaube ich.
> Vielleicht primitiv oder zynisch. Aber er
> entwickelt einen nicht, er hält nur auf.(H 206)

Such universal feelings are, it seems, taken to be as profoundly valid for these ordinary German soldiers as for
any other group of fighting men, but the authors wish to
go beyond this and emphasise those factors seen as uniquely significant in the German experience of the Second
World War, from a subsequent socialist perspective.
    The main point to be registered is that Nazi Germany
was responsible for unprecedented atrocities, both in the
conduct of hostilities and in its treatment of supposedly
inferior races in captivity. The plight of the Jews is
brought home to Hagedorn personally by the ostracisation
of Lea before the war and her subsequent incarceration,
while Holt gains a chilling insight into the horrors of
mass extermination in gas-chambers through Frau Ziesche's
accounts of her husband's activities.(WH 190-1) In some
scenes, however, and particularly in Die Abenteuer des
Werner Holt, the heroes are allowed first-hand experience
of the consequences of such criminal disregard for 'non-
Aryan' life. The gruesome episode in which Holt discovers
the dismembered remains of Slovakian partisans, murdered
by the SS in a sawmill, has been referred to elsewhere as
an example of baroque exaggeration, intended to appal the
hero into seeing the evil of his ways.[11] Fühmann's
narrator is equally shattered by the pointless murder of
the Ukrainian auxiliaries whose friendship has served to
convince him of the untenability of the notion of 'Unter-
menschen'. Nearer to home Holt, Weichmantel and Hagedorn
learn from those close to them of the torture and murder
of Communist Party activists, like the parents of Gundel
and Hella Hoff, and friends of the Hagedorns in Reiffenberg. Since the bulk of the war-action in these novels
takes place on the Eastern front, the main emphasis is
placed upon atrocities committed against Slavic nationali-
ties and individuals who are more often than not communists.
This would appear to reflect acceptance of Kurella's exhortation of 1957 to depict the war as essentially 'anti-
sozialistisch' rather than in its fuller international
complexity.
    Another crucial insight afforded to these typical
ordinary soldiers in the course of their active service
is that the unity of the 'Volksgemeinschaft' is a myth

when officers and the SS élite are under pressure.
Weichmantel's Prussian commandant, Major von Brietzow,
flees for his life from the battle-front, exhorting his
men to stick to their posts "bis zum letzten Mann" for
the sake of the "Heimat".(H 9-10) He then turns up after
the war in Berlin, attempting to establish a network of
newspapers for expropriated fugitives like himself from
the Eastern provinces of the Reich and seeking to restore
"die schicksalhaften Bande des Volkstums" and "die Dorf-
und Stadtgemeinschaften".(H 386) This kind of calculated
exploitation of the naive idealism of inferiors is
accompanied by a grossly self-indulgent life-style which
contrasts harshly with the material hardships of their
troops. Occasionally, of course, a non-commissioned
officer appears who is courageous, honest, and enjoys the
respect of his men, like Krell in Der Hohlweg: he is one
of von Brietzow's former serfs who quickly realises where
his true loyalties lie, after he has been captured by the
Russians and finds in them "ein Volk von Pädagogen".(H 76)

The SS is seen to consist of brutes and fanatics who
blindly believe everything that Hitler and Rosenberg ever
wrote and are merciless towards all who waver from total
commitment to the Nazi cause. In their almost uniformly
blond-haired, blue-eyed purity, they appear as a race
apart, and usually only on the periphery of the fictional
action. Even an enthusiastic fighter like Werner Holt
knows himself to be incapable of such "gläubigen Fanatis-
mus"(WH 324), no matter how much he may yearn for it at
times as a way of escaping his moral dilemmas. Like most
of his fellow-recruits, he is bored stiff by Leutnant
Wehnert's lectures on the mysteries of race and blood.
(WH 427-32) In the last days of the war, however, where
the focus of these novels lies, members of the SS are
always threateningly evident, forcing the wounded and
disheartened into suicidal defence of the devastated
fatherland and executing anyone showing any sign of de-
serting or betraying it. There is no attempt at psychological analysis: the SS is a manifestation of evil incapable of transformation under any more humane political
system, and accepting this becomes a means towards com-
prehending how the appalling atrocities of the Hitler
years could have occurred.

There is, of course, a more positive side to the education of potential socialists than this form of aversion
therapy. One of the first stages in the process of extending isolated doubts about aspects of the war into
broad disillusion with the whole nationalist cause, is
the realisation that there is an organised German opposition to Hitler. Information about its existence tends
to come through broadsheets and radio broadcasts prepared

by deserters who have joined the Russians. Although
soldiers like Fühmann's narrator are initially uncon-
vinced, they find it a powerfully unsettling experience:

> Es war ein Wirbel, ein Sog, jede Antwort floß
> fort: ich fühlte plötzlich, daß ich überhaupt
> nichts wußte, ich wußte ja nicht einmal,
> warum ich hier in Rußland lag und warum die
> Kameraden vor Stalingrad fielen und warum
> Deutsche auf der anderen Seite waren und was
> das für Deutsche waren ... ich wußte in
> dieser einen schweigenden Minute, da jeder
> den Atem anhielt, daß eine Frage wie ein Keim
> in mein Hirn gesenkt war, die nicht mehr
> herauszureißen war.(J 127-28)

Such doubts are further accentuated by the news of the
attempted assassination of Hitler on 20th July 1944
planned by the group of high-ranking officers led by
Oberst Graf Stauffenberg. Noll interweaves extracts from
Hitler's radio broadcast announcing his providential escape from injury with Holt's incredulous reactions, before
having him hauled off for interrogation by the SS about
his association with Uta and her father Oberst Barnim.
The latter, it emerges, has just been executed for capi-
tulating to the Russians.(WH 278-291) Fühmann devotes a
full episode to the event, describing how the narrator,
working as a telegraphist in Athens, reacts to the stream
of obsequious messages of devotion forwarded to the
'Führer' by fear-stricken Generals afterwards (J 129-46),
and Schulz hints that Lea's uncle, Füßler, has links with
the plotters.
     The more decisive insights, however, come through
direct experience of the dissenting views and actions of
trusted friends. In the climate of fear and regimentation
of opinion which stifles discussion, even in the most
private spheres, it is usually only in desperate situations
that any frankness occurs. The younger figures, Holt and
Weichmantel, are guardedly warned before they depart on
active service of the need for some scepticism to avoid
the "Überbewertung des starren Prinzips"(WH 325) and the
uncritical acceptance of military clichés.(H 13) The
important discussions, however, take place at the front-
line after some awareness of the atrocities and double
standards referred to above has been gained. With
Hagedorn and Otto Siebelt, a gentle auto-didact who has
fought beside him for two years against the Russians, it
is essentially a question of remembering the inherent
goodness of man in the midst of senseless death. One
phrase stands out in Hagedorn's mind - "Es steckt etwas
im Menschen, das will reden"(S 315) - and helps him to sur-

vive   after Siebelt's death in 1943.

The more typical situation is one which goes beyond
considerations of self-preservation and raises the question
of the morality of desertion. In <u>Werner Holt</u> and <u>Der
Hohlweg</u>, it is the trusted friend of earlier years - Sepp
Gomulka and Gert Eckert respectively - who reaches the
point of total rejection of Nazi Germany and tries to
persuade the hero to defect with him to the Russians.
The evidence of SS butchery in the sawmill has finally
persuaded Gomulka that further involvement with the German
army will inevitably implicate all of them with the "Ver-
brecher" and "Mörder", since "ganz Deutschland [ist] wie die
Sägemühle".(WH 459-60) Yet no matter how much Holt knows
about the evils of the Third Reich, he cannot relinquish
his German identity and place himself at the mercy of a
ruthless enemy. His only instinctive action is to prevent Wolzow from shooting down Gomulka as he deserts, in
a scene intended to encapsulate the three predominant
responses of German youth to this final crisis of the
Third Reich. In <u>Der Hohlweg</u>, the coldly rational Eckert
is primarily determined not to throw away his life in the
impossible defence of a meaningless position, and sets
out on the perilous journey across no-man's-land with
Weichmantel in pitch darkness. While Eckert succeeds, the
terrified Weichmantel is only too relieved to be disturbed
by a patrol of his comrades and find his way back, against
all reason, to the ravine.

The effect, therefore, of such disillusioning experiences
and the realisation that there is a - highly dangerous -
way of escaping from the nightmare, is the limited one of
leaving the central figures anxious for survival but still
desperately confused, as the war enters its last weeks.
In Fühmann's case, the hope is cherished almost until the
end that some miracle, like the involvement of the
Americans and Russians in a bloody confrontation or the
launching of the long-anticipated 'Wunderwaffe', will yet
allow the Germans to win. Holt inclines towards fata-
listic acceptance of the need for suffering, before people
like himself can discover their true selves:

> Ich weiß alles. Kommunisten werden hin-
> gerichtet, Juden mit Giftgas erstickt,
> Kriegsgefangene geschlagen und zu Tode
> gehungert, Polenkinder ins Reich verschleppt,
> Ukrainer ins Ruhrgebiet deportiert, junge
> Mädchen erschossen, Partisanen zu Tode
> gefoltert ... Jetzt gibt es kein Ausweichen
> mehr. Ich kann nicht mehr zurück. Ich muß
> durch die sieben Höllen ... Vielleicht muß

>   das so sein, damit wir endlich wir selbst
>   werden.(WH 395-6)

Weichmantel, who is extremely lucky to escape from the
ravine with a head-wound from a grenade, is only interested,
like Hagedorn, in avoiding further fighting. As both of
them see the end in sight, they formulate vague aspirations as to their future conduct: Weichmantel, full of
hope that an era of love and brotherhood will follow, sees
it the duty of all who survive to become "das Gewissen
der Welt"(H 80), while Hagedorn, with a powerful sense of
collective guilt and the need to forget the past, also
wants to look forward to a better future - "nach vorn
denken".(S 75)
    But mere survival is fraught with hazards and is seen
to involve both good luck and a willingness to show some
of the decisiveness missing earlier. Weichmantel has to
knock out the SS man Koch, who has forced him out of con-
valescence in hospital to guard a bridge, in order to escape into the anonymous mass of refugees. Hagedorn is
compelled to flee for his life from Saliger after being
charged with dereliction of duty. Holt and Fühmann's
narrator both watch their immediate companions in the
final turmoil being lynched by fellow-Germans, and are
fortunate enough to fall into enemy hands just afterwards.
These tense days marking the end of the war contain moments
of truth for all of these figures, which tend to be couched
in clichés all too familiar from earlier Socialist Realism.
Holt at last sees through the folly of his blind adherence
to 'Schicksal':

>   Es war, als zerbreche etwas in Holts Brust ...
>   die Binde fiel von seinen Augen, das dunkle
>   Zimmer wurde hell ... wie Schuppen fiel es
>   ihm von den Augen.(WH 529-31)

Hagedorn has the sensation of distancing himself from the
false 'self' that the Third Reich has brought into existence and discovering the real identity rooted in his
earlier life:

>   Es war ihm, als wäre er aus der eigenen Haut
>   geschlüpft, als ginge da ein fremdes, seelen-
>   loses Wesen durch den Nebel, ein Schatten
>   von ihm, als flöge der wirkliche Rudi Hagedorn
>   wie ein Schuhu darüber hin ... Es war ihm,
>   als könne sich der Schuhu dort oben wieder in
>   einen Menschen verwandeln, in den wirklichen
>   Rudi Hagedorn mit kurzen Hosen und ewig ver-
>   schrammten Knien ...(S 141)

Fühmann too realises in an escapist mood that his real

affinities lie outside Germany in his Czech homeland (J 167) and Weichmantel anticipates, as part of a general process of "Anderswerden", the rejection of a dissonant past.(H 167)
These are convincingly insubstantial feelings, not overloaded with ideological significance out of keeping with the experience of the main characters at this stage. The basic points about the criminality of aggressive nationalism, the exploitation of idealism to preserve the hegemony of bourgeois and capitalist interests, the burden of guilt for atrocities resting upon the SS and the officers, have of course been made emphatically, and not without a great deal of unsubtle characterisation and premature revelation of war-crimes. There is, however, a clear recognition - most striking in Das Judenauto, where there is no 'positive' German figure to suggest a political alternative before May 1945 - that the process of education into socialism could not realistically have got under way until the nightmare of war had relented, and would then hardly be other than slow and complex for individuals whose recent life had been so full of fear and disillusionment.

Patterns of post-war development

The depiction of the progress of typical individuals in the aftermath of German capitulation in May 1945 clearly presented major problems. The broadly similar pattern of experience up until the end of the war was threatened by the sheer variety of fortunes thereafter. Fühmann was completely remote from Germany in Russian captivity until 1949, while those who lived through the political turmoil and material hardships of the intervening years had problems of a different order. Some reference clearly needed to be made to the gulf between the Socialist ideal and the failings of the system introduced by the Soviets in their zone of occupation, yet these novelists were committed, within the framework of the socialist 'Entwicklungsroman', to bring their central figures at least to the brink of willing integration into German socialist society. Even in the works which had presented the protagonist's development through the Third Reich from the perspective of the end-of-war crisis, like Der Hohlweg and Wir sind nicht Staub im Wind, post-war progress now had to be depicted in a strictly chronological manner. Except under the rather loose episodic structure of Das Judenauto, there was little scope for the authors to pass over periods in which the moral growth was negligible. The tension between following the logic of characteristics emphasised

in the pre-1945 'self' and avoiding an unedifying portrayal of Soviet authority must have been considerable.
The solution which presented itself comes as little
surprise to students of a literature in which complaints
have always been voiced about the inadequacies of prevailing social reality as a setting for great ideas and
noble personalities. The "herumziehendes Komödiantenvolk
und armselige Landleute" who frustrated Goethe's epic
ambitions for Wilhelm Meisters Lehrjahre [12], and the
sceptical ex-soldiers and hard-pressed bureaucrats amongst
the ruins of post-1945 Germany may have a great deal more
in common than first strikes the eye, in their inability
to inspire confidence in the future. Indeed, just as the
liveliness and realistic detail in the earlier stages of
the classic novels of Goethe and Keller are threatened by
the temptations of allegorical abstraction as their heroes
approach maturity, so the educationally decisive scenes
set nominally in the Soviet Zone tend to occur remote from
recognisable historical reality. This situation develops
almost inevitably in Führmann's novel, where the backcloth
is the featureless and timeless one of a labour-camp in
Russia. Even where the central figure is apparently
brought face to face with the diversity of life in each
sector of occupied Germany (Die Abenteuer des Werner Holt),
or in divided Berlin, (Der Hohlweg), the impression of
authenticity is soon disturbed. It is evident that the
untenable aspects of life outside the Soviet Zone are
being starkly highlighted, while the ideological problems
of the age are considered behind closed doors within the
new world of socialism. The tendency towards this kind
of abstraction is greatest in Wir sind nicht Staub im
Wind, in which external action is reduced to negligible
proportions and rounded off with an incredible melodrama,
while representatives of broadly existentialist, humanist,
and socialist viewpoints discuss their differences at
length in rural tranquillity.
Historical time is also in danger of being telescoped
as a means of reducing to acceptable proportions the
hero's meanderings between the ideological alternatives.
The foundations for successful integration into the Soviet
Zone are thus laid within a few months of the end of the
war for Hagedorn or during the following year for
Weichmantel. Ironically, Dieter Noll's determination to
make things difficult for his hero meant that Holt was
still far from achieving stability in 1946 - but Noll
had needed two volumes to make the point and was faced
with the unpalatable task of extending his ponderous
narrative into a third. Only Führmann extends the path of
post-war development as far as the establishment of the
GDR in 1949, and then with results that he was later to

72

regard as a regrettable "Stilbruch".(J 221)
     Working under pressures of this kind, the authors again
tend to make use of character-types to chart the course
of their hero's future development between an easily recognisable set of alternatives. They also avoid involving
them in the painful historical realities of demontage,
forced collectivisation, labour squads and the like. The
first and obvious stage of this process is to give the
now confused 'bourgeois individualist' a clear idea of the
logical consequences of his youthful attitudes in adult
behaviour. Although none of the heroes was ever seriously
tempted by bourgeois materialism, Noll provides Werner
Holt with an extended, cautionary look into his mother's
wealthy surroundings in the second part of the Roman einer
Heimkehr. There is, one suspects, a deliberate attempt to
present a modernised Buddenbrooks in this portrayal of the
world of Hamburg industrialists, but it is so undifferentiated in suggesting that the Rennbachs profited hand-
somely from the Third Reich, and are now happily exploiting
the post-war chaos, that it rarely rises above caricature.
Holt's three months in this environment are predictably
unproductive, and necessary to his development only to the
extent that they allow him to break irrevocably with his
mother and join his father in the Soviet Zone, even though
the people there are, as yet, "nicht weniger fremd".
(WH 2, 249)
     The restoration of bourgeois business practice is more
of a background phenomenon in Der Hohlweg and Wir sind
nicht Staub im Wind, but an accusing finger is pointed at
the American forces of occupation for placing ex-Nazi
officers in key jobs without making any serious effort to
re-educate them. Von Brietzow's rise to the editorship
of the Jugend-Rundblick in Berlin, with his callous abuse
of authority at the 'Hohlweg' suppressed by the assassination of his chauffeur Krause in the internment camp, is
an obvious case in point. The real temptation offered by
the Western world is that of neglecting social and political responsibilities in favour of the cultivation of the
self. An absolute choice between two ideologies now faces
both the generation of parents who have helplessly watched
the rise of Nazism and its barbarities, and their children
dreaming of Hyperion and Karl Moor until war destroyed
their bourgeois illusions.
     The obsolescence of the ideal of "Bildungshumanismus"
is spelt out most plainly by the Czech Marxist Hladek in
Schulz's novel, who emphasises its "praktische Wehrlosig-
keit" and sees it as something peculiarly German - "die
ohnmachtgeschützte Innerlichkeit deutscher Art".(S 417)
This insight is of course readily confirmed by the vagueness of his partner in discussion, the recent religious

convert, van Bouden, who wants to devote his intellectual
energies to explaining the doctrine of original sin, or
by de Bruyn's declining aristocrat, Oyst-Winterfeld, who
who talks about "freie Entwicklung von Persönlichkeit"
for the intellectual elite(H 260), but has no interest in
seeking justice for the people as a whole. It requires a
more incisive grasp of the historical process to recognise
the necessity for establishing new links with the Communist
Party and the working class, as academics like Hagedorn's
mentor Füßler and Holt's father, or enlightened officers
like Major Hochreither in Das Judenauto, demonstrate.

For the younger figures, however, it takes somewhat
longer to realise the ultimate sterility of the Romantic
dream of self-fulfilment through the perfect relationship.
The heavily idealised girls from younger days, Holt's Uta
Barnim and Hagedorn's Lea, re-appear, after periods when
all contact has been lost and their death seemed unavoidable,
to expose the "Trieb zur Selbstzerstörung" which Hladek
saw as the danger to sensitive young people nourished on
"Bildungshumanismus" before 1945.(S 417) Both have lost
all hope for humanity, and are wasting away in a life
without happiness, obsessed with writers like Rilke and
Trakl who express their sense of existential despair.
Uta, in her Schwarzwald retreat, finds her only purpose
in life in tracking down her father's murderer, while
Lea - less bleakly - helps to disabuse Hagedorn of his
illusions as he reviews his past in letters to her. The
fact that she is still amenable to the counsels of Hladek
and Füßler may yet allow her to revise her belief that
man is nothing more than "Staub im Wind"(S 121, 359),
towards the affirmation contained in Schulz's title.
Weichmantel's dreams also take on more substantial form
in his love for the two daughters of the Oyst-Winterfeld
family, Claudia and Thea, whom he meets on the confused
trek away from the front as the war ends. The delicate
Thea turns up months later in Berlin as an actress with
a theatrical troupe which is hopelessly tainted with
bourgeois decadence. In this "Asyl für geistig Obdach-
lose"(H 493), the players' devotion to the works of
Nietzsche and Dostoyevsky makes them incapable of any
genuine exchange of feeling, as Weichmantel discovers when
he makes love with Thea and feels they are both merely
playing roles in a fragile dream world. His efforts to
bring her back to reality are doomed to failure, since he
is up against the theatre company and Thea's increasingly
reactionary family, so she ends the novel remote from
Weichmantel and in a state of suicidal despair.

While these insubstantial hopes are being inexorably
deflated, the figures who represent the emerging socialist

society take on clearer contours, and a more explicit
didactic tone is introduced. Schulz, Noll and, to a
lesser extent, de Bruyn strive to foster the notion of a
community made up of disparate personalities, but unified
in its efforts to persuade individuals with potential to
accept its values - recalling the purposeful interventions
of the 'Gesellschaft des Turms' in Goethe's Wilhelm Meister.
The height of contrivance is reached in Wir sind nicht
Staub im Wind, on the day when Hagedorn decides to take
courage in his hands and visit Lea, and thus submit his
Hyperion fantasies to the test of reality. Instead of
finding her alone as he hoped, he breaks into Dr. Füßler's
birthday celebrations where the guests include not only
Lea's father, van Bouden and the shrewd Hladek, but a
delegation from the new communist administration in
Reiffenberg, made up of Ernst Rottluff and Ilse Pohl, KPD
stalwarts and old friends of the Hagedorns, together with
the local Russian cultural attaché Grischin. The purpose
of the delegation's visit is to present Füßler - appro-
priately - with a Cotta edition of Goethe's works and
inform him of his re-appointment to the headmastership of
the Goethe-Schule. There is, however, more than a hint
of benevolent destiny in a situation where the confused
ex-soldier suddenly finds himself in the company of those
who represented the highest aspirations of his home environment before the disaster of Nazism, and now stand
united in working for a better future.

It is equally unmistakable that Hagedorn enjoys their
special esteem as an exceptionally promising individual
who has already demonstrated his integrity. Füßler spares
him no embarrassment in making this rhetorically clear:

> "Sehen Sie: Das ist er, der Rudi Hagedorn,
> einer meiner Schüler, einer, der aus armen
> Verhältnissen kam, einer der ganz wenigen,
> von denen ich sagen kann, das Korn, das auf-
> zuwerfen mir vergönnt war, fiel nicht auf
> steinigen Acker. Es gehören schon Mut und
> klare Besinnung und Gewissenstreue dazu,
> meine Freunde, meine lieben Gäste, wenn sich
> einer als junger Mensch in scheinbar
> glänzenden Zeiten einer gesicherten Laufbahn
> entschlägt, freiwillig abgeht von der Schule,
> in die der Ungeist eingezogen ist ..."(S 336)

After praising Hagedorn's desertion from the army as
further evidence of his humanity - "sich bewähren wollen
als Mensch, sich überwinden wollen als Kreatur" - and
calling Goethe to his aid to describe the liberating
effect of overcoming past failings, Füßler expresses his
hope that Hagedorn will strive onwards into the "Morgen-

licht des neuen Sittentags".(S 337) The plebeian Rottluff, less concerned with fine phrases, is gently reproachful that Hagedorn has not yet renewed contact with "alte gute Bekannte" like himself, and has neglected his parents, failings noted with disappointment by "ganz Reiffenberg". (S 339) As the gathering disperses, Hagedorn is left in the room to reflect on his progress and seek inspiration from Goethe, with the latter's "Prometheus" coming conveniently to hand.

This occasion marks the turning-point in Hagedorn's development, leading to his initiation into the philosophical discussions between Füßler, Hladek and van Bouden, and to Rottluff's confidence-inspiring gesture of recommending him for a crash-course in teacher training. It is not yet the end of his confusion, since Schulz acknowledges that the effects of such guidance will be gradual and even sometimes counter-productive. But it does clearly encourage the view that the forces in control of the new socialist state have the insight and patience to develop to the full the potential of its younger citizens. The second book of Die Abenteuer des Werner Holt also gives this impression, but without allowing the network of guiding spirits to be as tightly organised or as exemplary as Schulz has it. Links with the past are preserved through Professor Holt and Sepp Gomulka's father, who is in close contact with Holt's two loves, Uta and the young orphan Gundel, as legal advisor and guardian respectively. Holt's father is however rather cold and pedantic, while Dr. Gomulka has remained in the West in Nuremberg, happy to let Gundel move to the Soviet Zone once the war is over. Coincidence plays its part in bringing Holt together again with his favourite teacher from the military training school in the Ruhr, Gottesknecht, who had once tried in vain to dampen his ardour and preach the virtues of survival through the "sieben Höllen" of war into a better future - "damit wir endlich uns selbst werden".(WH 307) But the task of leading Holt towards his true self needs the proletarian orientation provided by new figures like the stalwart Müller, close to death after years in concentration-camps, yet managing a chemical works and tireless in his efforts to win over sceptical youths. Müller is equally effective in combating intolerance within the ranks of the Party, pointing out to young activists like Horst Schneidereit how Holt's resentment of authority is typical - "ganz nach dem nationalen Standard" - and must be overcome by persuasion rather than ultimata if the new state is to survive. (WH 2, 52)

Müller's outstanding personal example of purposeful hard work is well supplemented by the theoretical instruc-

tion Holt receives from Zernick, the secretary of the
local Kulturbund. Although Holt meets him by chance, the
argumentative and impetuous Zernick turns out to be a
close friend of Müller's: he wastes no time becoming acquainted with Holt's father, Gundel and Schneidereit, so
that the circle of helping figures around Holt is neatly
closed. The book that Zernick first places in Holt's
hands is Becher's Abschied, with its obvious similarities
in pointing the way forward for the previous generation,
which Holt is quick to bring to Gottesknecht's attention
as "das Thema unseres Lebens".(WH 2, 293) Although Müller
dies before his efforts to help Holt have borne fruit, he
leaves instructions that Holt should be given a copy of
the Communist Manifesto. Holt's communion with Marx,
Engels and the spirit of Müller in the isolation of a
country boarding-house, as he reads feverishly through
the night, seems set to transform his life:

> Die Gedanken dieses Buches stürzten ihn in
> eine Erregung, deren er in dieser Nacht nicht
> mehr Herr wurde. Jeder Satz traf ihn mit der
> Wucht der Wahrheit, der man nach langer Suche
> unversehens begegnet.(WH 2, 322)

Yet no matter how climactic such scenes may appear within
a carefully nurtured development, the fortunes of Holt
and Hagedorn depend more in the end on the fluctuations
of their relationships with the opposite sex. The only
external action in Schulz's novel is stimulated by
Hagedorn's two attempts to escape the emotional dilemma
brought about by his continuing obsession with Lea during
the pregnancy of his devoted, but homely, Hilde. Each
time he suffers at the hands of the marauding ex-soldiers
who are seen to represent the real threat to the stability
of the Soviet Zone: he is lucky to survive the assault
which knocks him out of a moving train on the second
occasion. It appears that this severe blow to the head
is the only way to bring Hagedorn to his senses, as an
onlooker colourfully observes:

> Manchmal geht's kunterbunt zu ... manchmal
> muß einer erst vom Zug fallen und sich den
> Schädel aufschlagen wie ein Hühnerei, damit
> sich's wieder zusammenlebt und zusammenklebt.
> (S 514)

Although Hilde adds to the melodrama soon afterwards with
an attempted suicide resulting from her misunderstanding
of an old letter of Hagedorn's to Lea, their stability
and Hagedorn's willing integration into socialist society
are assured from this point on. Holt, on the other hand,

is still drifting at the end of Part 2 of his 'adventures'
because he has failed to win the love of Gundel, who has
fluctuated between the ideologically solid, but unimaginative, Schneidereit and the obstinate Holt throughout - an
apparently insoluble conflict which gives the book its
static and repetitive quality.

In both these novels then, there is a major weakness
resulting from the author's inability to find a plausible
way forward for a hero who has already received sound
practical and ideological assistance from a range of outstanding individuals. It is as if Noll and Schulz accepted
the need to emphasise only the positive aspects of post-
1945 society in the interests of 'Parteilichkeit', yet
were unable to work out a pattern of development for their
typical figure which lay between the dramatic 'conversions'
experienced by the heroes of the 'Aufbauromane' and despair at the initial Soviet disregard for the future of
their Occupation Zone, which must have affected even dedicated communists during the years of harsh reparations.

Where this experience falls outside the personal recollection of the author, as in Führmann's case, he can
present the transformation of his characters as more gradual and abstract. The anti-fascist instruction initiated
by German defectors, and the example of the Russians –
working harder than their prisoners on reconstruction projects, showing themselves as "nette Kerle", arousing new
interest in literature and music – set the process of
change in motion through "dieses ... tote Stück Zeit im
Menschenleben, das so eintönig war wie ein russisches
Schneefeld".(J 205) The general sense of scepticism about
the socialist reconstruction in Germany prevails beyond
the creation of the SED in 1946, with Führmann suggesting
a widespread antipathy to "Vermassung".(J 191) His
narrator is nevertheless soon to be transformed, after
being moved to an anti-fascist school in Latvia, where
his reading of Marx washes away the illusions of the past
"wie Schuppen von den Augen".(J 206) Führmann devotes his
final episode to the experience of the newly-created GDR
at Christmas 1949, with an immediate sense of identity -
"heimgekehrt in meine Republik" - and an atmosphere of
conviviality, alive with "Wandlung" and "wehmütige Weih-
nachtslieder"(J 214-5) - reminiscent of the beginning of
Becher's Tagebuch 1950. The climax is reached as he learns
about the benefits of land-collectivisation, in a conversation with a liberated serf, and is inspired to compose
an effusive poem in the latter's honour:

> Land war: Für tausend Knechte Lebensraum,
> Land war, ach Land - und war doch nichts als
> Traum,

> bis dann die große Zeit der Wende war -
> es kam des Knechts, des Bauern, größtes Jahr -
> "Hier nimm dein Land - dein Eigentum - greif zu!
> So faß es doch! Wach auf - der Herr bist du!"
> Nun steht er da breitbeinig, starr und stark,
> nun fährt er durch sein Land, durch seine Mark,
> er, heimgekehrt als Herr auf eignen Grund ...
> (J 218)

Amidst this profusion of wise guidance and affirmation,
only one voice, that of Günter de Bruyn, introduces a
problematic element which makes the resolution of post-
war alienation dependent upon rather more than realising
the wisdom of socialism or overcoming personal resentments
like Holt's jealousy of Schneidereit. In the second half
of Der Hohlweg he returns to the issue which first attracted
Franz Fühmann's attention in Kameraden, and is implicit
in the portrayal of the experience of all the 'Entwicklungsroman' figures during the Third Reich, namely the inevitable gulf between finely-worded ideals and immediate
realities, whatever the ultimate morality of a given ideology may be. Without in any sense blurring fundamental
distinctions between National Socialism and the
socialist system introduced into Germany by the Russians
after 1945, de Bruyn suggests, through his depiction of
the fortunes of Wolfgang Weichmantel after May 1945, that
it is more difficult to harmonise personal needs with
social objectives than novels like Wir sind nicht Staub
im Wind would allow.

Resistance to 'große Worte' as a basis for identity

Where Schulz and Noll endeavour to insulate their hero
from the evils of the outside world within a community of
individuals concerned with his welfare at every level,
they also feather the nest with emotionally reassuring
values, which help to keep the harshness of material conditions within tolerable proportions. Even when the extent of post-war misery is hinted at, as in Gottesknecht's
discussion with Holt about "unser elendes, zerrissenes
Deutschland ... bettelarm nach den Demontagen ... diese
furchtbare Zeit"(WH 2, 420), or in one of Hagedorn's
letters to Lea, it is accompanied by an exhortation
against despair and towards a kind of spiritual renewal
nurtured on suffering and self-conquest:

> Der Traum ist aus. Wir haben den Krieg ver-
> loren und haben die Sieger im Lande. Und alle
> schröpfen uns nach Herzenslust. Überall, auch

in der Fabrik, wo mein Vater arbeitet, werden
die modernen Maschinen mit einem Kreuz aus
Ölfarbe versehen. Sie sollen demontiert und
fortgeschafft werden. In der Werkstatt, wo
ich arbeite, wird fast nur für die Besatzungs-
macht gearbeitet ... Aber wenn wir uns auch
jetzt die Seele von Robotern einsetzten, um nur
am Leben zu bleiben, so wären wir auch unsere
eigenen Totengräber ... Ich bin fest überzeugt,
daß wir nur dann als Menschen und als mensch-
liches deutsches Volk fortleben, wenn wir uns
aus dem WELTGEIST erneuern.   (S 321-2)

Hagedorn is in any case the least seriously threatened of
these figures. Not only is he endowed with "plebeische
Gesundheit"(S 417), but he has also been able to return
to his 'Heimat' and re-establish the sense of natural
harmony and continuity lost temporarily during the Third
Reich. The clouds above Reiffenberg float past "wie
die unablässige, stumme Heerfahrt der Zeit aus einer unendlichen Ferne in andere unendliche Fernen", and he re-
discovers his youth "in einem mächtigen Gefühl der Urver-
trautheit mit diesem Stück Erde, mit diesem Stück Himmel".
(S 265-6)   The new, dynamic feature on the landscape is
the Russian camp. Past and future are fused in an organic
process of development.
    When political allegiance means that links with the
'Heimat' must be sundered - West Germany in Werner Holt
and the 'Sudetenland' in Das Judenauto - there is a powerful need to compensate by embracing the adopted homeland
in emotional terms. Fühmann actually succeeds in feeling
"heimgekehrt" before he arrives, while Holt - like Hans
Gastl in Abschied - finds it relatively easy to turn his
back on his origins, sensing "daß es gut war, lachend Abschied zu nehmen"(WH 2, 260), but that it is less simple
to give his oft-asserted sense of 'Anderswerden' concrete
form. Holt's powerful yearnings for a sense of 'wholeness' and 'home' are, of course, inextricably bound up
with the success of his relationship with Gundel. He regards her as his only "Halt und Hilfe" in life, describing
himself in a revealing juxtaposition of phrases as "krank
nach Gundel, krank vor Heimweh".(WH 2, 455)
    The contrast in Der Hohlweg to these vague sentiments
is quite striking. Weichmantel's recollection of the
years before 1945, while rarely as vivid as that of
Fühmann's narrator, is dominated by his sense of having
been led astray through the abuse of concepts like 'Heimat'
and 'Gemeinschaft' by those in power. In the first section
of the novel, von Brietzow abandons his men with an exhortation to defend the homeland (H 10), and as the war

ends Weichmantel has little sympathy for the aristocrat
Oyst-Winterfeld's vision of a community of liberated individuals, because his earlier experience is that of
having been continually "[gepreßt] in Gemeinschaften".
(H 196)   It is therefore hardly surprising when he reacts
strongly against the efforts of Hella Hoff, the enthusiastic
young activist protected by Weichmantel's mother during
the last months of the war, to enlist his support in
working for the "friedliche und demokratische Zukunft des
deutschen Volkes". Weichmantel is instantly sceptical of
any appeal based upon the rhetoric of "große Worte":

> Ein Satz, in dem deutsch und Volk und Zukunft
> vorkamen, hätte er ernsthaft nie über die
> Lippen gebracht; denn bei Deutschland klang
> das "über alles in der Welt" mit, und bei Volk
> hörte er "Reich und Führer" dazu. Und er ver-
> stand nicht, wie ausgerechnet dieses Mädchen
> so etwas sagen konnte. Ihre Ungehemmtheit
> beim Aussprechen großer Worte, deren mangelnde
> Konkretheit durch Begeisterung überkleistert
> wurde, erinnerte ihn unangenehm an das
> jugendlich-stolze Pathos edel blickender
> Hitlerjungen, an ihre bemüht harten, von
> strengem Optimismus besonnten Gesichter und
> an ihre Lieblingsworte wie: Volk, Nation und
> Vaterland, Ehre, Ruhm und Treue, Blut und
> Boden.(H 287)

Although he recognises the unfairness of this word-asso-
ciation, he has to emphasise that "[diese Gedankenverbin-
dung] war da, und ließ sich ebensowenig verdrängen wie
die Erinnerungen an die Nacht im Hohlweg oder die Angst
um die Mutter". He refers further to "nebulose Begriffe"
and "unklare, begeistert hervorgestoßene Abstrakta" which
undermine the process of rational perception. The fundamental insight which the years of Nazi domination have
given him and which he regards as crucial to the "Über-
windung der Vergangenheit", is that the way forward is
through "eine gesunde Skepsis gegen große Worte ... und
die Schärfung und der Gebrauch des Verstandes".(H 287-8)
   Weichmantel's return to Berlin and the Mark Brandenburg
that he knew so well as a youth does not only mark a sense
of continuity restored, but also a new alertness against
the misleading dreams of the past, "die verführerische
Luft vergangener Tage", from which he must now "endgültig
Abschied ... nehmen", however difficult this may appear.
(H 272)   His mother emerges as a perceptive and sympathetic woman who provides an emotional anchor through the
difficult post-war months, but without being idealised.

She acts as a further foil against the naive enthusiasm
of Hella and her friends in the Free German Youth (FDJ),
suggesting even that if people like Weichmantel support
the new regime, it will be in spite of, and not because
of, its insistence on regimentation and rhetoric. (H 516)
That there are good grounds for scepticism is admitted
clearly by Karl Blaskow, who, although playing the role
of guiding father-figure towards Weichmantel, is far more
sensitive to the inadequacies of the new regime. Blaskow
stresses the disparity between the Marxist ideal and the
Party's tendency to elevate superficial conformity to
higher status than honest doubt:

> Auch ich bin manche Stunde verzweifelt, wenn
> sich vieles Neue in Formen entwickelt, die
> mich anwidern, wenn ich eilige Bußfertigkeit
> sehe, Kriecherei und Unduldsamkeit, wenn die
> Karrieristen mit Parteibuch sich nach oben
> drängeln, wenn Lippenbekenntnisse und
> gespielte Begeisterung mehr gelten als
> ehrliches Suchen. (H 451)

While Blaskow has the faith to overcome such doubts through
self-criticism, without losing his sense of purpose, his
comments do help to expose the artificiality of the notion
of harmonious community, upon which so much emphasis is
placed in novels like Wir sind nicht Staub im Wind, and
create a more differentiated image of the early days of
the Soviet Zone.

Overall, Der Hohlweg moves cautiously towards an assertion of the need for intellectuals like Weichmantel to
enjoy some freedom of movement beyond the confines of
ideological wishful thinking, since the attainment of an
enduring identity within the socialist state depends on
the gradual development of confidence that its insistence
on loyalty does not conflict fundamentally with individual
expression of reasoned criticism. Once Weichmantel has
outgrown the passive attitudes which lead him to spend
the early post-war months just as "verträumt" (H 311) as
he had been earlier, steeped in the elitism of writers
like Hölderlin, he proves his basic integrity by opting
out of the Jugend-Rundblick. He still maintains an independent position between the "dumme[n] Hochmut der Anti-
kommunisten" and the "gläubige Marxisten" from a perspective "im Lager der Pessimisten". (H 469) There is a convincing logic about Weichmantel's development from the
moment at the end of the war when he is gripped with a
powerful sense of moral responsibility that he, with his
fellow-survivors, must become "das Gewissen der Welt".
(H 80) His natural affinities lie with the intellectuals
and artists, like Eckert and Thea, rather than with Hella

and the proselytising FDJ; his chief concern is to counter
act the indifference of Eckert and Thea to the fate of
Germany. [13]   Thus when Hella endeavours to rush him into
making a political choice, which would place a barrier
between him and these cultured friends, by reminding him
of the 'Hohlweg' and the necessity which it symbolises of
deciding between the two alternatives, he is struck by he
disregard for the individual dimension in the acquisition
of truth:

> "Vielleicht sind deine Wahrheiten nicht meine.
> Ich glaube, daß man sie sich selbst erwerben
> muß und nicht servieren lassen kann. Ich mag
> keine Speisen, die in einer Zentrale gekocht
> und von begeisterten Mädchen weitergereicht
> werden."(H 528)

This last encounter with Hella still leaves Weichmante
a long way from overcoming his mistrust of the state's
dependence on cliché and regimentation. But the novel is
brought to an end only after his hopes of influencing his
cultural peers for the better have suffered a crucial
blow. Thea and Eckert betray him by starting a relationship behind his back, and then implicate themselves un-
forgivably in the reactionary plans of her father and
von Brietzow for a 'Vertriebenenzeitung'. Unfortunately,
in confronting Weichmantel with this major disillusionment
just a year after his escape from the ravine, de Bruyn
seems to have allowed himself to disregard the sources of
conflict within the socialist state to which he had drawn
specific attention in the novel. For as Weichmantel trie
to come to terms with his personal disappointments, he
seeks - and finds - the restful tranquillity of a 'natural
country community, and a protective web is wound around
him. He leaves Berlin for the now liberated village of
Brietzow, although he has previously preferred the variety
and stimulation of city-life. He is thus reunited with
other wartime friends, Hans Springs, the 'decent' officer
Krell, and Lena, his nurse and confidante, in the atmosphere of "wohltuende Sachlichkeit und einfache Güte"
which he sensed on an earlier visit there.(H 357)   The
wholesome benefits of 'Heimat' and 'Gemeinschaft' may not
be proclaimed or demonstrated in the novel's brief epi-
logue, but there is an inference that Weichmantel is now
safe in an island of harmony and stability, remote from
whatever difficulties the state as a whole may be undergoing.

The idyll is briefly threatened when it seems that
Weichmantel will have difficulties with the unimaginative
local school-inspector. He applies for a teaching job,
but makes it clear that his motive is "durchaus nicht

Begeisterung für unsere Politik", but simply that the new state offers the best available guarantee against "einen Rückfall in die braune oder graue Krankheit der Deutschen". (H 552) But here Karl Blaskow intervenes to ensure that Weichmantel is treated as a special case and given the job. Even though there is still a hard time ahead for him, the final impression is that the major difficulty has been resolved with his departure from Eckert and Thea, and that he is now on the "richtige[n] Weg.(H 551)

Although this conciliatory ending tends to undermine de Bruyn's endeavour to present a view of character-development affected as much by the alienating aspects of the socialist take-over as by the realisation of individual error, he still succeeds in going further than his fellow-novelists in showing that identity is not synonymous with integration into a superficially uniform community. He seems deliberately to play down the 'organic' class basis of identity, although Weichmantel's deep attachment to his mother, who respects his sensitivities from her perspective of uncomplicated support for the state, shows that heredity can be a significant factor. De Bruyn also avoids the 'leap of faith' into the new world, which, as Becher and Fühmann have shown, frequently only stores up difficulties of allegiance for a later stage. The convenient device of signifying the achievement of maturity by building up a stable relationship, on the Hagedorn-Hilde Panitzsch model, is no solution for Weichmantel, not only because he insists upon working out his attitudes independently, but also because his affection for Hella is kept within bounds by his resistance to her naive conformity.

The inadequacy of the parochial notion of 'Gemeinschaft' for an intellectually gifted figure like Weichmantel is also exposed. The metropolis may produce feelings of "Fremdheit und Beengtheit ... Verlorenheit und Einsamkeit" for a country lad like Hans Springs (H 441), but Weichmantel says of Berlin that he is "an diese Stadt [ge]fesselt", enjoying the pace and variety of life and finding it "irgendwie abenteuerlich".(H 458-9) De Bruyn has no evident need for the superlatives of 'wholeness' in presenting his sober reflection of the limitations of the post-war years. He does admittedly refer at times to changes in his hero's disposition and in his environment in terms of the meaninglessly vague 'Anderswerden', but without raising it to major thematic proportions as Becher did in Abschied.

These may all seem relatively modest points, when it is seen how Der Hohlweg depends elsewhere on caricature and simplified contrast in its overall structure and then concludes with the conflict-eliminating idea of the pro-

tective community. But in presenting the identity conflict of an intellectual as a continuing process, with no
easy resolution of the scepticism nurtured by excessive
exposure to propaganda, de Bruyn was introducing a greater
degree of differentiation into his depiction of individual
growth and of the new socialist society than his contemporaries had wished or dared to acknowledge.

'Erpreßte Versöhnung' and its literary consequences

T.W. Adorno's well-known response to Lukács' Die Gegen-
wartsbedeutung des kritischen Realismus [14] ends with a
firm rejection of the latter's qualitative distinction
between Critical and Socialist Realism. The 'genuine'
reconciliation of the hero with his socialist environment,
which Lukács contrasts with the resignation, escapism and
forced conformity found in the bourgeois 'Entwicklungsroman', is seen by Adorno as dangerous utopian thinking,
which makes no allowance for the alienation experienced
even by dedicated socialists in post-war Eastern Europe.
Despite Lukács' courageous criticism of the schematic
simplifications of Stalinist cultural policy, he was
underestimating the problems of removing the bureaucratic
apparatus in order to begin the transition towards genuine
communism. Adorno conceded that Lukács would have viewed
Russian society as "zwar noch widerspruchsvoll, aber
nicht antagonistisch", but was too conscious of the purely theoretical basis of Lukács' definition of the socialis
'Entwicklungsroman' to accept this:

> Das Postulat einer ohne Bruch zwischen Subjekt
> und Objekt darzustellenden und um solcher
> Bruchlosigkeit willen ... "widerzuspiegelnden"
> Wirklichkeit jedoch, das oberste Kriterium
> seiner Ästhetik, impliziert, daß jene Versöhnung
> geleistet, daß die Gesellschaft richtig ist;
> daß das Subjekt ... zu dem Seinen komme und in
> seiner Welt zu Hause sei.

By the time the East German novels conforming to this
aesthetic had been published, Lukács was no longer in a
position of cultural-political authority to deal with
Adorno's point that his image of socialist society was
"bloße Lüge". It was clear, however, that these novelists
had been under pressure to convey their hero's social
integration as more imminent and securely founded than
Lukács would ever have wished.

Lukács himself revealed in his essay of 1964 on
Solzhenitsyn's <u>One Day in the Life of Ivan Denisovich</u>
that he had modified his position on the appropriateness
of the 'Entwicklungsroman'. He now accepts that it was
premature to call for novels containing the totality of
the post-war epoch, as reflected in the concrete experience
of representative individuals, before its realities had
been explored more modestly and incisively in shorter prose
works like <u>Ivan Denisovich</u>. He is quick to point out that
this emphasis on the value of the 'Novelle' as a precursor
to the conquest of reality by the broadly-based epic does
not amount to a retreat from his consistent elevation of
the latter: he describes it merely as "ein erstes Abtasten
der Wirklichkeit auf der Suche nach den ihr angemessenen
großen Formen". [15] It is however an undoubted - if
belated - recognition of the validity of the more explora-
tory approach to contemporary realism advocated by
dissenting Marxist critics like Benjamin and Brecht since
the 1930s.

The difficulties and compromises into which the East
German 'Entwicklungsroman' authors had been led, by
accelerating the development of their central characters
or depicting the progressive forces in the GDR as uniformly benign, became increasingly evident in the following
decade. In a situation all too reminiscent of Becher's
problems with <u>Wiederanders</u> in the 1950s, these younger
writers had to face the overwhelming problem of how they
might take their characters in further volumes beyond the
threshold of commitment, into active involvement in the
GDR.

Dieter Noll and Max Walter Schulz, whose novels are
more schematic in almost every aspect than those of
Fühmann and de Bruyn, were the two authors to announce
their intentions of writing sequels. A round table discussion in <u>Neue Deutsche Literatur</u>, considering the
prospects for <u>Werner Holt</u>, coupled praise for Noll's determination not to produce another of those "sozialistische Heilsgeschichten, in denen der Weg 'per aspera ad
astra' allzu geradlinig verläuft", with timely criticism
of the weaknesses of his second volume. [16] There was no
recognition, however, that the root of the problem might
have lain in the contradiction between the anachronistic
structures of the socialist 'Entwicklungsroman' itself
and Noll's intentions. Not surprisingly, the third volume
of <u>Werner Holt</u> never materialised, and Noll had no consolation in his creative cul-de-sac (apart from the continuing popularity of the earlier volumes) until he managed
to complete a new novel, <u>Kippenberg</u>, in 1979.

Schulz's plan of 1962 for a continuation of <u>Wir sind</u>
<u>nicht Staub im Wind</u> sounded ominously like Becher's ori-
ginal hopes for an <u>Abschied</u> sequel. The first novel contained the "epische Exposition der Charaktere und der Ver-
hältnisse": what he now wanted to write was "einen Ge-
sellschaftsroman, der die Nachkriegsentwicklung einiger
heute vierzigjähriger deutscher Menschen in den Mittelpunkt stellt".[17] When <u>Triptychon mit sieben Brücken</u>
finally appeared - twelve years later, in 1974 - the
narrative present had shifted from 1945 to the days
following the suppression of the 'Prague Spring' in 1968,
with Rudi Hagedorn patiently explaining to Lea, now his
second wife, the necessity of Soviet intervention in
Czechoslovakia, and the problems of post-war reconstruction
had been consigned to the distant past. In the meantime,
Schulz had confirmed the ideological orthodoxy of his
portrayal of Hagedorn's rapid social integration at the
end of <u>Wir sind nicht Staub im Wind</u> by becoming one of
the SED's leading cultural politicians over the creatively arid years 1965-71.

For Franz Fühmann, in contrast, the harmonious climax
of <u>Das Judenauto</u> had quickly come to represent a creative
error he was determined not to repeat. His embarrassed
feelings about the final episode of <u>Das Judenauto</u> came to
light in the brief afterword which he wrote for the
Western edition of 1968. He admits how strikingly it de-
viates from the principle of self-irony he adopted for
the rest of the book, in favour of "eine Haltung absolu-
ter Übereinstimmung zwischen dem Individuum und der von
ihm als Lebenssphäre gewählten Gesellschaft". Although
he makes it clear that he did enjoy this sense of exalta-
tion and harmony in returning to socialist Germany, he
suggests, with a hint of disillusionment, that such moments are rare and "nicht auf den Alltag übertragbar".
(J 221)

The most illuminating insight into the situation of
conflict under which these 'Entwicklungsromane' were
written has come from Günter de Bruyn. In a short essay
in the anthology of writers' comments on their first book,
<u>Eröffnungen</u> (1974), de Bruyn confirms just how serious
the distortion of personal experience within an inflexible
ideological framework actually was.[18] He describes the
dominant feeling which he shared at the end of the war
with his youthful contemporaries who had known nothing
other than the Third Reich, as that of sheer relief at
having survived, as "das Glück der Anarchie". It took
years before these sensations were finally dissipated,
years in which consciousness was determined by "Abwesen-
heit von Ideologie" and alienation from newly-imposed
authority was complete - "Natürlich sind Mächte da, denen

man ausweichen muß, aber fremde, die einen innerlich nichts
angehen". The subsequent commitment to the socialist
cause is seen not as a movement towards self-fulfilment,
but - initially at least - as a betrayal of this "Urerleb-
nis innerer Freiheit", since it involved compromising
high-minded personal vows taken during these days of ela-
tion (akin presumably to Weichmantel's aspiration to become part of 'das Gewissen der Welt').

De Bruyn points out, in a powerfully self-critical
vein, how little of this has survived in Der Hohlweg.
Alluding to the pressures of contractual obligations and
admitting his own ambitions to achieve literary success,
he makes it clear how dependent he became upon the officially approved conception of 'representative' experience.
The "vorgegebenes Schema" is, of course, the one which is
all too evident in these novels as a whole:

> Der Krieg als entwicklungsfördernde Katastrophe,
> die zwei deutschen Freunde, die zu Ost-West-
> Feinden werden, die guten Mädchen und die guten
> Altgenossen als Leitersprossen der Helden-
> entwicklung, das gewaltsame Erfassenwollen
> sozialer Totalität.

According to the same scheme, the period of anarchic
happiness and resistance to authority which was so vivid
and unique for de Bruyn had to become one of "Verzweif-
lung" and frantic "Suchen", with a positive resolution
firmly in prospect. As an inexperienced writer, de Bruyn
had far too little self-confidence to resist the wisdom
of his ideological advisers and accept "das Wunder ...
daß Eigenstes, genau dargestellt, sich als Allgemeines
erweist". As a consequence, the literary product is
seriously lacking in authenticity: in a nice phrase, he
describes how he "[mogelte sich] auf 552 Seiten herum" in
distorting his state of consciousness after the war.
Understandably, anxiety about stepping out of line politically made him even less inclined to trust his own memories, and he ended by avoiding the issue through devoting
more attention to secondary figures who might superficially
create an impression of totality:

> Hemmung, sich selbst zu offenbaren, und Angst,
> Falsches, Unerwünschtes oder Mißverständliches
> zu sagen, lassen Tiefe nicht zu, fördern
> Flucht in die Breite.

He seeks no credit for his efforts to by-pass some of the
schematic clichés, referring to them disparagingly as
"rührende Versuche which reveal even more clearly his
dependence upon the given framework.

De Bruyn concludes firmly that it was unforgivable,
even for a literary beginner like himself, to complete a
novel after realising that he had "sein Thema ans Schema
verraten". But his predicament points equally to the
falsity of the premise upon which writers like him were
driven to overreach themselves, in attempting to emulate
the novels viewed as the foundations of their cultural
heritage. Instead of standing as monuments to the coming
of age of East German literature and demonstrating the
continuity of the tradition of the 'Entwicklungsroman'
from Goethe to the socialist present, works like Der
Hohlweg appear over-ambitious and inauthentic. With so
much predictability in their structures, especially where
'typical' experience is most obviously at odds with
historical realities, they reveal just how stifling the
cultural-political annexation of traditional genres for
primarily didactic purposes can be to creative perception.
De Bruyn recognised too late that he was on the wrong
track - his 'Hohlweg' having proven to be a 'Holzweg', as
the title of his essay indicates - in aspiring to produce
a work of epic proportions. The completed novel became a
hollow edifice, a betrayal of the original literary
stimulus and of his own past:

> Damals trieben pädagogischer Eifer, literatur-
> theoretische Desorientierung und falsch
> gewählte Vorbilder mich dazu, den Roman
> größer machen zu wollen, als der Autor war.
> Ich schrieb über meine Verhältnisse. Noch
> fehlte mir die Erfahrung, daß gut nur werden
> kann, was man, sich selbst gehorchend,
> schreiben muß, nicht, was man will oder soll.

Although he was awarded the prestigious Heinrich-Mann-
Preis for Der Hohlweg in 1964, the novel had long since
ceased to exist for him: "Als das Buch gedruckt war, war
es für mich tot. Nie habe ich es wieder ansehen mögen" -
a severe judgment from the author who had succeeded best
in breathing life into constricting 'Entwicklungsroman'
structures, and one which obscures the degree of progress
Der Hohlweg represents over the 'Aufbauromane' of the
1950s.

The fundamental inadequacy of these novels as a group
lies in their perpetuation of the illusion - created by
works like Abschied - that a deep personality crisis can
be resolved through a decisive move towards political
commitment. Nevertheless, the rapid recognition - at
least by Fühmann and de Bruyn - of the perils of denying
subjective experience is an indication of the determination of some younger GDR authors to discard this tenet of

orthodox Socialist Realism forthwith. Significant progress was to be made in the later 1960s beyond these derivative 'Entwicklungsromane' towards establishing new standards of originality and authenticity. [19]

CHAPTER 3

CONTINUITY AND CONFLICT IN THE GDR'S DEVELOPMENT

The unforeseen cultural revolution

Most of the SED's cultural-political pronouncements in
the period between its reassertion of total authority in
1957 and the proclamation of the 'Bitterfelder Weg' in
April 1959 suggested that a major redefinition of the
writer's status and social function was taking place.
The keynote of the Fifth Parteitag in July 1958 was the
(apparently Maoist) emphasis on the 'sozialistische Kulturrevolution': the division of labour between elitist
intellectuals and workers would be ended and literary
creation would become a collective process, serving as a
vehicle for accelerated political education.[1] The encouragement of 'schreibende Arbeiter' implied that their
efforts would be every bit as good as those of professional
writers, and thus demonstrate that full-time creative employment was an expendable luxury. This rhetoric of
permanent revolution emanating from a rigid Stalinist
hierarchy proved, not surprisingly, to be little more than
"ein rein verbale[r] Radikalismus".[2] On the one hand,
ordinary workers were not given the opportunity to speak
their mind; on the other, many 'Berufsschriftsteller' who
were initially eager to become part of a literary collective focussing on the GDR's industrial achievements came
to recognise the untenability of official stereotypes and
the need to place greater reliance on their independent
perceptions.
Behind all the talk of cultural revolution and decadent
Western influences, the SED's primary concern was to prevent the re-emergence of the articulate critical voice
within its own ranks represented by the intellectual
leadership during the 'Thaw' of 1955-56. Its task could
scarcely have been easier: the death of Brecht, followed
by the political disqualification of Lukács and Becher,
had removed - virtually at a stroke - the three dominant
intellectual personalities during thirty years of debate
on German socialist culture. The cultural politicians
now felt confident enough to mount a crude attack on ivory
tower theoreticians remote from economic and social realities.[3] Yet the bankruptcy of their understanding of
how the credibility of Socialist Realism might be restored
in the eyes of their potential mass audience remained
glaringly evident. Apart from their unacknowledged

borrowing of Lukács' conception of the socialist 'Ent-wicklungsroman', they saw no alternative but to return to the discredited industrial reportage/fiction of the earlier 1950s and hope that younger writers capable of greater subtlety than the Hans Marchwitza of Roheisen might inject some vitality into the genre. The best example of de-sirable new writing they could summon up for the Bitterfeld Conference was Regina Hastedt's Die Tage mit Sepp Zach (1959), which is based entirely on the clichés of the egocentric author, the heroic activist and the unified proletarian community, with the author's subsequent in-tegration into this selfless, emotionally supportive world attaining the force of a religious conversion. The first anthologies of the work of the 'schreibende Arbeiter' were no better. Even though Werner Bräunig's slogan for the Bitterfeld Conference - "Greif zur Feder, Kumpel, die sozialistische Nationalkultur braucht dich!" - conjures up the image of manual workers enthusiastically describing their experience, most of the contributions were from 'white-collar' journalists and Party officials purveying conventionally affirmative reportage.[4]

The first indication of renewed resistance both to this reduction of literature to ideologically subservient status and to the challenge to the professional writer represented by the 'schreibende Arbeiter' actually emerged at the Bitterfeld Conference. Erwin Strittmatter was the only main speaker there who still represented some degree of continuity with the personalities and the literary inno-vations associated with the 'Thaw'.[5]   As the new First Secretary of the Writers' Union he coupled his assurance that many of his colleagues were volunteering for in-dustrial placements with a plea for the cessation of the intimidation to which authors wishing to depict serious conflicts were being subjected.[6]   By May 1961, when the Fifth Writers' Congress was held, this renewed process of self-assertion had gained momentum and Strittmatter felt able to present himself, with some irony, as a 'schreibender Arbeiter' who had had to undergo a long apprenticeship before having the satisfaction of having something worthwhile published, and thus ask for the "lesender Arbeiter" to be protected henceforth from "die Selbstverständigungen und das gut gemeinte Gestammel seiner Arbeitskollegen aus der anderen Abteilung".[7]

This circumspect attempt to restore some respect for literary quality and to show the need for critical differentiation in the depiction of the GDR of his day came too late to influence the first wave of 'Bitterfelder Weg' prose following the exodus of young writers in 1958-59 to building sites, factories and collective farms.

The impossible task the cultural politicians had set them
of reconciling glorification of the status quo with an
authentic portrayal of the GDR's workforce meant that the
work published in 1961 was still full of contradictions.
Brigitte Reimann's Ankunft im Alltag and Erik Neutsch's
Bitterfelder Geschichten are - as their titles alone
suggest - still programmatic celebrations of industrial
progress, with clearly identifiable positive and negative
characters. Franz Fühmann's Kabelkran und blauer Peter
and Karl-Heinz Jakobs' Beschreibung eines Sommers also
contain strongly affirmative scenes, but reveal that the
emphasis on subjective experience on the 'Bitterfelder
Weg' had a liberating potential for GDR literature which
the cultural politicians had scarcely foreseen. Both
works are first-person narratives with little of the omniscient certainty and the schematic harmonisation of personal and industrial achievement hitherto basic to 'Auf-
bauliteratur'. Fühmann provides an honest journalistic
account of the problems faced by a physically maladroit
intellectual attempting to integrate with workers from an
entirely different background, amidst the bewildering
technology of the Warnow shipyard. Jakobs presents the
challengingly non-conformist perspective of a fictional
protagonist with undeniable leadership qualities. Tom
Breitsprecher may be an example to the young volunteers
on the pioneering construction project in the rural backwater of Wartha, but he also falls foul of Party authority
both for his criticisms of the tendency in literature and
the mass media to substitute 'Schönfärberei' for factual
description of working conditions, and for his involvement
in an adulterous relationship. Jakobs' combination of a
disconcertingly complex narrator, a lively colloquial
narrative and a deliberately open-ended conclusion introduced a new quality of "Lebenswirklichkeit" into the portrayal of GDR society, as Christa Wolf pointed out in an
important supportive review.[8]   Although both Kabelkran
und blauer Peter and Beschreibung eines Sommers still betray their original conception as pieces of industrial
reportage - modestly concentrating on a brief episode set
in the recent past which allows little scope for the analysis of character development - they represent a significant progression towards the literary authenticity which
was to initiate the GDR's real cultural revolution within
a few years.
    The sense of a new beginning, of participating in a
coordinated plan for the industrial transformation of the
GDR - after years of political uncertainty and economic
hardship - which the Bitterfeld Conference had marked, was
seriously threatened by the time this first wave of storie

were published. 1960 had seen the ruthless completion of
the SED's highly unpopular programme of land collectivisation as well as the repressive industrial legislation contained in the new 'Arbeitsgesetzbuch'. The barometer of
instability, the numbers of 'Republikflüchtige', which
had dropped markedly in 1959, rose steadily again to an
average of almost 20,000 a month in 1960-61 and led to the
building of the Berlin Wall in August 1961 as a desperate
means of ensuring the GDR's very economic survival.[9]
The early 'Bitterfeld' prose, mainly set in the encouraging
days of 1959, could ignore all of this, whereas for those
writers who were still, late in 1961, evolving a fictional
response to their industrial experience, the untenability
of the rosy optimism of a work like Ankunft im Alltag was
self-evident. Not surprisingly, there was little significant prose published in the period immediately after this
crisis. It was only after the SED's Sixth Parteitag in
January 1963 had announced comprehensive internal reforms,
introducing the 'Neues Ökonomisches System der Planung und
Leitung' (NÖS) and thereby recognising the importance of
individual initiatives to stimulate fresh growth of the
GDR's economy, that the second, decisive wave of
'Bitterfeld' fiction began to appear.

The novels which represent the most noteworthy achievements on the 'Bitterfelder Weg' include two by authors who
had risked little in their 1961 debut, but who were now
intent on presenting a more complex view of GDR society,
Brigitte Reimann's Die Geschwister (1963) and Erik Neutsch's
Spur der Steine (1964). They are complemented by novels
by two other young writers associated independently with
the limited progress made in the cultural debate since
the end of the 'Thaw', and with modest reputations as
creative writers outside the 'Bitterfeld' framework,
Christa Wolf's Der geteilte Himmel (1963) and Hermann
Kant's Die Aula (1965).[10] They all appeared within a
year or so of the liberalisation of cultural policy which
followed in the wake of the NÖS, although in the case of
Die Aula there was a further gap of a year between its
serialisation in the youth magazine Forum and the book
edition. Like the 'Entwicklungsromane' treated in the
previous chapter they form a distinctive group - published
close to one another in response to specific cultural-
political stimuli, and sharing a number of structural and
thematic features which reveal the tensions between
official expectations and creative self-assertiveness.
These tensions are now more pronounced than in the 'Entwicklungsromane', because the works cannot be isolated
either from the crisis of August 1961 or from the fresh
hopes for reform engendered by the reforms of 1963, and

once again there are significant differences in the radical potential of each novel which can be revealed through
comparative analysis. The means of extending the narrow limits of the SED's
original conception of the 'Bitterfelder Weg' had been
indicated at the Fifth Writers' Congress, where a link had
at last been forged between what had hitherto passed in
the GDR as mainstream Socialist Realism and the cultural
heritage of German socialism. Anna Seghers - one major
creative influence from the Exile generation to survive
1956 relatively unscathed - gave the main address to the
congress on the subject "Die Tiefe und Breite in der Literatur". It is a surprising essay for anyone who identifie
Seghers the literary critic principally with the forthright arguments she expressed in her correspondence of
1938-39 against Lukács' conception of realism, because it
is another unadmitted, but unmistakable, endorsement of th
latter's strategy for modifying the utilitarian view of
literature held by Party cultural bureaucrats - a view
which had changed depressingly little between the 1930s
and 1961. Furthermore, Anna Seghers herself was now a
cornerstone of the literary establishment rather than a
voice remote from the sources of Soviet authority, as she
had been in her exile years. Her emphasis was, however,
not on the 'Entwicklungsroman' centred on the political
turning-point of 1945, since she regarded a work like
Noll's Werner Holt as too restricted in scope and un-
healthily preoccupied with the war itself. She appeared
to be reviving the dream of the Socialist Realist epic
with the panoramic scope and the quality of a Tolstoy
novel, which would take stock of the entire post-war era -
Lukács' 'großes proletarisches Kunstwerk' in all but name.
This meant the addition of a dimension of social and individual development which would take account of the conflicts as well as the continuity within this process, and
thus make the hindrances to the attainment of stable
identity under socialism the subject of serious fictional
analysis for the first time:

> Wenn ein Schriftsteller unseres Landes seinen
> Beruf ganz versteht, seine Umwelt darstellt
> und ihre Vergangenheit, die Gesellschaft, die
> Landschaft, die Arbeit, die Liebe, dann wird er
> auch in der Wirklichkeit seines Landes und seiner
> Tage wahrnehmen, wo und wie sich der Sozialismus
> herausbildet und vorwärtsentwickelt, unter allen
> möglichen Widersprüchen, unter allen möglichen
> Schwierigkeiten, mit allen möglichen Hindernissen.

She succeeded in attaching great importance to maintaining
traditional standards of literary quality, without implyin

that there were obvious classical models to be emulated, and thus avoided creating new pitfalls such as those into which two generations of German socialist writers had been, and were still being, led through excessive adherence to <u>Wilhelm Meister</u> and other outstanding 'Entwicklungsromane'. By coupling literary quality with creative autonomy she was reinforcing the underlying principle of all Lukács' criticism, reminding her audience that "Parteilichkeit" is inherent in any work with the requisite "Tiefe" in its perception of social development and cannot be "[montiert] nur von außen als politische Aussage", and that "Breite der Wirkung" is inseparable from creative excellence. [11]

Neither Seghers nor any other speaker at the Writers' Congress could have anticipated the psychological upheaval which they, like the whole GDR populace, were to undergo within a matter of months following the building of the Berlin Wall. It meant the end of any residual illusions that the achievement of genuine socialism in the GDR would be anything other than a prolonged uphill struggle. It was to be a time for retrospective analysis rather than creative projection into an uncertain future, and a situation in which the authors would be forced to rely more than ever before on their independent perceptions rather than the received wisdom of the Party line. The result was a series of novels in which the narrative voice becomes more subjective and rooted in the identifiable present-day of 1961 or 1962, taking stock of the fluctuating progress made since the establishment of the GDR in 1949, and only then passing judgement on the nature of the society arising from the crisis of 1961. With the exception of Neutsch's <u>Spur der Steine</u> they did not, however, aspire to become 'epics' on the scale of the theoretical 'großes proletarisches Kunstwerk': Wolf, Reimann and Kant showed a greater awareness of the latent contradictions between a more authentically personal narrative perspective and a nineteenth century panoramic breadth of content, and were about to shift the balance in East German literature perceptibly towards the former. [12]

The narrator as mediator

One of the most important respects in which these novels extend the subjective vein introduced in 1961 by Jakobs and Fühmann is at the narratorial level: there is a close relationship, if not total identity, between the narrator and the central character. In one case, <u>Die</u>

Geschwister, the main figure, Elisabeth, is unambiguously
the first-person narrator, while the third-person perspective of Die Aula scarcely disguises the fact that the
narrator is almost indistinguishable from Robert Iswall.
In Der geteilte Himmel a deep emotional involvement in the
progress of the more idealised Rita Seidel is unmistakable
but the (female) narrator is reticent about her own identity. In these three novels the narrator is correspondingly
not a mouthpiece for state authority, but a mediator
standing between the experience of representative GDR
citizens and the SED's ideological understanding of events
He is quite open-minded about the competence and the
morality of socialist authority and allows a range of
attitudes to be presented in relatively objective terms.
Above all, he goes beyond the simple moral categorisation
of individuals into 'socialist' and 'bourgeois', identifying a spectrum of often incompatible attitudes within
the socialist camp, and presenting in detail problem-cases
like those of Manfred Herrfurth (Der geteilte Himmel),
'Quasi' Riek (Die Aula) and Uli Arendt (Die Geschwister).
In Spur der Steine, appearances of narrative conventionalit
prove deceptive to the extent that Neutsch also gives
prominence to the fall from grace of an exemplary Party
secretary, Werner Horrath.

The fact that the narrative perspective is both retrospective and rooted in a recognisable present underlines
the authors' determination to take stock of the aspirations
of those willing to participate in the construction of a
new socialist world after the nightmare of the Third
Reich. The amount of direct comment upon the GDR of the
fictional present is still limited, but the reader is
left in no doubt, especially in Die Geschwister and
Der geteilte Himmel, as to the critical stage reached in
the state's existence. The former is set shortly before
the erection of the Berlin Wall, the other shortly after,
and both reflect all the associated anxieties and uncertainties. Yet to judge from Die Aula and Robert Iswall
frame of mind during his travels through both Germanies
in the spring of 1962, it would appear that none of his
generation of graduates from the 'Arbeiter- und Bauern-
fakultäten' (ABF) were affected by this major crisis.
Kant is ultimately more concerned with a critical record
of the GDR's pioneering years than with the turmoil of
the immediate past. His adoption of 'cinematic' flash-
back techniques, his experiments with montage and stream-
of-consciousness recollections, together with his satirical
wit, appear to place him at the forefront of the literary
avant-garde, [13] but his view of the present is conventional
ly affirmative.

Despite the differences in narrative perspective, Erik Neutsch is comparable to Christa Wolf and Brigitte Reimann through his concentration of interest upon the two-year span between the initiation of the 'Bitterfelder Weg' and the 'Republikflucht' crisis of 1961, and in the striking variation in the fortunes of his basically sympathetic central figures. But the background in <u>Spur der Steine</u> is so solidly filled by the expanding chemical works at Schkona that the vexed question of leaving the GDR, as faced by Manfred and Rita in <u>Der geteilte Himmel</u> and Uli in <u>Die Geschwister</u>, never clouds the horizon. Christa Wolf reduces her factory to "ein kreischendes, schmutziges Durcheinander, ein Gewinkel von Hallen und Schuppen und Häusern, kreuz und quer von Gleisen durchzogen" (GH 40), in order to do justice to her characters. Neutsch, in striving over 900 pages for the panoramic breadth of a great Socialist Realist epic, pays insufficient attention to the demands of psychological consistency in the development of his protagonists Balla and Horrath.

The expression of 'Parteilichkeit' has become a matter of considerable subtlety for these authors, as they recognise the necessity of establishing independent ground as constructive mediators between their large readership and SED authority. One of the revealing nuances in this shifting of ground is the use which the writers make of the collective first-person statement, through the 'Wir' perspective, in endeavouring to create a sense of community with the reader and his experience, while demonstrating a basic self-identification with the GDR.

In <u>Die Geschwister</u>, Elisabeth, the gifted artist in her mid-twenties, frequently reveals her eagerness as narrator to speak for her generation as a whole. Her pride in their achievements seems at times rather too effusive, in a situation where she is desperately endeavouring to dissuade her younger brother Uli from defecting to the West. Uli's feelings of constriction - "wie ein Gefangener, hinter einem Gitter von Dummheit und Bürokratie" (G 116) - and resultant disaffection, are met with a response which sounds dangerously naive:

> Warum, dachte ich, scheuen sich die jungen
> Leute meiner Generation vor großen Worten
> und dem Ausdruck großer Gefühle? Waren wir
> damals, in den ersten Jahren nach dem Krieg
> und nach der Gründung der Republik, nicht mit
> mehr Ernst und Leidenschaft bei der Sache?
> Wir hatten Augen zu sehen, wie die neue
> Ordnung feierlich und rot heraufstieg, und
> die zornigen jungen Männer waren noch nicht
> erfunden und nicht die saloppen Anbeter

ihres mißverstandenen saloppen Idols, die
mit einer attraktiven Tut-mir-leid-Fisch-
Bewegung unsere schöne Glut zertreten hätten.
(G 119)

Soon afterwards, however, impressed perhaps by the weight
of her brother's grievances, Elisabeth indicates that her
generation's identity is also based on opposition to the
state's insensitive authority:

Wir wollen nicht Vertrauensseligkeit. Wir
fordern Vertrauen. Die Männer und Mädchen
meiner Generation haben neue Maschinen kon-
struiert und Wälder gerodet und Kraftwerke
gebaut ... Wir haben ein Recht auf Vertrauen.
Wir haben ein Recht, Fragen zu stellen, wenn
uns eine Ursache dunkel, ein Satz anfechtbar,
eine Autorität zweifelhaft erscheint.(G 141)

This endeavour of a young adult to mediate between the
'younger generation' and the rhetoric of 'authority',
and to identify alternatively with each, bears fruit in
terms of the novel, since Uli's conflicts are resolved
through his decision to remain in the GDR, but the contradictions inherent in this stance are not seriously examined
Although Elisabeth argues that her commitment to socialism
has resulted from her industrial experience of the system's
vitality, Uli suspects, with good cause, that emotional
and utopian factors are just as important:

Betsy hat Gemüt ... Betsy denkt mit der Seele.
Für sie bedeutet Sozialismus hienieden Brot
genug für alle Menschenskinder und Rosen und
Myrten zugleich.(G 245)

Elisabeth's recourse to this instinctive optimism, her
reliance on 'große Worte' in her dealings with her sceptical brother at this crucial hour for the GDR's survival,
is made more acceptable to the extent that it follows a
succession of grim battles with authority in the recent
past, in which she has proven her capacity for equally
tenacious critical argument.

The effusiveness of her affirmation becomes evident,
however, in contrast to the more distant third-person
perspective of novels like Der geteilte Himmel and
Die Aula, in which statements of a personal nature are
used economically and to greater effect. In Christa
Wolf's novel, the narrator occasionally slips over, almost imperceptibly, to the 'Wir' form, when she wishes to
underline feelings she shared with her readers in the de-
pressing weeks after the erection of the Wall. At the
beginning and again at the end of the novel, she refers

in the present tense to the difficulties of returning to
everyday normality, but seeks to provide reassurance that
this can be achieved:

> Wir gewöhnen uns wieder, ruhig zu schlafen.
> Wir leben aus dem vollen, als gäbe es über-
> genug von diesem seltsamen Stoff Leben, als
> könnte er nie zu Ende gehen. (GH 7-8)

The narrator's relationship with Rita is given some foundation early on. The implication is either that they both
come from the same village, or that the narrator feels
close enough to fuse her identity with Rita's:

> Als [Manfred] damals vor zwei Jahren in unser Dorf
> kam, fiel er mir sofort auf ... Da wußte ich
> bald so gut wie jeder andere, daß der junge
> Mann ein studierter Chemiker war...(GH 11)

The ambiguity here is not resolved, but it provides one of
many indications that Rita merits sympathetic support and
is part of a tightly-knit community. The other few occasions when the narrative 'Wir' is heard reveal, in contrast, its usefulness as a device for placing the main
action in a sober historical perspective and underlining
the narrator's identity with her readership. It first
occurs at the moment when the progress of Rita and Manfred
seems to promise a conventional happy ending:

> Sie liebten sich und waren voll neuer
> Erwartung auf ihren zweiten Winter ...
> Einen dritten gemeinsamen Winter gab es
> nicht ... Wir wußten damals nicht - keiner
> wußte es - was für ein Jahr vor uns lag.
> Ein Jahr unerbittlichster Prüfung, nicht
> leicht zu bestehen. Ein historisches Jahr,
> wie man später sagen wird. (GH 116)

It is only after Rita has been through the depths of despair, bringing her close to death and necessitating a
long recuperation, that the narrator again links herself
with the reader, on the basis of their inherent capacity
to find the spiritual resources to overcome even the
bleakest of crises:

> [Rita] hat schlimme Tage durchgemacht, und
> das ist nicht zuviel gesagt. Sie ist gesund.
> Sie weiß nicht - wie viele von uns nicht
> wissen - welche seelische Kühnheit sie nötig
> hatte, diesem Leben Tag für Tag neu ins
> Gesicht zu sehen, ohne sich täuschen zu lassen.
> Vielleicht wird man später begreifen, daß von
> dieser seelischen Kühnheit ungezählter gewöhn-

licher Menschen das Schicksal der Nachgeborenen
abhing - für einen langen, schweren, drohenden
und hoffnungsvollen geschichtlichen Augenblick.

(GH 256)

This feeling of solidarity scarcely needs further rein-
forcement, and the narrator is able elsewhere to give at
least the impression of maintaining a more impersonal
standpoint. Such limited 'Parteilichkeit' cannot be understood as a specific endorsement of the state leadership:
the communal 'Wir' is not expressed in terms of generations, or of activists against sceptics, or in any other
limited sense. At a critical hour like this, the simple
need for emotional unity throughout the population is
paramount.

In Die Aula, Hermann Kant creates a much stronger impression that his narrator has been fully involved in the
fictional action yet is endeavouring to preserve a degree
of distance - despite the weight of biographical evidence
suggesting that there is little difference between Robert
Iswall and his creator, in their progress from the
Greifswald ABF in 1949 to a position of respectability in
the cultural world of 1962. The narrator seems to suppress
his natural inclination to use the first-person plural to
describe the achievements of the graduates of a unique
institution, realising the need for some more precise
means of differentiation He knows there are significant
areas of contradiction in the fortunes of his ABF colleagues
and in his identification with the state. The ideologically inexplicable case of 'Quasi' Riek, the most politically
active of Iswall's fellow-students, who then went to the
West and became a publican, illustrates the value of the
more neutral third-person perspective. For propaganda
reasons the state would rather forget that Riek ever
existed, but this is unacceptable to the intelligent and
well-informed citizen that Iswall is:

> Möglich, daß es einigen alles sagte, wahr-
> scheinlich, daß viele genug wußten: Klarer
> Fall - bei uns gelernt, auf unsere Kosten,
> abgehauen, Kneipier geworden ... ist ein
> Schuft und war immer schon ein Schuft ...
> War er aber nicht, war ein Kerl wie keiner
> sonst. Hatte mal kranke Lunge, aber ein Herz
> hatte er wie das von Trullesands Tante, ein
> Herz aus Vollkornbrot. Und hatte einem sogar
> einmal das Leben gerettet.(A 180)

At the same time, a unique success story, such as the
rise of the forester Jakob Filter to a top post in a
government department, seems the right topic for the

climax of a speech intended to celebrate the obsolescence of the ABF in the education system of 1962. The narrator stands back, and Iswall reveals the full extent of his partisan pride, making full use of the 'Wir' form to present the ABF's success as symbolical of that of the GDR as a whole:

> Die anderen haben gesagt, wir könnten all
> dies nicht, und wir haben ihnen gesagt, was
> wir können. Ihnen ist das Grinsen vergangen,
> und wir lächeln. Wir können alles, was sie
> können und allein zu können meinten. Das ist
> bewiesen.(A 362)

Thus the delicate balance between 'Parteilichkeit' and the objective presentation of a more catholic range of viewpoints is sought in Die Aula, as deliberately as in Der geteilte Himmel and Die Geschwister. This is reflected equally in the blend of considered loyalty to the state, and active endeavour to improve its deficiencies, found in each of the central figures, Iswall, Rita and Elisabeth, which makes them relatively credible in their exemplary status.

Erik Neutsch is the exception, in Spur der Steine, in having no narrator persona, surprisingly perhaps, since the reportage-length stories in his earlier Bitterfelder Geschichten had been introduced by journalists or workers directly involved in events, who were able to place a stamp of authenticity on the neatly resolved conflicts they described. Although Spur der Steine is on the surface an objective third-person narrative, it is the most tightly organised of these novels in the way it demonstrates steady progress towards an ever-rosier future. The sense of continuity inherent in the title is underlined by the simultaneous 'growth' of industry and most of the characters, and a number of the characters also conveniently serve as the author's mouthpiece at significant moments. The partisan 'Wir' is thus used extensively, but the narrative standpoint is now clearly within the ranks of the Party, and explicitly loyal to the leadership. This is, after all, the only novel to allow the hierarchy to speak for 'the people' not once, but on three occasions.

The Minister-President, Otto Grotewohl, sets the tone in the opening section:

> Von unserer Republik geht der Friede für
> Deutschland aus. Wir bauen bereits die
> Straße, die in eine lichte Zukunft führt und
> die früher oder später die gesamte Nation
> beschreiten wird. Jeder muß Aufbauhelfer
> sein, mit seiner Arbeit, an seinem Platz.

> Die Verantwortung, die wir tragen, ist von
> wahrhaft geschichtlicher Größe ...(SS 15)

Herman Jansen, First Secretary of the Party for the Halle
region, provides the guiding voice of central authority
at the Schkona site, and gives a major public speech in
the middle of the novel (SS 500-4). To round matters off,
Walter Ulbricht presides over a celebratory dinner in the
final pages, marking the success of the project in its
first two years. Individual members of the Party, like
Werner Horrath and Katrin Klee, are seen by the uninitiated
to have special qualities and a unique strength deriving
from their ideological commitment. As the rebellious
Balla recognises, in a typical instance of the author's
analysis intruding upon the perceptions of a more limited
character:

> Es schien, als wirke etwas in ihrem Wesen,
> was sie stets stärker und glücklicher machte
> als ihre Gegner. Mit einer aufreizenden
> Gelassenheit, mit einem überheblichen Stolz
> ertrugen sie jede Schikane ...(SS 112)

Workers like Balla lay the foundations for their identity within their brigades, but lack a sense of wider purpose because they do not feel otherwise involved in the
state. The decisive step outside this isolation is viewed
as a process of "über sich selbst [hinaus] wachsen".(SS 734)
For Balla this is no straightforward integration, but
rather a matter of broadening the Party's base, by representing the interests of the workers more satisfactorily
than has previously been the case. He - and with him, it
seems, Neutsch - expresses their criticisms of the inflexibility of work-norms and of the stifling of initiative (SS 584), or of inefficiencies in planning, to the
extent of confronting the taboo of strike action: "Wollen
wir betonieren, kommt das Holz, wollen wir schalen, krie-
gen wir Kies. Engpaß auf der ganzen Linie ... Ich sag
Ihnen ... es ist zum Verzweifeln".(SS 677-8) The Party
itself is far from faultless, although the problems are
seen to lie with individual failures like the works-
manager Trutmann and the bureaucrat Bleibtreu. Once a
character like Balla joins the ranks, his 'Wir' becomes
a powerful force unifying the interests of the Party and
the working-class. His transformation really begins when
he acts as envoy to the engineer Hesselbart with an offer
of new managerial responsibilities following Trutmann's
demise. Balla almost surprises himself by announcing
"Mich schickt die Partei" and then continuing "Wir bitten
Sie, Ihren Urlaub abzubrechen. Wir brauchen Sie ...".
(SS 732) Thereafter, his identity is unshakably firm,

and he never hesitates to upbraid the sceptical, even of
the stature of the artist Voss:

> Man kann nicht das Dumme mit noch Dümmerem
> ausrotten wollen. Glaub mir, wir werden mit
> echten Schwierigkeiten fertig, mit Wider-
> sprüchen, die wir nicht überbrücken können,
> durch die wir hindurch müssen. Warum sollten
> wir es nicht auch mit den Fehlern, die nicht
> zu sein brauchen? ... Wir, du und ich und wir
> alle, wir schaffen es ...(SS 747)

In the end it is Balla who represents the voice of collec-
tive unity against the despair of his former mentor,
Horrath, in a complete reversal of their earlier roles.
(SS 797-8)

What disrupts the surge forward towards total harmony
in the novel is precisely this issue of Horrath's decline.
It is striking that the single break in the narrator's
apparent objectivity occurs at the point where Horrath's
crisis begins, when he proffers an extended general observation, highlighting a vital flaw in the state's
centralised organisation. Firstly, he describes the
authority hierarchy as a living organism, responding to
signals received from every individual cell which forms
part of the whole:

> Ein Ministerium ist ein Kopf für einen großen,
> weitverzweigten, höchst kompliziert einge-
> richteten Organismus. Wie ein Kopf Augen und
> Ohren, Sinne für den Geruch und den Geschmack
> hat, so verfügt auch das Ministerium über
> eine Anzahl von Nervensträngen, die sein
> ganzes Ressort durchziehen und es überwachen
> ... juckt es im kleinen Zeh, erfährt es der
> Kopf.(SS 169-70)

He then asserts that errors in planning and decision-
making occur only where the contact between the nerve
cells and the brain has temporarily broken down. The
concrete problem of the dispute between Horrath, as
innovating Party secretary, and the unimaginative Trutmann
is viewed as a genuine contradiction between "Plandiszi-
plin" and "[Steigerung] der Arbeitsproduktivität".(SS 171)
The genius of bureaucratic compromise decrees that the
protection of state office-bearers is just as important
as productive modification of the economic plan, with
the result that, while Horrath's proposals are adopted,
he receives a formal reprimand which sullies an otherwise exemplary record.

This bureaucratically neat resolution of a serious conflict becomes an important factor in undermining the

identity of a dedicated socialist. There may be other
significant factors as well, but the nature of Party
authority is questioned here just enough to disturb the
overall sense of unity which the novel gives and to create
reservations as to the representativeness of Balla's 'Wir'.
This shows Neutsch to have something of the critical distance of the other Bitterfeld authors, even though the inadequacies of authority are scarcely evident in his portrayal of individuals within the Party leadership.

Narrative structure is thus in itself of considerable
significance in this fiction, reflecting for the first
time since the war fiction of 1955-57 an awareness of the
problematic nature of the author's identity. The commitment to the communal 'Wir' of the GDR is never at issue,
although there is considerable subtlety in the definition
of a position of 'Parteilichkeit' which also embraces the
feelings of a readership still unsure about its support
for the state. The tone of mediation comes over as something genuine and emphatically new, vital to the health
of literature in East Germany as well as to the authors'
individual sense of creative independence.

The reckoning with the Stalin era

The way may have seemed open since 1956 - since
Khrushchev's public revelation of Stalin's crimes - for
a critical portrayal of life in the Stalin era in the GDR,
and particularly of the nature of the Party's authority,
but it was only in the context of the scrutiny of past
mistakes initiated by the political and economic reforms
of 1963 that a closer literary analysis of internal factors affecting the GDR's troubled development seemed
feasible. The novelists completing their work in 1963-4,
engaged in the process of raising the confidence of their
readership in the state, needed to depict at least some
of the ways in which the regime had earlier alienated so
many of its workers and intellectuals.

The location of turning points between past aberrations
and the more hopeful present, and the determining of
periods of conflict and moral growth in relation to wider
historical developments, was not as attractively uncomplicated as in the 'Entwicklungsromane' describing the
period around 1945. Even a more independent conception
of 'Parteilichkeit' presupposed that a personal crisis
would not be allowed to coincide with historical events
which augured poorly for the GDR, in the way it had in a
novel like Mutmaßungen über Jakob (1959) by the émigré

Uwe Johnson, where the fictional setting is the autumn of 1956. (The crisis of 1961 was, of course, the exception, since, for Christa Wolf and Brigitte Reimann at least, it was simply too recent to be ignored.) The historical detail is thus generally imprecise, but it does make the broad nature of the conflicts comprehensible. The phenomenon of Stalinism is considered through character and incident, so that the elements of continuity and conflict in the GDR's existence can be weighed against one another for the first time. Culpable mismanagement of economic planning and unpardonable treatment of individuals by representatives of Party authority are described, alongside the exemplary actions of psychologically more complex leaders and workers, in a spirit of debate about the future course of socialist society. There are still cases of glaring contradiction between the presentation of comparable situations in one work and another, but certain basic impressions of the legacy of Stalinism emerge from the range of perspectives and characters offered.

In the GDR, the Stalin era effectively began in 1948, with the SED's abandonment of its initial conception of a broad anti-fascist base, which could have allowed an independent German version of socialism to develop. The Party's endeavours to plan economic growth thereafter seem to have been overshadowed by its ruthless persecution of anyone suspected of subversion, not least long-standing socialists with dissenting views. With the network of Party functionaries from village and factory-floor level upwards assuming an exclusive right to decision-making, justified in terms of the emergency situation, the cultural-political image of full community participation was at its furthest remove from actuality. [14]

These years must have put those in Party office to the ultimate test of demonstrating whether they could inspire understanding and trust, in a situation which allowed little scope for extended debate or reasoned dissent. The period obviously also offered unique opportunities for the 'Radfahrer' mentality to flourish, since unquestioning obedience to superior authority and mindless implementation of official policy at lower levels could easily become virtues in their own right. [15] The existence of such amoral careerism had been acknowledged in the 1950s 'Aufbauromane' (notably Eduard Claudius' Menschen an unsrer Seite), but only in order to reassure the reader that such villains were no more than an ineffectual minority. The 'Entwicklungsromane' tended to stop short of any depiction of Stalinist aberrations, with little more than the concerned comments of idealised personalities like de Bruyn's Blaskow in Der Hohlweg to show that the problem existed at all. The Bitterfeld

novels, especially the more explicitly historical <u>Die Aula</u>
go much further, providing psychological analysis of the
bureaucratic mentality and giving a more credible impression of its prevalence in the state's early years -
with the result that they inevitably raise the highly
pertinent question of the extent to which its worst features have been eradicated by the 1960s.

Kant challenges the hitherto basic assumptions about
continuity and consistency in the Party leadership, in
depicting a power conflict in existence since the foundation of the Greifswald 'Arbeiter- und Bauernfakultät' in
1949 between anti-fascist veterans and the rank-obsessed
functionaries fresh from the Cold War 'Parteischule'.
(He nevertheless glosses over the historical crisis-points
within this struggle which Erwin Strittmatter, for example
depicts effectively in his <u>Ole Bienkopp</u>.[16]) Robert
Iswall's self-assured dealings with authority figures
suggest that the GDR is now sufficiently established to
view its past errors in critical depth and consign its
bureaucrats to positions of insignificance, but he tends
not to explain when or how the change for the better
occurred.

The composition of the selection committee which accepts
Iswall into the Greifswald ABF certainly suggests that the
hard-liners are in the ascendancy, with the head of the
faculty, Völschow, and the classicist Angelhoff as local
Party secretary both seeking Iswall's approval of Stalin's
view that "die Kader entscheiden alles".(A 30) Only the
historian Riebenlamm takes time to offer the private reassurance which finally ensures Iswall's commitment to the
ranks of the mature students. Völschow and Angelhoff tend
to act in tandem whenever an ideological issue has to be
resolved. They reveal the near hysterical suspicions of
the era in their interrogation of Iswall after his sister's
defection to the West (A 97 - 100), and actually compel
their students to spend three days formulating a 'Selbstkritik' because an article in <u>Neues Deutschland</u> has
omitted the word 'demokratisch' in its publication of a
purely rhetorical telegram from Stalin which should have
read - "es lebe und gedeihe das einheitliche, unabhängige,
demokratische, friedliebende Deutschland".(A 281) Kant
appears to crystallise his views on the retrogressive
effect of such leadership, in the scene depicting a march
organised by the students to agitate for the renaming of
Greifswald's main square as 'Platz der Befreiung'. Althoug
nominally at the head of the parade, Völschow and Angelhof
spend most of the time walking backwards, abusing a student for showing 'kleinbürgerlich' and 'revanchistisch'
tendencies in daring to question the value of the marathor

'Selbstkritik', instead of leading the way forward con-
structively. (A 283)

The balance is however restored towards more ideal
leadership with the students' discovery that the district
Party secretary Haiduck has rather more admirable qualities. At every point, this knowledgeable veteran of the
Spanish Civil War presents an encouraging alternative to
the dogmatic restrictiveness revealed in the ABF.
Haiduck's attitude is one of basic trust in the individual's
judgment and sense of responsibility, whether or not he
is a 'Kader':

> Liebe Genossen, Mißtrauen vergiftet die Atmos-
> phäre, Wachsamkeit reinigt sie. Ein wachsamer
> Mensch beobachtet genau, rechnet scharf, denkt,
> denkt, denkt, fragt immer nach den möglichen
> Folgen seiner Schritte, aber er geht - manch-
> mal rückwärts, manchmal seitwärts, aber im
> ganzen immer vorwärts. Wachsamkeit hat mit
> Mut zu tun. Mißtrauen hat mit Angst zu tun.
> Mißtrauen schießt auf Gespenster. Das ist
> Munitionsvergeudung, und die ist strafbar. (A 164)

Haiduck is consequently furious when the strictures of
Völschow and Angelhoff lead to the defection to the West
of Fiebach, the student brave enough to question their
methods, on the basis that the loss of a single potential
leader far outweighs the emotional satisfaction provided
by this symbolical renaming of a town square. But because
his socialism is far more flexible than the prevalent
Party line, Haiduck too exposes himself to Stalinist vin-
dictiveness. The last the reader hears of him is that he
is publicly attacked around 1953, on the grounds that he
at one stage favoured a "besonderen deutschen Weg zum
Sozialismus" - regardless of whether he continues to hold
such views and of the fact that they were also official
SED policy until 1948. (A 355)

Haiduck's fate is not revealed any more than are the
fortunes of Völschow and Angelhoff after Iswall's 'Jahr-
gang' graduates in 1952, as if it were possible to draw
a veil over the intervening decade, until Iswall, in preparing his speech, begins his reckoning with the ABF.
Haiduck's plight is, however, compared by Iswall to that
of his mother and step-father, Nußbank, who are hounded
unjustifiably by a bureaucracy deaf to all reasoned
pleading. They eventually leave for the West shortly before the upheavals of June 1953, to escape from what
Iswall himself calls "die Kafkatour". (A 357) This is also
the period when Quasi Riek, the chief organiser and spokes-
man for the ABF, disappears to the West, thus creating the
unsolved mystery amidst a series of exemplary careers.

There seem no grounds for attributing Riek's defection to
such Stalinist excesses - indeed there are hints that he
may even be involved in espionage - but one plausible
motive would be his inability to find a basis for the
strong sense of identity established in the ABF in the
wider context of GDR society.(A 353)

The attention devoted to Riek is a further proof of the
Bitterfeld authors' determination to present a convincingly complex view of the socialist past. But one of the
weaknesses of Kant's novel is that he does not go on to
reveal, in terms of his characters' development, how progress came to be made. Iswall's years of academic study
in Berlin after 1952 and his beginnings as a journalist
are summarised in a paragraph which mentions decisive
moments like "Chruschtschows große Rede" without showing
how they affected his subsequent thinking.(A 402-4) It
may be that the conception of a struggle within the Party
between dogmatists and humane dialecticians is ultimately
too simple, and that suggestions of a neat resolution
would misrepresent the extent of their necessary co-
existence under the Soviet system. Kant shows the continuity of each basic type over the 1949-62 period, through
the figures of Meibaum, who begins as the pedantic warden
of the student hostel and rises to the post of principal
of the ABF, and Riebenlamm, Iswall's most inspiring
teacher, who is now chief school inspector for the region.
Iswall's comments on the Meibaum of 1962, especially as
regards the latter's desire to excise unflattering details
from any account of the past, certainly imply that the
bureaucrats can now be resisted in a cavalier fashion:

> Den Film spielen wir nicht mehr, Meibaum.
> Entweder du willst eine Rede von Iswall, oder
> du willst keine Rede von Iswall, so liegen
> die Dinge, und eine von Meiwall oder Isbaum
> kriegst du nicht! ... Sich über Meibaum
> ärgern - dazu gehört schon etwas! Der Mann
> ist komisch, ist er von Anfang an gewesen ...
> Meibaum war immer ein Bürokrat und er
> ist es geblieben. (A 237-8)

The historical vagueness in Die Aula may also be partially explained by the fact that Kant, in common with
Christa Wolf and Brigitte Reimann, was concerned with re-
gistering the general improvement in the ideological
climate, in terms of the literary and academic spheres in
which they were most intimately involved. An obvious
critical target was therefore the would-be 'Künstler',
who hitherto supplied the synthetic image of reality
approved by the SED's cultural politicians, and was

showered with material advantages and public praise in
return.

Reimann clearly used her own industrial experience extensively in presenting Elisabeth's fortunes as one of
the youngest artists committed to the 'Bitterfelder Weg',
leading a 'Zirkel malender Arbeiter' at a lignite-combine.
After the initial encouragement of finding workers like
Lukas, a brigadier discriminating and enthusiastic in his
appreciation of art, Elisabeth is confronted with Ohm
Heiners, an unimaginative exponent of what Elisabeth calls
the "Romantik der schwieligen Faust", reducing each worker
he paints in his dull greys and browns to a "hirnlosen
Produktioner" or a "finsteren Roboter".(G 161-3) He has
no conception of the changing nature of work since the
1930s, which has made the skilled technician more of a
contemporary 'Vorbild' than the muscle-bound labourer.
Heiners, however, forbids criticism of his work, on the
grounds of his proletarian pedigree, and is bitterly intent
upon preserving his position of privilege. Lukas makes the
point, through an apt adaptation of the title of Leonhard
Frank's novel Links, wo das Herz ist: "Der Mann hat 'ne
kitzlige Stelle unterm Jackett, links, wo die Brieftasche
sitzt".(G 181) From his artistically primitive perspective,
Heiners attacks Elisabeth for the 'subjective' and 'forma-
listic' tendencies in her work, only to be met with a
courageously expressed personal credo, appropriate to the
Bitterfeld generation as a whole:

> ... deine Sorte von Realismus könnte ich auch
> mit einem guten Farbfilm 'runterknipsen.
> Mein Auge ist aber keine Kameralinse, und ich
> bin kein Photoapparat, ich bin ein Mensch mit
> Empfindungen und mit einem bestimmten Verhält-
> nis zu dem Menschen, den ich male, und der
> gemalte Mensch hat auch seine Empfindungen
> und seine eigene Einstellung zum Leben, zu
> seiner Arbeit, zu seiner Familie, und das alles
> muß man in einem Porträt festhalten - viele
> Schichten statt einer glatten Fläche.(G 172-3)

Heiners' resentment of Elisabeth's success with her art-
group and his jealousy of her superior skills finally
make him resort to character-defamation - the culmination
of Reimann's bleak depiction of art and the artist as
fostered under Stalinist principles. But the climate is
seen to have changed sufficiently to allow the Party
secretary, Bergemann, to ensure that justice is done to
Elisabeth, with Heiners sent off to the backwoods out of
harm's way.

The situation is even more reassuring in Die Aula,
through the confident manner with which Iswall handles

authority-figures like Meibaum and his newspaper editor
Kuhlmann, and evades their attempts to censor his work.
Kant has a counterpart to Heiners in Frau Tuschmann, who
writes 'Novellen' as if life could be organised with
mathematical precision on a fictional billiard-table, with
characters as polished and predictable as billiard-balls.
Thus Iswall is able to plead for the complexity of life
in tones which closely echo Elisabeth's:

> Mathematik war eine großartige Sache ... sie
> war nützlich beim Billard und bei anderen
> Dingen, aber eine Geschichte schreiben konnte
> man damit auf keinen Fall, denn die hatte es
> mit dem Leben, und das hatte Buckel und Risse,
> und die Menschen hatten sie auch.(A 34)

Although Iswall seems to live up to this rejection of
simplified reality in his criticism of Stalinism, something
vital is lacking in his portrayal of the cultural world
of the early 1960s. He is never directly confronted with
figures like Frau Tuschmann, and when he is present at a
meeting organised by the Writers' Union to allow an 'exchange of experience' between older and younger writers,
he substitutes caricature for an exposition of the inherent
tensions.(A 336-48) The predilection of authors with
names like Gertrude Buchhacker for long-winded historical
novels, 'poetic' studies of heroic figures in the GDR's
cooking-oil industry, rambling gossip packaged as 'Volks-
tümlichkeit', and so on, is patently intended to expose
them to the reader's ridicule. It also suggests, im-
plausibly, that the up-and-coming Iswalls enjoy a kind of
anarchic independence from their authority. Satire of
this kind is too far removed from actuality to be taken
seriously. The identifiable jibes elsewhere at Erik
Neutsch and Max Walter Schulz for the programmatic delibe-
rateness of their works are scarcely more than mildly provocative: the ambitions of the "junger Autor" to write a
900 page novel "Doch ewig bleiben die Steine" suggest to
Iswall an ideological reversal of Gone with the Wind,
while Schulz's 'Entwicklungsroman' is innocuously disguised as a 'Lehrlingsromanze' entitled "Das bläst der
Wind nicht fort".(A 267)
    Christa Wolf probes more deeply into the legacy of the
past, shifting the emphasis from the literary to the academic world, through Manfred's situation as a research
chemist at Halle university and Rita's experience at her
college of education. Here the threat to progress comes
as much from the attitudes of a reactionary academic hierarchy as from the Party's attempts to restrict the subject
matter, and both sides are implicitly condemned. On the
one hand, products of the FDJ and the 'Parteischule', like

Rudi Schwabe and Mangold, reduce all intellectual matters
to simple ideological terms. Schwabe is appointed as the
Party's representative in the university registry - an
"Allroundfunktionär" who has never pursued "einen anstän-
digen Beruf".(GH 90) Mangold has been given leave from
his previous unspecified bureaucratic activity to train
as a teacher, and intimidates fellow-students like Rita
with the sheer weight of doctrine he has learnt by heart.
Schwabe may have sympathetic traits, yet is the "aus-
führendes Organ" for disciplinary sanctions which can
threaten the career of outstanding students like Manfred's
colleague Martin Jung.(GH 182-3) Mangold has avoided the
post-war indecision of his generation by total immersion
in ideological abstraction, which he worships as infallible
truth:

> Alle mußten jetzt sprechen ... Aber immer noch
> redete nur Mangold, dem man guten Glauben
> wohl zubilligen mußte. Er sprach über die
> Parteilinie, wie Katholiken über die
> unbefleckte Empfängnis reden.(GH 174)

The only saving feature in the college is that the students
have, in Erwin Schwarzenbach, a tutor who is able to expose the dangers of such inflexibility in a constructive
manner.
   Those in academic authority in the elite world of the
university's science faculty are no less a detrimental
force than the Party's uncritical servants. The hierarchy
here is composed of arrogant bourgeois materialists, with
a questionable past in the Third Reich, who exploit the
situation in the GDR, where experts in the field of
chemical research are desperately needed. The Professor
and his elderly colleagues operate a semi-feudal system,
demanding "Götzendienst" from their students and
researchers.(GH 144) Manfred has become entangled in this
struggle for patronage, but only after finding to his cost
earlier that public criticism of the system - "Über Fehler
im Studienbetrieb. Über den tollen Ballast, der uns be-
lastete. Über Heuchelei, die mit guten Noten belohnt
wurde" (GH 176) - exposed him to vicious counter-attack.
Nevertheless, when Rita first sees him in this environment,
at a Christmas party, it is a distressing experience for
her which marks the end of the "Verzauberung" in their
relationship.(GH 150)
   The academic world threatens to become as disillusioning
for Rita as it has been for Manfred in the 1950s. It is
only through the example of Schwarzenbach, the man who
first recognised her potential in the rural obscurity
where she spent her adolescent years, that its new vitality is finally affirmed. As Rita prepares to face the

world again, late in 1961, after her recuperation,
Schwarzenbach visits her and tells her about an article
he has just had published on the theme of dogmatism in the
classroom. It has culminated in a plea for educationalists
to become "Sozialisten" rather than "Nachplapperer", on a
basis of open discussion rather than by dictating 'truths'
to their students. Schwarzenbach has already been criti-
sised by Party sources, on the grounds that the time is
not yet ripe - just after August 1961 - for the expression
of internal conflicts. His rhetorical response, as
challenging as those of Elisabeth and Iswall, is that the
breakthrough into 'Vielschichtigkeit', and the revelation
of the 'Buckel und Risse', must occur now, precisely after
the moment of deepest crisis:

> Zum erstenmal sind wir reif, der Wahrheit ins
> Gesicht zu sehen. Das Schwere nicht in Leicht
> umdeuten, das Dunkle nicht in Hell. Vertrauen
> nicht mißbrauchen ... Sozialismus, das
> ist doch keine magische Zauberformel. Manch-
> mal glauben wir, etwas zu verändern, indem wir
> es neu benennen ... Die reine nackte Wahrheit,
> und nur sie, ist auf die Dauer der Schlüssel
> zum Menschen.(GH 252)

The one discordant note in this fairly uniform expression of the need for a radical break with the methods
and the typical personalities of the 1950s is struck in
Spur der Steine. Neutsch was evidently less inclined to
emphasise insights arrived at by intellectuals from their
protected perspective on everyday life. He does include
an artist within the broad panorama of the novel, but in
a more ambivalent light. Eberhard Voss has not had a
smooth career, pilloried as a 'formalist' years before
he takes on the task of depicting industrial life at
Schkona, but still determined to use the collage techniques
he favoured then. At one point, he looks like becoming
the author's mouthpiece, communicating as effectively with
the culturally ignorant Balla as with the intelligent
young graduate Katrin Klee. He offers the central interpretation of the novel's title, in clarifying to Katrin
what Balla meant by the 'Spur der Steine' linking together
the many building projects he has worked on:

> Dieser Balla hat mir vor kurzem gestanden ...
> er habe so etwas wie die Spur der Steine
> erblickt, des Aufbaus, seiner Hände Arbeit,
> und damit den Aufbau seines eigenen Ichs. Es
> ist sicherlich richtig, aber es ist noch mehr.
> Die Steine ziehen eine Spur, die nicht nur
> durch das Land geht, Häfen, Talsperren,

> Fabrikhallen ... Sie quält sich mitten durch
> uns hindurch, und sie ist mit keiner vor ihr
> vergleichbar. Wie auch sollte es anders
> sein, wenn man sich selber aufbaut.(SS 671)

Later, though, the vital sense of identity with the GDR
is seen to be lacking in Voss. His experience of Stalinist
'Kulturpolitik' at its most philistine is not questioned,
yet his discussions with Herman Jansen suggest that the
artist needs to change more than the state's attitude to
culture. The Party's regional secretary may be old-
fashioned in his ideas about art, but his criticisms are
always perceptive:

> Ich habe dir dein erstes Atelier eingerichtet.
> Ich ahne auch, wie du über die Partei denkst:
> Alle zwei Jahre eine Welle gegen mich ... Aber
> du wärst nicht unser Genosse, wenn wir dich
> nicht ganz für uns gewinnen wollten, dich mit
> deiner Kunst.(SS 609)

Despite such reassurance, Voss is confronted with a further
crass injustice when his portrait of Katrin Klee, uni-
versally held to be the best exhibit in a state exhibition,
is only given third prize. Some unnamed figure of ministerial status has overruled the jury's judgment on the
grounds that Voss' previous work contained "spätbürger-
liche Rudimente", even though the actual portrait bore no
sign of his collage methods. His bitter response to this
malevolent interference is however seen - by Balla - to be
as reprehensible as the interference itself (SS 747), as
Neutsch reveals his readiness to denigrate the artist who
has previously filled a significant didactic role. Such
inconsistency in characterisation may arise from Neutsch's
desire to show that he has not glossed over the writer's
problematic relationship with authority, while emphasising
that the injustice suffered by Voss is a regrettable fall
from established standards, rather than a typical example
of the Party's methods of ensuring superficial conformity.
   Neutsch does provide a caricatured image of the aberrations of the recent past in Bleibtreu, the dullard
who finds himself entrusted with the responsibilities of
Party secretary on the Schkona site as Horrath loses his
grip, and comes close to disaster on the day when Balla
leads a spontaneous strike and Katrin Klee criticises the
local Party leadership in the press.(SS 709-10)
Bleibtreu's significance is however negligible in comparison to that of the vastly experienced Herman Jansen,
whose whole career since the 1920s has been exemplary -
"sein Leben ist die Geschichte der revolutionären Arbei-
terbewegung Deutschlands" (SS 230) - and who is an inspi-

rational force, whether in private discussion or on an
open-air platform, capable of making even Balla in his
most sceptical phase feel "wie frisch gewaschen".(SS 504)
Furthermore, Jansen's abilities are seen to be shared
by both Otto Grotewohl and Walter Ulbricht at significant
points of the novel. Ulbricht, in his conversation with
Balla, is a model of understanding, well aware of the
ordinary worker's hardships and doubts. He is also put
in the position of vindicating the Party leadership and
their methods since 1945, without fear of contradiction:

> Der Vorsitzende durchschaute [Balla], erriet
> die Bedenken und Zweifel, die ihn, Balla,
> lange bewegt hatten. Doch er schien sie ihm
> nicht zu verübeln.
> "Aber glauben Sie mir. Niemandem von uns ist
> es leichtgefallen, sich neuen Aufgaben zuzu-
> wenden, zum Beispiel einen Staat zu leiten.
> Und trotzdem sind wir vor der Verantwortung ,
> nicht zurückgeschreckt. Wenn nicht wir, wenn
> nicht Sie, wenn nicht die gesamte Arbeiter-
> klasse, wer sonst?"(SS 924-5)

Such explicit support for the state leadership is clearly
the exception amongst this Bitterfeld fiction, and places
in doubt Neutsch's determination to present the Stalin
era in credible dialectical terms, since the overall
achievement, the 'Spur der Steine', dwarfs the individual
problems of a Voss or a Horrath, however significant they
may prove when regarded in isolation.

The cumulative evidence of these novels nevertheless
demonstrates the untenability of the propagandistic assertion that the GDR could have become an integrated community
from the outset, and a new - if highly incomplete - sense
of development through conflict emerges. The relationship
between Party officials and the intelligent, creative individual is seen to be crucial to progress towards the
communal ideal, since the Party's insistence on discipline
and uniformity has been misguided, especially where it
allowed a bureaucratic mentality little changed from the
Third Reich to flourish. It has also been directly
counter-productive where it has prevented people with a
basic socialist commitment from fulfilling their potential,
to the detriment of the GDR's economic growth as well as
of individual morale.

The limits of community

This new perspective on the tortuous road to socialism
in the GDR ought finally to have rendered the conceptual
framework of harmonious 'Gemeinschaft' redundant. It
comes therefore as a disappointment to find some of the
compositional simplifications of earlier Socialist Realism
recurring even in the most impressive of the Bitterfeld
novels. The 'pathetic fallacy' of using nature-analogies
to reflect the situation of the main characters plays a
significant part in Spur der Steine and Der geteilte
Himmel, in relation to Hannes Balla and Rita Seidel.
Balla's twelve years of post-war 'Wanderschaft', before
he arrives with his brigade at the Schkona site in 1959,
are presented as aimless and rootless. Although he has
been involved in major building projects all over the
GDR, they are seen as "Station[en] in der Fremde", in
keeping with his mercenary motives for working there.
(SS 118) This surprisingly negative first reference to
the 'Spur der Steine' can also be explained by the convenient fact that Schkona is close to Balla's birthplace,
the village of Angersfurt, where his parents still live,
so that 'Heimat' is initially only meaningful for him in
this private sense. Ironically, of course, Balla achieves
his fondest material ambition, the purchase of a Wartburg
car - his "blaue Blume"(!) - just when the example of
selfless dedication to communal goals, which Werner Horrath
offers, has led him to see himself as an "Auswanderer im
eigenen Land", and starts him longing for the stability
of a "warme[s] Nest".(SS 350-2) The 'natural' process of
Balla's moral growth is soon evident to those around him,
like Katrin Klee, who views him as "gewandelt, als sei er
aus der rauhen Schale seiner Verderbtheit gesprungen wie
eine Kastanie aus ihrer Kapsel".(SS 382) The narrator
extends the image in describing Balla's new social insights as "überreife Früchte, denen der leiseste Windzug
genügte, manchmal sogar nur die eigene Last, um von den
Zweigen zu brechen".(SS 424) As the spring of 1960 begins,
full of hope and fresh life, the swallows return from their
winter migration to remind Balla that human life is also
a cyclical process of "Wanderschaft" and "Heimkehr".
(SS 472-5) Before long, he is setting off to inspect
Soviet industrial innovations as a representative of his
country, to cap a meteoric rise to fame. The image of
the 'Wandervogel' dominates the climax of the novel in
the spring of 1961: the Russian trip, in the company of
Katrin, brings about a major extension of his horizons as
a "Wanderschaft um die Welt".(SS 843) At the same time,
his "Heimat" is suddenly "weit geworden" and then to be
found "überall" (SS 939, 945), even though the hope that

a deepening of his friendship with Kati would satisfy his
longing for domestic roots seems to have been thwarted.

Neutsch, however, unlike Christa Wolf, leaves little
room for the idyllic view of nature as a contrast to the
industrialised modern world. He almost seems to warn
against the liberation of human feelings in nature during
the course of the affair between Kati and Werner Horrath,
which begins in a park in Schkona and goes into decline
during their brief winter retreat in the chilling country
air of Lohenstein. The inability of Horrath to reconcile
this experience with his public life as a dedicated Party
secretary and his apparently stable marriage, is central
to his moral disintegration; for Kati, it is bitterly disillusioning, but not quite as disastrous. Neutsch's un-
problematical exemplary figures like Balla and Jansen seem
to find fulfilment within the rapidly expanding industrial
landscape described in the novel's opening scene, where
the atmosphere is "geschwängert vom fauligen Geruch der
Schwefelgase".(SS 10) For them, the only prospects of
respite are in the works dormitory or on the road to the
next assignment.

The paradox of Neutsch's often hackneyed use of nature-
metaphors, in conjunction with his lack of interest in the
world of nature and the private life of many of his characters, points to a poverty of literary imagination as well
as to a restrictive view of what constitutes personal
wholeness in a modern industrial context. Christa Wolf,
on the other hand, seems to overdo the description of
Rita's harmonious one-ness with nature and her origins so
much that her 'Heimat' becomes totally divorced from the
industrial and academic spheres she subsequently enters.
The introduction to her earlier existence, from the novel's
distinctly unidyllic perspective of late 1961, has all the
qualities of a fairy-tale:

> Rita[lebte] mit Mutter und Tante in einem
> winzigen Häuschen am Waldrand ... Sie war
> zufrieden mit ihrem Dorf: Rotdächrige Häuser
> in kleinen Gruppen, dazu Wald und Wiese und
> Feld und Himmel in dem richtigen Gleichgewicht,
> wie man sich's kaum ausdenken könnte.(GH 11)

As a later reference shows, everything in this world has
been "einfach" and "überschaubar" for Rita, with something of the purity and completeness of the last day of
Creation(!), allowing her to grow up with an "Unberührt-
heit der Seele".(GH 77) Nothing in the rapid expansion
of her experience - through her relationship with Manfred,
her work in the factory or her studies - serves to place
this perfection in the kind of parochial light which
would offer any possibility of comparison with Neutsch's

Angersfurt. In fact, the inhabitants of the village, even Rita's mother and aunt, who brought her there in 1945, are never characterised. During a brief visit, Rita gains great consolation from the fields, the birds and the sky, and feels she has "alles ... was ein Mensch braucht" (GH 169), but it is all curiously static and insubstantial.

The weather and the seasons change in keeping with Rita's mood. The autumn of 1960, when she first realises there is something lacking in the existence she shares with Manfred, is "trüb" and "dumpf", shrouded in acrid fog: relief comes only when she seeks out her mentor Schwarzenbach and finds in his home a vitality lacking in the Herrfurth household. (GH 123-30) May 1961 is chilling-ly cold, with the deeply overcast sky giving forth "eine unbestimmte Drohung", stirring up "unterirdisch ... eine trübe Flut von Lüge, Dummheit, Verrat" which threatens "durch Häuserritzen und Kellerfenster auf die Straße [zu] sickern" (GH 201) - a passage which reveals all the dangers of attributing an undeniably man-made crisis to mysterious metaphysical sources. Rita's recovery in the sanatorium in the autumn of 1961 is described in rather more plausible psychological terms, and yet the day which marks the de-cisive turning-point is "der erste, klare, kalte Herbst-tag nach einer stürmischen Nacht". (GH 130) The birds again play their symbolical role, with the accent now on the freedom and grace of the swallow striving for the heavens (GH 217, 236), in contrast to the tortoise which Manfred sees fit to bring Rita as a present from Bulgaria: "der stumpf-traurige Blick der uralten Augen" becomes re-pellent to her after Manfred goes to the West. (GH 212)

Interestingly, Neutsch and Wolf also use the same his-torical event, the first manned space-flight, carried out by Yuri Gagarin in April 1961, to demonstrate the univer-sal scale of the growth of socialism which they present as a 'natural' development in individuals like Balla and Rita. The small-scale achievements to which they have contributed are thus seen as being organically related to this dramatic technological breakthrough. The point is made ponderously in Der geteilte Himmel, with "die Nachricht", as it is mysteriously termed in the lengthy build-up, coinciding with the test-run of the latest light-weight railway carriages produced in Rita's factory. The three central characters - Rita, Manfred and the young works-director Wendland - are on board, travelling "quer durch das Land" through "das Gewebe des Alltags" (GH 188), and arguing whether socialism can succeed in an industrial state like the GDR. The perfection of the space flight is not fully shared at the microcosmic level, since the brakes are not as effective as they should be: for the more emotional Rita, however, the general feeling of

identification - "Ich gehöre dazu, dachte sie" (GH 196) -
with 'her' carriages and thus with the sputnik, is sufficient at this stage. In Spur der Steine, the achievement
in space becomes the climax of Balla's four-week encounter
with Soviet technology, which has already given him a new
vision of the "Spur der Steine ... die noch vor mir liegt"
(SS 879) As Balla happens to be on the point of flying
back to the GDR when he hears the news, Neutsch is able
to reveal the same interrelationship in the socialist
world between individual growth, the technology of everyday
life, and mankind's cosmic potential.(SS 891) The 'sozialistische Menschengemeinschaft' under Soviet leadership is
thus seen as working, with nature's benevolent support,
towards the perfection of the hero's world.

This harmonisation in Der geteilte Himmel and Spur der
Steine is revealingly associated with the figure intended
as the main 'Vorbild', in whose characterisation the author'
personal experience is no more than distantly reflected.
Although there is a close emotional relationship between
the narrator and the heroine in Der geteilte Himmel, with
Rita's origins similar to those of Christa Wolf herself,
time is curiously telescoped for the ten-year-younger
Rita. She gains her practical knowledge of industrial
life at the threshold of adulthood, and her idyllic
'Heimat' represents a total contrast to the Stalinist
1950s, which were the formative years for Wolf's own generation. It is as if Wolf wanted to demonstrate how life
could have been for those born around 1930, if the starting
point for socialism had been the spirit of the 'Bitterfelde
Weg' rather than the Cold War, while confining the disheartening quality of intellectual life in the 1950s within
her characterisation of Manfred. Neutsch would appear to
have put different aspects of himself in the artist Voss,
the Party secretary Horrath and the proletarian activist
Balla, each of whom takes over the burden of the positive
hero for parts of the novel. But while the stars of Voss
and Horrath wane with psychologically disturbing alacrity,
the transformation of the self-centred Balla in the opposite direction is even less credible. The idea of Balla,
within a matter of months, giving articulate guidance to
Voss and Horrath, and exchanging ideas with the SED
leadership, not to mention his conversion to Mozart,
places him in the realms of the ideal. He still has much
in common with Becher's utopian figures, whatever the
documentary basis for Spur der Steine might suggest to the
contrary.

Both Rita and Balla form interesting exceptions to
what could be regarded as an autobiographically determined
norm for the central figures in these novels. Balla is
the only manual worker to be studied in depth: other

figures may have proletarian or peasant origins, like Jakob Filter in <u>Die Aula</u> or Joachim Steinbrink in <u>Die Geschwister</u>, but have risen to positions of responsibility well before the narrative present. Rita represents the younger generation maturing into the 1960s, in the same way as Neutsch's graduates Katrin Klee and Kurt Hesselbart, for whom social integration will be far less problematical. By far the major group of characters, however, is made up of those aged roughly between 25 and 35, and engaged in intellectually demanding work - Elisabeth and Joachim in <u>Die Geschwister</u>, Manfred, Ernst Wendland and Erwin Schwarzenbach in <u>Der geteilte Himmel</u>, Werner Horrath in <u>Spur der Steine</u>, and ABF graduates like Robert and Vera Iswall, Gerd Trullesand, and Quasi Riek in <u>Die Aula</u>. They are thus slightly younger than the heroes of the 'Entwicklungsromane' dealt with in the previous chapter, and were just able, with the exception of some of Kant's figures, to avoid active war-service. They were fortunate, in Iswall's eyes, still to have both "ein heiles Fell" and "ein reines Gewissen" as peace was established.(A 246) As Manfred recalls in <u>Der geteilte Himmel</u>:

> Lässig beendeten wir die Schule. Damals waren
> wir Fünfzehnjährigen die älteste Klasse, in
> der keine Gefallenenliste hing.(GH 59)

This small age-difference might have been quite crucial to their survival, but has certainly not meant any rapid or 'natural' integration into an embryonic socialist society. They are more isolated, both from any benevolent influence of 'nature' and from many of the social groupings that make for a sense of community. The feeling of continuity based on close family ties and an unchanging 'Heimat' is rarely present for those who, in Manfred's words, make up "die politische Generation".(GH 90)

The point is frequently made that they have special identity problems. Neutsch emphasises, in relation to both Horrath and Balla, that "die Dreißigjährigen suchen täglich nach dem Neubeginn", with an insecurity which goes back to the war years.(SS 261, 796, 900) Horrath believes that his generation has had exceptional difficulties in overcoming the indoctrination to which it was exposed in the Third Reich:

> Die vor uns haben es einfacher, sie wußten
> stets von der Konsequenz der Widersprüche,
> die nach uns leichter, ihnen wird nichts mehr
> verschleiert.(SS 797)

Manfred sees the problem differently, in terms of a self-protective moral indifference developed against the ideology of the Hitler Youth, and never overcome, which places a real barrier between himself and Rita's generation:

> Wozu erzähle ich dir das alles? dachte er.
> Versteht sie überhaupt, was damals los war?
> Sie war ja noch nicht mal geboren ... Komisch:
> Irgendwo zwischen ihr und mir fängt die neue
> Generation an. Wo soll sie begreifen, daß
> man uns alle frühzeitig mit dieser tödlichen
> Gleichgültigkeit infiziert hat, die man so
> schwer wieder los wird?(GH 56)

Many of them, like Horrath, Trullesand and Riek, have
grown up as orphans; others become alienated from the
petit-bourgeois attitudes of their parents, usually
evident in the form of opportunism and materialism, as in the
Herrfurth household, which is reduced for Manfred to a
"Lebenssarg" (GH 29), or in the homes which Iswall's
mother and sister set up with their husbands in Hamburg,
which leave him feeling "das ist doch keine Familie mehr".
(A 124)

The political re-division of Central Europe after 1945
means that some of this generation were born outside the
GDR's boundaries, Iswall to the West, Horrath and
Trullesand to the East, and have thus no geographical
base in the state. Most of them are town-dwellers, if
not from birth, then after establishing themselves in the
GDR - Christa Wolf's figures in Halle, Elisabeth Arendt's
brothers and Werner Horrath in Rostock, Robert Iswall and
some of his colleagues in Berlin - while cultural centres
like Weimar, Leipzig and Dresden appear regularly on the
fictional itinerary. There is however little attempt to
define the nature of city life in a socialist context:
Iswall, for example, is at the centre of intellectual life
in Berlin, but offers almost no idea of what happens outside his working day as a journalist. Christa Wolf raises
questions of urban alienation - "wie leicht kann einer
hier verlorengehen" (GH 32) - and the destructive side-
effects of industrialisation, through Rita's initial impressions of Halle:

> [Der Fluß] war, seit Manfred ihn als Kind ver-
> lassen hatte, nützlicher und unfreundlicher
> geworden: er führte watteweißen Schaum mit
> sich, der übel roch und vom Chemiewerk bis
> weit hinter die Stadt den Fisch vergiftete.
> Die Kinder von heute konnten nicht daran
> denken, hier schwimmen zu lernen, obwohl die
> Ufer flach und von Gras und Weiden gesäumt
> waren.(GH 35)

Particularly in Wolf's case, the acceptance of the need
for industrial growth is reluctant, and tends to interfere

with her schematic contrast of socialist and capitalist
society on the familiar 'Gemeinschaft' - 'Gesellschaft'
basis. This is most evident during Rita's unsuccessful
reunion with Manfred in West Berlin, where the city is
utterly infertile and colourless.

The one marked difference between city-life in East
and West is that the figures in the GDR tend to enjoy
steady emotional relationships, which reduce the risk of
urban isolation - Iswall has a stable marriage and a
child, Elisabeth has the strength of her love for Joachim,
and Rita, initially, lives with Manfred. Difficulties
occur, however, when a commitment to a new industrial project leads characters, in <u>Spur der Steine</u> or <u>Die Geschwister,</u>
to unfamiliar towns dwarfed by the scale of technological
progress. The workers live in primitive huts, while the
planners and administrators are billeted in down-at-heel
rooms in the town. For those compelled to move without
their spouse, like Horrath, the problem of stability and
integration becomes acute, since there are few natural
means of recovering from the tensions of a desperately
hard working-day. Even where there is housing available,
in the exceptional case of the unmarried Katrin Klee and
her son, the lack of contact between neighbours in a
multi-storey block of flats is seen to be as grim in the
GDR as anywhere else. Despite age similarities, there is
no "Mietergemeinschaft": as Katrin bitterly notes, "die
Geräusche in diesem Haus waren einander schon vertrauter
als die Menschen".(SS 755)

In such a distinctly unwelcoming environment, the in-
cessant pressures to increase productivity, and thus ensure the GDR's economic survival, threaten the quality of
life implied by concepts like 'Gemeinschaft'. The variety
of reactions to the issue of Party membership amongst the
characters who make up the young administrative and
creative elite in these novels reflects the extent of
such tensions between ideals and expediency. Those who
joined the SED in its Stalinist days have clearly grown
in stature above the Mangolds and the Bleibtreus, but their
initial motivation seems to have been rather similar.
Werner Horrath, in the depths of his crisis, refers to
his espousal of Marxism as a liberation from fascist be-
liefs, which failed however to bring about a decisive
break from the methods of National Socialism. In 1961,
he is still trying to shake off "diese innere Gefangen-
schaft von, sagen wir, mindestens fünfundzwanzig Jahren".
(SS 796)   Other characters, like Schwarzenbach and
Wendland in <u>Der geteilte Himmel</u> or Iswall and Jakob Filter
in <u>Die Aula</u>, have made this transition at less cost to
their personal stability. But a fair proportion of these
potential leaders are not members of the SED at the

fictional outset, and for well-founded reasons, even though
they may well take the decisive step in the near future
(with the obvious exception of Manfred).

Manfred's scepticism is shown to be the self-protective
façade of an idealist who has been made to suffer for
justifiable criticisms of the Party's leadership in the
past. He is, like Rita, one of "die Empfindlichen", whom
the Party needs more than dogmatic loyalists of Mangold's
ilk: the likely reason why even an exemplary younger
figure like Rita is not yet a member is its insensitivity
to individual needs.(GH 128-9) Elisabeth, in Die Geschwister
stands between the Party and the disillusioned, represented
by her younger brother Uli, who has been prevented from
obtaining employment simply because he studied under a
professor who later left the GDR. She recognises the validity of his complaints, but criticises him for his lack
of patience and understanding, mindful of the endless
"zermürbende Nachtarbeit" which most Party members willing-
ly undertake.(G 144) Elisabeth's experience, as a non-
member, of full support from the Party secretary at her
workplace against the activities of an establishment
figure like Heiners, together with her successful relationship with the dedicated Joachim, is encouraging, but not
necessarily representative. In Der geteilte Himmel, it is
Martin Jung - exmatriculated from university for political
reasons - who expresses regret that Manfred left the GDR
just before the erection of the Berlin Wall, in words
which probably reflect the mixed feelings of the authors
themselves:

> In unserem Betrieb ist gerade eine Kommission
> der Partei. Sie interessiert sich für unsere
> Maschine. Hätte Manfred nicht die acht Monate
> durchhalten können? Das macht mir am meisten
> zu schaffen, wenn ich an ihn denke: Wenn er
> hiergeblieben wäre, und sei es durch Zwang:
> Heute müßte er versuchen, mit allem fertig zu
> werden. Heute könnte er ja nicht mehr aus-
> weichen ...(GH 180)

Generally speaking, the Bitterfeld authors, while seeing
socialist progress in terms of the interaction of productive personalities like Manfred and a more responsive
Party structure, accepted this short-term inevitability
of some degree of coercion, to ensure the state's economic
stability, but without seeking thereby to modify their
well-founded criticisms of the SED's exercise of power in
the past.

The nucleus of a new communal self-consciousness for
the technological post-Bitterfeld era is seen to be developing from below, within the industrial brigades. The

brigade is seen as a democratic microcosm - "ein kleiner Staat für sich".(GH 49) Its functioning is described in Der geteilte Himmel and Spur der Steine, with noticeably less of the harmonisation which detracts from the characterisation of Rita and Balla. The starting-point for the portrayal of the brigade tends to be a feeling of alienation from authority, apparently little changed since capitalist days. The workers are capable of outstanding feats of productivity, but essentially for material reward, although some may derive satisfaction of a private kind from their achievements. They represent a cross-section of generational experience: both these novels include a father-figure, an ex-Nazi officer, a young and timid Party member, and a likeable apprentice within groups of eight and twelve men respectively. (Neutsch, however, makes matters less complicated by including a pair of incorrigibly evil elements to retard the brigade's corporate development.) The brigadier looks after his men's interests first and foremost, which can mean tricking the management into keeping work-norms ridiculously low, or obtaining materials illicitly in times of shortage. The group's identity is an old-style 'Zunftgeist', based on their common skill and on pride in their leader: they are pleased to be known as 'die Ermischleute' or 'die Ballas'.

The economic reforms of the late 1950s have a significant influence upon this situation. On the one hand, the new competitive element is introduced, challenging brigades to campaign for the title 'Brigade der sozialistischen Arbeit'; on the other, there is the potentially unsettling move to establish a sophisticated shift-system for new projects - 'die komplexe und industrielle Bauweise' - with a system of larger brigades representing various complementary skills rather than a single specialism.

Christa Wolf restricts herself to the homogeneous brigade making window-frames for railway-carriages, which can thus gain the satisfaction of seeing its work integrated into the finished product under the same factory roof with an organic coherence. Rita is proud to bring Manfred along to see where "die Geburt des Wagens begann".(GH 186) The new spirit of socialism in the GDR is exemplified by a change of leadership in the works management (Wendland's promotion having been accelerated through his predecessor's flight to the West), and by the efforts within the brigade, stimulated by Rolf Meternagel, to increase productivity. Meternagel's refusal to abandon his commitment to the state and to comrades who have earlier treated him cruelly, despite his "rückläufige Kaderentwicklung" (GH 74) and demotion from his position as 'Meister', make him a leader of greater stature than

Ermisch, who is merely "ein guter Brigadier für gute Zeiten".(GH 70) By the end of the novel, the brigade has come a long way towards developing a sense of common identity, extending to their leisure activities, as in the works party where they feel "bei sich selbst zu Gast" (GH 110), a process which augurs well for the GDR as a whole.

Erik Neutsch places his brigade in a more complex industrial setting, and yet suggests a more conclusive transformation of attitudes over the same two-year period. Balla's eight-man team of carpenters, most of whom have worked together for years on building-sites throughout the GDR, is so united that he can count on their unpaid support to build a byre at weekends on his father's farm. Nevertheless it is Balla who actually takes the lead in splitting them up to allow the introduction of the new shift-system at Schkona. The carpenters continue to live together in their hut and develop their socialist consciousness as a group (with the exception of the malevolent newcomers Galonski and Bolbig). Balla's attainment of ideological maturity, together with the achievements of his now committed socialist brigade on the burgeoning Schkona site, is only the beginning for Neutsch. Most of his original brigade take on new responsibilities elsewhere - studying at college, entering the army or the 'Parteischule', as Balla himself becomes a kind of roving ambassador for the new GDR. The concluding comment of his father figure Büchner - "überall ist einer aus der Brigade, überall" (SS 939) - suggests a continuing process of growth and multiplication of socialist cells on this model through the country.

This confidence in the brigade structure within industry is not contradicted elsewhere, not least perhaps since involvement at brigade level was the point of departure for the 'Bitterfelder Weg' generally and had a special significance for these authors. There is certainly a feeling that the sense of personal involvement in the state's technological development is more easily achieved here than in the rural context of land-collectivisation around 1960, which is only treated in Spur der Steine, within the sub-plot involving Balla's father. The majority of the central characters, however, in their positions of economic, political and intellectual responsibility, have to develop outside a tangible collective unit of this kind. Their fortunes compel a more profound consideration of the extent to which it is possible to regard success in working life as the key to wholeness of personality. They also work against the understanding of 'Gemeinschaft' in purely external, environmental terms, in the way they reflect the interdependence of private fulfilment and public achievement.

The private dimension to self-fulfilment

The assistance of friends and mentors incorporating
genuine socialist morality is insufficient in itself to
ensure the progress of the protagonists towards stability
and happiness. The question of whether each figure has
also succeeded in establishing an enduring relationship
with a member of the opposite sex effectively becomes a
touchstone of their personal maturity. There are, however, no illusions about marriage as an institution, and
no taboos about sex before or outside marriage, of the
kind evident in earlier 'Aufbauromane' such as Roheisen:
physical involvement is now viewed as a scarcely dispensable test of the potential strength of a relationship.
The painful break-up of a long-standing liaison is a recurring experience, and while the authors endeavour to
explain emotional conflict and alienation in psychological
terms, they also admit to some degree of irrationality in
human behaviour in intimate spheres. This threatens to
place the whole question of personal relationships outside
the control of an otherwise planned socialist society.
Indeed, the attempts made by the Party to resolve sexual
issues are portrayed, in Spur der Steine, as distinctly
counter-productive.

There is nothing remarkable in the fictional first
romances which prove to be insubstantial, except that
the partner invariably reveals bourgeois insensitivities,
which serve to show the protagonists that their future
involvements should have a secure socialist basis. Robert
Iswall soon regrets giving up weekends of political agi-
tation with his ABF colleagues for the pastor's daughter
Inga; Elisabeth quickly tires of her apolitical friendship with a student at West Berlin's 'Freie Universität';
Katrin Klee makes the painful realisation that the handsome artist Schmidt, a fellow-student, is incapable of an
emotional response to her. The relationship between Rita
and Manfred also falls into the category of 'unsuccessful
first love', but is treated in far greater depth. Rita
reveals the aspirations of the younger generation, seen
also in Katrin and Elisabeth, to involve itself tireless-
ly in building a new society, and to experience "außerordentliche Freuden und Leiden, außerordentliche Gescheh-
nisse und Erkenntnisse" in return.(GH 16) Manfred, the
academic from the city, seems to offer access to the
mainstream of life, and Rita sees her role as helping
him to cast aside his self-protective mask of scepticism.

For a time, their hopes approach realisation, and the intensity of their shared love gives him a previously unknown sense of stability and identity within the GDR:

> Das Unvergängliche in ihrer Liebe trat immer
> schärfer hervor, frei von Täuschung, Wunsch
> und Irrtum, durch Wissen und Entschluß
> gesichert. Das ist kein schwankender Boden
> mehr, auf dem ich gehe, dachte Manfred. Sie
> schafft es, sie macht mich im Leben fest.(GH 84)

This feeling stimulates Manfred's most productive and satisfying period of research work and also comes at the time when his sense of belonging to a genuine academic community is strongest. It is the same assurance that he is needed which finally convinces Elisabeth's brother that he should stay in the GDR, at the height of his personal crisis in Die Geschwister (G 249), and sends him back to his studies with fresh determination. For Manfred, however, the feeling of "Übereinstimmung mit der Welt" (GH 104) is short-lived: the fact that he never again experiences it lies partially with the insensitivity of GDR authority in rejecting the modified 'Spinning Jenny' developed by Manfred and Martin Jung. At the same time, Manfred's refusal to fight this adverse decision, regarding it fatalistically as an "Orakel" (GH 146), is unforgivable. It marks the beginning of Rita's loss of confidence in his will to transcend his "tödliche Gleichgültigkeit" (GH 56), a goal seen to be realisable only with her support and within the GDR. Rita's later rational recognition that Manfred has committed moral suicide in going to the West may not prevent her from coming close to actual death, in a desperate withdrawal from what seemed a lifelong commitment, but it represents the decisive turning point in her life:

> Er hatte aufgegeben. Wer nichts mehr liebt
> und nichts mehr haßt, kann überall und nirgends
> leben. Er ging ja nicht aus Protest. Er
> brachte sich selbst um, indem er ging.(GH 242)

The ending of liaisons in which one partner is unable to live up to the standards of socialist morality is fully understandable in a literature which rejects the notion of love as something independent of morality and environment. A situation, however, in which the marriage of committed socialists loses its vitality and breaks down through the involvement of a third socialist, is clearly more complex in its potentially disruptive effect upon the community. It inevitably affects all aspects of the life of each individual involved. In Spur der Steine, Werner and Marianne Horrath are separated after eight years of married life in Rostock, when he is transferred as Party secretary to the Schkona works, a couple of hundred miles away. Theirs seems to be a model relationship - indeed, in the story Der Neue, a first draft for parts of Spur der Steine, the equivalent relationship was exemplary. [17] Marianne teaches in a nursery school and is also a dedicated Party member, characterised by her "vernünftigen, ruhigen Mut" (SS 59) and her "geduldige Ausgeglichenheit".(SS 299) He has, however, been so committed to his Party work, accepting assignments all over the GDR without demur, that they have only spent a fraction of their married life together. They once accepted this sacrifice of private happiness with idealistic determination:

> Fünf Prozent unseres Lebens, wenn es hoch-
> kommt, Liebste, gehören uns, denn auch die
> Arbeit erfüllt uns, und seit Jahren werden
> wir auseinandergerissen. Laß uns so tun,
> als könnten die fünf Prozent uns hundert-
> prozentig entschädigen ...(SS 126)

They have gradually lost the vitality of their earlier life together, as Werner realises too late - "dauernd konnte er jedoch nicht verhindern, daß das Feuer einmal verlöschte".(SS 304) His assignment in Schkona proves the toughest of them all, with the strains of organising 20,000 workers, and, in particular, the rejection of his carefully worked out amendments to the development plan for the chemical works, suddenly threatening his unquestioned loyalty to everything the Party stood for. It is at this point that he finds Marianne lacking, since all her affections and sympathy are geared to offering him an escape from his torment, rather than helping him to resolve what has become a major identity crisis. Horrath's friendship with Katrin Klee rapidly develops into total involvement. What makes the difference is Katrin's ability to understand his despair and discuss it with him, to a point where he can transcend it - and in this sense she proves an outstanding representative of her generation. She succeeds where Marianne fails - "[Kati] allein hatte ihm geholfen, zu sich selbst zu finden".(SS 198)
   This is the moment of truth for Horrath, where a doubt is raised whether socially constructive activity and the pursuit of personal fulfilment can be reconciled within the framework of the Party and its view of morality. As Horrath sees it much later in the novel, he now has the possibility of a "Neubeginn" (SS 900), of liberating himself from the self-repression which has afflicted his generation through the Third Reich and the Stalin era, but the opportunity is lost. Whether it is real or an

illusion in Horrath's tortured mind, the destructive
factor is "der unerbittliche Moralkodex in unserer Partei".(SS 461) Horrath's insistence upon separating his
feelings for Kati from his public 'self' marks the start
of a pathetic disintegration of personality. Even Kati's
pregnancy fails to bring him to an open expression of his
feelings: he simply continues his secret assignations
with her, and compounds it all through the "größte Lüge"
of concealing their affair from Marianne during their
rare reunions.(SS 304) His moral paralysis, culminating
in the grotesque scene in which he presides, Oedipus-like,
over Kati's humiliation for refusing to name the father
of her child, is almost beyond psychological belief.

Neutsch underlines the dire consequences of such moral
turpitude. After the trial of Kati, Horrath recognises
that "ein Kollektiv hat Grenzen, die Liebe übersteigt sein
Urteilsvermögen, denn die Liebe ist nicht kollektiv", but
it is too late. He has condemned himself to an isolation
which is "schon ein halber Tod, eine verheerende Krankheit, die den Menschen auszehrt und den Charakter aus-
höhlt".(SS 550) Horrath deludes himself that he can somehow salvage his "Verhältnis zur Partei", and a limited
existence with Marianne, from the ruins of his affair with
Kati, even though he sees that losing her has meant for
him a loss of "Persönlichkeit".(SS 626) The decline of
his competence at work and his eventual dismissal complete
a rapid fall from grace, which leaves him in a state of
"Selbstverachtung".(SS 799) The novel gives little
assurance that there is an effective way to reverse this
process of disintegration: as Horrath himself says -
"einen dritten Anfang gibt es nicht".(SS 900)

Amongst the central figures who finish on a high note,
the absence of a stabilising relationship in Balla's life
makes him very much the exception. It is almost surprising
that Neutsch resisted the temptation to allow a close involvement with Kati to begin during their Soviet tour.
He evidently recognised that it would have been implausibl
so soon after her sufferings at Horrath's hands, quite
apart from the contrast in their backgrounds, to do more
than stress their mutual understanding. At the conclusion
of Spur der Steine, Kati will be "noch lange eine Genesen-
de", while Balla leaves on his travels through the 'Heimat
without establishing his emotional roots.(SS 941-5)
Rita, in Der geteilte Himmel, is much further on the road
to recovery than Kati, with a circle of sympathetic friends
and the possibility of a liaison with Wendland to provide
an enduring stability. Wendland himself is now more conscious of the need to strike a balance between work-
dedication and private fulfilment, after the failure of
his earlier marriage to Meternagel's daughter. Although

he is the epitome of reliability, his interest in Rita has
already made him, for the first time ever, invent an excuse
to avoid a business meeting.(GH 206) He has not expressed
his feelings openly during the difficult months of Rita's
reckoning with Manfred, but they have certainly been inti-
mated to the reader.

The potential strength of such a union of kindred
spirits makes up part of the measured affirmation with
which Der geteilte Himmel ends. The unambiguous optimism
which emanates from the narrative present in Die Aula or
Die Geschwister is no less attributable to the emotional
security enjoyed by Robert Iswall and Elisabeth Arendt.
In both these novels, the central figures and their part-
ners, Vera and Joachim, have demanding professional
careers, the journalist and the oculist on the one hand,
the artist and "vielleicht der jüngste Werkleiter in der
Republik" (G 40-1) on the other. For each couple job-
satisfaction and emotional harmony are mutually inter-
dependent. Even before marriage, Elisabeth confidently
accepts the inevitability of periods of separation:

> Als [Joachim] fortging, küßten wir uns nicht
> einmal - mit solcher Sicherheit wußten wir,
> daß dies nur der erste von Tausenden Abenden
> war und daß wir Jahre und Jahre vor uns
> hatten, mit all ihren Stationen der Zärtlich-
> keit.(G 91)

Robert and Vera have already enjoyed several years of
marriage, which have afforded both of them a sense of
continuity since their ABF days. The one lingering threat
to Robert's sense of wholeness is his fear that he forced
a wedge between 'Freundschaft' and 'Liebe' in bringing
about the removal to China of his close friend Gert
Trullesand, when he supposed him to be a rival for Vera's
affections.(A 314-5) Robert's reunion with Trullesand
and his wife Rose, which forms the last section of Die
Aula, provides the reassurance that his earlier jealousies
were largely unfounded, and that they all still enjoy a
natural closeness as 'Genossen', unaffected by a ten-year
separation.

The balance is thus fairly evenly divided in these
novels between stability and crisis in the emotional development of central figures whose socialist morality is
not in doubt. For the first time, the virtue of self-
denying commitment to work is relativised by the presentation of the perils of neglecting to 'work', with a
different kind of assiduity, at private relationships.
The 'Anderswerden' of joining the Party and helping to
create the socialist state is no more than the first step
in a long struggle for self-understanding and a well-founded

identity, which cannot be rationally guided by the Party. This differentiation in the portrayal of socialist man in his private life and recognition of its bearing on social productivity fully complements the probing historical analysis of the Party's role and the GDR's development in these novels. The optimistic tenor of earlier Socialist Realism may be retained: apart from the genuine pathos in the plight of Werner Horrath and Manfred Herrfurth, the experience of alienation or despair is relatively short-lived, and the socialist community, for all its limitations, is still generally supportive. The thematic boundaries have, however, been courageously extended and - ironically, in terms of the original conception of the 'Bitterfelder Weg' - the focus has switched away from industrial achievements and towards the more compelling literary issue of the private, moral dimension of socialist identity.

The parting of the ways: the Eleventh Plenum

Largely as a result of the Bitterfeld novels, GDR literature was, in 1964-65, drawing markedly closer to the elusive Socialist Realist ideal of genuine popularity and critical sophistication. The chief editor of Neue Deutsche Literatur, Wolfgang Joho, acknowledged that the "Volksdiskussion um Literatur" was unprecedented.[18] Even though this discussion was largely centred on the content of the novels, with little regard being paid to the related modifications in narrative structure, there was also evidence of a new analytical quality in literary criticism in the GDR, and a willingness in the Federal Republic to overcome deeply ingrained prejudices about the qualitative potential of GDR literature.[19] The reaction of the SED leadership to this differentiated literary depiction of the GDR's socialist progress was initially cautious, but not entirely disapproving. At the second Bitterfeld Conference, in April 1964, Walter Ulbricht asked for a movement away from the "Blickpunkt des empirischen Betrachters" and (back) towards the "Blickwinkel des Planers und Leiters". He thought it right that social contradictions should be depicted, although in a manner which showed them more capable of resolution than a work like Der geteilte Himmel had. Special praise was accorded to Erik Neutsch, whose Spur der Steine was published in a large edition to coincide with the conference: the Bitterfeld novelist least critical overall of the Party's management of the GDR's development was still the one incarnating "den neuen Typ einer

sozialistischen Künstlerpersönlichkeit".[20]
 The authors saw themselves vindicated in their independent judgments of where the balance should be struck between retrospective criticism and affirmation of the
state's potential. They were determined to continue making
their own decisions as to what constituted 'Parteilichkeit', artistic quality and historical truth. Franz
Fühmann had led the way with his open letter of March
1964 to the Minister of Culture, Hans Bentzien, which
called for a halt to the artificially harmonious depiction
of the industrial world. Since most serious authors had
insufficient first-hand knowledge to provide an authentic
portrayal of "die differenzierten Gestalten des Arbeiters
heute und hier in ihren Lebensmilieus, ihren Gedanken,
Träumen, Wünschen, Sehnsüchten, Glücks- und Leidempfin-
dungen", they should cease perpetuating myths and concentrate on fundamental aspects of their private experience.
Echoing Lukács, he made a qualitative distinction between
the provision of politically useful information in works
of reportage, and the primary task of "künstlerische Gestaltung".[21]   Christa Wolf had the cultural-political
climate of the GDR in mind when, during the second
Bitterfeld conference, she compared the creative writer
to a trapeze-artist operating without a safety-net. None
the less she adhered to the conviction which she had had
Erwin Schwarzenbach express at the climax of Der geteilte
Himmel: that the decisive action of erecting the Berlin
Wall had ushered in an era in which 'die reine, nackte
Wahrheit' must prevail:

> Die Wahrheit über [die sozialistische Gesell-
> schaft] zu verbreiten schadet ihr nicht,
> sondern nützt ihr. Zum erstenmal in der
> menschlichen Geschichte stellt sie keinen
> unüberbrückbaren Widerspruch mehr dar zum
> humanistischen Wesen der Kunst.

Wolf gave this general belief a more specific connotation
the following year, in making it clear that literary truth
must of necessity be subjective, reflecting "die Hand-
schrift, die Sprache, die Gedankenwelt des Künstlers".[22]
 It is difficult to overestimate the significance of
this public debate with the SED leadership and the strength
of these convictions which had so quickly become articles
of faith for many of the GDR's new generation of authors.
A momentum for literary reorientation had been established
which threatened to sweep aside all the surviving clichés
behind the SED's 'Kulturpolitik', as the publication of a
work like Der Bau, by Heiner Müller, early in 1965 indicated. A matter of months after the SED accolades for
Spur der Steine, Müller was confronting issues which

Neutsch had glossed over, in a radical adaptation of his
novel for the stage. Where Neutsch had contrived to round
off his fictional action in the months before the erection
of the Berlin Wall, Müller makes August 1961 his starting
point: not only does he portray the shattering effects
the events of that month had throughout the GDR (and more
graphically than Wolf had done in <u>Der geteilte Himmel</u>);
he also shows how little change the introduction of the
'Neues Ökonomisches System' in 1963 brought to the hard-
bitten labourers in the construction industry. Through
Barka, his counterpart to Neutsch's Balla, he makes it
clear that the transition from "Eiszeit" to "Kommune" is
a tortuous one, and still far from complete.

<u>Der Bau</u> affirms the revolutionary strength of the poli-
tically enlightened working-class, as exemplified by Barkas
brigade, but it suggests that there are still fundamental
identity problems for individual socialists, more profound
than the Bitterfeld fiction had acknowledged in drawing
attention to the private dimension of self-realisation.
Müller recognises that the desperate economic pressures
had hitherto made unremitting hard work the primary reality for the GDR's activist heroes, and turned many of them
into totally one-sided personalities. Balla's proud vision
of the 'Spur der Steine' as a symbol of his personality
growth becomes a nightmare of self-destruction in Barka's
key speech:

> Sind sie hinter dir auch her, Elmer, in der
> Nacht, Stein auf Stein und Wand auf Wand, die
> VEBs, die du gebaut hast, jagen dich von Bau
> zu Bau über den Globus, der sich dreht, du
> mußt sein Tempo halten, wenn du stehenbleibst,
> rollt er dich ins Leere. Du hast angefangen,
> du mußt weitermachen. Beton will Beton. Du
> bist der Bagger, und du bist der Baugrund,
> auf dich fällt der Stein, den du aufhebst,
> aus dir wächst die Wand, auf deinen Knochen
> steht der Bau, noch den Strom ziehen sie aus
> dir, mit dem die Turbinen das Land unterhalten.
> Das ist so, Elmer, Fleisch wird Beton, der
> Mensch ruiniert sich für den Bau, jedes Richt-
> fest ein Vorgeschmack auf die Beerdigung ...[23]

The reaction to <u>Der Bau</u> - and equally challenging
writing by Stefan Heym, Wolf Biermann and Werner Bräunig -
at the Eleventh Plenum of the SED Central Committee in
December 1965, showed that the leadership was no longer
able to cope with the constructive criticism it had
sought to encourage through the reforms of 1963. Despite
the fact that the Bitterfeld novels had introduced a new
dialectical view of personal and social development into

GDR literature, it was the "Mißachtung der Dialektik der Entwicklung" which Erich Honecker, in the name of the Central Committee, held to be intolerable. The Party could not accept the depiction of contemporary reality "nur als schweres, opferreiches Durchgangsstadium zu einer illusionären schönen Zukunft", and the writers were accused of undermining public morale by their "Popularisierung von Schwierigkeiten". Most incredible of all to the writers' ears must have been the revival of the dualistic moralism of the Stalin era:

> Unsere DDR ist ein sauberer Staat. In ihr gibt
> es unverrückbare Maßstäbe der Ethik und Moral,
> für Anstand und gute Sitte. Unsere Partei
> tritt entschieden gegen die von den Imperial-
> isten betriebene Propaganda der Unmoral auf,
> die das Ziel verfolgt, dem Sozialismus
> Schaden zuzufügen.

This insidious imperialist 'Unmoral' was responsible for declining standards of discipline at work and lack of respect for authority as well as for sexual promiscuity, love of beat music and brutality, and the writers were contributing to its growth.[24] The only moderating voice at the Plenum was that of Christa Wolf, and her efforts cost her the hope of full membership of the Central Committee.

This was, culturally speaking, the GDR's darkest hour, because it revealed how readily the politicians could re- treat to ideologically entrenched positions taken up in the Cold War, at a time when a new quality of critical commit- ment to the state was emerging, with the help of the crea- tive achievements and the public courage of the writers. It demonstrated also how fully the struggle for a more profound understanding of identity, community and conti- nuity in literature was a political struggle against SED authority, and how little the nature of that authority had changed in East Germany's first two decades. The writers' hopes of mediating between the Party and the less committed majority of the population were crudely dashed, and there seemed no alternative for some of them but to withdraw temporarily from the public limelight. Others - even those like Neutsch and Kant who had shown themselves more willing, in the last analysis, to make the course of fictional events approximate to the Party line, were to face considerable difficulties in the years to come. As the subsequent literary evidence shows, however, at least half of the authors examined in the previous two chapters - Wolf, Reimann, de Bruyn and Fühmann - were firmly resolved not to return to the unhappy compromise between idealisation and critical analysis represented

by their Bitterfeld novels - <u>Der geteilte Himmel</u> and
<u>Die Geschwister</u> - and their 'Entwicklungsromane' - <u>Der</u>
<u>Hohlweg</u> and <u>Das Judenauto</u>.

CHAPTER 4

A LIFETIME'S EXPERIENCE IN THE 'SOBER LIGHT OF DAY'

The task of self-discovery

In Fritz Rudolf Fries' novel Der Weg nach Oobliadooh (1966), there is an episode in which the central figure, Arlecq, acting as a simultaneous interpreter during an international conference held in the GDR in the late 1950s, demonstrates how ideologically conformist utterances degenerate into predictable cliché through excessive repetition. Instead of listening to the Cuban delegate's marathon speech about North American imperialism, Arlecq switches off his receiver and fabricates a German version of his own. His relaxed presentation is clearly appreciated by the German speaking delegates, and he has no difficulty in anticipating the climax of the Cuban's speech:

> Als Arlecq den Ton wieder aufdrehte, sagten
> sie, sein Redner, er, noch immer das gleiche,
> lief die Linie ihrer Gedanken zusammen: im
> Kampf für den Weltfrieden. Der Beifall der
> Delegierten wurde stehend geboten.

Fries' refreshing picaresque novel, published a few months after the Eleventh Plenum of the SED's Central Committee, but only in the Federal Republic, was, for all the apparent universality of Arlecq's irreverent dismissal of "scheißblöde[s] Fortschrittsgequassel", confidently written as a retrospective critique of a less enlightened era.[1] It was ironical that his satire came to relate with equal force to the ideological state of affairs reestablished in the GDR for the second half of the 1960s, when many newly successful writers found themselves for the first time totally at odds with SED cultural policy.

From 1966 until 1971 SED spokesmen such as Kurt Hager (in the Politbüro), Klaus Gysi and Hans Koch (in the Ministry of Culture), and Max Walter Schulz (at the Institute for Literature in Leipzig) - who were gradually taking over the role of defining the cultural-political line from Ulbricht, Abusch and Kurella - acted as if the productive atmosphere which had give rise to the Bitterfeld novels had never existed. The depths of hackneyed predictability were plumbed at the Sixth Writers' Congress in May 1969 when, in the main address, Schulz expressed a Stalinist confidence in the inspirational potential of the two-dimensional hero with a pre-formed identity, in an untroubled socialist community:

> Im Volk lebt das Ideal von Gut und Schön und Wahr
> im Bild des Helden, im Bild des kühnen, klugen
> Menschen, der eine gute Sache vertritt, der die
> Situation ... meistert, der zum Riesen aufwächst im
> Kampf mit den Gewalten, der ein Mensch bleibt auch
> in seinen Schwächen, der die Angst überwindet vor
> Ritter, Tod und Teufel, der im Unterliegen dennoch
> siegt ...

The threat to the autonomy of creative writers represented
by the talk a decade earlier of cultural revolution and
'schreibende Arbeiter' was renewed in the guise of the
principle of collectivity: the "Kollektivwesen Literatur"
was to be coordinated through the Ministry of Culture,
and the primary task for writers was that of achieving
"freie vielstimmige parteiliche Übereinstimmung".[2]
With the milestone of the 20th anniversary of the GDR in
sight, there was exaggerated praise both for suitably
monumental Socialist Realist epics like Anna Seghers'
Das Vertrauen (1968), regardless of whether they met the
qualitative expectations aroused by the Bitterfeld fiction
and for the small-scale replicas created by the stories
in Werner Bräunig's Gewöhnliche Leute (1969) or Erik
Neutsch's Die Anderen und Ich (1970).
Neutsch's view, in the title story of his volume, that
uncritical adherence to "die bewährten Traditionen" did
not mean that these works were "voller Klischees"[3] was
one that a significant number of his literary colleagues
continued to repudiate in the face of this retrogressive
'Kulturpolitik', even though the means had to be more
circumspectly 'literary' than in the more forthright
debates of 1964-65. In the formal terms of their subsequent prose-writing this resistance was demonstrated
by further decisive moves away from the traditional framework of the socialist 'Entwicklungsroman' or the Tolstoyan
epic. And although such moves may also have appeared to
signal a definitive break with the theory of realism deriving from Lukács, they significantly did not reflect a
desire to abandon the organic understanding of personality
and self-realisation which lay behind his rigid views on
literary form. The primacy of the free development of
individuality still provided a vital strand of moral and
aesthetic continuity, between the extremes of the SED's
neglect of the private sphere and the 'Western' view of
identity as an inherently pluralistic question of role-
adoption.[4] The dominant theme of non-conformist GDR
writing after 1965 thus becomes the threat to identity
represented by a socialist society which has failed to
develop according to expectations: as the propagandist

conception of a spontaneously created socialist community recedes, the problematic dimension of the organic unity in the personal experience of the generation subjected in turn to Hitler's Reich and the Stalinist GDR begins to be seriously scrutinised.

The question of alternative literary forms is healthily unresolved at the outset, although the growing influence of Bertolt Brecht (whose critical writings were just becoming fully accessible in the GDR of the mid-1960s[5]) is now unmistakable in this respect. It is the Brecht for whom literary realism is a constant process of adaptation and experimentation, as the author seeks to clarify the nature of social progress - according to the principle of "neue Formen" for "die neuen Inhalte"[6] - who particularly interests the Christa Wolf of 1966, in her brief essay "Brecht und andere". Brecht's importance lies not so much in the potential his creative writing offers as a source of models to be imitated, as in the way it inspires self-confidence, the "Ermunterung zu eigenen Entdeckungen". [7] The middle 1960s proved to be an important period of private stocktaking in this empirical vein for Wolf and fellow-authors such as Erwin Strittmatter, Günter Kunert and Günter de Bruyn.[8] Wolf's major essay of 1966, "Tagebuch - Arbeitsmittel und Gedächtnis", conveys with exemplary clarity the radical reorientation taking place in the aftermath of the Eleventh Plenum.[9] In Wolf's words, her generation has now passed the age of innocence - "den glücklichen Zustand früher Unbefangenheit" - and henceforth needs to assess the GDR "bei nüchternem Tageslicht, von Wunschbildern befreit". The process of socialist transformation is in danger of stagnating at the very time when it should have been accelerating, now that the division of Germany has become an incontrovertible reality. Authors are therefore charged with a special responsibility to keep "das revolutionäre Prinzip" alive.

Christa Wolf was now convinced that subjectivity was the key to the 'typicality' in pursuit of which her generation would previously have altered or ignored crucial aspects of their experience: her own problems were part of the "Durchschnittsproblematik gewöhnlicher Menschen". This was for her a fruitful phase of "Tagebuchfreudigkeit", devoted to recording her observations of people, places and nature, recording anecdotes and documentary details of everyday life and, above all, using her diary to assist the process of remembering precisely events from her own past. She was also eager to learn from the authentic writing of fellow authors, quoting, in this essay, illuminating points from other diaries, including Becher's Tagebuch 1950, and, in another essay of 1966 on

Ingeborg Bachmann's subjective prose, [10] revealing how
great her need was to establish previously unrecognised
literary affinities which could not be contained within
conventional ideological demarcation lines. Indeed, Wolf
creates a new demarcation line of her own between the
quality of authenticity she detects in Bachmann's stories
or Becher's diary, and fiction which is based on "Erfindungen
über das Innenleben unserer Mitmenschen". As her own
diary was not being kept with publication in mind (even
though her essay makes many references to its content),
it would avoid the "voreilige Schlüsse" of consciously
'composed' prose, and help to resolve the issue vital to
the liberation of GDR literature from its constricting
dependence on approved cultural models: "Wie ... soll
man heute schreiben?"

Wolf emerged from this period of creative introspection
with a piece of 'short prose' which arises directly from
one of her self-imposed diary disciplines - "genaue Aufzeichnungen über einen bestimmten Tag". Her Juninachmitta
(1967) stands out amidst the spate of writing in the
various shorter prose forms which signals the major qualitative leap forward about to occur after the crisis of
1965. It is a distillation of the mood of this period,
describing - as it steadily undermines the initial impression of summery domestic tranquillity - how the
narrator's longing for a stable sense of identity continues
to be thwarted. The garden in which she spends this week-
end afternoon in June with her family is a sphere of
creativity on the imaginative as well as the practical
level. But the garden is too close to the Berlin air
corridor and the state border to permit more than temporary
respite from ideological conflict and the destructive
potential of modern technology. The immediate human environment is equally alien: neighbours and passing
acquaintances, as well as unseen figures like the elder
daughter's teacher, are all stunted personalities,
obsessive, unimaginative, trivial, materialistic. Death
and violence are everywhere: in the book the narrator
reads, in the newspaper, in the railway disaster which
has just taken a friend's life, and even the garden's
modest harvest seems destined to decay. As in a nightmare
past fears reassert themselves, and the narrator feels
again "wie leicht mir immer noch ... der Boden unter den
Füßen wegsackt".[11] As the day ends, her only respite from
this debilitating anxiety comes through the reassurance
of domestic routine and by extension, of the act of
writing itself.

Juninachmittag, like Wolf's well-filled diary of the
middle 1960s, is part of what she described as a
thorough course of "Training" for a major "Kunstwerk".

However important essays and short prose of this quality
may be in heightening awareness of the inadequacies of
earlier GDR fiction - "den Kern der Wirklichkeit, den das
Kunstwerk sucht, kann nur das Kunstwerk freilegen".
Significantly, Wolf was not alone in seeking to express
this 'average' citizen's sense of identity under threat
in more explicit terms. By the late 1960s a new group of
prose-works with broadly similar features was emerging,
intent on redefining the relationship between the socialist
society of their day and personal identity, in a more subjective light. Günter de Bruyn's Buridans Esel (1968)
received uncertain official sanction at the time when
monumental novels such as Das Vertrauen were being made
the focus of literary discussion. Wolf's Nachdenken über
Christa T. (1968) was to become the most controversial
work of the decade, and it appears that the political
storm it provoked around the time of the Sixth Writers'
Congress in 1969 contributed to the surprising rejection
for publication of the superficially comparable Das
Impressum by Hermann Kant, after most of it had been
serialised in the youth magazine Forum. Kant's novel
eventually appeared in a slightly modified form in 1972,
while a fourth novel based on the same generation's experience, Brigitte Reimann's Franziska Linkerhand, was
published in its uncompleted form in 1974, soon after the
author's death from leukaemia, although it too had been
substantially written by the late 1960s. [12]
   These novels still reflect the standard concern in
German socialist writing since the exile years for the
structure of personal development, but now far removed
from the exemplary patterns derived from earlier 'Entwicklungsromane'. The dimension of the narrator has been
markedly extended, and there is now an undeniably autobiographical basis to what is still described as fiction.
The relationship between the narrator and his protagonist
is more intimate and correspondingly less 'controlled'
than in the Bitterfeld fiction, while relatively little
attention is devoted to 'typical' subsidiary characters
and socio-economic details regarded as essential to the
balance achieved in these authors' previous work. The
narrative standpoint, in a recognisable GDR of the middle
1960s, encompasses, in a more intensive, subjective manner
than before, the experience of the author's lifetime. As
a result, the interplay in the central character's life
between self-discovery, social integration and the goal
of total self-realisation is now more contradictory and
open-ended than ever before. The depiction of the GDR in
the narrative present bears little trace of earlier heroic
struggles on the ideological barricades, and begins to
take in the problems of a technologically advanced urban

existence. The continuity of thematic interest is unmistakable, but the questions being asked of socialist
society are now radical and uncompromising ones.

Fiction and 'subjective authenticity'

   The new confidence in the validity of private experience
reflected in the short prose of the middle 1960s was to
have a fundamental bearing on the structure of the novels
upon which Wolf, de Bruyn and Reimann were working in the
period immediately afterwards. There is now less of the
sense of strained compromise found in the Bitterfeld novel
at the level of the narrator between partisan omniscience
and the search for a distinctive individual voice. As the
fiction is subject to the practical limitations of individual knowledge and perception, it is no longer an
effective vehicle for the transmission of ideological
certainties. The more the undramatic "Alltag" of the increasingly stable 1960s is recognised as the appropriate
setting for the fiction,[13] the more the complexities of
the self can receive its main focus.
   The effects of this radically changing conception of the
scope of the novel are well illustrated by the modification
to which Brigitte Reimann's Franziska Linkerhand was subje
from the time she began writing it late in 1963. [14]
Reimann saw it initially as a more serious attempt than
in either Ankunft im Alltag or Die Geschwister to come to
terms with her deep frustrations amidst the chaos and
anonymity of the new town of Hoyerswerda, by projecting
them into the more exemplary development of a younger
figure. Franziska Linkerhand, as a newly qualified architect, might eventually succeed in bringing about practica
improvements in this bleak environment where an intellectual like Reimann could only express moral concern.
Indeed, if Reimann's 'Bitterfelder Weg' experience since
1957 could be telescoped into a matter of months in the
early 1960s, then the problems of Franziska's "Neustadt"
might appear capable of speedier resolution. Reimann
knew that the rhetorical nature of her affirmation of the
GDR in Die Geschwister needed to be checked, and thought
at first of imitating the objective chronological style
of Emile Zola. Life was to be made difficult for her
idealistic heroine: her working environment was to be
"entsetzlich alltäglich", and there would be "keine
heldenhaften Schlachten, sondern die kleinen, zermürben-
den Streitereien". At the same time, however, it would
be a story of "Ganz Große Liebe" which would end in
Franziska's reconciliation with this highly imperfect

society.

Reimann had excerpts from <u>Franziska Linkerhand</u> published in the GDR and in a Western anthology,[15] but the response in this period of fruitful East-West cultural contacts was less than enthusiastic - there was, for example, a stinging Western reference to her "freundliche Mittelmäßigkeit". Thus, by the summer of 1965, Reimann had decided to rethink her novel and to make a much bolder break with convention than she had earlier envisaged:

> ... ich habe schon aufgehört, mich darüber zu
> ängstigen, schlage alle Lehren in den Wind
> und versuche zu schreiben, was ich fühle und
> denke (also weg, weg vom verbreiteten Wunsch-
> denken), wie ich das Leben um mich sehe,
> nehme mir das Recht auf subjektive Sicht,
> auch auf Irrtümer ...[16]

When she gave her next interview on the novel, in 1968, Reimann had found an effective means of expressing this subjective perspective in the narrative structure. There was now to be a framework first-person monologue, in which a slightly older Franziska, living in temporary, self-imposed exile from Neustadt, addressed her most intimate thoughts and feelings to 'Ben', an artificial figure based upon her lover Trojanowicz.[17] This meant that her earlier life, and particularly her year in Neustadt, were being viewed at a critical distance, and implied that the novel could not close with anything more than the possibility of her return to her career and social productivity.

This radical change of plan raised questions of narrative consistency which she was unable to resolve before her death. The contrast between Franziska's more mature self as the narrator and her earlier life until the crisis in which she leaves Neustadt to live with Trojanowicz, is conveyed through changes from the first person to the third, and the virtual identity of the older Franziska and Reimann is suggested by the presentation of the novel itself as the work of Franziska during her period of exile. At times, however, another impersonal narrative voice can be detected, providing psychological insights which Franziska could scarcely have enjoyed into the mind of the novel's third pivotal figure, Schafheutlin, the chief architect in Neustadt. Reimann evidently wanted to anticipate the growth of a relationship between the heroine and her initially unattractive superior which would eventually be an important factor in her decision to return to Neustadt, but could not demonstrate this adequately from Franziska's perspective (e.g. FL 195-7, 400-2). Even though such contradictions might have been

overcome in a final revision of <u>Franziska Linkerhand</u>,
their obtrusive presence in the published version provides
an unusual insight into the difficulties involved in
abandoning schematic structures in favour of a more authen
tic, restricted viewpoint.

The consistency which Reimann failed to achieve is im-
pressively evident in <u>Buridans Esel</u>. De Bruyn's narrator
makes great play of the fact that he is an independent
"Berichterstatter", investigating into the life of his protagonist, the librarian Karl Erp - and yet he is suspicious-
ly omniscient about Erp himself. In the course of Erp's
marital crisis, which forms the external 'action' of the
novel, he is an intimate recorder of the progress of Erp's
relationship with the young library assistant, Fräulein
Broder, and authoritatively reveals the contradictions in
Erp's thought-processes throughout his months of indecision.
However much he maintains that his "Bericht" is restricted
to "die platte Wirklichkeit" (BE 118), his standpoint is
a more committed one, and such categorical statements are
often highly ironical. In fact, even though Erp is decidedly anti-heroic in his moral response to this crisis,
there is a considerable biographical unity linking de Bruyn,
his narrator and his fictional counterpart. The narrator's
identity with de Bruyn is implied in references to earlier
fiction like <u>Der Hohlweg</u> (BE 75), while Erp's life follows
the pattern of de Bruyn's own development in many essential
respects, roughly up to the point when he became a full-
time writer in the early 1960s. The tensions begin when
Erp achieves the career success which de Bruyn could also
have enjoyed as head of a Berlin library, and then succumbs
to the temptations of an indolent, self-indulgent life-
style - in obvious contrast to de Bruyn's subsequent progress. Erp stagnates as a personality in a situation of
conflict which allows him a real opportunity to re-
vitalise his existence, while the author's privileged
awareness of the narrowness of the dividing line between
loss of self and growth of personality within Erp gives
the novel its ironical force.

De Bruyn was fully aware that this complex narrative
structure took the question of 'positive' or 'negative'
characteristics outside the previously insulated sphere
of fictional action and confronted the reader with the
task of passing his own final judgment on Erp. He
justified this procedure in an interview given shortly
before the publication of <u>Buridans Esel</u>:

> Um der Vielfalt der Wirklichkeit nahe zu
> kommen, mußte ich die schöne Oberfläche
> gedanklich aufrauhen. Ich brauchte eine
> Form, die Raum bot für Reflexion, für Kommen-

> tar, für Abschweifung, für Für und Wider ...
> Der Erzähler wird beweglicher, der Leser
> aktiver, er muß mitdenken, mitarbeiten.

The confidence he expressed in the powers of the "denken-
der Leser", now mature enough to insist upon the "ständig
wachsende Differenzierung" of character, was crucial to
the development of the novel in the GDR. In relation to
Karl Erp's fortunes, it was of vital importance that
"Identifizierung" and "Distanzierung" should stand "in
einer dialektischen Wechselwirkung", and that - in the
spirit of Brecht - the reader should become "die Zentral-
figur, an der sich alles entscheidet". [18]

  Nachdenken über Christa T. proceeds from a rather more
unusual authentic basis - the attempt to write "eine Art
von posthumem Lebenslauf" of a close friend (after her
death from leukaemia), which became something far more
profound as the author grew aware of the remarkable
parallelism between her own life and that of her contemporary at school and university. It was not just the
knowledge of time spent together at various crucial stages
of both their lives, but also a unique similarity in their
inner responses to all the upheavals their generation -
the children of the Third Reich - had had to face since.
There were of course many points of divergence in their
fortunes and temperaments, but it was this awareness of a
shared identity, constantly heightened by Wolf's researches
into the past of the person she came to call 'Christa T.'
which made the unforgettable impact upon her:

> Ich stand auf einmal mir selbst gegenüber, das
> hatte ich nicht vorgesehen. Die Beziehungen
> zwischen "uns" - der Christa T. und dem Ich-
> Erzähler - rückten ganz von selbst in den
> Mittelpunkt: die Verschiedenheit der Charak-
> tere und ihre Berührungspunkte, die Spannungen
> zwischen "uns" und ihre Auflösung, oder das
> Ausbleiben der Auflösung ... Nichts mit Händen
> Greifbares, nichts Sichtbares, Materielles, aber
> etwas ungemein Wirksames. [19]

This experience had major implications for the way in
which Nachdenken über Christa T. was conceived: not as
a documentary account of this relationship, but as a
literary invention which would attempt to recreate the
complicated interplay of self-recognition and differentiation involved - and in doing so confront the reader with the
elusiveness of identity. Wolf's choice of a first-person
narrative standpoint is essential to this purpose, and yet
almost a paradox in a novel so aware of "die Schwierigkeit
'Ich' zu sagen".(CT 214-6)

It is therefore significant that the narrator makes extensive use of the first-person plural to chart the modifications in the relationship between Christa T., herself and 'society' in its various manifestations, sometimes exploiting the unspecific ambiguity of the 'Wir' form, which may at one moment refer generally to her generation or the GDR, then to the shared feelings of smaller groups. There are times when Christa T. stands separate from the wider social group with which the narrator identifies, and the gulf between the two is emphasised: in their school days in the Third Reich, the narrator is timidly conformist (CT 10-14), while at university in Leipzig in the early 1950s Christa T. seems to shirk her collective responsibilities.(CT 46) On other occasions, the 'Wir' statements reflect the unanimity of the two friends, as sensitive representatives of their generation, against negative aspects of life in the GDR - opportunism, bureaucratic government and the like - which are in urgent need of reform (e.g. CT 33-6, 167-9). Thus, when the narrator does use the 'Ich' form, it stands out starkly, like the moment she chooses to assert the importance of Christa T.'s life in the authentic complexity with which she has presented it:

> Ach, hätte ich die schöne freie Wahl erfundener Eindeutigkeit ... Nie wäre ich, das möchte ich doch schwören, auf sie verfallen. Denn sie ist, als Beispiel, nicht beispielhaft, als Gestalt kein Vor-Bild. Ich unterdrücke die Vermutung, daß es nicht anders erginge mit jedem wirklich lebenden Menschen und bekenne mich zur Freiheit und zur Pflicht des Erfindens. Einmal nur, dieses eine Mal, möchte ich erfahren und sagen dürfen, wie es wirklich gewesen ist, unbeispielhaft und ohne Anspruch auf Verwendbarkeit.(CT 57)

It is clearly not fiction as such which is under attack here, but rather the indefensible simplification and distortion of character in conventional Socialist Realist fiction.

Wolf went further than either Reimann or de Bruyn in outlining a theoretical framework - and a literary tradition - for this new subjective realism, in her essay "Lesen und Schreiben" of 1968.[20] Developing her views on the inspirational force of Brecht's writing, she argued that authors like herself should now apply the principles of his epic theory to their prose writing, making it a vehicle for the stimulation of "dialektische[s] Denken in Modellen". It would once again become "eine 'epische' Prosa", investigating a reality in which nothing can be "selbstverständlich", instead of reinforcing "alte Denk-

inhalte". Those neglected authors in Lukács' canon of
realistic prose, Büchner and Dostoyevsky, had paved the
way in showing that the narrative world is four-dimensional:
in addition to the three dimensions of the fictional action,
"Prosa" needs "die vierte, 'wirkliche' [Dimension] des Er-
zählers". This is the subjective level at which the vital
link between fiction and reality is established and maintained - "die Koordinate der Tiefe, der Zeitgenossenschaft,
des unvermeidlichen Engagements, die nicht nur die Wahl
des Stoffes, sondern auch seine Färbung bestimmt".

Essential to this method is the complex relationship
between the narrator and his central figure, the interplay
of identification and distancing to which de Bruyn also
referred in his remarks on <u>Buridans Esel</u>. The examples
Wolf provides have a central bearing on her own situation
in conceiving <u>Nachdenken über Christa T.</u>: in Büchner's
<u>Lenz</u> fragment, there is his remarkable empathy with the
'Sturm und Drang' figure, while <u>Crime and Punishment</u> represents Dostoyevsky's self-salvation through working out
his apparently insoluble conflicts in the figure of
Raskolnikov. It is striking, in view of Wolf's recognition
that genuine literature must derive from urgent inner
necessity - "Für einen bestimmten Autor gibt es in einem
bestimmten Augenblick nur einen einzigen Stoff" - that
three of the most gifted authors of her generation should
independently seek to create this four-dimensional prose
in the late 1960s. The phrase "subjektive Authentizität",
which Wolf subsequently introduced into literary parlance
in the GDR,[21] is an extremely apt term to describe the
distinctive narrative quality of these novels.

The shift from 'objective' omniscience and the pursuit
of extensive totality brings with it a new recognition of
the limitations of individual powers of perception.
Difficulties previously held to be symptomatic of bourgeois
decadence are now seriously faced. Memory, for example,
is seen to be problematic. Günter de Bruyn shows an awareness of its unreliability in the scenes where Karl Erp is
brought back by his father's death into contact with the
past in his native village of Alt-Schradow. The narrator
makes a firm distinction between his analysis of the
"Erpsche Vergangenheit" and Karl's "Erinnerungsbrille",
which is always tinted in relation to his moods.(BE 188)
This is not, however, made into a major theme in <u>Buridans
Esel</u> or <u>Franziska Linkerhand</u>, where the main focus is on
the recent past with all the advantages of near-autobio-
graphical insight, in the way that it is in <u>Nachdenken
über Christa T.</u>. Wolf is concerned with the whole life-
pattern of a figure who has led a separate existence,
however parallel it may have run to that of the narrator.
As she made clear in her "Selbstinterview", it was a matter

of counteracting "die trügerische Erinnerung" with whatever documentary information could be unearthed - in
Christa T.'s case her diaries, letters and literary sketches
together with her revealing dissertation on Theodor Storm's
'Novellen' - and taking account of the opinions and information supplied by others. The opening lines of the
novel warn against the trap of the "Vergessen, das man Erinnerung nennt".(CT 7) The great danger, in social intercourse as in literature, is the tendency to reduce the
past to a series of neatly rounded "Geschichten", endowed
with a significance which incidents in real experience
never have, in order to boost each individual's sense of
the meaning in his own life. It is a temptation to which
the narrator and her educated friends are in no way immune,
as they sense that an important turning-point in their
development as GDR citizens has been reached, once the
crisis of 1961 has been resolved:

> Wir begannen, über unsere Erinnerungen zu
> verfügen. Wir entdeckten auf einmal - keiner
> von uns älter als fünfunddreißig -, daß es
> schon etwas gab, was den Namen 'Vergangenheit'
> verdiente ... Es war unvermeidlich, daß wir
> anfingen, uns Geschichten zu erzählen,
> Geschichten, wie sie in einem auftauchen,
> wenn die Wasser sich verlaufen. Dann ist man
> ein wenig erstaunt, daß diese Geschichten
> alles sein sollen, was übrigbleibt, und man
> sieht sich gezwungen, sie ein wenig auszu-
> schmücken, eine hübsche kleine Moral in sie
> hineinzulegen, und ihren Schluß vor allem ...
> zu unseren Gunsten zu gestalten.(CT 209-11)

The goal is to create a "Vergangenheit, die man seinen
Kindern erzählen kann".(CT 211) The best protection
against such unavoidable human weakness is to remain, as
Christa T. and the narrator appear to have done in the
decisive moments of their maturity, "unbestechlich"(CT 206)
and aware "daß man an seiner Vergangenheit arbeiten muß
wie an seiner Zukunft".(CT 181) It may seem paradoxical
that invention has an important part to play in this process, but the special justification of literature is that
it can convey a truth which documentary methods can only
hint at: the creative writer's task involves "erfinden
... um der Wahrheit willen".(CT 31)
    Just as serious as the distortion of the past through
the unreliability of memory is the reduction of the personality of others caused by the subjective need to cate-
gorise according to a limited range of basic 'types'.
This problem, previously treated in depth in 'Western'
novels like Uwe Johnson's Mutmaßungen über Jakob and

<u>Das dritte Buch über Achim</u>, now becomes important in the
GDR as these novelists begin to dispense with stereotype
'characters'. There is a refreshing admission of the
danger of 'taking possession' of other individuals in order
to make the fictional world more coherent. Christa Wolf's
narrator is aware of the enormous responsibility on her
shoulders when she says of the dead Christa T. - "Ich ver-
füge über sie ... Sie bewegt sich, wenn ich will"(CT 7) -
yet knows that her images amount to no more than a dubious
"Schattenfilm". For Franziska Linkerhand, on the other
hand, it is a comforting self-delusion that the 'Ben'
to whom she addresses her innermost feelings is an idealised image of her lover Trojanowicz, which she has
assiduously cultivated since she first saw him in Neustadt.
Such is Franziska's subjective delight in the figure she
sees as "meine einzige Liebe" on the mere evidence of
appearances (FL 145), that she avoids direct contact with
Trojanowicz for months, so as not to place this wish-
fulfilling image at risk. (This behaviour is, by implication, a psychological reaction to a disastrous marriage,
which made her fearful of another disillusioning commitment.) When she does finally get to know Trojanowicz,
her carefully nourished fiction must inevitably give way
to impenetrable reality:

> Ich war bestürzt, als habe dich erst der N
> unwiderruflich zu einem Teil der wirkliche
> Welt gemacht, die ich sehen, fühlen, riechen,
> schmecken kann ... Ich konnte nicht mehr über
> dich verfügen. Ich wußte nichts mehr von dir
> - in dem Augenblick, als du dich bekannt-
> machtest, wurdest du das Unbekannte Land,
> unwegsam (die Stromtäler und Geröllhalden der
> Erfahrungen, die vergangene Jahre zurück-
> ließen, und die tropischen Wälder der
> Erinnerungen), schwer erforschbar, vielleicht
> nie bis ins Landesinnere zu durchforschen.(FL 350)

Remarkably perhaps, their relationship does succeed for a
limited period, revitalising Franziska's life, but it is
still the fictitious 'Ben' with whom she communes in her
novel and who eventually survives the disintegration of
her relationship with Trojanowicz. In using 'Ben' as a
deliberate artefact Reimann is as aware of the problem of
character as Wolf, but is less sure whether truth can be
achieved by stripping off all the external layers of personality. Her observation is provoked by the recollection
of an experiment in portrait painting carried out by her
friend Jakob:

> An der Wand lehnten drei Porträts, immer der-
> selbe Mann und immer ein anderer, als wäre
> bei jedem nächsten Bild eine Schicht vom nur
> Äußerlichen, jedermann sichtbaren abgeblättert,
> bloßgelegt, was man sonst den anderen verheim-
> licht, vielleicht nicht einmal sich selbst
> gesteht. Ist das denn Wahrheit in der Kunst,
> wenn man einen Menschen so preisgibt? Ich
> weiß nicht, Ben; ich weiß nicht mal, was
> Wahrheit ist.(FL 85-6)

Günter de Bruyn seems less sure of his ground in the
matter of characterisation. On the one hand, as a leit-
motiv, he asserts that Erp's wife Elisabeth is inscrutable -
"Wer kennt sich in Elisabeth aus" - and approaches her
character with speculative caution; on the other, he,
offers extended insights into the development of Fräulein
Broder (e.g. BE 58-62), which tally with Erp's assessment
of her as a "Musterexemplar einer nächsten Generation".
(BE 52) Thus, although de Bruyn's narrator often wittily
undermines the images which his characters have of themselves and of each other, he still shows some reluctance
to abandon the notion of the 'Vorbild'. His portrayal of
Fräulein Broder recalls the idealisation of youth in a
figure like Rita in Wolf's Der geteilte Himmel, while
authority is also placed in an exemplary light in the
person of Fred Mantek, Erp's former boss in the library,
who now works in the Ministry of Culture.

Wolf and Reimann act more decisively against this neat
equation of economic productivity and moral distinction.
Their portrayal of the social environment in which
Christa T. and Franziska Linkerhand move suggests that
there are no positive figures to guide their fortunes in
a decisive way. Those who have gained official recognition
like the chief architect Schafheutlin or the author
Blasing in Christa T.'s provincial town, are seriously
flawed personalities, while the majority still struggle
to find a role which is socially constructive and will also
allow them to develop their personal potential. With the
fictional focus directed on the problematical central
figure, any suggestion that her difficulties could be resolved by the example of a conventional 'Vorbild' would
detract seriously from the open-ended impact of the novels.
Christa Wolf makes the point explicitly:

> Wer den Kopf jetzt wegwendet, wer die Achseln
> zuckt, wer von ihr, Christa T., weg und auf
> größere, nützlichere Lebensläufe zeigt, hat
> nichts verstanden. Mir liegt daran, gerade
> auf sie zu zeigen. Auf den Reichtum, den sie
> erschloß, auf die Größe, die ihr erreichbar,

auf die Nützlichkeit, die ihr zugänglich war.
(CT 171-2)

The extent of the maturing process that Wolf, Reimann and de Bruyn had gone through as novelists is demonstrated by the gulf which now separates their work from Hermann Kant's Das Impressum. Kant continues to use the narrative perspective he established in Die Aula: the protagonist, David Groth, the forty-year-old chief editor of the fictitious Neue Berliner Rundschau, who has just been appointed to a ministerial post in the GDR government, is also the narrator. Even though the narrative frequently switches with apparent purpose from the first person to the third, there is no significant tension between Groth's earlier and present-day 'self'. In fact, one of the most unsatisfactory aspects of the structure is the gap of almost ten years between the end of the account of Groth's life and the narrative present in 1967, omitting the years when Groth proved his entitlement to the editorship of a leading magazine and then to take on ministerial responsibilities.[22] The contrast to Buridans Esel is almost total, since the years when Groth's development is unthreatened are precisely those when the life of Karl Erp begins to fall apart.

As a son of the oppressed working classes in the Third Reich, Groth grows up naturally into the new socialist state - his progress from errand boy in the Rundschau is a "stetig steigende Kurve".(I 10) The only indication of unease in the 'fourth dimension' of the narrator is on the level of Groth's protest that his curriculum vitae in the SED's files represents less than the whole truth about him, when the actual differences seem insubstantial.(I 7-10) Groth as narrator is confident about his assessment of others and his recollection of past detail: indeed, his anecdotal style comes dangerously close to reproducing the artificially rounded 'Geschichten' of which Christa Wolf was so critical.

Furthermore, whereas Wolf makes frequent use of the 'Wir' prespective as a means of breaking down the conventional image of neatly interlocking levels of 'Gemeinschaft', David Groth's first person plural reflects an uncomplicated integration in every sphere. His marriage is synonymous with "Gemeinschaft, Gemeinsamkeit, Gegenteil zu Einsamkeit" (I 130); he is at one with his generation of pioneering activists and with the Party he has served loyally for twenty years, apart from a few short-lived conflicts. The Rundschau is run smoothly under his leadership, harnessing the varied talents of its workforce in a relaxed way: each working week consists of "fünf Tage Produktion und Klatsch, fünf Tage Fortschritt, und keiner

merkt es".(I 213) His identity is firmly rooted in the
proletarian tradition into which he grew up, and it is
the same "unsereins" who now form the GDR government.
(I 37-44)   He feels able to speak for the whole state in
refuting the clichés of Western propaganda:

> In diesem Land herrscht Diktatur. Wir stöhnen
> hier unter dem Zwangsregime der Wissenschaft.
> Hier wird man mit der Leselampe gefoltert.
> Die Despotie preßt uns in die Gelehrsamkeit.
> Der Druck bedient sich des Buchdrucks.
> Qualifizierung - das Wort schon sagt es.
> Theorie ist die Praxis hiesigen Terrors.
> Forscher zimmerten unser Joch. Lehrer
> bewachen unsere Schritte. Unser Profoß ist
> Professor. Wir führen ein Hirnzellendasein.
> Für Denken gibt es ein Soll. Wir sind die
> kybernetisch besetzte Zone.(I 27)

In the final flourish of Das Impressum, Groth's 'Wir'
takes in the whole of mankind - "jeder von uns ist der
dreimilliardste Teil dieses Wir".(I 476) With such untroubled solidarity in every sphere of his experience, it
is clear why Groth's development has been so easy.

Kant's undiluted partisanship is also reflected in his
choice of an outstanding figure from the ranks of the
state's leadership as his hero. Groth alone is intended
to represent the GDR's overall progress in terms of the
'objective' typicality which Wolf, Reimann and de Bruyn
had all by now rejected - even his name is significant
in the way that those of the heroes of earlier 'Entwicklungsromane' were. In the passage in which Groth ostensibly dismisses such simplifications as "allzu literarisch",
it emerges that he has been named David after a Jewish
benefactor who later falls victim to Nazi racialism, while
the family name is seen to have a certain kinship with
the Biblical Goliath. Although he may distance himself
from the family's naive hopes - "David Groth möge werden
David und Goliath in einem und also unbesiegbar" (I 45) -
this reading suits the novel's overall intentions ad-
mirably.

Given such a conventional narrative framework, it is
difficult to understand how Kant's limited critical interest
in the detail of Groth's life was regarded as sufficiently
threatening to have the novel withheld from publication
for three years, only to re-appear in a form "weitgehend
identisch" with the original.[23] It may be noteworthy
that he makes a mildly irreverent attack on the Stalin
cult of the early 1950s, or depicts the events of 17 June
1953 in a less incredible manner than Anna Seghers had
done in Das Vertrauen, or is involved in gently satirical

attacks on the Party leadership - but the novel remains a
rather static collection of anecdotes. There is nothing
of the creative urgency to reflect a new view of identity,
and thus of the contemporary limits of community, in Das
Impressum. For Wolf, Reimann and de Bruyn, on the other
hand, it was now a question of how much validity such
value concepts, already appreciably qualified in recent
fiction, could be seen to have in the GDR of their own
day.

The threat to identity within the GDR

However much stereotype methods of character depiction
are undermined in these novels, there is still no desire
to question the Goethean view of the unique, organically
developing identity with which each individual is endowed.
For Christa Wolf, the special quality of 'epic prose' is
its capacity to penetrate to "das innerste Innere" of the
reader's being and stimulate the growth of the "Kern der
Persönlichkeit". She argues that in any technologically
advanced society the dangers of individuality being reduced to streamline uniformity are considerably increased,
and that literature will have an ever more important role
to play in helping to preserve the "Kontakt der Menschen
mit ihren Wurzeln" and strengthen "Selbstbewußtsein".[24]
De Bruyn's primary motivation in writing Buridans Esel is
to confront the issue of "Persönlichkeitsverlust"[25] in
a gifted individual who neglects his inner development.
For Reimann too, it is essential for Franziska Linkerhand
to re-discover the "natürliches Selbstbewußtsein" of which
her bourgeois home environment has deprived her, causing
the instability and vulnerability of her adult self.(FL 125)
Presuppositions of this kind about identity, in combination with the complex autobiographical motivation of
their novels, meant that they would now have to take
account of factors influencing the growth or retardation
of the self over a lifetime rooted in the Third Reich and
extending over the Stalin era into the middle 1960s. This
would be far more challenging than the isolation of the
primary processes of coming to terms with socialism after
1945 in the earlier 'Entwicklungsromane', or the less personalised differentiation of the GDR's development through
the 1950s in the Bitterfeld novels - which had nevertheless
also paved the way for this comprehensive reckoning with
their own past.
It was inevitable that the extension of narrative
retrospection to cover more than thirty years would mean
that childhood in the Third Reich would be presented in a

fragmentary manner which would provide less 'information' about the period than the 'Entwicklungsromane', but which would equally compel the authors to concentrate upon features essential to their understanding of identity. Perhaps the most striking aspect in the depiction of this period is the isolation of their central characters from any influence which might make them aware of an ideological alternative to their fascist environment. At a time when, as Wolf suggested, they were totally cut off from their cultural heritage, including the moral, educative force of the classical 'Entwicklungsroman', there was little scope for the 'bourgeois individualism' exhibited by Rudi Hagedorn in Wir sind nicht Staub im Wind or Wolfgang Weichmantel in Der Hohlweg. In fact, as de Bruyn now points out, the predominating influence of Nazi literature - "dieses Loch, das noch gefüllt sein muß" (BE 72) - is in far more urgent need of analysis. There is one obviously didactic scene in Das Impressum, in which David Groth's father, a decent man who has suffered grossly for his modest integrity, passes on some basic truths, just before he despairingly commits suicide in uniform. David learns that it is the working class which must bear the heavy burden of fighting for social justice, regardless of the personal cost:

> Nun bin ich kein so großer Apostel für Tapfer-
> keit und Gerechtigkeit; wenn man ohne sie
> einigermaßen leben könnte, würde ich sagen:
> Laß sie sausen - was hilft die Gerechtigkeit,
> wenn du hungerst, und was hilft dir Heldenmut,
> wenn du sterben mußt; wer ins Bilderbuch
> kommen will, mag sich damit befassen, wir sind
> nicht dafür zuständig. Nur meine ich jetzt,
> wir sind dafür zuständig; es bleibt uns gar
> nichts anderes übrig, als gerecht und nicht
> feige zu sein, anders geht es uns an den
> Kragen ...(I 89)

Otherwise, there is no indication that guidance could have been forthcoming from parents - even those with evident moral courage, like the school-teacher fathers of Christa T. and Karl Erp - or schoolfriends, which might have pointed to a socialist alternative. The older mentor figures central to the 'Entwicklungsroman' tradition are now seen not to have existed in Hitler's Germany within the horizons of such receptive protagonists.
  The only personal relationship of any consequence is that between Christa T. and the narrator in Nachdenken über Christa T., in which the latter comes to admire her new classmate because she alone has preserved a conscious- ness of self, in opposition to the systematic levelling

processes at work everywhere else. Christa T.'s self-
assurance is signalled by the defiant manner in which she
trumpets through a rolled-up newspaper as she walks along
the street, while her peers and elders stand apart in embarrassed silence. For the narrator, this action brings
a shock of recognition that natural independence is
threatened with extinction - "ich fühlte auf einmal mit
Schrecken, daß es böse endet, wenn man alle Schreie früh-
zeitig in sich erstickt".(CT 16) This insight is, however,
as short-lived as it is profound. The chaos brought about
by the final disintegration of the Third Reich is imminent, destroying all contact between the two friends for
years. For Christa T., self-expression is of course a
more subtle business than the trumpeting which first
attracts the narrator's attention: the diary which she
starts keeping at the age of ten represents her attempt
to preserve the world of original experience from the
destructive intrusion of external forces, first registered
when the family cat is killed before her eyes by a drunken
house-tenant. The narrator, assisted by popular etymology,
sees Christa T.'s writing as deriving from "ihr Hang, zu
dichten, dichtzumachen die schöne, helle, feste Welt"
(CT 27), thereby linking creative writing and the defence
of an inherently harmonious identity.

The fact that the totalitarian endeavour to obliterate
the subjective sense of self was carried on in the name
of a quasi-metaphysical 'Volksgemeinschaft' is confronted
in these novels with a full awareness of the ambiguity of
such abstract concepts, previously hinted at in war-
stories such as Franz Fühmann's Kameraden. Wolf's narrator admits the extent to which she identified with the
school "Gemeinschaft" fostered through organisations like
the Hitler Youth and characterised by the group's "dümm-
liches Grinsen" when faced with an individual like Christa
T..(CT 10-14) Karl Erp flees from his father's puritan
insistence upon personal responsibility, attracted by
"die Wärme der Begeisterung" into "die Verantwortungs-
losigkeit der Gemeinschaft".(BE 194) The progression
from this condition of communal irresponsibility to the
battle front is taken as a grim inevitability for eligible
males like Erp, and not worthy of detailed recollection.
David Groth demonstrates his atypicality further when he
manages to avoid battle action through his Schweikian
cunning, accepting the humble position of "getreuer
Knecht" to an air-force general who is impressed by his
knowledge of weaponry. For all the others, survival is a
matter of sheer good fortune. It is only through the
horror of 'private' details like the corpse of the baby
which Christa T. sees abandoned by the roadside that the
final collapse of the Third Reich is depicted. In any

case, the chaos had been documented in the 'Entwicklungs-romane', whereas the vexed question of the transition to-wards self-identification with the socialist cause after the war had become crucial.

There is now no real dispute over the fact that the socialist reconstruction of the Soviet zone of occupation was greeted with scepticism by a generation whose instinc-tive idealism had already been ruthlessly exploited. Equally, a point appears to have been reached relatively quickly when collective needs again took priority over the protection of a disorientated self. De Bruyn, whose achievement in <u>Der Hohlweg</u> was to expose the inadequacy of the rhetoric of 'große Worte', has Karl Erp recall, in similar vein, "die lächerlichen Aufbauparolen, die man erst ernst nimmt, als die ersten Erfolge sich zeigen". (BE 57)   Groth soon finds his feet, supporting the 'Auf-bau' through the medium of the <u>Neue Berliner Rundschau,</u> while the other main characters are confronted with the dilemma of a 'conversion' to the cause in the terms of the 'Anderswerden' basic to socialist thinking since Becher's day. As Christa Wolf sees it, the creation of a 'new' self was essential to personal as well as to eco-nomic recovery, but dangerous in the longer term because it presupposed that the 'fascist' self could somehow be excised. The realisation that socialism is "der Weg zu uns selber" (CT 41) is unshakable for the generation which grew up into the GDR, as is their pride in having helped to make "die neue Welt" a tangible reality.(CT 66)   With hindsight, however, the problematical aspect of the 'An-derswerden' comes into focus. The separation of the bourgeois 'them' from the socialist 'us' may seem the way to salvation, but it fails to take account of the organic continuity of personality:

> Den Schnitt machen zwischen 'uns' und 'den
> anderen', in voller Schärfe, endgültig: das
> war die Rettung. Und insgeheim wissen: Viel
> hat nicht gefehlt, und kein Schritt hätte
> 'das andere' von uns getrennt, weil wir
> selbst anders gewesen wären. Wie aber trennt
> man sich von sich selbst? Darüber sprachen
> wir nicht.(CT 36)

Brigitte Reimann, the youngest of these authors, appear to avoid this question entirely by making Franziska some four years younger again, and thus born around 1937. Franziska's growth from childhood into the GDR seems a harmonious natural process - "ich wuchs wie eine Pflanze" (FL 33) ... "ich war selig eingeordnet".(FL 35)   She has a liberating sense of not needing to go through the agonie. of adjustment her bourgeois elders face:

> ... für mich, dachte ich, wird alles anders
> sein, und wenn ich das Leben, wie ich es mir
> damals vorwegträumte, in ein Bild umsetzen
> wollte, würde ich ein Pferd zeichnen, ein
> Pferd in rasendem Galopp, frei, wild, ohne
> Zaumzeug, die Mähne im Wind und mit Hufen,
> die den Boden nicht berühren ...(FL 36)

This proves to be naive self-deception: although she is
a world of experience away from her older brother Wilhelm,
and can wear the "blaue Bluse der Romantik" with with her
friends in the FDJ with boundless enthusiasm (FL 59), the
tensions between her fundamental identity and socialist
society have only been delayed. By the time she begins
her architectural studies in the middle 1950s she has been
made harshly aware of the fact that she is no more a
natural citizen of the GDR than her brother. On official
forms they must describe themselves as "Sonstige" since
they are neither farmers nor workers, and the new world
suddenly seems dependent on an updated version of Calvinist
predestination.(FL 63) Franziska and Wilhelm nevertheless
make the leap of faith and become part of the pioneering
generation, along with Christa T., Karl Erp and their
friends, enjoying the privileges of higher education and
in turn giving unstintingly of their time in youth organisations and voluntary labour on the farms. These are the
years when the individual and the collective are most
fully unified: as Wolf's narrator says, "an die Stelle
des Ich kann ... das Wir treten, niemals mit mehr Recht
als für jene Zeit".(CT 65)
   They were also years punctuated violently in the GDR
by the workers' revolt of June 1953 and the 'Thaw' of
1955-56, when the need for a dimension of individual responsibility in determining the future of socialism was first
articulated. Placing the struggle against dogmatism in a
more precise personal context was, however, still a highly delicate matter, and produced a wide range of responses
in these novels. For David Groth, the 17th June 1953 is
less memorable for his bewildered opposition to the rebellious workers than as the day when he decides to marry
the photographer Franziska Grewe: that evening, "so ein
würgender Tag" can be kept at a distance by their private
"freies Gelächter".(I 412)[26] In relation to Karl Erp's
development, it doesn't merit a mention, perhaps because
it happens during his period of energetic dedication to a
new career and marriage, when he is totally "er selbst".
(BE 17) In contrast, Christa T., studying in Leipzig,
sinks into a near-suicidal depression because of the
contradictions between her private values and those of the
world around her: "Da sie an der Welt nicht zweifeln

156

konnte, blieb ihr nur der Zweifel an sich".(CT 92)
(Franziska Linkerhand uses almost exactly the same phrase
in describing her brother Wilhelm's predicament at this
time (FL 62).)

The problem here is whether such a denial of self is
ever.more than temporarily justifiable, and whether an
environment which demands this might eventually bring
about a total loss of the continuity essential to the
survival of personality. Franziska seems less worried by
the long-term effects of an era when "wir verleugneten
uns, hielten uns Augen und Ohren zu und sagten ja, ja, ja
zu allem" (FL 62), and would rather consign such "alte
Geschichten" to oblivion. Wolf's narrator, however, insists more urgently that time alone will not be sufficient
to eradicate the Stalinist mentality, which tends to be
self-perpetuating. The new world of socialism quickly
becomes the "neue Welt der Phantasielosen. Der Tatsachenmenschen. Der Hopp-Hopp-Menschen", in Christa T.'s phrase.
(CT 66)   Through a terrible lack of self-certainty
stretching back to the Third Reich, this generation has
allowed itself to become subject to a bureaucratic "Mecha-
nismus" which would have it obliterate its personality -
"sich auslöschen. Schräubchen sein".(CT 72)   It is only
after the "plötzlicher Lichtwechsel" caused by Khrushchev's
revelations in 1956 about the Stalin era that a minority,
like Christa T. and the narrator, regain confidence that
their personality can be restored if they now accept
individual moral responsibility for the future course of
socialism.(CT 168)   They do not, however, suffer for their
new convictions as severely as Franziska's lover Trojanowic
does. Although his past is only pieced together in
speculative fashion by Franziska, what stands out is that
his exemplary development from proletarian Berlin to an
academic career in Leipzig is abruptly halted in the repression which followed the Hungarian uprising. Trojanowic
is one of those "erschüttert" in 1956 into seeking radical
reform (FL 531), who then spends four years in prison on
a charge of assisting subversion - experiences which help
to drive him later into the "schwindelhafte Existenz eines
Außenseiters".(FL 501)

Most members of this generation continue to accept
self-limitation in the face of a basically unchanged
authority structure. David Groth runs foul of Party
authority because of his "Neigung zu politisch gefähr-
lichem Einzelgängertum" (I 325), but the circumstances
are relatively unthreatening. The message for the reader
of Das Impressum, as provided by a proletarian veteran,
is nevertheless quite clear - the Party's collective
wisdom must always be accepted by the individual:

> ... eines ist für einen Genossen die furcht-
> barste Scheiße, in die er geraten kann: daß
> er meint, er ist schlauer als die Partei.(I 342)

This kind of conformism, as seen by Groth himself, is
based upon "Prinzipientreue" rather than "Dogmatismus"
(I 377), but is never put to the test in a crisis in which
socialist principles are themselves at issue. The only
other central character whose career progresses through
these years without a hitch is Karl Erp, but here the
lack of tension only masks the superficiality of his
achievement of socialist identity, with each step towards
stability adding to a dangerous "Gleichförmigkeit".(BE 16)
The point at which socially productive activity can lose
the quality of individual commitment is almost indefinable,
but in Erp's case the problem increases as life takes on
the trappings of affluence. The acquisition of a villa
in the exclusive 'Spreesiedlung' in Köpenick makes Erp
himself aware "wie schnell und gern man sich anpaßt, wenn
die neue Umgebung einem paßt".(BE 13)
   While Erp's decline is influenced by social factors,
there is also the more deeply rooted aspect of conformism,
arising from the retardation of democratic consciousness
amongst previous generations of Germans, which is seen as
a continuing threat to the development of personality in
the GDR. There are details in Franziska Linkerhand and
Nachdenken über Christa T. which bleakly reveal how prevalent the levelling processes of 'Anpassung' were in almost every sphere of life in the 1950s. Franziska's first
boyfriend, the uninhibited jazz-player nicknamed 'Django',
who preferred to leave university rather than accept the
offical line on decadent Western influences, ends up as
an utterly conventional school-teacher, who has 'died' as
an individual:

> Django hat sich eingerichtet, er ist tot, er
> geht durch die Straßen, belehrt seine Schüler
> über Gammastrahlen, zieht jeden Morgen ein
> reines Hemd an und ist mausetot.(FL 41)

Wolf's narrator is highly conscious of the critical point
in the GDR's existence when optimism and trust were over-
taken by "Berechnung, Schläue, Anpassungstrieb".(CT 71)
Almost at every turn, Christa T.'s unwillingness to conform unquestioningly is greeted with 'wiser' advice to
accept things as they are. Her depression in the summer
of 1953 is regarded by the university doctor as a neurosis
deriving from "mangelnde Anpassungsfähigkeit an gegebene
Umstände".(CT 92) When she begins teaching and is horrified
that her pupils are only interested in achieving the good marks
awarded for reproducing clichés, her headmaster sees her

as one of those "leicht erregbare Gemüter" whom he always
needs to "dämpfen".(CT 131) Years later, in the hope-
filled 1960s, Christa T. is again shocked to hear that one
of her brightest ex-pupils thrives on an attitude of "Anpassung um jeden Preis" as "der Kern der Gesundheit", in
a complete abdication of responsibility for what she sees
as "unsere moralische Existenz".(GT 141-3)

Conditions like these suggest a degree of alienation
from the 'natural' self which in ideological terms ought
to be inconceivable in socialist society. But where there
is such little scope for overt non-conformism, figures
like Christa T. are seen to have no option but to indulge
in a rather tentative kind of role-playing to avoid stagnating as individuals. This does not mean a dissolution
of the organic self into the 'pluralistic personality'
widely depicted in positive terms in West German novels
of the 1960s, but rather a temporary expedient until the
ideological climate becomes more conducive to self-
realisation.

The sections of <u>Nachdenken über Christa T.</u> which describe her life from the middle 1950s onwards return constantly to the complicated relationship between role-
playing and identity. Disappointed with her lack of
success as a teacher in Berlin, she adopts a policy of
"erst mal ein paar Rollen durchprobieren, ehe man sich
festlegt".(CT 151) In choosing the part of the heroine
of Sophie de la Roche's <u>Geschichte des Fräuleins von
Sternheim</u> at a fancy-dress ball, she is weighing up her
capacity to emulate the latter in making something positive out of a dreary married life in provincial obscurity
- before agreeing to become the wife of the veterinary
surgeon Justus, who has a remote practice in Mecklenburg.
Her "Spiel mit Varianten" seems relatively brief, but the
need for a more solid commitment is evidently more pressing
in a socialist environment than in the pluralist West.
Christa T. accepts her role as "Tierarztfrau", yet continues to see herself as "jemand mit Aussichten, mit ge-
heimen Möglichkeiten".(CT 171-3) Although she appears
to consolidate her married self in becoming a mother
and designing a new home in picturesque surroundings,
these attempts "sich inniger mit dem Leben zu verbinden"
(CT 193) are threatened by provincial pettiness and boredom. The crisis which develops is sparked off by adultery
but it concerns her whole identity: she has lost the
secret which made her uniquely "lebensfähig" - "das Be-
wußtsein dessen, wer sie in Wirklichkeit war". The brief
liaison with a young forester serves to begin the process
of growth again, making her "plötzlich wieder sie selbst".
(CT 199) But she later realises that everything in her
past life - and not just her consciously adopted roles -

has been preparing her for the recognition that she can
only fulfil herself by synthesising it all in her creative
writing:

> Was sie im Innersten wollte, wovon sie träumte
> und was zu tun sie seit langem begonnen hatte,lag
> offen vor mir, unbestreitbar und unbezweifelbar ...
> Ihr langes Zögern, ihre Versuche in verschiedenen
> Lebensformen, ihr Dilettieren auf manchem Gebiet
> deuteten in dieselbe Richtung, wenn man nur
> Augen hatte zu sehen. Daß sie ausprobierte,
> was möglich war, bis ihr nichts mehr übrig-
> blieb - das wäre wohl zu verstehen.(CT 215)

About the same time as Christa T. seeks protection in
marriage from less palatable forms of 'Anpassung',
Franziska Linkerhand attempts to purge the sins of her
bourgeois forebears by rushing into marriage with the
handsome working-class lad Wolfgang Exß. But instead of
securing her identity, this leads the young student into
a nightmare of violence, drunkenness and non-communication
with a husband who has nothing in common with her proletarian 'Menschenbild'. The role she takes on in trying
to leave behind her "Doppelwesen" (FL 34) as a middle-
class child in the workers' state creates a far more
serious split in her personality, between her existence
as a student of architecture and the traditional sub-
missive role which Exß expects her to fill. Indeed, the
dichotomy is so psychologically destructive to Franziska
that it appears to have the irreversibility of an organic
process about it:

> Sie fühlte, wie ihr Leben auseinanderriß, als
> sei das ein organischer Vorgang, als habe
> sich ihr Inneres in zwei zerstörerische Wesen
> gespalten ...(FL 88)

As the marriage falls apart, she finds herself living a
"provisorische[s] Leben zwischen Risiko und Ergebung".
(FL 95) Thereafter, the lack of anything more solid
upon which to base her identity than her unflagging
commitment to socialism gives Franziska's fortunes the
openness of role-experimentation. The decision to give
up a professional career in the city for the hardship of
a pioneer's life in Neustadt, and the subsequent abandonment of her architectural work there for a private
existence with Trojanowicz, both reflect this principle
of provisionality, which accepts the stresses of instability as an integral part of living life to the full.
She does, however, find herself at times so involved in
her role in Neustadt that she feels the desire to restrict
herself to this productive self, which is "ungeteilt",

and forget her private "angstvolle[s], bedrohte[s] Ich".
(FL 379)   But this is patently impossible, and, as time
passes, her yearning for the stability she feels must
follow when she manages to re-integrate her self becomes
more pronounced.

It was nevertheless radically new to suggest, in relation to this central period in the development of both
Christa T. and Franziska Linkerhand, that role-playing
could become in socialist society both necessary and productive, and did so for many in the years after 1956, when
the opportunity for a decisive improvement in the quality
of individual life appeared to have been missed. At the
same time, the cases of Trojanowicz and Schafheutlin point
to the dangers which occur when the dynamic, flexible
aspects of role-playing are forgotten. Trojanowicz has
taken a job driving a tip-truck after his release from
prison, and seems determined to keep his intellectual
interests to himself. Before she knows anything about
his past, Franziska is suspicious of his "angebliche
Identität mit einem Kipperfahrer" and is disturbed by behaviour intended to create a "Distanz zur eigenen Person".
(FL 383-5)   Schafheutlin, in contrast, has tried to
suppress vital aspects of his personality in taking on
"die Rolle eines Vorgesetzten".(FL 138)   The glimpses
into his earlier life suggest a well-balanced person,
fond of travel and literature, who has sacrificed too
much since, in the service of an unimaginative central
bureaucracy.

The schematic weakness of Reimann's novel is that
Franziska is depicted as being a person uniquely suited
to bring each of these diametrically opposed role-players
back to a higher self-unity. Schafheutlin determines to
liberate himself from a sterile marriage, with the ideal
of harmonising his public and private selves through life
with Franziska. Yet he remains so deeply associated with
the authority which frustrates all Franziska's plans to
give Neustadt a desperately needed social centre that she
commits herself instinctively to the relationship with
Trojanowicz. In their year together, as each comes to
terms with the past through their creative writing, she
hopes that Trojanowicz will 'write off' his negative self
in his novel, that "je weiter [dein anderes Ich] sich
entfernt, desto näher rückst du wieder dir selbst".(FL 537)
It is only when his "innere Erstarrung" becomes manifest
(FL 501), that Franziska considers the possibility of a
new "kluge Synthese" (FL 582), in Neustadt and in partner-
ship with Schafheutlin, but this is where the novel breaks
off.

161

In Buridans Esel, Erp's "Persönlichkeitsverlust" is
indicated by the way in which he never puts more than part
of himself into his various roles as "Chef", "Familien-
autorität", "Familienvater", "Schwiegersohn" and so on.
In his romantic encounters with Fräulein Broder, as in his
eventual return to wife and family, he tries to present
the most favourable image of himself. He has little enough
success, as the narrator reveals in characteristic ironical
fashion: when Erp loses his way in the labyrinth of the
Berlin tenement in which his prospective mistress lives,
his clumsy presence is announced to most of Fräulein
Broder's neighbours, and his illusion of himself as a
model of amorous discretion is sadly tarnished:

> ... er hatte sich so benommen, wie er war,
> und gar nicht so, wie er gesehen werden
> wollte. Sich ihr so zu zeigen, schien ihm,
> hätte das Ende vor dem Anfang bedeutet, und
> deshalb schwieg er sich über die ganze
> Geschichte aus.(BE 50)

His wife is no more convinced when he creeps back to her
months later as the "Mann, der bei Jericho unter die
Räuber gefallen ist und Anspruch auf seinen barmherzigen
Samariter hat".(BE 244)
    Not surprisingly, the idea that role-playing is a
natural part of everyday experience, involving neither
radical experiments nor any break in the continuity of
personal development, is found only in Kant's Das Impressum.
To the perceptive eyes of his wife Fran, Groth is always
"dieser David" whom she knows intimately:

> Und so war dieser David immer da; auch wenn
> er fort war zu einer Konferenz in Äquatornähe
> oder entschwunden in die Schlacht gegen
> sorgloses Mittelmaß; er blieb erkennbar als
> dieser David unter dem Staub und zwischen
> den Girlanden der Jahrestage, blieb erkenn-
> bar auf entfernten Tribünen und im Getümmel
> der Kongresse, Auschüsse, Komitees, Jurys
> und Delegationen, blieb David, der Mann von
> Fran, auch unter hundert Charaktermasken ...(I 133)

The rounded view of personality to which Kant clings here
stands in patent contradiction to the findings of his more
critically minded contemporaries. Identity, as de Bruyn,
Reimann and Wolf illustrate in their novels through a
variety of effective examples, had been seriously threatened
by historical, social and ideological factors in the socialist context of the GDR between 1945 and the early 1960s.
The idea of the qualitative superiority of life in the
GDR over life in the West is, however, preserved, since

neither the organic concept of personality nor the ultimate goal of self-fulfilment through socialism is sacrificed. The nature of the self is still very much a political issue, but for the first time there is a significant
degree of common ground between writers in East and West
Germany in the priority they give to the problematic
aspects of identity.

The urban context of contemporary socialism

In the narrative present of the middle 1960s, with the
GDR becoming a technologically sophisticated society, the
language of 'Gemeinschaft' and 'Heimat' was finally seen
to be ideologically inappropriate as well as creatively
obsolete. In these novels, the liberating step is taken
beyond the anachronistic transposition of modern socialist
society into a pre-industrial framework of small communities and unspoilt nature. Fictional analysis had by now
revealed enough that was disjointed and counterproductive
in the GDR's development to make it obvious that concepts
overladen with associations of continuity were better
avoided - indeed, they could be seen as standing in the
way of a convincing depiction of what was qualitatively
new about East German society. The progress achieved since
the Bitterfeld novels is marked by the absence of inauthentic central characters cocooned by nature, home and
the socialist community, like Rita in Der geteilte Himmel
and Balla in Spur der Steine. Significantly, this refusal
to make use of ideological cliché in the depiction of
spheres of which the authors had insufficient subjective
experience led to the disappearance of the worker-hero
and his environment from their fiction. Instead, there
is much more foreground emphasis on working environments
not far removed from those of most full-time writers -
the newspaper office, the library, the town-planning
department, the classroom - as well as upon their own
immediate creative problems, as East German fiction moves
into the urban world of the professionally qualified
minority.
The common feature in the career pattern of the central
characters is a decisive move from a rural or small-
town background to the city on the path to maturity.
David Groth leaves home after his father's suicide in
1943 and wastes no time, as peace is restored, in beginning
his long involvement with the Neue Berliner Rundschau.
For the others, educational reasons predominate: Karl
Erp, like Groth's wife-to-be Fran, moves to the metropolis
around 1950, the one to train as a librarian, the other

as a photographer; Christa Wolf's narrator and Christa T.
study together in Leipzig in the early 1950s, then also
live for a time in Berlin; Franziska Linkerhand studies
architecture in an unspecified city a few years later.
The home environment they leave behind is, to the extent
it is described at all, not seen to represent their 'roots'
in any significant way. The only novel in which contact
with the past is seen to be maintained is <u>Buridans Esel</u>,
in which Erp's feelings as he returns to his native
village of Alt-Schradow are as ambivalent as they are in
most other respects:

> Das Dorf war für ihn ein Sack unnützen Krams,
> den man auf die Flucht mitgenommen hat: Er
> hindert, man verflucht ihn, aber die Kraft
> zum Wegwerfen fehlt. Deshalb seine Sehnsucht
> nach der Arbeit auf dem Lande, aber auch seine
> Angst davor, deshalb sein Rückzug an die
> Peripherie der Stadt, aber auch seine Senti-
> mentalität auf der Heimfahrt.(BE 189)

Although Erp, following his father's death, comes to a
less woolly appreciation of what family continuity means
to him, the need for independent self-awareness is generally seen in these novels to be more important. David
Groth's comments on "böses Erbe" (I 36) and the tenacious-
ness of outmoded values illustrate the point: historically,
the community has been a repressive force, a constant
threat to individuality and progress, in the shape of
"das Ungewohnte, das einsame Neue, das abweichende Talent,
das verstörend Andere".(I 304) (Kant, however, still
expects his reader to differentiate between bourgeois
and proletarian communities.)
The relative lack of contact the protagonists have
with home and nature after forming their distinctive
selves in the city suggests a more positive view of urban
culture than was previously possible under the dualistic
conception of 'Gemeinschaft' and 'Gesellschaft'. There
is now also the major problem of introducing socialism
into what are seen to be country backwaters. Erp may
cherish a dreamy notion of "Leben und Arbeit auf dem Lande,
wo die Kulturrevolution noch merklich Revolutionäres
hatte, wo es war, als setze man in eine Brache den Pflug,
wo man mit den Menschen auf du und du stand" (BE 157),
but the thought of abandoning his life in Berlin for this,
even with the genuinely committed Fräulein Broder, is unpalatable for him. Franziska Linkerhand, on the other
hand, determined to break decisively with her past,
accepts the bleakness and monotony of life in the eastern
provinces in the pioneering spirit.

The small town in Mecklenburg to which Christa T. and
Justus move has preserved a rigid class system and is
riddled with corruption. She feels trapped in this
"toten Kreis" and almost loses her sense of self under
the strain - "Sie sah sich in eine unendliche Menge von
tödlich banalen Handlungen und Phrasen aufgelöst".(CT 199)
For this "Waldschwärmerin" of earlier years (CT 12),
nature and society at times enter into the polar opposition of the Romantic era, since the unspoilt environment
of forests and lakes helps to restore the damage which
a stagnant society inflicts upon her personality. The
fear that little has changed since the nineteenth century
haunts Nachdenken über Christa T., with "Poesie" and
"Persönlichkeit" at risk in "eine von Niedergangstendenzen
und Epigonentum gezeichnete Zeit" (CT 121), just as
Christa T. saw them to be in the age of Theodor Storm -
although Wolf does show a newly critical, liberating
atmosphere establishing itself in the GDR of the 1960s.
She still comes close to attributing a metaphysical
quality to man's relationship with nature, but has moved
away from the superficialities of the benevolent organic
community.

This does not mean the abandonment of the notion of
community altogether: it is still stressed by Kant and
de Bruyn that the superiority of East German society is
directly related to the encouragement of the co-operative
spirit in every sphere of work or leisure activity.
Community, in other words, is now of an institutional
rather than an organic nature. While the uncomplicated
team-spirit of the industrial brigades in the Bitterfeld
novels is no longer evident, productive harmony still reigns
in the Neue Berliner Rundschau and the public library.
Individuals may appear to be irreconcilably different, yet
wise leadership, with which the Party is fully identified,
moulds them into an effective whole. This is most neatly
depicted in Das Impressum, despite the obvious multiplicity
of functions which need to be integrated to ensure the
successful planning, production and distribution of a
leading magazine. Although the 'Oberste Abteilung' (a
euphemism for the Politbüro) frequently interferes with
articles on ideological grounds, and bitter exchanges en-
sue, there is continuing broad agreement on long-term
aims. The journalist's goal of being "umsichtig, ein-
dringend und unbeirrt auf die Wahrheit hin" (I 246) is not
viewed as problematic. Groth, as chief editor, takes a
personal interest in all his staff, and knows them well
outside their roles as employees. The magazine is thus
more than just a 'Betrieb': those who work for it grow
in stature as their product builds up its reputation.

The pyramid of power functions effectively here: Groth
has close personal relations with many leading Party
members - proletarian veterans like Xaver Frank, 'Kutschen-
Meyer', and Fritze Andermann, and rigid ideologues like
Johanna Müntzer, who are all 'Vorbilder' for him despite
his awareness of their individual limitations. On the
threshold of elevation to their ranks himself, Groth is
confident that popular mistrust of "unsere Oberen" can
easily be overcome by a process of education.(I 35f.)
De Bruyn presents a similarly unified image of "unsere
verständige Gesellschaft" (BE 209), if on a more modest
scale. Any problems which arise in his fictional library
- like Erp's extra-marital liaison with his young colleague -
are sensitively dealt with by senior ministry officials
like Fred Mantek, who is an old friend as well as a "Vorbild".(BE 159) De Bruyn may be felt to play down the extent of his mentor's influence, by describing him as a
"reitenden Boten" (BE 219) as he arrives with a scheme to
save Erp from exile to the provinces, at a time when Erp
is already retreating from his dynamic new relationship
into the comfortable routines of the past. This is however no more than the healthy ironisation of mentor-figures
who take on the role of benevolent destiny too deliberately, familiar since <u>Wilhelm Meisters Lehrjahre</u>.

Far less of this implicit confidence in the achievement
of "eine auf den Menschen orientierte Gesellschaft" (BE 221)
by the middle 1960s is found in <u>Franziska Linkerhand</u> and
<u>Nachdenken über Christa T.</u> Everything about Neustadt in
Reimann's novel seems as provisional as the narrator's
own life at this stage. The basic conflict between
functionalism and the pursuit of a new quality of life
constantly causes destructive frictions in the town-
planning office. Economic pressures make cheapness and
quantity the criteria for house-building,and result in the
impoverished existence of most of the new citizens of
Neustadt. Those who, like Franziska, know that a living
environment which is not planned with regard to the multiplicity of individual and social needs will cause at least
as many problems as it eliminates, make depressingly little
impact on an inflexible bureaucratic machine. The point
may have been reached here, as in <u>Nachdenken über
Christa T.</u>, where it becomes a moral imperative to confront
the 'Tatsachenmenschen' before they do irreparable damage
to the imaginative and creative faculties of the individual.
If, as Wolf had directly experienced at the Eleventh
Plenum in 1965, the SED leadership was itself too heavily
weighted towards the functionalist position to be a
genuinely unifying force, then it is hardly coincidental
that there is no affirmation of the state's institutions
in her novel. The collective 'Wir' of her narrator is,

as indicated above, a more subtle and discriminating one.
Franziska Linkerhand's longing to be more tangibly integrated into society increases towards the end of Reimann's
novel - the sound of some favourite jazz music in a Berlin
street is enough to release it:

> ... ich empfand eine starke Sehnsucht, bei
> diesen Leuten, Studenten vermutlich, dort oben
> zu sein, oder mich unlösbar einer Familie,
> Freunden, einer Landschaft, dem Land verbunden
> zu fühlen, und ich dachte, was ich je
> gearbeitet habe, sei dieser Sehnsucht ent-
> sprungen, dem Wunsch nach dem Aufgehoben-Sein,
> das ich noch nicht, das ich noch immer nicht
> erreicht hatte. (FL 580-1)

Otherwise, she too is able to regard her independence as
a productive condition and not as an indication of lack
of maturity.

Even the continuing dependence of Kant and de Bruyn on
some aspects of community cannot disguise the broad shift
of emphasis towards an urban perspective on human relations
The city is now acknowledged as being the setting for
self-liberation from rural parochialism, and the natural
environment of the specialists upon whom much of the GDR's
future depends. It also provides the context for the
analysis of negative phenomena of the 1960s such as alienation and the growth of a new class-structure.

Nowhere are the opportunities and the problems associated with the urbanisation of socialist society more
revealingly juxtaposed than in Reimann's Neustadt.
Franziska arrives with all the idealism of the young graduate that human relations can be transformed in a
planned environment. She expects towns to be "Organismen
... die für das Zusammenleben so wichtig sind wie eine
gemeinsame Sprache, Gesetze, moralische Normen".(FL 270)
What she finds, however, is "ein städtebauliches Debakel".
(FL 351) In her frequent arguments with Schafheutlin,
the economic and social priorities, the collective and
individualistic views of man are thrashed out, but the
"kluge Sythese" lies somewhere in the remote future. Her
brief experience of Neustadt shows the cost of this urban
experiment in human terms: the alienation of individuals
and families who are "zusammengepfercht" (FL 157) in
featureless blocks of flats; the boredom of a town where
the only social entertainment is the Saturday night dance
and there are no basic amenities; the symptomatic violence,
vandalism and excessive drinking, and the alarming suicide rate, which includes her own close friend Gertrud.
It is only in an emergency that a spontaneous community
spirit emerges, when neighbours come together to deliver

a baby after the ambulance has lost its way in the dark, anonymous streets.

For the resourceful Franziska, there may be a stimulating quality in being "fremd in einer fremden Stadt" (FL 159), but not for the resentful workers, some of whom have been forcibly removed from Berlin to Neustadt after the erection of the Wall.(FL 147) When she embarks almost single-handed on a campaign for a civic centre, she receives considerable support from "Leute, die sich eine Heimat wünschen".(FL 577) Yet the continuing lack of progress on this vital issue is finally instrumental in persuading Franziska to leave Neustadt with Trojanowicz. Her actions underline Reimann's message that the GDR's future is threatened by this official failure to generate a sense of communal identity in its new towns.

Neustadt may seem worlds away from East Berlin, with its proletarian traditions and metropolitan culture, but there are common problems. Some of the most graphic scenes in <u>Buridans Esel</u> are those in which Fräulein Broder's environment is depicted. She lives in one of the city's old 'Mietskasernen', with its own labyrinth of staircases and courtyards. The building is sadly antiquated for the needs of modern society and has a generally disreputable air, yet its location near the heart of Berlin's cultural life since the eighteenth century makes its survival important, when so many of the GDR's links with its 'bürgerliches Erbe' have been lost. The problem is that many of its proletarian inhabitants, for all their uniqueness as 'characters', have failed to change their attitudes in acknowledgement of the new socialist order:

> ... dort oben hatte die neue Ordnung noch nicht
> gesiegt, dort herrschten noch immer das Chaos
> und die Gesetzlosigkeit der offiziell längst
> erledigten Nachkriegszeit ...(BE 46)

Indeed, the "Hausgemeinschaft", in the name of which some of the younger tenants mischievously arrest Karl Erp after he leaves Fräulein Broder's flat late one night, is little more than an institutional structure.

The serious problems of Neustadt and proletarian Berlin point to the wider issue of the extent to which a meaningful community consciousness can be achieved in technologically advanced societies. It is the era of the "Fernsehgesellschaft" (BE 162), and television itself has brought about major changes in social habits, making city-dwellers in particular blind to the cultural opportunities around them:

> ... die meisten Berliner ... [verkriechen]
> sich heutzutage, genau wie die Landleute, nach

der Arbeit in ihre Wohnungen ..., um sich
durchs Fernsehen weltweite Kontakte vorzaubern
zu lassen.(BE 24-5)

Neustadt, of course, is worse off because there is not
even the illusion of alternative entertainment, and has
become "eine Siedlung von Fernsehhöhlen".(FL 351) In
contrast to the close friendships said to exist outside
working hours amongst the staff of the Neue Berliner
Rundschau, de Bruyn describes Erp's desperate efforts, in
the years before the widespread availability of television
to break down "das ungeschriebene Großstadtgesetz der ab-
soluten Trennung von Arbeits- und Wohnplatz".(BE 25)
Thus, for the many unable to overcome these obstacles, the
idea of the "Großstadtparadies" (BE 238) is entirely misleading. On the other hand, when intelligent and energetic
young people give up their natural urban surroundings to
assist in the cultural revolution in the provinces, there
is a considerable element of self-sacrifice involved. In
one of Franziska's blackest moments in Neustadt, she finds
herself longing for the features of city life which are so
glaringly absent there:

> Ich liebe Städte.
> Irgendwo auf der Welt muß es Städte geben und
> den Widerschein ihrer Lichter am Himmel und
> Trottoirs und Menschengedränge, in das du
> dich wie ein Schwimmer wirfst ...(FL 250)

Such a range of attitudes suggests that there is something akin to a class barrier, based on educational attainment and job responsibilities, separating those for whom
city life is an enriching experience and those for whom it
is alienating and harmful to their personality. The proletarian environment of de Bruyn's 'Mietskaserne' is still
in some ways reminiscent of the overwhelming metropolis in
the work of Döblin, and yet for the intellectuals and
economic leaders with whom the novels are primarily concerned, the opportunities and stresses are rather more
similar to those of contemporary Western society. The
trappings of affluence are less widely available, but there
is some recognition that the urban elite now have greater
access to consumer goods and comforts. Even though this
has the effect of blurring the previously rigid distinctions between bourgeois and socialist life-styles, it is
an aspect of contemporary society which can no longer be
ignored. Karl Erp is of course the most problematical
member of this new elite. The acquisition of a villa in
the 'Spreesiedlung' positively encourages his complacency
and conformism - a fact which might serve to confirm long-
standing socialist assumptions about the relationship

between a luxurious environment and moral decadence, since
Erp's career seems exemplary up to this point. On top of
this, there is de Bruyn's satirical exaggeration of the
intolerability for Erp of the noise, dirt and primitive
amenities of Fräulein Broder's tenement. Yet, as suggested
in the previous section, the problem is more deeply rooted
in Erp's past, in tendencies which he has suppressed rather
than mastered in the 'Aufbau' years. When the narrator
finally has Erp reduce his dilemma to the old classical
formula of "die zwei Seelen, ach, in seiner Brust" (BE 233),
his lack of genuine growth in earlier years is exposed.

Neither property owning nor affluence are seen to be
per se reprehensible. The house which Christa T. and
Justus build beside their lake in Mecklenburg seems at
first a dubious proposition to the narrator, who has "etwas gegen eigene Häuser". Yet a project requiring tremendous determination and patience, in a state where building
materials and fitments are desperately scarce, is later
seen to have a very positive value in consolidating
Christa T.'s badly shaken identity.(CT 191-3) More
affirmatively still, the privileged life led by de Bruyn's
Fred Mantek in his "fernbeheizte Luxuswohnung" in the Karl-
Marx-Allee (BE 172) presents no threat to his outstanding
commitment to the state, and is seen to be no less than he
deserves. This effective social separation of the elite
is, however, still resisted in some quarters. The Groths
are more egalitarian in choosing to live in a new block of
flats, where the occupants represent a social cross-section,
while Franziska Linkerhand displays the fundamental hostility of the younger generation towards preferential treatment for any group within the state (except that she is
later grateful to receive priority treatment in moving
within Neustadt to an older, more pleasant apartment).

Other factors also contribute to the isolation of the
intelligentsia. In a situation where there is still a
wide educational gulf separating them from most other
workers, they have to cope with proletarian resentments
and prejudices. Franziska often faces this antagonism in
Neustadt: "... daß die Intelligenz alles besser hat, daran
hat man sich doch schon gewöhnt. Euch blasen sie noch
Staubzucker in den Hintern".(FL 247) Such reproaches positively spur her on to break down the educational barriers,
to the extent that she spends half her leisure time giving
free tuition to her neighbours, but she is not supported
by her older professional colleagues in this determination
to overcome these new class differences. Christa T. finds
it much more enjoyable to communicate with the simple
farmers of the local LPG than with the class-conscious
townspeople nearer at hand. As Justus explains to the
narrator:

> Ihr erzählten die Bauern alles, ich weiß nicht,
> wieso ... [sie] saß an der Theke und zog den
> Bauern ihre Geschichten aus der Nase. Die
> ließen sich nicht bitten, weil sie merkten,
> daß sie sich nicht verstellte, sondern wirklich
> vor Lachen beinahe vom Stuhl kippte, wenn sie
> ihr von Küster Hinrichsens Hochzeit erzählten ...
>
> (CT 218)

The preservation of this level of communication is vital,
but is only brought about by this conscious striving against
the distancing effects of specialisation. Kant gives a
deceptive impression of boldness in using the word "Ent-
fremdung" in regard to Groth's position as part of the
elite, only to withdraw it immediately for 'tactical'
reasons.(I 376) For Groth, the problem has a dual
aspect: the state's leaders are overburdened with
responsibilities and thus a prey to the manifold stresses
summed up in the word "Managerkrankheit" (I 355), and
suffer at the same time from being cut off from the community at large. Kant often seems to be arguing that the
isolation enforced by an elevated sense of duty cancels
out the personal freedoms which intellectuals like Groth
acquire in rising above the restrictions of their home
environment.

This could, however, be viewed as special pleading for
the political leadership, and should not obscure the fact
that these novels are otherwise very much concerned with
the dimension of personal freedom to which the specialists
of the 1960s now have access. In addition to bearing their
heavy responsibilities for the moral as well as the economic health of the GDR, they do now have greater opportunities to fulfil themselves as individual socialists. Their
urban awareness of the need to encourage individuality once
a secure socialist consciousness has been established has,
moreover, led them to develop yardsticks for self-realisation
which go far beyond the conventional notion of self-
integration into an already existent community. The more
inappropriate the idea of 'Gemeinschaft', whether in institutional or in organic form, appears, the more formidable
the challenge to realise the dream of the 'whole man'
which unites the classical and Marxist traditions in German
culture.

The dream of wholeness

It is especially appropriate in the context of this
study that Christa Wolf should have prefaced Nachdenken
über Christa T. with the fundamental question raised in
Johannes R. Becher's Tagebuch 1950: "Was ist das: Dieses
Zu-sich-selber-Kommen des Menschen?".[27] The section of
the diary from which this is taken is one of those sub-
titled by Becher "Aus dem Leben eines bürgerlichen Menschen
unserer Zeit", in the evident expectation that the transitional period for socialists like himself of middle-class
origins, before the achievement of the goal of personal
wholeness, would be a brief one. It was highly revealing
that unforeseen problematical aspects of identity and community should provoke the same unanswered question a generation later. The fact that Wolf returns to it is a clear
reminder that there has been no abandonment of the highest
aspirations for the quality of individual life under socialism, and implies the recognition that the priorities
of establishing the GDR as a viable political and economic
entity had previously allowed little scope for the many-
sided needs of the individuals committed to that task.
The distance between 'finding oneself' 'as a socialist
and realising one's human potential had finally become the
subject of critical scrutiny. As Wolf suggested in her
"Selbstinterview", "die realen Grundlagen für die Selbstverwirklichung des Individuums" had been established, yet
there was still the same "tiefe Unruhe der menschlichen
Seele" which Becher had regarded in 1950 as "nichts anderes
als das Witterungsvermögen dafür und die Ahnung dessen, daß
der Mensch noch nicht zu sich selber gekommen ist". Wolf's
concern was that the differentiated approach to the GDR's
development initiated in the earlier 1960s should now be
pursued as a matter of urgency:

> Unsere Gesellschaft wird immer differenzierter.
> Differenzierter werden auch die Fragen, die
> ihre Mitglieder ihr stellen - auch in Form der
> Kunst. Entwickelter wird die Aufnahmebereit-
> schaft vieler Menschen für differenzierte
> Antworten. Das Subjekt, der sozialistische
> Mensch, lebt immer souveräner in einer Gesell-
> schaft, die er als sein Werk empfindet: nicht
> nur denkt und weiß, sondern empfindet.[28]

This was, in ideological terms, a much more challenging
line of argument than that running through the Bitterfeld
fiction. There, the personal crises for which East German
society was seen to shoulder at least part of the responsibility - those of a Werner Horrath or a Manfred Herrfurth
- were still seen as isolated cases of parochial vindictive-

ness, moral inflexibility, bureaucratic incompetence and
the like. For most of the other characters, fulfilment in
the sphere of personal relationships still harmonised neatly with productivity at work to lay the foundations for an
enduring self-unity. Now, the relationship between the
individual and social authority was being elevated by Wolf
on to a more complex, even antagonistic plane, and all the
convenient fictional formulae for self-realisation were
being studiously avoided.

The same cannot, however, be said of Das Impressum and
Buridans Esel, which are actually in some respects less
critical of society and the SED's leadership than the
Bitterfeld fiction. Kant, resorting readily (as Neutsch
had done for the motto of Spur der Steine) to the Brechtian
line that "die Mühen der Gebirge" had been left behind in
1945, so that the remaining problems were mainly "die der
Ebenen" (I 19), suggests that the discrepancy between the
Marxist ideal and the East German reality is not a cause
for particular concern:

> Wollte man dem Sozialismus am Zeuge flicken,
> könnte man ihm vorwerfen, daß er das Reich der
> Träume beschnitten hatte. Beschnitten oder
> besiedelt oder bebaut, jedenfalls mit Wirk-
> lichkeit besetzt und so verändert.(I 105)

Groth's utopian dreams are for the victory of the socialist
cause throughout the world rather than about how wholeness
can be achieved under prevailing conditions in his own
land. Indeed, the additional chapter included in the re-
vised version of Das Impressum, on the life of Groth's
contemporary Gerhard Rikow,[29] is probably intended as an
indirect commentary upon Christa Wolf's preoccupation with
the unfulfilled aspirations of the unknown Christa T..
Rikow too has just had his life tragically cut short by
leukaemia, and Groth - recognising the exemplary quality
of a career dedicated to industrialising East German agri-
culture, of a man who became a government minister at a
remarkably early age - considers how he might write a
suitable biographical article for the Rundschau. Rikow's
'qualities' are unambiguous: he has been both "ein unver-
besserliche[r] Optimist" and "ein tätiger Träumer"(I 433-4),
and there is no hint of even the minor discrepancies between the life of a leading "Persönlichkeit" and the private self which Groth finds in his own case.(I 7-10,360-1).
For Kant, the personality of the artist is clearly less
important than the achievements of the economic leader -
writers have the pragmatic task of boosting the morale of
the working-class and should above all, like the admirable
Bienhofer (modelled superficially on Erwin Strittmatter),
preserve their links with the people and the Party organi-

sation.(I 357-8, 379-80)

In <u>Buridans Esel</u>, the question of self-realisation is
not taken for granted in this way, but certainly reduced
to the central figure's capacity to fulfil his evident
potential within the benevolent framework of "unsere verständige Gesellschaft". The onus is on Karl Erp to re-
integrate his personality, not on society to correct the
kind of deformations acknowledged in the work of Wolf and
Reimann. The fact that Erp is capable of attaining wholeness is emphasised in the account of his love-making with
Fräulein Broder:

> Da wurden zwei eins,
> spürten einander, fügten sich ineinander,
> flossen ineinander, jauchzten, schrien mit-
> einander, hatten endlich nicht mehr das
> Gefühl, nur Hälfte zu sein, wurden ein Ganzes
> und hatten doch nie zuvor die Macht und Herr-
> lichkeit ihres eignen Ichs so sehr empfunden.
>
> (BE 136)

The signs of resurgence are there too in Erp's new-found
pleasure in his working life, but he finally founders in
a situation where society allows him an unhindered freedom
of choice. It is a definite weakness of the novel that
the ultimate issues of personality development are not
placed in a dialectical relationship with the state of
socialist society in the middle 1960s.

In fact, only in <u>Franziska Linkerhand</u> and <u>Nachdenken
über Christa T.</u> is this relationship between individual
growth and society effectively conveyed. Neither protagonist can approach wholeness in an environment which in
various respects alienates them, and both refuse a self-
restricting accommodation with the Party's authority
structures and economic priorities. Significantly, the
profound "Unruhe" which grips each of these apparently
frail women long after their basic socialist identity is
assured has a uniquely productive influence on those with
whom they come into contact. To Wolf's narrator, Christa T.
offers "das Beispiel für die unendlichen Möglichkeiten,
die noch in uns lagen" (CT 210-11), while those involved
with Franziska during her energetic year in Neustadt are
confronted in different ways with the one-sidedness of
their existence.

One-sidedness, that loss of inner unity when the self
is split into a succession of disparate roles, when working
and private life are divorced, is dangerously prevalent.
It is not of course synonymous with career specialisation,
which is seen to be essential in individual and social
terms: it is rather that the pressures towards outer conformism are, as indicated earlier, so severe that few

people have realised their unique potential through the
first twenty years of East German socialism. The lack of
a 'Vorbild' in either novel, like the absence of fictional
figures incarnating Party authority (even though many of
them are sincere SED members), points to the limited progress
towards self-perfection by this stage. It also leaves the
extent of the SED's contribution to refining the sensibilities of East German citizens - whatever its achievements
in the economic field - in an ambivalent light.

Although both novels suggest that important qualitative
improvements were becoming possible by the middle 1960s,
the GDR appears hitherto to have been, like Neustadt,
essentially 'provisorisch' as far as its capacity to foster
the pursuit of the ultimate human goal is concerned.
Franziska, Christa T. and their friends are part of the
gifted minority involved in creative labour, and yet their
experience of wholeness has been , at best, fragmentary
and short-lived - Franziska in the moments when she is
'ungeteilt' in her work or totally at one with Trojanowicz
Christa T. with family and friends on the Baltic coast
(CT 188-9) or engrossed in her writing (CT 214-7), rare
occasions when she can say 'Ich' in the face of her fundamental uncertainties about identity. How much more difficult, by implication, must it have been for those less
privileged to grow into harmonious personalities.

Wholeness is thus taken decisively out of the sphere of
propagandistic simplification as to what the GDR could
have achieved since 1945, and viewed again - as it had
been by the Weimar classicists and Marx alike - in its
long-term, ideal dimensions. In consequence, the continuity between the philosophical deliberations of Johannes
R. Becher, in his Tagebuch 1950 as in Abschied, and the
conception of Nachdenken über Christa T. or Franziska
Linkerhand, becomes evident on another level. The dream of
self-realisation, still remote on account of the imperfec-
tions of socialist society - however much it had by now
developed beyond the version with which Becher was confronted in Soviet exile - could again only be pursued on
an aesthetic plane. The special role of the writer and
his literary product, defended, albeit fitfully, by Becher
against the Party's predilection for affirmative literature
and reasserted by the next generation against the original
intentions of the 'Bitterfelder Weg', is a fundamental
tenet for the Christa Wolf of Nachdenken über Christa T..
It is a central theme of her essay "Lesen und Schreiben"
that significant prose arises from the author's "Sehnsucht nach Selbstverwirklichung": writing may prove to
be the only way to give expression to a complex awareness
of self - "der Zwang des Aufschreibens, als vielleicht
einzige Möglichkeit des Autors, sich nicht zu verfehlen".

Literature alone can record those fragmentary moments of
heightened self-unity which characters like Franziska and
Christa T. experience empirically, as the author liberates
himself from time and space, and blends past, present and
future into a coherent whole. The enormous intellectual
efforts involved bring about a transcendence of individual
limitations - "über sich selbst hinaus ... wachsen" - but
are also, paradoxically, the means of self-discovery -
"sich ... erreichen". [30]

It was in this spirit that Wolf chose to focus attention
upon the economically and politically insignificant life
of Christa T., and reveal the exemplary quality of her
striving for selfhood behind the lack of career commitment, the instability of her domestic situation, and all
the other apparently negative features of her existence.
Christa T.'s creative writing has grown out of the highest
human striving - "dieser lange, nicht enden wollende Weg
zu şich selbst" - firmly rooted in her East German environment but also transcending its present limitations in the
"viele Leben" and the "mehrere Zeiten" which it embraces.
(CT 221-2)   Her artistic vocation is no freely chosen
one which can be laid aside at will - as the narrator's
definition of Christa T.'s temperament suggests, her basic
"Sehnsucht" arises from an irrepressible "Sucht, zu sehen"
(CT 112), and she is equally addicted to the search for
meaning in life - "sinnsüchtig ... deutungssüchtig".(CT 180)
Such elevated claims for her progress towards wholeness
through the medium of literature are open to the criticism
that the excerpts from her writing quoted by the narrator
give little indication of any ability.   This anomaly can
really only be resolved if, as Heinrich Mohr has suggested,
Wolf's novel itself is seen as representing the identity
of Christa T. and the author on a higher creative plane.[31]

Reimann shows herself less inclined to isolate aesthetic
progress towards self-knowledge from renewed social en-
gagement, conscious perhaps of the weakness in Wolf's novel
that the two processes are not seen to be inter-dependent.
Franziska's period away from Neustadt, during which she
writes her autobiographical novel, is full of self-doubts
about the validity of her literary endeavours, making it
at best a "Zeit der Besinnung".(FL 481)

In the end, she places her novel at society's disposal
as a contribution to the quest for "die kluge Synthese
zwischen Heute und Morgen, zwischen tristem Blockbau und
heiter lebendiger Straße, zwischen dem Notwendigen und dem
Schönen" (FL 582), with the implication that she can only
begin the task of self-realisation once she returns to
Neustadt.   There is, however, a grim irony in this contrast
between the two novels, since Franziska rejoins the everyday struggle for a better life in the manner which was

denied to Brigitte Reimann, while Christa Wolf has continued since the publication of <u>Nachdenken über Christa T.</u>
to demonstrate the courageous commitment to the intellectual well-being of East German society which her heroine
was prevented from developing by her premature death.

Of these two outstanding novels, the more aesthetically
sophisticated <u>Nachdenken über Christa T.</u> occupies the
pivotal position in the progress of East German fiction.
In continuing to treat the question of personal wholeness
as a major theme, it stands firmly in the classical tradition, as mediated for German socialist culture by Lukács
and Becher, and still depends on their elevated view of
the writer and of the totality attainable in the 'Kunstwerk'. [32] And yet the subjectivity of its focus, the
open-endedness which breaks through the conventional
framework of fictional totality, and the critical differentiation of character and environment within socialism, all
suggest the need for a radical departure beyond the classic
al form of the 'Entwicklungsroman'. It represents the
culmination of some forty years of cultural-political debate and literary practice. In making authenticity the
new keynote of East German prose, Wolf was bringing to an
end a period which had seen so much well-intentioned recourse to outmoded models for depicting the individual and
his relationship with society, that works of literary meri
and critical force were no more than fortunate exceptions
to the rule. She had also shifted the balance between
'exemplary' and autobiographical perspectives so decisively towards the latter as to ensure that the explicitly
personal analysis of her generation's lifetime would
become a major preoccupation of the 1970s, in works such
as Franz Fühmann's <u>22 Tage oder die Hälfte des Lebens</u>
(1973), her own <u>Kindheitsmuster</u> (1976) and Stephan Hermlin's
<u>Abendlicht</u> (1979), which consolidate her outstanding
achievement in <u>Nachdenken über Christa T.</u>.

CHAPTER 5

THE SPECTRE OF THE 'DEUTSCHE MISERE'

Büchner's 'Lenz' as literary model

Christa Wolf's recognition, in her essay "Lesen und Schreiben", of the importance of Georg Büchner's Lenz as the model for contemporary 'epic prose', has proven even more decisive for the subsequent course of GDR fiction than my earlier reference to its bearing on the 'subjective authenticity' of works like Nachdenken über Christa T. or Franziska Linkerhand was able to indicate.[1]   These novels, empirically exposing the bankruptcy of the 'Entwicklungsroman' formula for the portrayal of Wolf's generation's experience of the GDR, were written as a challenge to the cultural dogmatism of the final years of the Ulbricht era (1965-71).   Their association with Lenz took the conflict much further.   It signalled a fundamental rejection of the historical authority on which Ulbricht's cultural policy was based - the conception of the GDR's literary heritage derived from Lukács' essays of the exile years and still not significantly modified, despite Lukács' own subsequent loss of favour since 1956-57.

Lukács, it will be recalled, had been able in the 1930s to impose his idea of the form a future German socialist literature should take by winning the historical argument over the centrality of the Wilhelm Meister tradition and the insignificance of 'experimental' works such as Lenz.[2] Furthermore, in his assessment of the most important era within the German cultural heritage (1770-1830), Lukács had accorded a monopoly of authority - similar to the one he sought for himself in the 1930s and 1940s - to the judgements of Goethe and Schiller on what represented the 'healthy' and 'progressive' tendencies of their day.   This meant, for example, that he had passed lightly over the "aristokratische[n] Zug" evident in the unsympathetic treatment the Weimar classicists had meted out to contemporaries such as Lenz and Hölderlin, whose aesthetic and moral priorities conflicted with their own.[3]   Wolf's espousal of Lenz, a generation later, demonstrated that she was no longer prepared to accept this one-sided emphasis on the classicism of Goethe and Schiller, and all that still implied for the literature of her own day.   And conversely, it also gave her a welcome opportunity to legitimise her own dissenting aesthetic and moral perceptions, by showing them to be in accord with those of some of her

literary forbears whose significance within the GDR's
cultural heritage now urgently needed to be recognised.

The historical assumption behind Lukács' exile writing
was that the 'deutsche Misere' - the state of political
and social backwardness which had frustrated the attempts
of German authors since Goethe and Schiller to translate
radical humanistic ideals into contemporary realities [4] -
would be rapidly overcome with the establishment of a
German socialist state. Once the political foundations fo
a genuine 'Gemeinschaft' had been laid, the quality of
identity anticipated in the 'Entwicklingsroman' would come
significantly closer to realisation. The idea of 1945 as
the decisive break with the 'Misere' had remained fundamental to the first two decades of East German literature,
even though its authors had become progressively less eu-
phoric in their accounts of the 'Anderswerden'. The
fictional framework had remained almost invariably the
life-span of the authors themselves, without a more precise
point of reference to the German past than the confidence
that they were in the process of transforming the utopian
aspirations behind 'timeless' literary works into personal
realities. The cultural and political stagnation of the
middle 1960s was, however, now forcing the GDR's leading
creative authors to counter the unabating rhetoric of
socialist 'Gemeinschaft' by more polemical methods than
those insensitively rejected at the Eleventh Plenum. [5]

It would nevertheless have been a startling volte-face
if Wolf had actually suggested that the experience of personal crisis and psychological breakdown central to
Büchner's Lenz, or the protagonist's sense of total alienation from society, now had a comparable 'timeless' relevanc
to the contemporary GDR: for Lenz is the polar opposite
to Wilhelm Meister in the perspective it adopts on the individual's chances of self-fulfilment and on the possibility of progress beyond the 'deutsche Misere'. But she
was not indulging in indiscriminate negative generalisations
of this kind in drawing fresh attention to Büchner's work:
through her elevation of Lenz to the status of an alternative literary model she was primarily exposing the
untenability of the expectations of a rapid transformation
of experience after 1945 - expectations which had not yet
been subjected to historically informed scrutiny in GDR
literature.

Wolf's determination to broaden the base of the cultural
heritage had undoubtedly been strengthened by the active
intervention of Anna Seghers in the debates of the 1963-65
period, as the authors themselves attempted to initiate
their own modest cultural revolution. Seghers, the only
opponent of Lukács from the 1930s still in a position to
change the course of GDR literature, had herself drawn

attention to <u>Lenz</u>, recalling the unique importance it had
had for her generation of radical young writers as "eine
Art Vorspiel der modernen deutschen Literatur". In 1965,
both in her speech to an international writers' conference
at Weimar and in an interview with Wolf, Seghers demonstrated
the need for a fresh exploration of German cultural traditions outside the parameters of the 'Entwicklungsroman'.
The previously neglected line of prose narrative she outlined - from Kleist and Hoffmann, via Heine and the Büchner
of <u>Lenz</u>, to Kafka - was in her view distinguished by its
precision and its closeness to the realities of "eine
düstere Zeit" (in implicit contrast to the work of Goethe
and Schiller). Furthermore, her list of stylistic models
overlapped significantly with her roll of honour of creative personalities whom she saw as the victims of the same
dark era - including Kleist and Büchner again, alongside
Lenz, Hölderlin and Karoline von Günderrode.[6]

These were virtually the same assessments overruled by
Lukács thirty years previously[7] and consigned to obscurity ever since: a matter of months later, the Eleventh
Plenum attempted to suppress the cultural debate in which
these 'historical' arguments had such a crucial legitimising
role to play. Christa Wolf's generation might have been
forgiven for feeling, after December 1965, that socialist
cultural history was, dishearteningly, repeating itself.
This is certainly the underlying mood of her subsequent
essay of 1968 on Anna Seghers, "Glauben an Irdisches",
which dovetails neatly with "Lesen und Schreiben". In
"Glauben an Irdisches", Wolf stresses the strand of continuity linking Seghers' thinking of the 1930s and the present
day (after justifying the cultural conservatism of the
middle stage of Seghers' career - from the early 1940s
until about 1963 - as arising from a decision to concentrate on her responsibilities as a teacher rather than on
the pursuit of literary authenticity). Her analysis of the
Seghers-Lukács correspondence of 1938-39 not only recalls
how historical personalities were used then as pawns in a
modern cultural conflict, but also indicates that the basic
issue is "erstaunlich dauerhaft". The radical artist,
working "unter kunstfeindlichen gesellschaftlichen Ver-
hältnissen", still has to choose between personal integrity - which inevitably brings conflict with authority and
hinders creative development - and retreat from social
responsibility - which enables him to produce misleadingly
rounded, 'classical' works:

> [Man] spürt...bei [Seghers] eine mehr als historische
> Beziehung zu Zweifeln und Verzweiflungen, die über
> hundert Jahre zurückliegen. Eine Ahnung davon, daß
> man scheitern kann, daß eine Entscheidung verlangt

werden könnte zwischen Auflehnung, rückhaltloser
Teilnahme an den Kämpfen der Zeit und dem abgerundeten
vollendeten Werk, dem die Zerrissenheit der Zeit und
ihr Reflex im Künstler nicht mehr anzumerken sein
darf. Die Dringlichkeit dieser Frage ist nach dreißig
Jahren noch zu spüren ...[8]

Viewed in this context, Wolf's espousal in "Lesen und
Schreiben" of Lenz - a work which not only challenges the
inherent optimism of Wilhelm Meister but also has as its
protagonist one of the artistic victims of what is conventionally termed the 'Goethe era' - indicated that the
time had come for a radical reassessment of the pace and
the quality of progress towards socialist self-realisation
in the GDR.[9]

Lenz must have been initially attractive to Wolf as a
literary demonstration that the experience of intense relationship between two kindred personalities, which is at
the heart of her Nachdenken über Christa T., can transcend
the barriers of time and space. She saw the distinctive
quality of Büchner's portrayal of the historical JMR Lenz
- "der volle Einsatz der eigenen moralischen Existenz" -
as arising from his sense of the remarkable similarity
between his own mental disorientation (during his political exile in Alsace in 1835) and that of his protagonist
(in the same Alsatian mountains of 1778, following the
disintegration of the aesthetic revolution of the 'Sturm
und Drang'). Büchner, in Wolf's view, saved himself from
the historical Lenz's fate of permanent mental derangement
only by preserving a precarious narrative separateness from
his fictional Lenz:

Die Variante Wahnsinn-Lenz kann dem nachgeborenen
Büchner nicht ganz fremd gewesen sein. Er kann sie
durchgespielt haben, um ihr zu entrinnen.

Historical distance, she recognised, did not affect the
totality of Büchner's identification with Lenz in this
"Schmelzpunkt" of past and present experience. Her rejection of post-1965 cultural policy evidently led her to
extend this line of argument into a stark general observation that the kind of overwhelming personal crisis undergone by Lenz and Büchner is a phenomenon of "Restaurations
zeiten" - an emotive term with much deeper resonance than
Seghers' earlier references to "Krisenzeit[en]" or "Über-
gangszeiten".[10] It was for Büchner

...ein Konflikt, in dem sich die tausendfache
Bedrohung lebendiger, entwicklungshungriger und
wahrheitssüchtiger Menschen in Restaurationszeiten
gesteigert spiegelt: der Dichter, vor die Wahl
gestellt, sich an unerträgliche Zustände anzupassen

und sein Talent zu ruinieren, oder physisch zugrunde
zu gehen.

This statement is not further amplified, but it seems to
imply that the desperate choice between humiliating compromise and self-destruction did not disappear with Büchner
in the 1830s, any more than did the underlying process of
revolutionary aspirations frustrated by the restoration of
repressive regimes.

The distinctive stylistic features of <u>Lenz</u> which Wolf
has in mind (even though she does not illustrate them
effectively in this brief analysis) are the following:

- it is based on a verifiable documentary source
(Pastor Oberlin's account of Lenz's visit), from which the
author quotes extensively, while bringing his imaginative
resources fully to bear in fleshing out the narrative
skeleton it provides. The finished work is thus a remarkable blend of historically authentic evidence and the
author's profound sense of affinity with his protagonist.

- the narrative perspective switches subtly (in what
Wolf describes as the "vierte Dimension") from the narrator's third-person description of Lenz's crisis to phrases
which are ostensibly narratorial in form, and yet express
Lenz's own thoughts and feelings directly - a pioneering
achievement in the development of the technique of 'free
indirect speech'.[11] The opening description of Lenz's
journey through the mountains is an obvious example:

Den 20. Jänner ging Lenz durchs Gebirg. Die Gipfel
und hohen Bergflächen im Schnee, <u>die Täler hinunter</u>
graues Gestein, grüne Flächen, Felsen und Tannen.
Es war naßkalt: das Wasser rieselte <u>die Felsen
hinunter</u> und sprang über den Weg. Die Äste der
Tannen hingen schwer <u>herab</u> in die feuchte Luft.
Am Himmel zogen graue Wolken, aber <u>alles so dicht</u> -
und dann dampfte der Nebel <u>herauf</u> und strich schwer
und feucht durch das Gesträuch, <u>so träg, so plump.</u>
(65) [12]

- Büchner's language, and especially his range of metaphors to convey Lenz's perceptions, is uniquely vivid and
violent (Wolf uses phrases like "frisch und kühn", "phan-
tastische Genauigkeit"). This is nowhere more so than
when Lenz is exposed to the ravages of the wintry elements:

Nur manchmal, wenn der Sturm das Gewölk in die Täler
warf und es den Wald herauf dampfte, und die Stimmen
an den Felsen wach wurden, bald wie fern verhallende
Donner und dann gewaltig heranbrausten, in Tönen,
als wollten sie in ihrem wilden Jubel die Erde
besingen, und die Wolken wie wilde, wiehernde Rosse

> heransprengten, und der Sonnenschein dazwischen
> durchging und kam und sein blitzendes Schwert an
> den Schneeflächen zog, so daß ein helles, blendendes
> Licht über die Gipfel in die Täler schnitt ...
> riß es ihm in der Brust ...(65)

The concluding phrase here points the way to Büchner's
climactic image of a sensitive personality and his world
rent asunder:

> Alles, was er an Ruhe ... geschöpft hatte, war weg:
> die Welt, die er hatte nutzen wollen, hatte einen
> ungeheuern Riß: er hatte keinen Haß, keine Liebe,
> keine Hoffnung - eine schreckliche Leere ...(81)

Lenz is a work of such unforgettable intensity that
the mere echo of its opening and closing sentences is
enough to release a powerful stream of associations of
mental crisis: "durchs Gebirg gehen" becomes a metaphor
for reaching the point of no return; "so lebte er hin"
(84) marks the final decline into pathetic helplessness
and, for Wolf, is a challenge to future generations to
revolt against the conditions which allow this tragic wast
of human potential to occur.

It would also be totally appropriate to Wolf's reading
of Lenz that the narrative reaches its intellectual peak
with Lenz's attack upon a culture which has lost all touch
with reality because of its obsession with 'exemplary'
characterisation (71-73) - an "Idealismus" which was to
develop beyond Lenz's lifetime into Weimar Classicism,
and, in turn, influence Lukács' conception of Realism.

Lenz is, of course, a text which makes heavy demands on
the reader wishing to understand the personal, social and
cultural factors which have brought its protagonist to the
plight described so graphically in Büchner's narrative,
and it leaves many points open to interpretation. Christa
Wolf's exclusive emphasis on the socio-political causes
of Lenz's breakdown is highly debatable, and yet it is on
this reading (following Anna Seghers) that she bases her
idea of a recurrent pattern of revolutionary idealism
driven to self-destruction in 'Restaurationszeiten'.
Purely as an analysis of Lenz, this part of "Lesen und
Schreiben" would scarcely repay prolonged scrutiny. Its
real importance derives, however, from the fact that both
the subject-matter and the style of Lenz, as understood
by Wolf for her definition of 'epische Prosa', have had
a crucial bearing upon five examples of East German
creative prose: Johannes Bobrowski's Boehlendorff (1965),
Gerhard Wolf's Der arme Hölderlin (1972), Volker Braun's
Unvollendete Geschichte (1975), Christa Wolf's own Kein
Ort. Nirgends (1979) and Erik Neutsch's Forster in Paris

(1981).

In contrast to the previous three chapters, this group of closely related texts does not represent a range of almost simultaneous responses to a commonly perceived literary task. They have been published at significant intervals over a period of almost two decades, and can be viewed as a seismograph for the fluctuating confidence of the GDR's established authors, now fully conscious of the continuing burden of their German past, in their state's capacity to transcend the 'deutsche Misere' in the longer term. For this reason, these texts will be treated as a sequence of responses to important changes in the cultural and political environment, which have convinced their authors of the 'epic' applicability of the Lenz model to present circumstances and then determined the manner in which they have each adapted it.

A society fit for 'moral beings'?

Christa Wolf makes a revealing mistake in her analysis of Lenz. In discussing the 'fourth dimension' of the narrative - the level at which the author's affinity with his protagonist is formally acknowledged - she praises Büchner's skill at switching perspectives: "... wie [er] nicht zufällig unvermittelt, von einem Satz zum anderen vom 'Er' zum 'Ich' übergehen kann". Büchner's use of free indirect speech is, however, more subtle than this: the only instances of first person speech in Lenz occur in conversational passages rather than at dramatic moments of heightened awareness. One plausible reason why Wolf slipped into this error is that her recall of Lenz may have been influenced by a work written by the GDR's most original literary talent of the 1960s, Johannes Bobrowski. His Boehlendorff [13], published in 1965, is a variant on Lenz which first revealed its rich potential as a creative model for GDR authors (over and above the continuing vitality of the original, upon which Anna Seghers had placed greater emphasis). And in Boehlendorff there are decisive moments when Bobrowski switches from third person to first person narration.

Bobrowski's protagonist, living in destitution in the Baltic provinces of the early 19th century, is introduced at second hand by a narrator whose function appears to be that of recording fragments of parochial gossip about an obvious outsider. Then, quite unexpectedly, the mood becomes lyrical and atmospheric: an unspecified 'Ich' emerges, fusing the anxieties of the narrator and his historical counterpart in the present tense:

Regen. Das ist der Regen. Der Regen regnet. Hinter
dem Regen die Leere. Die kommt weiß. Haar, weiß,
eines Geschöpfs ohne Augen, das sein Gesicht, weiß,
heraufhebt über den Rand. Über den Rand. Welchen
Rand? Die Erde war früher eine Scheibe, dann eine
Kugel. Jetzt ist sie wieder eine Scheibe. Und wo
ich hintrete, sinkt sie ein, unter meinen Füßen, die
schwarze Erde gibt nach, mehr als die weiße, sinkt
ein, wo ich umhergehe ...(107-8)

Boehlendorff's problems reach crisis point in natural
surroundings as hostile as those described at the beginning
of Lenz, in a passage which echoes both the deceptively
sober first sentence and the violent imagery of Büchner's
opening scene:

In dieser Nacht ist Boehlendorff unterwegs. Wird ihn
einer sehen, wie er über die Heide rennt? Über ihm
jagen Wolken, verdecken den Mond, geben den Mond
wieder frei, sein Licht schießt wie eine Meute Hunde
im Kraut umher, als wichen sie einander aus, oder
stießen zu, hierhin, dorthin, jetzt wirft es sich
weit voraus wie auf einer Fährte ...(112)

There is no doubt that Christa Wolf was, by 1968, closely
acquainted with Boehlendorff and would have had excellent
grounds for including it in her assessment of the potential
for 'epic prose' in the GDR. Her husband Gerhard had
championed Bobrowski's cause during the latter's tragically
brief period of public recognition in the GDR (between
1961 and his death in 1965), and continued to do so with
critical distinction thereafter. He had drawn
specific attention to the links between Lenz and
Boehlendorff, and had described the salient features of
Bobrowski's prose in terms which are strikingly similar to
his wife's subsequent general comments on 'epic prose'.[14]
In the hostile literary climate of the late 1960s there
may have been good reasons why Christa Wolf did not refer
directly to Bobrowski's achievements: in any case, it was
a debt she was soon to acknowledge generously.

Boehlendorff might so easily have been a second Lenz.
Bobrowski's impressive range of poems on the 'unglückliche
Dichter' of past centuries reveals a special interest in
the Goethe era and an obvious identification with the same
generation of victims singled out by Anna Seghers. His
poem "JRM Lenz", although stimulated by a performance of
Brecht's adaptation of Lenz's Der Hofmeister - "das ABC
der Teutschen Misere"[15] - which he saw in 1963, suggests
a primary indebtedness to Büchner. It uses the opening
sentence of Lenz to signal the onset of the poet's crisis
- "Geht übers Gebirg" - and seems to consider emulating

Büchner's narrative, before acknowledging the futility of
such an aspiration:

> War einiges zu reden,
> erinnere ich mich,
> aber das ist geschehen,
> denk ich, ich hör,
> man hat es
> gehört. [16]

The historical Lenz was doubly important to Bobrowski,
since he was also (like Bobrowski himself) a product of
the German communities in the Baltic provinces, and
Bobrowski's overriding preoccupation as a writer was with
the historical exploitation of the indigenous population
by German colonists.

Bobrowski's creative frustration was, however, short-
lived, for within a year he had discovered an alternative
historical model who also fitted into both these categories
- Casimir Ulrich Boehlendorff (1775-1825) - after gaining
an impression of his life and work in a second-hand anthology of Baltic literature he had received as a birthday
present. Boehlendorff actually suited Bobrowski's intentions
better than Lenz: he was a more obscure figure who could
be treated with considerable poetic licence, and yet he
was remembered in German literary history as the recipient
of two of Hölderlin's most revealing letters (during the
latter's crisis of 1801-02), in the first of which Hölderlin
had underlined their closeness with the phrase "Wir haben
ein Schicksal". [17]

Boehlendorff could thus be associated with the generation of Hölderlin, Kleist and Karoline von Günderrode,
born between 1770 and 1780, for whom the French Revolution
had been a decisive early experience which had encouraged
them, at least on a personal, moral plane, to resist compromise with the corrupt society born of the 'deutsche
Misere'. They could all be viewed as having suffered
acutely in the post-1800 'restoration' signalled by
Napoleon's elevation to the emperorship of France, as
having been ostracised by Germany's cultural and social
establishment and driven finally to suicide or mental derangement. The historical Boehlendorff had been at the
centre of German political and cultural life for a short
period: he had witnessed the abortive Swiss revolution of
1797, been close to Hölderlin and Sinclair in Homburg
thereafter when the South German insurrection was planned,
had been a journalist with the Vossische Zeitung in Berlin
and published two plays. By 1803, however, he was back
in the Baltic provinces, with two decades of obscurity
and isolation ahead of him.

Bobrowski's Boehlendorff is a prose work as short and

deceptively fragmentary as his model. His 'epic' treatmen
of his material reflects the desire both to establish a
clear link with Büchner's <u>Lenz</u>, and to suggest his protagonist's capacity to transcend his existential crisis
through political action. This is reflected in the narrative structure, in which Bobrowski allows himself greater
variety of perspective than Büchner, at times closely
identified with his protagonist, at times conventionally
omniscient. Since part of his purpose is also to satirise
the social establishment by allowing typical personalities
to parade their prejudices in conversational exchanges, he
has to sacrifice much of the intensity of <u>Lenz</u>, which
arises from Büchner's rigorous restriction of the narrativ
to what Lenz experiences directly. The other significant
change is the establishment of a dialogue between author
and reader which, especially in the final part of the
story, confronts the reader with a Brechtian challenge to
draw active conclusions from Boehlendorff's failure.

Bobrowski's portrayal of Boehlendorff's personality is
very dependent on <u>Lenz</u>. The extraordinary intensity of hi
perceptions and his capacity to convey them in striking
metaphors is immediately evident in the passage quoted
above, which echoes the opening section of <u>Lenz</u>. But the
time-span is decisively different: while Büchner restricted himself to the three weeks early in 1778 covered by
his documentary source, Pastor Oberlin's account of Lenz's
visit, and never sought to grant more than a temporary
respite from the mental turmoil, Boehlendorff is allowed
to develop, over two decades and through a succession of
crises, retaining something of the élan of his earlier
radical aspirations. In this respect, of course, Bobrowsk
is able to exploit the fact that Boehlendorff lived in the
political aftermath of the French Revolution, as well as
implying that he displayed the same aesthetic radicalism
as the 'Sturm und Drang' Lenz - a notion which would have
been more credible if the historical Boehlendorff had been
a poet of the stature of his friend Hölderlin and not a
neglected epigone. So it comes about that the revolutionary question directed by Boehlendorff at a Prussian
province untouched by the spirit of change is one deriving
not from his own work but from the Tübingen idealism of
Hölderlin, Hegel and Schelling: "Wie muß eine Welt für
ein moralisches Wesen beschaffen sein?".(115) [18]
Boehlendorff's moral objective - helping to establish the
kind of society he saw emerging during the Swiss revolutio
of 1797 when "uns schien, alle Welt ginge umher mit offene
Armen"(111) - is not one to be abandoned because of the
immense psychological, social and economic strains of
remaining true to it.

In contrast to Lenz, who is haunted by 'voices', hiero-

glyphs and other indefinable threatening forces in his
isolation from society, Boehlendorff finally comes to an
understanding of the malady of his age by obsessively
reading the 'signs' left behind by previous generations:

> Alles aufgeschrieben. Im Buch der Geschichte auf den
> Scheunentoren. In den Wäldern zu lesen, auf den
> abgehauenen Stämmen, und auf der Erde, vor dem
> Regen.(112)

His "Spuren" and "Zeichen" are the evidence of the guilt
incurred by German colonists in their exploitation of the
Baltic provinces, building a civilisation, which, according
to Boehlendorff's recurring vision, will soon be destroyed
through an act of retribution as fearsome as the Old Testa-
ment Flood.

This chapter of the 'deutsche Misere' is illustrated in
a distinctly caricatured manner through Boehlendorff's
treatment, over years of rootlessness, at the hands of the
nobility, the church and the rising bourgeoisie. This
provincial ruling clique knows how to protect itself from
the agrarian and tax reforms initiated in far-off Berlin
after 1806 ("Deutschland" always being contrasted un-
favourably with "hier"). For them, the defeat of Napoleon
offers a sure return to the status quo - "es ordnet sich
alles" - whereas in Boehlendorff's eyes "es bequemt sich".
(114)   Their attitude to the younger generation which has
left its native backwater to study and has thus experienced
the radical changes in the world outside since 1789, is
patronisingly dismissive:

> Das geht ja schon eine ganze Zeit so, die jungen
> Leute fliegen aus, mit den glänzendsten Gaben, wie
> man immer wieder hört, machen Furore, dort draußen,
> und kommen uns schließlich unzufrieden und ungerecht
> zurück, dafür läßt man nun studieren ...(107)

Intellectuals like Boehlendorff who have sown their wild
oats "mit einem ganzen Schwarm Poeten" are tolerated only
as long as they bolster up authority as tame "Hofmeister"
or "Literaten" - producers of purely decorative verse.
If, however, they insist, as Boehlendorff does, on imple-
menting their moral idealism, they are ostracised as "verrückt".(120) 'Madness' here becomes much more than the
threat of mental derangement - considerable though that
threat remains - it is also the judgement of an uncompre-
hending and ruthlessly self-protective establishment upon
its critical opponents.

Bobrowski seems more than a little anachronistic in
portraying his fictional Boehlendorff as drawing political
conclusions from the treatment he receives. He goes underground for periods amongst the German peasantry, even

venturing as far as the "undeutsche Dörfer", emerging late
as a troublemaker to parochial authority. This activity,
though, is ultimately ineffectual, not just because he is
an isolated intellectual, but also because he is a German,
indistinguishable to non-Germans from other members of the
ruling minority - tainted by the sins of the fathers. His
suicide in 1825 is correspondingly assumed to be a final
gesture of despair.

Bobrowski's 'epic' treatment of Boehlendorff - blending
biographical fiction with timeless aspects of the poet's
predicament - ensures that the final, open-ended question
relates to the GDR of his own day:

> Und was tun wir? Errichten wir ein Monument? Eine
> Säule? Lassen jenen Satz einschlagen in den Stein:
> Moralisches Wesen, und: beschaffen sein, und: muß?
> Und setzen dazu, daß er Zeichen gelesen hat?(126)

As well as this implied criticism of the reverential and
ultimately stultifying attitude to authors who become part
of the official 'cultural heritage', the recurrent motifs
on which this fiction is based - "Wie muß eine Welt für
ein moralisches Wesen beschaffen sein?", "Ordnet es sich
oder bequemt es sich?", "Alles aufgeschrieben ..." - represent a warning to the GDR not to betray the moral principles on which social revolution should be based and
decline into another 'restoration'. Against the background
of the modest cultural revolution of 1963-65, the political
implications of Boehlendorff might not have appeared un-
usually challenging. But it had a unique pioneering
vitality, deriving from Bobrowski's skill in exposing the
GDR to the uncompromising moral scrutiny of the victims of
the 'deutsche Misere'.

Direct confirmation of Bobrowski's influence on Christa
Wolf's aesthetic deliberations in "Lesen und Schreiben"
was to come from both Christa and Gerhard Wolf in the
1970s. In her stimulating interview of 1972 with Joachim
Walther, which gave her a valuable opportunity to re-
capitulate her arguments on 'epic prose' and the exemplary
status of Büchner's Lenz, Christa Wolf also included a
specific reference to "Bobrowski's Thema", which for her
meant the unanswered question from Boehlendorff about when
the socio-political conditions for moral self-realisation
might be achieved. The elaboration of this issue is now
described as the supreme task facing GDR authors of the
1970s: it is their moral responsibility to ensure that
the GDR pursues the ultimate goal of "Selbstverwirklichung ihrer Mitglieder" with a genuine sense of urgency
- "ohne Rücksicht auf augenblickliche Schwierigkeiten".
[19]

Boehlendorff's open question and the issues it raises

have underpinned a significant proportion of East German prose writing since the early 1970s, giving substance to Christa Wolf's claim in a subsequent interview - "die Problematik, die in diesem Themenkreis steckt, auch der persönliche Konfliktstoff, reicht für die Literatur einer ganzen Epoche"[20] - which marked the upsurge of confidence in the GDR's potential for development after the Ulbricht era had finally ended in 1971. The full extent of this change can be gauged if we turn our attentions to the next literary adaptation of the Lenz model to appear, Gerhard Wolf's Der arme Hölderlin, which reflects the depths of despair to which many GDR intellectuals had sunk during the period which began soon after Bobrowski's death in 1965, and was to last until Erich Honecker took over the reins of leadership from Ulbricht in 1971.

A new German 'Zerrissenheit'?

The appearance of Gerhard Wolf's Der arme Hölderlin in 1972[21] can be viewed as the culmination of several years' productive involvement with Bobrowski's work, which took him beyond literary criticism and encouraged him to develop his own variant on the 'epic prose' of Boehlendorff. After his sensitive, but conventionally structured, exposition of Bobrowski's life and works in the monograph of 1967, Wolf had adopted the associative, montage approach of Beschreibung eines Zimmers (1971), in which reference to the minutiae of Bobrowski's working and living environment in suburban East Berlin is subtly interwoven with quotations from his writing, in a manner which reveals Wolf's intimate understanding of Bobrowski's personality and artistic methods. Der arme Hölderlin represents a third significant stage in this development, a literary biography arising not least from the desire to show that the warning to the GDR implicit in the open questions of Boehlendorff had become far more urgent in the repressive climate of the 1965-71 period.
In view of Bobrowski's reliance on the writings of Boehlendorff's friend Friedrich Hölderlin for his formulation of Boehlendorff's moral and political views, it was not a major switch of emphasis for Wolf to use Hölderlin's own sufferings as another yardstick for the assessment of the GDR's revolutionary progress. There was in any case nothing surprising about a renewed interest in Hölderlin as an exemplary figure at this time, since the bicentenary of his birth had been officially celebrated in the GDR (as in the Federal Republic) in 1970, although without any prior indication that the old cultural-political con-

flict between Lukács' condemnation of his political naivet
and Becher's praise of the patriotic force of his writing
had been resolved. Alexander Abusch's ceremonial speech,
which culminated in a rhetorical flourish by declaring the
GDR in its existing form to be the fulfilment of Hölderlin'
"Traum einer neuen Menschengemeinschaft", simply glossed
over the problem [22]; far more significant was the less
heralded radio-play by another of the GDR's cultural
pioneers, Stephan Hermlin, who, in 1969, had ended a
lengthy creative crisis with his <u>Scardanelli</u> [23] (the titl
of which recalls one of the 'pseudonyms' adopted by
Hölderlin during the long years of mental illness -
1807-43 - he spent in his tower in Tübingen).

Hermlin had played a vital role in the 1960s in fosterin
young writers and arguing the case (in the essays, broadcasts and interviews later collected as <u>Lektüre 1960-71</u>)
for a more cosmopolitan and sophisticated conception of
literature. The unique position occupied by Hölderlin in
Hermlin's understanding of German culture was spelt out
in an essay of 1969, in which he not only declared the
latter the greatest German poet, but also took up Anna
Seghers' argument that Hölderlin's mental derangement was
caused by the cultural and political backwardness of "eine
Nation, die ihren größten Dichter in den Wahnsinn trieb".
Hermlin then went on to accuse successive generations of
Germans of underestimating Hölderlin's "unerbittliche
Reinheit" and his "Ruf zur Revolution". [24] In his
approach to <u>Scardanelli</u> he recognised that Hölderlin - an
author whose work was still generally available and whose
life had been intimately documented in his own correspondence as well as by his many biographers - could not be
treated with the same poetic licence as the shadowy
Boehlendorff. The life of both writers was marked by an
abrupt separation from the mainstream of German cultural
and political life - Boehlendorff's by his departure from
Berlin to the Baltic provinces in 1803, Hölderlin's by his
certification as insane in 1806 - but, where Bobrowski had
fancifully envisaged a political development for Boehlendor
thereafter, Hermlin stuck closely to the historical evidence and concentrated on a retrospective consideration
of the factors leading to Hölderlin's breakdown. He did
opt for a montage structure, but one which reversed the
proportions of fictionalisation and authentic quotation
in <u>Boehlendorff</u>.

The other main difference is Hermlin's avoidance of
artificial emphasis on the timelessness of Hölderlin's
plight and of the ahistorical identification encouraged
by narrative sleight-of-hand such as Bobrowski's switches
from 'Er' to 'Ich' in mid-sentence. The 'fourth dimensio
of the narrator in this radio-play is more objective than

in <u>Boehlendorff</u>. Hermlin uses what could be called a
collective narrator, made up of the dialogue of two modern
voices (Stimme 1 and Stimme 2) and quotations from the two
best-known contemporary accounts of Hölderlin's life, those
by his landlord Zimmer and the poet Waiblinger. This
narrative structure may be designed to counter the conventional notion of 'madness', in highlighting many examples
of mental acuteness in Hölderlin's later years, but otherwise it allows the documentary evidence to speak for itself, in an account of his life between his student days,
in the revolutionary atmosphere of the early 1790s, and his
breakdown in 1806, offered in a sequence of largely chronological, but thematically distinct, scenes. Many of
Hölderlin's experiences thus described are, for sound
historical reasons, similar to those of Bobrowski's
Boehlendorff: the intellectual's commitment to the moral
ideals behind the French Revolution is followed by his
failure to transform the political realities of Southern
Germany in 1798-99; and the miserable existence of the
'Hofmeister' again represents the only means of economic
survival. Hermlin, however, also focuses on areas of
conflict which Bobrowski passed over: the sphere of personal relationships, where the enforced termination of
Hölderlin's clandestine love for Susette Gontard has
destructive emotional consequences, and the literary
world, in which so much despair results from the indifference of the cultural establishment - Goethe and
Schiller in the process of defining their Weimar Classicism - to unorthodox literary talents such as Hölderlin.

    <u>Scardanelli</u> provides the basis for a sound historical
assessment of Hölderlin. Hermlin is careful not to allow
it to become a purely partisan portrayal of Hölderlin as
the helpless victim of society: his readiness to differentiate is particularly evident in his account of why Goethe
and Schiller failed to support his protagonist.[25]
Consequently, when the motif of Utopia is introduced (and
not, as we shall see, for the only time in this context)
- "Und kein Ort für ihn, keine Stelle, nirgendwo, kein
Mundvoll Luft zum Atmen?"(29) - the narrative is investigating whether Hölderlin's total divorce from social and
cultural life might have been avoided. The temptation to
draw parallels with the GDR might nevertheless be
strengthened by the fact that this question forms the
climax of a section structured around excerpts from the
rhetorically forceful lament in Hölderlin's <u>Hyperion</u> on
the 'deutsche Misere', such as the following:

    Barbaren von alters her, durch Fleiß und Wissenschaft
    und selbst durch Religion barbarischer geworden,
    tiefunfähig jedes göttlichen Gefühls ... Handwerker

siehst du, aber keine Menschen, Denker, aber keine
Menschen, Priester, aber keine Menschen, Herrn und
Knechte. Junge und gesetzte Leute, aber keine
Menschen.

The fact that the 'timeless' accusing statement - "Ich
kann kein Volk mir denken, das zerrißner wäre, wie die
Deutschen"[26] - is omitted from this quotation may not
appear insignificant to the reader familiar with <u>Hyperion</u>:
there is, however, nothing in the narrative structure of
<u>Scardanelli</u> which encourages him explicitly to consider
'epic' analogies.

When Gerhard Wolf came to write his <u>Der arme Hölderlin</u>
he must have been intimately acquainted with Hermlin's
radio-play; he had, moreover, decided to adopt a technique
developed from Bobrowski's <u>Boehlendorff</u> for his treatment
of the Hölderlin material. A first reading of <u>Der arme
Hölderlin</u> will indicate that almost every detail of
<u>Scardanelli</u> has been incorporated into this extensive
prose portrait, almost as if it represented little more
than a first draft. Wolf's <u>Hölderlin</u> is thus, like
<u>Scardanelli</u>, a montage composition which draws heavily on
Hölderlin's letters, poetry and <u>Hyperion</u> in covering the
same historical period of 1792-1806, and which uses the
records of Waiblinger and Zimmer as a framework for a
retrospective consideration of Hölderlin's fortunes over
these years. There are changes in presentation: the
post-1806 framework is neatly distinguished from the
central period of Hölderlin's creative life as a succession
of ten short scenes punctuating the nine main chapters;
and the basic chronology of Hermlin's account is dis-
regarded, with the evident intention of making the year
1799 - with its revolutionary hopes and bleak disillusionment - into the book's climactic finale. Although the
analysis of Hölderlin's life which emerges is not significantly different (the political, economic, emotional and
cultural pressures contributing to his mental derangement
are separately highlighted in thematically organised sections, just as in <u>Scardanelli</u>), Wolf's more extensive
treatment enables him to provide a detailed picture of the
political and social context.

The most striking innovation comes at the level of the
narrator, where Wolf discards the collective, objective
framework of <u>Scardanelli</u> in favour of a more personalised
and challenging voice, which has unmistakable echoes of
the narrator in both <u>Lenz</u> and <u>Boehlendorff</u>. The period
during which Hölderlin's mental equilibrium is irretrievably destroyed is seen as the one between January
1801 and the summer of 1802, marked by the journey to
Switzerland to take up his final post as private tutor,

his last despairing approach to an uncaring Schiller, the abortive emigration to France and the death of his beloved Susette Gontard. Wolf clearly wishes to present this as another variant on the 'Lenz crisis', and signals this by beginning and ending the chapter with what are virtually Büchner's own words: "Im Jänner 1801 geht Hölderlin übers Gebirg", "Hölderlin ... lebt da so hin".(27-32)

Bobrowski and his Boehlendorff permeate the narrative. One of Wolf's most obvious additions to Hermlin's material is his introduction of Boehlendorff into the text as a close friend of Hölderlin's (sections 10 and 18), in scenes which reflect the painstaking research of a Bobrowski scholar into the historical facts behind the fictional Boehlendorff. His intention is to stress the typicality of Hölderlin's predicament, especially in the tenth section, which takes as its leitmotif Hölderlin's phrase in his letter of December 1801 to Boehlendorff - "Wir haben ein Schicksal" - and depicts the latter's insensitive treatment at the hands of the cultural and social establishment during his years in Berlin.

Then there are interpretative hints which the reader familiar with Bobrowski's work will not overlook. The origins, and the content, of Boehlendorff are evoked at the point when Wolf's account begins to overlap with Bobrowski's (i.e. in 1803, when Boehlendorff leaves Berlin to return to the Baltic provinces). Wolf quotes phrases from the account of Boehlendorff's life from which Bobrowski drew his inspiration, including the appeal of 1809 for financial support - "Auf diesem ungewöhnlichen Weg ... Infolge meines ökonomischen Unvermögens ..." - which opens Bobrowski's story. Wolf quickly breaks off, however, with the phrase "aber das ist bekannt", which recalls Bobrowski's disclosure of his source and his reasons for concentrating on Boehlendorff, rather than the better known Lenz (52, Boehlendorff 126). When Boehlendorff makes his second appearance in Der arme Hölderlin, he tells Hölderlin "ich werde alles aufschreiben", a phrase which derives from Bobrowski's motif 'alles aufgeschrieben' rather than anything Boehlendorff ever said. Once again, Wolf avoids going over familiar ground - Boehlendorff's experience of the Swiss revolt of 1797 - by assuming his reader's knowledge of Bobrowski's story - "Aber das wißt ihr ja selbst".(97-8)

Once this degree of common ground with Boehlendorff is established, it seems legitimate to inquire how Wolf seeks to achieve a comparable 'epic' effect to that achieved by Bobrowski with his challenging question - "wie muß eine Welt für ein moralisches Wesen beschaffen sein?" - which Bobrowski describes as the "Satz, den Boehlendorff mitbringt, wohin er geht". Not only does Wolf establish a

direct link with this motif, through a further quotation
from the fragmentary 'Systemprogramm des deutschen Idealismus' from which it comes: here the goal of restoring
"Poesie" to its original status as "Lehrerin der Menschheit" is declared.(76) He also draws attention to another
revolutionary slogan, a "Satz" which echoes as ineffective-
ly in the streets of Hölderlin's Southern Germany as
Boehlendorff's did in the Baltic provinces:

> Nur der Tod oder eine Regierungsänderung wird das
> Vaterland von den Ungeheuern befreien.(18)

If this 'Satz' is indeed intended as an equivalent of
Bobrowski's, then its implications for the GDR of the last
years of the Ulbricht era would obviously have been explosive. But - perhaps for this reason - it is left rather
more ambiguous, not repeated elsewhere to give it the status of a motif, not 'open' enough to prove anything' in
isolation, just another of the many moments in the text
which evoke an unchanging bleakness of experience.
Even without these specific analogies between the two
works, Der arme Hölderlin can be seen as a literary endorsement of Bobrowski's epic method. Another hint as to
how it should be read can be found in Wolf's analysis of
Bobrowski's prose style in his monograph of 1967: the
historical subject-matter "ist ... eigentlich nur Vorwand,
ist Verfremdung"; he is seeking the 'trigonometric point'
at which time loses its purely linear quality, with the
aim "Vergangenheit aktuell zu machen, Gegenwartsverant-
wortung am geschichtlichen Vorgang zu messen - hier wie
dort gleichzeitig zu sein"[27]; he further breaks down
the conventional division between past and present time
with his use of conversational present-tense narration.
Der arme Hölderlin is written with exactly the same awareness that moments of such 'timeless' identity will occur.
The reader is at times explicitly reminded of this possibility:

> In welcher Zeit lebt [Hölderlin] da, und in
> welchem Raum ...?(12)
> Da war Zukunft. Da wird Vergangenheit. Was ist
> Gegenwart?(41)

Although Wolf refrains from switching his narrative perspective in the manner of a Büchner or a Bobrowski from
the narrator to his protagonist, he makes extensive use
of the more overt 'Verfremdung' of letting the historical
Hölderlin speak for himself, in a montage of quotations
from his letters and his creative writing. Wolf thereby
uses the available historical evidence to maximum effect,
since Hölderlin's own writing records his most intimate
feelings as vividly as any subsequent author of bio-

graphical fiction could possibly ask. Hölderlin's highly
receptive, but chaotic state of mind during his visit to
France in 1802 - the period of his 'Lenz crisis' - is
evoked in a confusion of fragments from his letter of
November 1802 to Boehlendorff and his poems "Andenken"
and "Das nächste Beste"[28]:

> Das gewaltige Element, das Feuer des Himmels und
> die Stille der Menschen, ihr Leben in der Natur
> und ihre Eingeschränktheit und Zufriedenheit. Die
> letzten Tage bin ich schon im Frühling gewandert.
> Die schöne Garonne und die Gärten von Bordeaux.
> Sie werden glücklich sein, sagt mein Konsul. Die
> traurige einsame Erde. Die Hirten des südlichen
> Frankreich und einzelne Schönheiten. Wenn im
> Olivenland in liebenswürdiger Fremde die Sonne
> sticht. Männer und Frauen, die in der Angst des
> patriotischen Zweifels und des Hungers erwachsen
> sind ...
> Nicht ist es gut, seellos von sterblichen Gedanken
> zu sein. Mancher trägt Scheu, an die Quelle zu
> gehn; es beginnet nämlich der Reichtum im Meere.
> Offen die Fenster des Himmels und freigelassen der
> Nachtgeist, der hat unser Land beschwätzet mit
> Sprachen viel, unbändigen, und den Schutt gewälzet
> bis diese Stunde. (30-31)

It seems clear that Wolf intends the timelessness of many
such intensely personal statements to shine through the
contorted and dated manner of self-expression. In any
case, he makes his point about the continuing relevance
of Hölderlin's experience more explicitly at many important
stages in the narrative, with the help of rhetorical
questions, speculative comments and editorial reassurances,
following quotations which could be felt to have a distinctly modern applicability. It is no coincidence that
the quotations thus highlighted fall into certain categories, of which the most important are:
- firstly, a radical disillusionment with the authoritarian
state:

> Du räumst dem Staate denn doch zuviel Gewalt ein.
> Er darf nicht fordern, was er nicht erzwingen kann.
> Was aber die Liebe gibt und der Geist, das läßt sich
> nicht erzwingen. Das laß er unangetastet. Der weiß
> nicht, was er sündigt, der den Staat zur Sittenschule
> machen will. Immerhin hat das den Staat zur Hölle
> gemacht, daß ihn der Mensch zu seinem Himmel machen
> wollte.
> Das steht im Hyperion. (93)

- secondly, references to the alienated existence of ordinary citizens:

> Die Menschen fürchten sich voreinander, und darum
> gönnen sie sich wohl Speise und Trank, aber nichts,
> was die Seele nährt, und können es nicht leiden,
> wenn etwas, was sie sagen und tun, in anderen in
> Flammen verwandelt wird.
> Mit wem spricht [Hölderlin] da?(10)

- and finally, the destructive effects of the suppression of the morally inspiring voice of the poet:

> Bleibt ihm, als Asyl, nur noch Gesang?

> Ich begreife nicht, ruft er verstört, wie manche
> große, reine Formen im Einzelnen und Ganzen so
> wenig heilen und helfen - vor der allmächtigen,
> alles beherrschenden Not.

> Aber wer hört ihn da noch? Versteht, was er meint?

> Wie ein mächtiges Schicksal, das gründliche Menschen
> so herrlich bilden konnte, die schwachen nur mehr
> zerreißt.(106)[29]

This is much more politically provocative than <u>Boehlendorff</u> and its ambiguous question about a society capable of nurturing 'moral beings'.

<u>Der arme Hölderlin</u> can also be seen as a response to the crippling narrowness of the SED's cultural policy in the 'Restaurationszeit' 1965-71. More explicitly than in Christa Wolf's essays of 1968, it suggests similarities between the dominance of Goethe and Schiller as literary arbiters during Hölderlin's most productive years, and the bureaucratic control of culture in the GDR. Wolf not only emphasises the patronising attitude of Goethe and Schiller to poets like Hölderlin (scrutinising their correspondence, as Hermlin did before him); he also takes Hölderlin's two poems "An die klugen Ratgeber" as expressions of his response to this insensitive treatment. In another of the sections of <u>Der arme Hölderlin</u> to conclude with a challenging rhetorical question - "Wo? Wo seid ihr?" - terms such as "Kunstrichter" and "kluger Ratgeber" take on more modern connotations, as does Hölderlin's spirited response to Schiller's attempt to edit out the 'objectionable' parts of "An die klugen Ratgeber". There is another echo of <u>Boehlendorff</u> in the emphasis Wolf gives to Hölderlin's line - "Und mir, mir ratet nicht, mich zu bequemen ..." - and perhaps more than a hint of personal acrimony in Wolf's modification of Hölderlin's - "Jetzt mordet ihn der sanfte kluge Rat" - into the statement - "[Schiller]... streicht, mildert, mordet mit klugem sanftem Rat".(74-77) The totally negative image of Goethe and Schiller which Wolf chooses

to convey - especially in the light of Hermlin's more
balanced historical assessment of their role, in his
Scardanelli - has clearly much more to do with his polemical intentions than with his view of Weimar Classicism. [30]
  Viewed as a piece of creative writing, Der arme Hölderlin
gives rise to serious misgivings. Its conception is highly derivative, with much of the historical content taken
over from Hermlin and many stylistic features imitated
from Bobrowski (however understandable the desire to draw
attention to Bobrowski's achievement might have been). It
reads at times as an academic exercise - full of moments
of recognition for the initiated, and often disturbingly
eclectic - rather than a work of imaginative fiction in
the tradition of Lenz and Boehlendorff.
  In political terms, Wolf has obviously left himself
open to charges of didactic over-simplification and of
obscuring major achievements of GDR society where he treats
historically authentic material as a parable for his own
day. It would, however, be a great injustice not to
appreciate the reasons for its polemical excesses or to
suggest that a committed author like Gerhard Wolf intended
Der arme Hölderlin to read as a disguised assertion that
there is no essential difference between 'the state' in
1800 and today, or between Goethe and Schiller in their
capacity as 'Kunstrichter' and the GDR's cultural politicians, or that the famous description of the 'Zerrissenheit' of the Germans (revealingly omitted in Scardanelli,
but quoted directly by Wolf on p. 60) now applies directly
to the GDR. Nevertheless, its political implications are
as radical as those of any other piece of creative writing
published in the period following the official rejection
of Nachdenken über Christa T..

'Werther's sorrows' in a 'non-antagonistic class society'

  Virtually at the same time as Der arme Hölderlin
appeared, Gerhard Wolf's younger colleague Volker Braun
was pinpointing the weaknesses of texts which rely for their
contemporary political impact on the ambiguities of
"Sklavensprache":

    Ich habe ein großes Mißtrauen gegen die bei uns
    gängige Methode, antike Storie zu benutzen, um
    Probleme unserer Revolution abzuhandeln, ein Ver-
    fahren der Sklavensprache, die die Literatur bis
    heute fließend beherrscht. Es ist aber im Grunde
    nicht legitim, heutige Inhalte mit den Vorgängen
    der Klassengesellschaft zu transportieren, das
    ist unfair.

The far-reaching importance of this statement is that it was made by an outspoken opponent of a conventional Socialist Realism artificially cut off from historical problems in which the individual's conflicts are neatly resolved against a lifeless socio-political backcloth – stories constrained "im bloß Ökonomischen", where society is a "Milieu" rather than a "menschlich sich bildende Landschaft". For Braun, just as much as for Bobrowski, Christa Wolf and Gerhard Wolf, "Geschichtsbewußtsein ist Selbstbewußtsein", and the distinctive feature of genuine socialis literature – in contrast to the complete "Gedächtnisschwund of Western art – is its historical dimension, especially in the form of a critical involvement with its cultural heritage. [31] Implicit in what Braun was arguing, however is that prose-works like <u>Boehlendorff</u> and <u>Der arme Hölderlin</u> by hinting at analogies between the Germany of Goethe's day and the GDR, obscure the fundamental qualitative distinctions. (By the same token, of course, the weakness of Büchner's <u>Lenz</u> as a work of the mid-1830s would also be that its profound psychological insights into the creative personality in crisis dominate to the extent that it fails to reveal anything specific about the social conditions of his day, however clearly Büchner's own courageous politica. commitment is illuminated elsewhere in his writings.)

Braun argued that an historically conscious literature would show how each distinctive phase of man's progress towards socialism is characterised by a specific structure of political power. GDR authors creating this quality of literature would therefore need to reverse the proportions of 'present' and 'past' content established by Bobrowski or Gerhard Wolf, to enable the fictional action to be firmly anchored in the present-day GDR, with the crucial motifs from the cultural model being introduced into the text in a more disguised form – a technique which Braun had already developed most effectively in his own poetry and drama. [32]

What separates <u>Der arme Hölderlin</u> and Volker Braun's open advocacy of an historical approach involving direct criticism of the 'Machtstrukturen' of his own day, is, of course, the change of political leadership in 1971, when Erich Honecker took over as First Secretary of the Central Committee of the SED from Walter Ulbricht. The radical ideological and cultural changes announced by Honecker in the months following his elevation to the leadership effectively acknowledged how correct Christa Wolf's generation of authors had been to stand by the creative insights and moral perspective they had reached by the mid-1960s. Since their portrayal of GDR society after the watershed of 1965 had shown just how far removed it was from the propagandist conception of an harmonious community,

it must have been a welcome relief to them to see the
official designation of the GDR changed, at the Eighth
Party Conference in 1971, from "sozialistische Menschengemeinschaft" to "nichtantagonistische Klassengesellschaft".
They must have felt further encouraged by the vote of confidence in their independent powers of critical evaluation
offered by Honecker in December 1971:

> Wenn man von der festen Position des Sozialismus
> ausgeht, kann es meines Erachtens auf dem Gebiet
> von Kunst und Literatur keine Tabus geben. Das
> betrifft sowohl die Fragen der inhaltlichen Gestal-
> tung als auch des Stils - kurz gesagt: die Fragen
> dessen, was man die künstlerische Meisterschaft
> nennt.[33]

This improvement in the cultural climate was, however,
rather too rapid to be received without the underlying
suspicions reflected in the narrator's searching questions
to his readership in Der arme Hölderlin. As Braun argued
at a conference only three months after Honecker's pro-
nouncement, it was not enough to assert that there were no
taboos for GDR authors, when "unsere Klassenlage und Herr-
schaftsstruktur" were reflected in the taboos which
undeniably still existed in GDR society, such as the pro-
hibition of "Mitbestimmung" in every sphere. The qualitative difference which set the GDR above earlier societies
was, in Braun's view, that fact that its continued existence
did not depend on the preservation of such taboos: on the
contrary, "diese Gesellschaft kann nur weiterexistieren
und sich entwickeln, indem sie ihre Tabus aufgibt, das
heißt, indem sie sich selbst rigoros anrührt".[34]
Nevertheless, the climate of open discussion of past
errors in the field of cultural policy, which prevailed
between 1971 and 1975, encouraged the publication by the
GDR's established creative writers of the wealth of self-
analytical writing which, inter alia, was intended to
transform public attitudes to the groups of novels discussed in Chapters 2-4 of this study. Volumes such as
Meinetwegen Schmetterlinge, Eröffnungen, Was zählt, ist die
Wahrheit, together with the proceedings of the stimulating
Writers' Congress of November 1973,[35] are a vital element
in the understanding of the beginnings of the Honecker
era as well as of the earlier course of GDR literature.
The same generation of authors was now also encouraged to
move on to the next stage in the seemingly inexhaustible
process of taking stock of their own lifetime's experience,
producing works such as Fühmann's 22 Tage oder die Hälfte
des Lebens (1973), de Bruyn's Die Preisverleihung (1972),
Christa Wolf's Kindheitsmuster (1976) and Hermann Kant's
Der Aufenthalt (1977).

The distinctively new quality in these authors' work
of the 1970s is, however, its historical focus. Their
reluctance to depict the GDR of the 1970s in conventional
fictional terms seems partly to reflect the difficulties
(both of a literary and of a political nature) of portraying its distressingly slow progress towards the goal of
'Gemeinschaft'. But there were other compelling reasons
for this second major demonstration of independence from
official cultural policy (following the one discussed in
Chapter 4), which led these authors to turn their attentions to their German cultural heritage, and especially to
the age of Goethe. Apart from the preoccupation with
Büchner's Lenz and the temptation to identify with other
'suffering poets', they have contributed enormously to the
understanding and enjoyment of many German writers of this
era who had previously been neglected in the GDR because
of the narrowness of the classical canon. The variety of
their endeavours has been quite remarkable (and has served
as a further reminder of the mediocrity of so much professional literary criticism in the GDR): they have
written biographical essays, given commemorative speeches,
edited new editions of neglected authors' writing and
compiled anthologies - quite apart from their own extensiv
exploitation of this rich literary heritage in their own
creative work. And it should be stressed, in a chapter
which is drawing special attention to their literary involvement with the 'victims' of the age of Goethe - Lenz,
Boehlendorff, Hölderlin, Kleist and Karoline von Günderrode
- that there has been a marked degree of identification in
this literary-critical work with authors who can be regarded as its 'survivors' (and thus as rather more
encouraging models for today) - Jean Paul Richter,
Heinrich Heine, ETA Hoffmann and Bettina von Arnim.[36]
    It is no surprise, however, that the most popular and
influential work of the early years of Honecker's leadership was a further variant on the cultural stereotype of
the suffering poet, and one set in the contemporary GDR,
Ulrich Plenzdorf's Die neuen Leiden des jungen W. (1972-
73). It does seem ironical, with hindsight, that this
crucially important literary text was originally conceived
as a film script, and by an author not previously involved in the evolution of this historically rooted
realism. Die neuen Leiden certainly owes its reputation
to a combination of factors, and it has often been argued
that its impact has largely to do with Plenzdorf's stimu-
latingly original presentation of the language and the
everyday experience of GDR teenagers, and very little to
do with the parallels in his plot to Goethe's Die Leiden
des jungen Werther, or the quotations from Werther's
letters with which the text is liberally sprinkled.[37]

While this may be largely correct, it would be most un-
fortunate if its pivotal importance in the process of
establishing a new sense of cultural continuity in GDR
literature (whether consciously intended by Plenzdorf or
not) were to be overlooked as a result.

The significance of the Werther material has also been
extensively and authoritatively analysed, but without
locating Die neuen Leiden in the context of the desire of
other GDR authors to identify with poets in the Lenz tradition - or rather with the image of these poets they had
moulded from other literary and biographical sources.[38]
The temperamental similarities between Werther and the
other casualties of the same era of German history scarcely need to be underlined, nor does the close author-
protagonist relationship in Werther and Lenz (even though
the narrative means of expressing it are more distanced in
Goethe's novel). There is also no doubt about the gulf
separating the classical Goethe - the unsympathetic conformist portrayed in Der arme Hölderlin - from the radical
and subjective 'Sturm und Drang' Goethe, in the eyes of
East German authors of today.

The direct link between Der arme Hölderlin and Die neuen
Leiden is the way in which the narrator - here the young
Edgar Wibeau from his posthumous vantage point "über den
Jordan" - draws his reader's special attention to the
continuing relevance of the experience of his historical
hero. The tone is, of course, strikingly original.
Wibeau's conditioned irreverence towards quoting from the
'classics' arises from the over-valuation of uncritical
learning by rote in the GDR school system. But he is
also a narrator observed in the process of discovering
the timeless significance of material he originally exploits for its purely humorous potential. His unofficial
education begins when he overcomes his superficial hostility to the linguistically obscure manner in which Werther
expresses his feelings: "Leute! War das ein Krampf! ...
Das heißt, so ganz blöd war es auch wieder nicht. Ich kam
einfach nicht mit dieser Sprache zu Rande".(43) As his
sense of intimacy with "Old Werther" grows, so also
does he recognise basic similarities in their experience:
"Langsam gewöhnte ich mich an diesen Werther ... Der Mann
wußte Bescheid".(57) The quotations which are intended to
stand out are those which do more than establish enter-
taining analogies between Werther's relationship with
Lotte and Albert on the one hand, and Wibeau's with Charlie
and Dieter on the other. They convey a harsh message
about the impoverishment of individual experience, and the
impossibility of self-realisation, in an authoritarian
society dominated by the work ethic:

Es ist ein einförmiges Ding um das Menschengeschlecht.
Die meisten verarbeiten den größten Teil der Zeit,
um zu leben, und das bißchen, das ihnen von Freiheit
übrigbleibt, ängstigt sie so, daß sie alle Mittel
aufsuchen, um es loszuwerden.(41,73)

Und daran seid ihr alle schuld, die ihr mich in das
Joch geschwatzt und mir so viel von Aktivität vor-
gesungen habt. Aktivität! ... Ich habe meine Ent-
lassung ... verlangt! ... Bringe das meiner Mutter
in einem Säftchen bei.(14,74)[39]

While Gerhard Wolf, in his portrayal of Hölderlin, can go
no further than posing his rhetorical questions about the
applicability of his key quotations to the GDR, Plenzdorf
has embedded 'historical' statements like these in a text
in which the reader has every opportunity to relate them
to a specific East German context.
What emerges from Wibeau's experiences is in fact much
more encouraging: there is nothing inevitable about the
negative features of GDR society confronting him: it seem
more a matter of one of the two conflicting approaches
to socialism having gained the upper hand. The issue is
summed up in the difficulties his name appears to create
for those in authority: they invariably read it as
'Wiebau', with the inescapable connotations of 'Aufbau' -
post-war reconstruction and the work ethic - while the
hero himself regards his Huguenot roots as a distinctive
part of his identity which is threatened in a society with
a blinkered sense of its own heritage. The perspective of
the 17 year-old protagonist is (deliberately?) too restricted to offer him any political insights into the nature of
the authority he comes to reject. The remarkable thing
about his development is the ease with which he changes
course, from being a model pupil amidst the parochial
drabness of Mittenberg, to the life of a temporary drop-
out in his abandoned summer house in Berlin. This implies
the complete superficiality of an education system dependent on learning from the example of others ('das Vorbild')
to conform with the status quo ('sich einreihen') and thus
become a productive member of society ('Musterknabe') -
to use some of Edgar's most hated words.
As this system allows too little scope for fantasy,
experimentation, and humorous exposure of its faults, its
products become split personalities, whose public and
private selves are poles apart. Thus, as Plenzdorf would
have it, Edgar is simply giving himself the opportunity
to discover his 'true' self when he liberates himself from
the constraints of Mittenberg. The account which the
narrator Wibeau provides of his last months is contradictory, with moments of self-critical insight alternating

with adolescent self-dramatisation (in a perfectly plausible way). But the evidence does tend to suggest that his withdrawal from organised education, with scope for living on an empirical 'trial and error' basis for the first time, has a rapid maturing effect on his approach both to personal relationships and to work as a self-fulfilling activity (if also dangerous for the ill-prepared 'Selbsthelfer'). Furthermore, Edgar's identification with the GDR is never at risk. He is sure that the hero of his other favourite piece of literature, The Catcher in the Rye, whom he tends to confuse with its author, would feel perfectly at home there:

> [Dieser Salinger] soll zu uns rüberkommen ... Mittenberg war natürlich ein Nest gegen New York, aber erholt hätte er sich hervorragend bei uns ...(25)

Later he states quite categorically:

> Kein einigermaßen intelligenter Mensch kann heute was gegen den Kommunismus haben ...

It would all be much easier for adolescents like himself, he adds, if GDR authority would recognise that they need to throw over the traces in order to prove themselves:

> Aber ansonsten sind sie dagegen. Zum Dafürsein gehört kein Mut. Mutig will aber jeder sein. Folglich ist er dagegen. Das ist es.(59)

Edgar is no "verkanntes Genie" in the artistic sense, as he likes to pretend (18): his 'abstract' painting represents a piece of superficial role-playing, and he regards success in the world of culture as nothing better than a confidence trick. What he does possess, however, is the kind of personal vitality, the potential for relationships and innovation, which could be crucial to the GDR's development. It is this quality of 'genius' - liberated from its historical and elitist associations and directed towards the wider aspiration to achieve self-fulfilment in a socialist society - which Plenzdorf highlights through his critical portrayal of Edgar Wibeau.

The unfinished historical task

Where Die neuen Leiden disappoints is in its failure to make the analogy between Wibeau and Goethe's Werther more than superficial. In Wibeau's constant talk of his "Leiden" - "das war ein echtes Leiden von mir", etc. - the word has been devalued to mean little more than 'problem' or 'fad'. His actual sufferings at the hands

of society are relatively minor and capable of being resolved (had he not accidentally electrocuted himself).
Wibeau is not subject, as Werther is, to an inner conflict
from which he cannot escape and which ultimately destroys
him.

It is precisely this criticism which Volker Braun expresses, through the thoughts of another fictional GDR
teenager, in his Unvollendete Geschichte (1975), a work
intended to put into practice the conception of historical
consciousness which he articulated so persuasively after
1971. Early in 1974 (the fictional events can be clearly
dated from the textual evidence), the 18 year-old protagonist of Unvollendete Geschichte, Karin, finds herself
faced with a conflict which has many similar elements to
that of Wibeau but actually does threaten her entire
psychological equilibrium. Both are the children of Party
stalwarts (Edgar never meets his wayward father until he
leaves Mittenberg), and grow up under great moral pressures
to set an example to others at school and during their
vocational training. But while Edgar merely adopts the
public role of 'Musterknabe' until he blots his copybook
by dropping a metal plate on his supervisor's toe and
escapes from his home environment, Karin initially experiences a total accord between her own and her parents'
aspirations. When this harmonious, if sheltered, world
is suddenly disrupted by her parents' incomprehensible
antagonism to her boy-friend, the effects are correspondingly much more severe than anything Edgar undergoes.

It is in the midst of this crisis of divided loyalties
which overwhelms Karin for some months that she discovers
a copy of Die neuen Leiden (in her brother's bedroom -
a more conventional setting for a literary experience
than the 'Plumpsklo' in which Edgar discovers Werther).
Almost surprisingly, given its immense popularity amongst
young people in the GDR in 1972-73, she has not hitherto
read it, although she is aware of the defensive way in
which the Party leadership has reacted to Plenzdorf's
success. She recalls Honecker's phrase that writers who
attempt to force the responsibility for their own sufferings
upon society - "eigene Leiden der Gesellschaft aufzuoktroy-
ieren" - are not conveying what is qualitatively new about
the GDR of the 1970s.[40] Karin enjoys reading Die neuen
Leiden and finds it authentic, but it gives her no insights
into human suffering in the way that Goethe's Werther
(which she has studied as a set-text in school) did. In
a remarkably mature assessment of the differences between
the two works, Karin notes that Edgar only comes into
superficial conflict with society, whereas Werther's
experience rends him and his environment asunder:

> Das Ungeheure in dem <u>Werther</u> war, daß da ein Riß
> durch die Welt ging, und durch ihn selbst. Das war
> eine alte Zeit. Und doch war auch in all dem
> Äußeren ein <u>Inneres</u>, W. drang nur nicht hinein, ein
> tieferer Widerspruch - den man finden müßte! Wie
> würde ein Buch sein - und auf sie wirken, in dem
> einer heute an den Riß kam ... in den er stürzen
> mußte ...(45-6)

Naturally, <u>Unvollendete Geschichte</u> itself is the book
which Karin desperately needs at that moment - a more
profound updating of the sufferings of a Werther in a
contemporary socialist context.

The historical dimension which Braun's story shares
with <u>Die neuen Leiden</u> may not be obvious at first, but
this is because Braun has adhered, in most respects, to
his own principle of avoiding 'Sklavensprache' statements.
Yet Karin's thoughts do include a significant clue to
Braun's historical model: her observation on the "Riß"
which destroys Werther and his environment is a disguised
quotation from the moment in Büchner's <u>Lenz</u> when the
protagonist's mental balance is irretrievably upset:

> ... die Welt, die [Lenz] hatte nutzen wollen, hatte
> einen ungeheuern Riß; er hatte keinen Haß, keine
> Liebe, keine Hoffnung - eine schreckliche Leere ...[41]

As with <u>Boehlendorff</u> and <u>Der arme Hölderlin</u>, the paradigm
of the Lenz crisis is being applied to a kindred figure,
but, following Plenzdorf's example, Braun is demonstrating
that neither poets in general, nor the 'suffering poets'
of the Goethe era in particular, have a monopoly on this
degree of suffering.

Karin is portrayed by Braun as an exemplary teenager
for the GDR of the 1970s, as a complement perhaps to the
less conventionally dynamic Wibeau. She has many of the
classical qualities of the 'Entwicklungsroman' protagonist:
she is idealistic, introverted, passively exposed to the
influence of her elders and to the unpredictable accidents
of life. She is also a woman, in a state which has always
officially encouraged female emancipation, and an aspiring
journalist committed to the open discussion of issues
crucial to the future of socialism. It is therefore clear
that when the impressive progress of a true 'Vorbild' is
disrupted by the apparently irrational interference of
authority figures at home and at work, the resulting conflict will be far greater than anything faced by the more
precocious and sceptical Wibeau.

It becomes, indeed, a contemporary crisis of <u>Lenz</u> proportions. After her father's unspecific attack on the
character of her boy-friend Frank in the opening scene,

Karin's superficially harmonious childhood comes to an
abrupt end. The bus journey, in the New Year of 1974, to
begin her journalistic training, marks her loss of equilibrium:

> Am 2. Januar fuhr sie nach M. ... Sie schaute in die
> plane Landschaft hinaus, die großen Felder, ein
> dünner Schnee fiel und verschwand am Boden. Die
> zwei herverschlagenen Bohrtürme, wenige stille
> Dörfer, der Wald preußisch gerade ... Dann kamen
> andere Wälder, zerrissen zwischen Wiesen und Schauern
> Schnees, und jetzt erst ging es von zuhause fort,
> ihr war seltsam im Kopf. Es schneite stärker, die
> Dörfer wie zugehängt, die Bäume am Straßenrand
> rückten ganz fern und unwirklich weg. Sie fror.
> Sie hielt die Masten und Schneisen in ihrem Blick,
> das kam ihr nun alles zu, und konnte nichts halten,
> es flog alles dahin, alle Gewißheiten, alle
> Sicherheit.(14-15)

The landscape is far removed from Büchner's Alsace, and
bears the marks of the GDR's industrial development and
a Prussian sense of order, but the echoes of the opening
section of _Lenz_ are again unmistakable, in the narrative
structure of free indirect speech, in the protagonist's
confused state of mind, and in the heightened awareness
of the wintry elements.[42]

Karin is, however, not alone in the intensity with which
she suffers this sudden disorientation. Although the
narrative closely follows each stage in her crisis, it
also offers revealing glimpses into her boyfriend Frank's
plight over the same period. When she dutifully phones to
break off their relationship, we initially only learn that
he is "verwirrt".(12) Later, though, the full impact of
this incomprehensible news is recalled with equal vividness by a narrator who is also privy to Frank's innermost
feelings:

> Als Karin so seltsam angerufen hatte - und er dachte:
> ich gefall ihr nicht, das ist alles aus! hatte ihn
> das tagelang gepeinigt, seine Gedanken wie ein Aus-
> schlag, der ihn juckte, er mußte darin kratzen,
> keine Arbeit lenkte ihn ab, sein Gehirn nur eine
> Wunde. Er hätte sich den Kopf einschlagen mögen.
> (31)

Frank's mother has just been quoted as viewing him as "zu
empfindlich", but the evidence of his life hitherto
suggests rather that it is a relief that his sensibilities
remain intact at all. For Frank too offers a deliberate
contrast to Edgar Wibeau in the confused adolescent rebellion he has undergone (as the product of another broken

home) - first sent to a reformatory as a petty criminal
and a "Rowdy", but then determined to become a productive
member of society, without reference to an alien Party
authority. His communist impulses are not natural, like
Wibeau's, but developed over years of introspection, with
the contradictory results that he can enthuse about the
idea of joining an international brigade to fight the
military junta in Chile, following Allende's overthrow,
yet admit of his life in the GDR - "Kollektiv - das hab
ich nie erlebt".(31)
    Frank's relationship with Karin is the first opportunity
he has had to liberate himself from his social isolation
and from the feeling of despair provoked by the arbitrariness of authority. Thus, when the same arbitrary, anonymous state tries to force the lovers apart, on the basis
of unspecified allegations about his character, the fragile
identity Frank has established quickly disintegrates again:

> Er hatte Angst, daß sie ihm abhaut. Und auf ihre
> Eltern hört, weil er VERDÄCHTIG war ... Was war ihr
> wichtig. Er konnte nicht in sie reinsehen. Er
> begriff nichts. Und wenn man gegen ihn ermittelte,
> und sie wußte es? Sie standen lange da. Er sah sie,
> sie gefiel ihm rasend, das offene Gesicht, das Haar,
> die Stirn - da, dahinter war alles, mit Händen zu
> greifen, er hätte sie packen können! Er stand ganz
> starr da. Was hielt er dann, außer sich an ihr.(39)

These are the only insights Braun affords his reader into
Frank's state of mind, since it only takes one further
indication of Karin's apparent willingness to abandon him
before he is driven to his suicide attempt. In the course
of his slow recuperation from the effects of a drug over-
dose and gas poisoning, he is never more than the frail
object of Karin's concern. Yet enough has been revealed
to suggest that Frank, as well as Karin, has undergone a
psychological upheaval of Lenz proportions.
    It is, however, in Karin's experiences over these months,
as all the certainties of her sheltered teenage world are
overturned, that the main force of the narrative is concentrated. The revelation of her mother's almost bourgeois
pettiness, her father's timorous vacillations, the
blinkered conformism of Party bureaucrats in the newspaper
office, and the general inability to respond to urgent
personal needs all combine to induce Karin's mental disarray, at the very time when she is undergoing the emotional and physical effects of pregnancy. Moments of
heightened awareness punctuate the text, capturing Karin's
extremes of feeling and perception in original images
which emulate Büchner's in their vividness and violence:
the sense of her brain about to explode in anger (50),

of being assaulted by physical objects during the nightmar
drive to Frank's bedside (54-55), the alienation from the
everyday normality of town life, which resembles a drunken
stupor (59-60), a dream-like feeling of paralysis during
subsequent hospital visits (77), and a torrent of anger in
her head after her outburst of Promethean rage against
"diese dicken oder dünnen Beamten,.denen der Schweiß aus-
bricht, wenn sie etwas verantworten sollen!".(78)

Yet for all the exact comparability of mood in each of
these passages to moments in Lenz, the crucial - and, for
Braun, historical - difference lies in the possibility
(to put it no more strongly) that Karin and Frank can progress beyond their individual crises towards the goal of
self-realisation. There is no final note of "so lebte er
hin" here. The protagonists (or at least Karin) have not
suffered irreparable mental damage as a result of their
experiences: for Karin, the idea of giving up her politically conscious self is a temptation which she is ultimate
ly able to resist and to recognise as "ein Selbstmord,
nicht des Körpers sondern des Denkens" which would leave
her "tödlich leer" (93-94): the process of "zu sich selbe
kommen" (71) is already under way. She has come to realis
that an upbringing based on the principles of 'self-control
and 'self-conquest' ("bei sich bleiben" 66, "sich überwinden" 71) has actually obstructed the real process of self-
discovery. As she begins to understand the depth of her
feelings for Frank, her fear disappears and she establishe
a firmer identity within the 'self-sacrifice' of love:

> Sie spürte ... mit Erstaunen, daß sie jetzt erst
> Frank zu lieben begann, so, daß sie darüber sich
> selbst vergessen konnte. Und sich noch deutlicher
> empfand dabei, als würde sie ihrer selbst sicher.
> Jetzt löste sich eine dicke Schicht von ihren
> Armen, ihrer Brust. Sie hatte keine Angst mehr.(95)

Through this complex pattern of parallels and contrasts
to Lenz, Braun has transformed the documentary substance
of his story[43] into a didactic model. In particular,
by extending his narrative focus beyond the main protagonist and avoiding the implication of a unique personal
predicament, Braun is able to suggest a crucial change in
the typical experience of the socialist 1970s in relation
to the earlier, prolonged 'deutsche Misere'. Even in the
sections focused entirely on Karin's predicament, the
narrator enjoys moments of superior insight and, at times,
attributes insights to Karin which scarcely accord with
her experience (such as her criticism of Die neuen Leiden)
The narrator's special attentions are also directed not
just towards Frank, but towards Karin's father, once his
comfortable assumptions of a lifetime of Party service

have been undermined by the new conflict between his roles
as father and local official. When he finally recognises
that uncritical acceptance of information handed down from
superior Party sources has brought him close to destroying
his own daughter, his own self-disgust makes him determined
to rediscover what the mass of ordinary citizens think and
feel. Interestingly, Karin's father's crisis is not presented in the manner of Lenz: he carries out a rational
self-analysis of striking linguistic sophistication:

> Die Wachsamkeit, ja - aber was hatte er bewacht,
> wenn er ein Kind verlor, und ein andrer wirklich
> draufging? Er hatte so sehr aufgepaßt, daß er
> nicht aufpaßte, was wirklich passierte. Sein
> Mittel vernichtete den Zweck, womöglich, die
> Sorge um den Menschen brachte den Menschen um -
> oder um was, wer fragt schon was?(83)

It seems central to Braun's view of GDR society that the
ageing generation of Party stalwarts should be shown as
capable of such insights and of translating them into
action. It is also fascinating that the dilemma of
JR Becher should re-emerge here as the starting point for
Karin's father's self-transformation. The poem of 1956/57,
"Entlastung", which he is amazed to discover in Volume 6
of Becher's Gesammelte Werke (published in 1973, just before the fictional action begins), appears to be the first
piece of literature to challenge his ideological certainties.(41-42) (Indeed, had the fictional present been
1975, the literary stimulus might just as easily have been
Wiederanders, in which the same experience of release from
high office triggers off Becher's narrator's liberating
reassessment of his identity.[44]) For a much lowlier
official than a Minister of Culture, accustomed to using
literature only as a source of self-confirming quotations,
this revelation initiates the process of self-questioning;
for the reader of Unvollendete Geschichte it could serve
as a reminder that two decades of opportunity to change
this authoritarian mentality had been wasted.

Thus Karin's father, as a Party pioneer of the post-
war years, becomes a representative figure in the same
sense that Karin and Frank, as members of the new generation born in the GDR, are. Braun's narrative is correspondingly more convincingly 'epic' than those of Bobrowski
or G. Wolf, especially at the various points of Unvollendete
Geschichte where he considers the dual meaning of
'Geschichte', as fiction and as history. He sees nothing
unique about the story itself: Karin's conflict is
described as a variant (however extreme) on the universal
theme of adolescent idealism forced to come to terms with
social constraints:

Vielleicht war das kein Fall, der in ein bestimmtes
Kapitel der Geschichtsbücher gehörte, sondern sie
erlebte nur zwingender, als Schock, was jedem Auf-
wachsenden geschieht, wenn er seine hochdampfenden
Vorstellungen von der neuen Gesellschaft zu Wasser
werden sieht. Wenn er sich endlich in die Möglichkeiten zwängt.(94)

The narrator also retains tight editorial control over his
material, conscious of the arbitrariness of imposing an
ending on any individual's 'unfinished story' and determined not to distort the significance of this particular
story by ending it at the wrong moment. He moves deliberately beyond the bleakest moments of Karin's isolation
- "hier konnte ihre Geschichte nicht enden" (84) - but
equally avoids the 'happy ending' of so much Socialist
Realist fiction, leaving the future of his protagonists
unresolved (even though, as indicated above, Karin seems
to be in the process of establishing a more solid identity) - "Hier begannen, während die eine nicht zuende war,
andere Geschichten".(98)
   On the historical level, Braun has clearly avoided all
simplified assumptions about continuity and human progress.
The disguised, but intimate analogy with <u>Lenz</u> is a constant
reminder of how little has changed as far as German
society's ability to harness the creative potential of its
most gifted citizens is concerned. The historical point
of reference is even extended greatly beyond the 'deutsche
Misere' through Frank's identification with an abandoned
hero of Classical Greece (via Heiner Müller's controversial
<u>Philoktet</u>). As Karin glances at the text of Müller's play
after Frank's suicide attempt, she has another lucid perception of the extent to which she is still caught up in
the seemingly endless era of man's inhumanity to man:

Sie las in dem Text, ohne ihn ganz zu begreifen,
er rauschte so hin, es war wie das ungeheure
Rauschen der Geschichte, abgrundfern, aber in der
sie weit oben noch schwammen.(75)

There are, however, substantial historical and contemporary
reasons for the GDR's failure to make a reality of socialist
ideals. These are outlined in the discussion between
Karin's father and the Party's Area Secretary - after the
disastrous human consequences of their misjudgement of
Frank have been revealed - which centres on the GDR's
unique problems as a state without a secure sense of
identity, founded on the ruins of the Third Reich and
incessantly threatened by the very existence of the German
Federal Republic:

Wir leben in zwei Welten, oder drei, und leben mit
drei Zeiten. Und eine schlägt mit der anderen nach
der dritten in uns oder neben uns ... Der Wettlauf
mit den Toten, wir Totengräber jagen dem Kapitalis-
mus nach über den Friedhof unserer Pläne ... Wir
sind nicht nur wir, wir sind wir und nicht sie, wir
gegenüber ihnen. Das ist die Spannung, die uns
kribblig macht, die Belastung, die uns jagt und
hemmt. Diese Geschichte - hat das ganze Land.(69)

But while Braun has shown previously that he accepts this
predicament as a challenge to socialism to prove its
superiority (in his poem "Wir und nicht sie"[45]), these
two dutiful servants of the state are all too eager to
view it as a justification for their siege mentality,
which, as Unvollendete Geschichte amply demonstrates, per-
vades the GDR in the form of the gulf between the Party
and the majority of doubting citizens. It is the failure
of the SED to distribute power and responsibility more
widely which links Karin's emotional outbursts against
'dicke oder dünne Beamte' with Braun's public statements
of the post-1971 period, and which can be viewed as the
chief criticism articulated in Unvollendete Geschichte.
   The counterbalance to this criticism is, of course,
Braun's suggestion that representative citizens like Karin
and her father are already beginning to draw radical conclusions from their experience, which could - if the SED
shows itself sufficiently receptive - form the basis of
progress towards genuine socialism. Beyond this is the
vision of a utopian society created by the unified efforts
of free individuals, which underlines the continuity between the exile optimism of Becher's Abschied and
Unvollendete Geschichte, despite the radical differences
in critical emphasis. The vision comes in a dream of
Karin's, which has the allegorical qualities of the fantasy
'Anderswerden' sequences in Abschied, a dream, however,
which she can 'not yet' recall afterwards - a revealing
'epic' irony on Braun's part. It takes the form of a
public tribunal in a factory, at which the bureaucrats
who have hindered the creation of the prototype 'new man'
(represented by Frank) are driven out, and an age of proletarian equality and happiness is ushered in.(85-89)
This remains the sustaining hope, some 35 years after
Abschied, in the face of the disheartening realities of
the 1970s in the GDR.
   The polemical force of Der arme Hölderlin, as reflected
in the narrator's rhetorical questions and Hölderlin's
anger at the 'Kunstrichter' Goethe and Schiller, is fully
sustained in Braun's story. Here again, a succession of
questions and exclamations is interpolated into the

narrative and directed aggressively at the cultural and
political hierarchy of the Party - "Was für NICHT DRUCKBAR]
Stimmungen!"(78) ... "Klammert euch an den Zaunpfahl,
Rezensenten!"(94). Some of these interjections derive
from Büchner, but now the explicitly political Büchner.
Braun provocatively raises the question of whether the
'Machtstrukturen' have changed essentially since the 1830s
through the rhetorical insertion of Büchner's challenge,
in the Hessischer Landbote, to the peasants of Hesse to
overthrow a corrupt hierarchy: "Was ist denn das für ein
gewaltiges Ding: der Staat?".(78) Christ's statement
(Matthew 18, 7) on the inevitability of evil and human
suffering, which Büchner quotes in horrified bewilderment
in his correspondence and in Dantons Tod - "es muß ja
Ärgernis kommen, doch wehe dem, durch welchen Ärgernis
kommt"[46] - is unconsciously inverted by Karin to suggest
that the naive view of socialist progress and happiness
is just as unbelievable following her experiences - "es muß
ja vorwärtsgehen; doch wohl dem Menschen, durch welchen
es vorwärtsgeht!".(93) There is no need for an aesthetic
debate on the model of Lenz's exchanges with Kaufmann in
Büchner's story: quotations like these demonstrate
Braun's radical rejection of the idealised 'classicism' of
Socialist Realism and show his determination to confront
the taboo subjects which Honecker had declared to be open
to serious literary treatment.

Braun went on to provide an illuminating glossary on the
cumulative significance of the allusions to Büchner's work
in Unvollendete Geschichte, in his essay "Büchners Briefe"
of 1978.[47] Here he sets out to demonstrate the profound
relevance to him of Büchner's political perceptions -
"Büchners Briefe lesend, muß man sich mitunter mit Gewalt
erinnern, daß es nicht die eines Zeitgenossen sind." In
Büchner's critique of the apparatus of German state repression, the self-perpetuating nature of bureaucracy,
the hypocrisy of officially fostered affirmative literature, and the bloody excesses of the French Revolution,
Braun recognises historical problems as yet unremedied in
the post-1917 socialist era. It is a situation crying
out for radical change and the use of "Gegengewalt", the
character of which may be "freundlicher" today, yet "mit-
nichten nachgiebiger". Braun's subject matter may still
be 'literary' (and assume a close knowledge of Büchner's
life and work), but the tone is more explicitly political
than in Unvollendete Geschichte: indeed, "Büchners Briefe"
could be viewed as the nearest thing we might expect to
find in the GDR to a radical pamphlet in the tradition of
the Hessischer Landbote - if it had actually proved
possible to publish it there.

The cultural-political climate had, however, again

changed significantly for the worse since Braun found his
'documentary' inspiration for <u>Unvollendete Geschichte</u> in
1974, and recognised the continuing applicability of the
<u>Lenz</u> model. His 'epic' fiction was to appear only once in
the GDR, in the pages of the journal <u>Sinn und Form</u> (5/1975),
and although it demonstrates that personal crisis and conflict with authority are not only inevitable but also
capable of productive resolution in the longer term, it was
clearly regarded as too 'negative' for the general GDR
readership. Despite the many similarities between <u>Unvoll-
endete Geschichte</u> and <u>Die neuen Leiden,</u> there were no
officially sanctioned public debates or academic colloquia
in 1975-76 responding to the stimulus of Braun's work.
Already, the breaking-point was being reached in the
Honecker era's tolerance of criticism of the present-day
GDR - even though that criticism was, in this case, historically differentiated and carefully woven into an outstanding, multi-layered piece of creative fiction. By
1978, therefore, the prospects for a polemic like
"Büchners Briefe" were virtually non-existent.

A haven amidst the storms

   During a public discussion in the East Berlin Academy
of the Arts at the end of 1975 - around the time when
<u>Unvollendete Geschichte</u> was being published in the
academy's prestigious journal - Christa Wolf felt able to
look back upon four years in which the cultural climate
had undergone a decisive change. When she referred back
to the frustrations of a "Zeit, in der sehr massiv dumme,
kunstfremde und feindliche Meinungen herrschen und immer
und überall vertreten werden", her words had the ring of
confidence that these were problems of the past, and that
a new era of progress had been initiated with Honecker's
rise to power in 1971.
   The standing conflict between artists and the "offizielle
Politik" seemed a thing of the past; it was now more
accurate to think in terms of a mutually fruitful relationship binding together writers like herself and a discriminating public. She now felt sure that "der Kampf um den
Realismus in der Kunst irgendwann aufhören oder leicht
sein wird".[48] She had just completed <u>Kindheitsmuster</u>,
a work which can be seen as the third stage - after
<u>Der geteilte Himmel</u> and <u>Nachdenken über Christa T.</u> - in an
exhaustive analysis of her own lifetime, with each novel
paving the way for the more rigorously autobiographical
approach of its successor. And although she was the author
who had originally pointed to the continuing significance

of Büchner's <u>Lenz</u>, she had not yet attempted a fictional
elaboration of her historical model of 'epic prose'. Her
husband Gerhard had, of course, already done so at the end
of the Ulbricht era, with the mixed results already
examined, and it is not unlikely that the <u>Lenz</u> theme no
longer appeared appropriate in the more encouraging years
thereafter. She had gone further with the idea of updatin
motifs from the 'anti-classical' cultural heritage, in her
collection of shorter prose published in 1974. But the
tone of her <u>Neue Lebensansichten eines Katers</u> is, like
Hoffmann's <u>Kater Murr</u>, essentially satirical, and even the
slightly Kafkaesque fantasy <u>Unter den Linden</u> has a conciliatory outcome. She had also in the meantime directed
her creative interests - in <u>Selbstversuch</u> - towards the
issue of female emancipation, in common with other
GDR authors like Sarah Kirsch and Irmtraud Morgner. [49]
Whatever her immediate plans might have been after the
completion of <u>Kindheitsmuster</u>, they were clearly disrupted
by the crisis which struck the East German cultural world
late in 1976 following the expatriation of Wolf Biermann.
Regardless of personal feelings about an artist so tempera
mentally different to herself, Christa Wolf recognised, as
did almost all the GDR's internationally respected authors
the fundamental threat this decision of the Politbüro pose
to the spirit of constructive self-criticism she had praise
the previous year. Wolf, together with her husband Gerhar
and Volker Braun, was among the twelve original signatorie
of the letter to Erich Honecker asking him to reconsider
his decision not to allow Biermann back into the GDR after
his concert tour of the Federal Republic - a letter and an
expression of writers' solidarity which would have been
inconceivable even a few years earlier.
The consequences of this intervention are well known:
Gerhard Wolf was apparently one of a small number of sacri
ficial lambs expelled from the Party and the executive of
the East Berlin branch of the Writers' Union, while Christ
may have been spared a similar fate by the fact that she wa
taken seriously ill at the height of the Party inquiry int
this 'rebellion'. [50] Although the exact details are
irrelevant, it seems that the feelings of profound despair
over the future of the GDR, which had plagued her after
the Eleventh Plenum in 1965, returned in the aftermath of
this next major cultural setback.
When she began writing again, the problem of 'Selbstverwirklichung' in the face of an authoritarian, technological society had taken on a new, grim urgency. In her
deeply sympathetic review of Maxie Wander's collection of
documentary interviews with women, <u>Guten Morgen, du Schöne</u>
(1978), Wolf refers to the wider issue of the "Subjekt-
werden des Menschen - von Mann und Frau" in a patriarchal

society which deforms human relationships and human lives:
the basic conflict is that between 'feminine' and 'masculine' qualities, where feminine is a synonym for creativity, for the capacity to love, while masculine implies
rationality and the obsessive technological progress which
depends on the destruction of nature (culminating in the
nuclear confrontation of today's superpowers).

In this essay, "Berührung", Wolf presents the problem
historically, in terms of the dominance of the masculine
principle since the era of the French Revolution, when this
"herrschende[s] Selbstverständnis" ignored the needs of the
underprivileged, in a mockery of the ideals of equality,
fraternity and liberty (or, in more personal German terms,
'Bildung' and 'Selbstverwirklichung'). It was around 1800
when women battled for equality in the cultural areńa,
with little success in the established genres of drama and
fiction, but leaving behind vivid documentary evidence of
their struggle, in what Wolf calls "d[ie] persönlichsten
und subjektivsten Literaturformen" - diaries, letters and
poems. The natural allies of these pioneers were male
writers who shared their hostility towards "eine unerbitt-
lich auf Effizienz eingeschworene Gesellschaft", but also
with little hope of achieving their personal goals. Their
collective fate is summed up as "Einsamkeit, Esoterik,
Selbstzweifel, Wahnsinn, Selbstmord".[51]

At this point Wolf has mentioned no names, but the
wheel has obviously again turned full circle to Anna
Seghers' view in the 1930s of the same revolutionary-
reactionary era and its heroic victims. In the light of
Wolf's feminist consciousness and the course taken by the
wider GDR debate on the cultural heritage in the second
half of the 1970s, her models for these two groups of intellectuals had effectively selected themselves. The only
woman mentioned by Seghers was Karoline von Günderrode
(1780-1806), an excellent example of the woman struggling
for self-emancipation against all the odds; and just as
Hölderlin, partly by virtue of the bicentenary celebrations
of his birth, was a key historical figure for East German
writers around 1970, Heinrich von Kleist (1777-1811), was
the obvious point of reference at this time.

Kleist, like Hölderlin, had been claimed for the official
'bürgerliches Erbe', and, once again, the basic incompati-
bility of Kleist's writing with the traditional, Goethe-
orientated view of classicism had been obscured. The
commemorative volume of essays was the subject of some
controversy, with the author of a rejected contribution,
Günter Kunert, publicly attacking its editor, while other
less overtly provocative pieces by GDR authors - including
Gerhard Wolf - were completely at odds with the official
image of Kleist.[52] There was also a direct link between

Günderrode and Kleist, although based on legend rather
than historical fact: the story that the two poets had
met near Mainz in the summer of 1804 had a symbolical
potential which Christa Wolf found irresistible. Her
Kein Ort. Nirgends [53], written in 1977-78 and published
in 1979, is centred on that day in June 1804 when such a
unique meeting of minds and sensibilities could have
occurred.

At first sight, it seems unlikely that this piece of
historical fiction might be related to the Lenz model:
there is an obvious contrast between the mood of inescapable
crisis associated with Lenz and the summery idyll which
the idea of the Kleist-Günderrode meeting conjures up.
The scope for intense identification between the narrator
and his protagonist(s) has receded: there are no scenes
which signal a direct parallel to the onset of mental turmoil, the "durchs-Gebirg-gehen" of the first sentence of
Lenz; and there are no stylistic echoes of Büchner's use
of free indirect speech in his opening scene (such as
Braun achieved so forcefully). The dominant mood of Wolf's
opening scene is elegiac. It establishes the historical
distance from the characters and events to be described,
and yet a new narrative level is created, alongside the
third-person commentator who will soon set the fictional
scene and organise the course of the action. This first-
person plural 'Wir' is, of course, a familiar voice from
Wolf's earlier prose and again evidently speaks for an
unspecified community of kindred spirits - but now also
initiates an extra-fictional dialogue with her protagonists,
'Ihr'. The initial impression is a grim one - blood,
silence, the denial of all the associations of peace in
death, the failure to learn from the self-sacrifices of
two centuries ago, and the temptation to abandon the hope
inherent in the writings of Kleist and Günderrode:

> Die arge Spur, in der die Zeit von uns wegläuft.
>
> Vorgänger ihr, Blut im Schuh. Blicke aus keinem Auge,
> Worte aus keinem Mund. Gestalten, körperlos. Nieder-
> gefahren gen Himmel, getrennt in entfernten Gräbern,
> wiederauferstanden von den Toten, immer noch
> vergebend unsern Schuldigern, traurige Engelsgeduld.
>
> Und wir, immer noch gierig auf den Aschegeschmack
> der Worte.
>
> Immer noch nicht, was uns anstünde, stumm. (5)

The reader's thoughts are inevitably directed to Wolf's
own situation - recovering after a period of intense personal stress - when she seized upon this topic. It is the
sense of recovery, in fact, which provides a vital clue to

the link between <u>Kein Ort</u> and <u>Lenz</u>. A closer examination of the historical circumstances of both protagonists in the summer of 1804 produces revealing parallels. Kleist was in Mainz convalescing after a nervous breakdown suffered in France late in 1803, the time when he burnt the manuscript of his <u>Robert Guiskard</u>, the drama praised by CM Wieland in extraordinarily glowing terms; Günderrode had also suffered inordinately in the recent past: her hopes of marriage had been dashed because of her refusal to conform to a conventional domestic role, and her first volume of poetry (published under a pseudonym to disguise the fact that the author was a woman) had been destructively reviewed in an influential journal. Material enough, then, for more than one variant on <u>Lenz</u>. And the other point inescapably associated with both their lives is that they later committed suicide: Günderrode in 1806, and Kleist, after repeated subsequent periods of inner turmoil, in 1811.

Seen in this light, the situation described in <u>Kein Ort</u> is not so much the storm of crisis as a temporary haven in the midst of a succession of threatening storms. Wolf's fictional protagonists are uncompromisingly committed to developing their full human potential in an age when they already know such aspirations are doomed to failure. Günderrode always carries a knife, determined never to endure humiliation; Kleist is sure that there will be no way of avoiding the stark choice between self-inflicted death and the conformism which would only be "eine andere Art von Tod".(14) To both of them, authority is omnipresent and implacably hostile, in a variety of 'timeless' abstract guises - "der Staat", "Mächte", "Preußen" and so on.

As artists, both are instinctively hostile to the notion of classical moderation which Goethe incorporates for the cultural establishment: anyone, they feel, who categorises art as either "gesund" or "krank", who can express (as in <u>Tasso</u>) his personality conflicts through neatly contrasted characters (106-7) and who lives a life comfortably insulated against human suffering, must be creatively sterile - "lebensfremd".(126) Their suffering, on the other hand, is the very substance of their art. For Kleist, the experience of the "Riß", of a hopelessly divided self, has been almost as shattering as for the Lenz of Büchner's story - he has only just managed to recover from his breakdown the previous November:

> ... [er unterdrückt] die zweite Stimme in [sich] ,...
> wie er es eisern geübt hat. Er hat seine Lektion
> gefressen. So lernt man nur, wenn es ums Leben geht,
> in Todesangst. In der Gewalt von Mächten, die keinen

> Zweifel lassen, daß sie uns vernichten können, weil
> in uns selber etwas, das wir nicht kennen wollen,
> ihnen entgegenkommt. Dieser Zusammenbruch im
> November. Der schauerliche Winter. Diese
> dröhnenden, niemals abreißenden Monologe in seinem
> armen Kopf.(14)

He later describes the "Riß" specifically as the "entsetz-
liche[n] Widerspruch, auf dessen Grund das Verderben der
Menschheit liegt".(102) Karoline von Günderrode, because
she is a woman and not torn apart by the economic pressure
to conform, is seen to have her identity intact. What is
destroying her is society's inability to understand her,
the total isolation which she will bring upon herself if
she seeks self-fulfilment outside the constricting bonds
of social convention:

> Sie kennt sich, sie kennt die Menschen, ist darauf
> eingestellt, vergessen zu werden ... Sie hat das
> Unglück, leidenschaftlich und stolz zu sein, also
> verkannt zu werden. So hält sie sich zurück, an
> Zügeln, die ins Fleisch schneiden. Das geht ja,
> man lebt. Gefährlich wird es, wenn sie sich
> hinreißen ließe, die Zügel zu lockern, loszugehen,
> und wenn sie dann, in heftigstem Lauf, gegen jenen
> Widerstand stieße, den die andern Wirklichkeit
> nennen ...(11)

They are united - as they discover in the course of their
day together when they manage to escape the world of polit
social intercourse - in their vision of "der ganze Mensch"
(119), in their understanding of concepts like "sich ...
vervollkommnen" (150), "ganz wahr sein mit sich selbst".
(148) They also know that these goals are all, in the
fuller, bleaker sense of the book's title, utopian:
"Unlebbares Leben. Kein Ort. Nirgends".(137)

The question of the authenticity of such thoughts and
conversational exchanges located in a fictional 1804 is
crucial to the interpretation of Wolf's novel. None of
the above quotations are recorded statements of Kleist or
Günderrode, however much they may be in keeping with what
is known historically of them. Yet <u>Kein Ort</u> is, in places
as crowded with genuine quotations - especially from the
two authors' correspondence - as <u>Der arme Hölderlin</u>. As
in Gerhard Wolf's work, there is no typological differentiation between the verifiable excerpts from the protagonists' own work and the author's narrative commentary,
but the problem is more perplexing in <u>Kein Ort</u>. Most of
Gerhard Wolf's additions to his montage of quotations
consist of linking commentary, providing a biographical
thread of continuity over a full decade of Hölderlin's

life, and leaving the poet's comments deliberately fragmentary. Christa Wolf, in contrast, opting for dramatic
concentration on the events of a single day, makes extensive use of inner monologue, flashbacks and conversational
exchanges. In each of these areas she tries to blend
authentic and imaginative material, although in doing so
creates stylistic problems, since genuine quotations -
from written sources - will often sound quite implausible
in conversation or inner monologue.

Christa Wolf's device for effecting an almost imper-
ceptible transition from the fictional action to the
'timeless' statements intended to draw the reader back
into the realities of his own day, is the narrative 'Wir'.
As much of the fiction consists of conversational exchanges, and as the main internal movement is the growing
recognition of Kleist and Günderrode that they have the
common identity which enables them to speak as 'Wir', the
opportunity to create Lenz-like moments of profound one-
ness involving the narrator as well, develops as the
action itself develops.[54]   For example, a verifiable
statement of the historical Kleist on the commercial and
militaristic obsessions of the new machine age[55] is
expanded shortly afterwards into a prediction of the
fictional Kleist about the coming of an "eisernes Jahrhundert" in which the artist will be a "Fremdling". This
is followed by a bleak narratorial comment on our disheartening lack of progress beyond this situation:

> Wir kennen alle alles.
> Kleist hat die Vision eines Zeitalters, das sich auf
> Gerede gründet anstatt auf Taten. Die Landschaft
> versinkt ihm, nüchternes Licht. Und da sitzen wir
> immer noch und handeln mit den Parolen des vergangenen
> Jahrhunderts, spitzfindig und gegen unsre stärkere
> Müdigkeit ankämpfend, und wissen: Das ist es nicht,
> wofür wir leben und worum wir sterben könnten.
> Unser Blut wird vergossen werden, und man wird uns
> nicht mitteilen, wofür.(100)

On the personal level, the elusiveness of identity, the
inadequacy of socially constrained relationships and the
inability to communicate form the major underlying theme,
and are presented as problems so unchanged since the
depths of the 'deutsche Misere' that the differences between the narrator and her characters become entirely
fluid:

> Frau. Mann. Unbrauchbare Wörter. Wir, jeder gefangen
> in seinem Geschlecht. Die Berührung, nach der es uns
> so unendlich verlangt, es gibt sie nicht. Sie wurde
> mit uns entleibt. Wir müßten sie erfinden ...

Unkenntlich bleiben wir uns, unnahbar, nach
Verkleidungen süchtig. Fremde Namen, die wir uns
zulegen ...

Ich bin nicht ich. Du bist nicht du. Wer ist wir?

(138)

Then comes the echo of the poignant phrase which establishes
the mood in the first scene of Büchner's drama of the
failure of revolution, Dantons Tod: "wir sind sehr einsam".
   This narrative perspective, which makes the compart-
mentalisation of 'fiction' and 'reality' impossible, is
the main weapon in Christa Wolf's 'epic' arsenal. The
provocative rhetorical questions which are so important
in this respect in Der arme Hölderlin are reduced here
to a couple of teasing challenges - "Wer spricht?" -
carefully placed near the beginning and end of the text.
(6, 144)   The other stylistic feature which underlines
the link between Kein Ort and Lenz are its metaphors.
The images used by Kleist and Günderrode to describe their
suffering may not be as dynamic as Büchner's, but they are
none the less violent for being more calmly expressed:
after his breakdown, Kleist recalls the sensation as that
of having been crushed and dismembered in a mill-wheel
(49), or as that of a machine being driven at top speed
at the same time as the brakes are applied (113), and
Günderrode feels that she is about to be crushed by iron
plates.(138-9)   Apart from these images, the text is
permeated with references to blood, suffering and violent
death, in a deliberately unrelenting manner.
   The only respite from this ubiquitous violence - the
haven amidst the storms - is the conversation shared by
Kleist and Günderrode at the approach of evening. Their
subject is man's future potential for untrammelled relationships, for overcoming the division of labour and thus
achieving real self-fulfilment. For them, this must remain Utopia - "Unlebbares Leben. Kein Ort. Nirgends" - as
the narrative underlines, by breaking off into a future
tense summary which demonstrates the inevitability of
suicide once this point of hopelessness has been reached.
(140-1)   In the final thought shared by the protagonists
- "einfach weitergehn"   - there is another echo of Lenz's
fate ("so lebte er hin"), which is strengthened by the
narrator's ominous closing words - "wir wissen, was kommt".
(151)
   As in Büchner's case, the redeeming effect of this
meticulous study of human breakdown is the possibility
that it might have served a cathartic function for the
author. Kein Ort leaves Christa Wolf's narrator still
dangerously close to despair at the seeming endlessness
of this 'deutsche Misere', yet prepared to cling defiantly

to a faith of which knowledge makes a mockery:

> Wir wissen zuviel. Man wird uns für rasend halten.
> Unser unausrottbarer Glaube, der Mensch sei bestimmt,
> sich zu vervollkommnen, der dem Geist aller Zeiten
> strikt zuwiderläuft. Ein Wahn?
>
> Die Welt tut, was ihr am leichtesten fällt: Sie
> schweigt.(150-1)

Like Volker Braun, Wolf has continued to explore this
profound sense of kinship with Büchner, as a vital point
of reference to today's GDR. The speech she made after
being awarded the (West German) Büchner-Preis in 1980 is
remarkably comparable to Braun's "Büchners Briefe", as a
complement to the fiction which precedes it and as a more
outspoken sequel. Wolf's speech is a passionate plea,
supported by references to the female characters in
Büchner's plays as well as to Lenz, for the feminine principle and against the madness of a male rationality which
finds its ultimate expression in the nuclear bomb. She
harnesses literature, recalling its main (and unofficial)
function in the GDR as "Lebenshilfe", to the moral and
humanistic cause of "Friedensforschung", in the conviction
that if it fails internationally in this task, the only
task remaining will be that of "Sterbehilfe".[56]
    This is the awesome potential culmination of the 'Lenz
heritage' in the world situation of renewed Cold War confrontation in the early 1980s - and shows in the starkest
possible terms why the continuing elaboration of Lenz has
been such a dominant feature of recent GDR literature.

Despite everything - Utopia today?

    The historically based critique of the contemporary
GDR underlying the texts examined in this chapter has not
gone entirely unanswered. Erik Neutsch, one author who
conspicuously refused to join the protest of 1976 against
the expatriation of Biermann, has since attacked unnamed
"Autoren, die ... Geschichten schreiben ohne angemessenen
geschichtlichen Sinn für das, was in diesem Land geleistet
worden ist.".[57]   In reaching this conclusion, he too
had taken Georg Büchner as his point of departure - in the
essay of 1975, "Reise zu Büchner". Neutsch's pilgrimage to
Büchner's birthplace, the village of Goddelau near
Darmstadt, was the occasion for an attack on the absence
of any public recognition in the Federal Republic, for
example in terms of a museum, of Büchner's importance.
Neutsch's point was to prove how much more effective the

"Rezeption des kulturellen Erbes" was in the GDR (and thereby express regret that so many radical German forbears were born outside its boundaries).

With regard to Büchner's reception in the GDR, he made the apt comment that Büchner is "der literarische Vorfahr von so ziemlich der Hälfte aller in der DDR lebenden und schreibenden Schriftsteller", and took care to add - "Jeder nimmt ihn auf seine Weise in Anspruch" - indicating his own preference not for <u>Lenz</u> but for the "revolutionären Atem von <u>Dantons Tod</u>".[58]   Without developing this view, he concluded his essay by informing his reader that he was on his way to Mainz to see what he could unearth about Georg Forster, another obvious example of a revolutionary writer neglected in the FRG.

The first fruits of this research came in the form of another essay, "Georg Forster heute", published in 1979. Neutsch begins with a consideration of the subjective motives which lead authors to seek out literary forbears - in exploring the basis of their "Geistesverwandtschaft", they are simultaneously asserting the "Aktualität" of their chosen models.   In Neutsch's list of kindred spirits the Goethe era is well represented, although only the more politically radical of Anna Seghers' 'suffering poets' remain: Lenz, Hölderlin and Büchner are included, but there is no mention of Kleist or Günderrode, suggesting a negative reaction both to the GDR's Kleist cult of the later 1970s and to figures who might be regarded as excessively egotistical.

Neutsch's choice of Georg Forster (1754-94) serves to highlight the surprising neglect hitherto of virtually the only German writer of the French Revolutionary era to translate his concern for 'Bildung' and 'Selbstverwirklichung' into concrete revolutionary action.   Neutsch lays stress on both aspects: he quotes with admiration Friedrich Schlegel for his early recognition that "Vervollkommnung" is "der feste, durch seine ganze schriftstellerische Laufbahn herrschende Grundgedanke"; later, he presents Forster as the "Berufsrevolutionär" who, in the last year of his life, is willing to sacrifice his literary work, his domestic happiness, his health and his fortune to the French Revolutionary cause.   Ultimately, this recognition of the historical necessity of the revolution, whatever its failings, is seen as the factor which makes him a "Mensch von überdurchschnittlicher charakterlicher Größe".[59]

Forster is therefore an exemplary figure by virtue of his revolutionary achievements and his readiness to sacrifice his own life for the cause.   This account of Forster's life, however, gives little indication of how Neutsch understood his personality; it was only when

Neutsch published his biographical novel <u>Forster in Paris</u>
in 1981, with the focus on the last few months of Forster's
life, that he seems to emerge as another Lenz, for it is
Büchner's story which again provides the structure and the
dominant motifs.[60]

Forster's coach journey in November 1793 from the Swiss
border to Paris marks the onset of his final crisis; he
has just failed in his despairing attempt to retrieve his
marriage (his wife and children remain with her lover in
Switzerland); he is already an exile, with a price on his
head, since the collapse of his German revolutionary dream
of a Mainz Republic in the summer; he has sacrificed his
middle-class respectability and his career as librarian
for a garret in Paris; his German friends have abandoned
him, and even a fellow revolutionary exile like Adam Lux
has lost faith and finished under the guillotine; and
finally, he has a serious bronchial illness which is
getting steadily worse.

The atmospheric conditions of his journey through the
Jura mountains are closely modelled on Lenz's - the massive
threat of the mountains, the fog and rain, the pressures
on his brain and chest - after the opening sentence has
unmistakably signalled Neutsch's intentions:

> Am Sechsten des Monats Frimaire kam Forster von
> Pontarlier ... Die Erinnerung drückte ihn nieder. Mit
> dem Abstand von heute lag sie auf seinem Kopf wie eine
> Last, so, als wollten sich nachträglich die
> Enttäuschungen rächen, die kalten und kargen,
> verregneten, bleich von Nebeln umhüllten Berge des
> Juramassivs über ihn stürzen und seinen Mut
> verschütten. Er spürte die Brust sich verkrampfen ...
> (5-6)

Later, on the plains closer to Paris, the sense of autumnal
decay offers a contrast, but little relief from his anguish. Neutsch dutifully searches for violent images to
convey mental turmoil - the vice tightening mercilessly
on Forster's head (9) - but in doing so exposes his creative limitations, as, for example, when he wants to describe Forster's unsuccessful attempts to obliterate the
image of his wife Therese from his consciousness:

> Nein, er zweifelte nicht, daß es ihm niemals gelingen
> würde, ihr Bild aus seinen Gehirnfasern zu reißen,
> aus dem heißen Lavastrom seiner Gedanken ...(8)

When Forster reaches Paris, he never succeeds for long in
warding off an anguish conveyed in terms all too familiar
from <u>Lenz</u>: he is "ausgebrannt, leer, stumpf" (54), he is
"entsetzlich einsam" (66); one night he is plagued by
"eine seltsame Unruhe in sich, Anspannung aller Nerven,

ängstliche Beklommenheit, und zum ersten Mal ... sogar
Furcht vor dem Tod".(80) At times he feels the superhuman
strength of a Gulliver in Lilliput, but then, like Lenz
after his Promethean outburst at the deity, Forster is
paralysed by the indifference and emptiness of the
universe:

> Es war ... als säße er auf einem fremden Stern.
> Als zeitige jeder Schrei von ihm nur ein brummiges,
> mißmutiges, gelangweiltes Achselzucken des Weltalls.
>
> Wie sollte sich da nicht auch in seinem Innern eine
> gähnende Leere ausbreiten?(122)

Inexorably, his illness overwhelms him, until the narrator
signals the point of no return - "... so siechte er hin".
(139)

Forster in Paris includes the obligatory conflict with
Goethe, although - in contrast to Der arme Hölderlin and
Kein Ort - it is his bourgeois decadence, "die unverschämte
Eitelkeit und Saturiertheit" (109), rather than his omni-
potence in the cultural establishment, which is important.
An authentic meeting (of August 1792) is recalled, when
the fictional Forster suspects (as Wolf's Kleist has already done in her fictional 1804) that Goethe is merely a
dilettante, living off his early successes; and in another
revealing imitation of the same Kleist, Forster feels
himself capable of divesting Goethe of his "Lorbeerkranz"
(109) - although it is implied that Forster would actually
have done so, had he had the chance to return to his
writing.

Another change of emphasis which reflects Neutsch's
position vis-a-vis the GDR's cultural policy is that 'the
state' is not portrayed as an omnipresent threat to
Forster's self-realisation. His Forster has liberated
himself successfully from German repressiveness and discovered a new sense of identity with the revolutionary
state in Paris. Only in Neutsch's novel is 'the state'
personalised, through Forster's meetings with leaders such
as Saint-Just, in which they find themselves intellectually in agreement about the necessities of the hour. The
only difficulty acknowledged is that these contacts with
individuals so totally engrossed in organising a revolution cannot develop into the deeper friendships Forster
has lost elsewhere. Gradually these contrasts build up
to a significant revision of the 'epic' understanding of
Lenz shared by Neutsch's colleagues. Braun's central
'Wir und nicht sie' theme [61] returns, but in order to
affirm the arguments of the Party's Area Secretary rejected in Unvollendete Geschichte: here, Saint-Just makes

it clear that the "Verschwörung des Auslands ist total"
and leaves the Jacobins no alternative but to deal ruthlessly with waverers like Forster's friend Adam Lux.(52-3)
 Bobrowski's dubious suggestion that Boehlendorff became
involved in radical politics in his later life pales into
insignificance beside Neutsch's idyllic presentation of
the revolutionary proletariat in Paris and his depiction
of a politically active working-class in Germany. Workers
like Peter Schridde in Mainz are shown confronting the
ruthlessness of feudal authority and, half a century before the publication of Büchner's Hessischer Landbote,
adopting its slogan - "Krieg den Palästen - und Friede
den Hütten".(76) Schridde is an inspirational force in
the life of the middle-class intellectual Forster, and
seen (despite the evidence to the contrary, even in
Büchner's 1830s) to strengthen him decisively in his revolutionary commitment.
 Neutsch also disputes Büchner's view of the Robespierre-
Danton conflict over revolutionary ruthlessness. Forster,
although fully aware of the complexity of the choice to
be made between moderation and excess, ultimately sides
with Robespierre's view that any sign of weakness will
destroy the basis of the revolution (128); he accepts the
inevitability of injustice and errors in the short term,
but feels confident that history will judge them sympa-
thetically. This crucial assertion of Forster's is in
fact historically correct, and can be found, like much
else in the text, in his correspondence,[62] but Neutsch's
narrator associates it directly with the Robespierre-
Danton conflict in order to make Forster's endoisement of
the excesses of the Terror more clear-cut than it ever
was historically. Immediately after this, one of the rare
'open' statements within the narrative occurs, with the
unspecified 'Wir' underlining the moral to the GDR
audience:

> Ein Mensch, durch die Revolution zum Handeln
> gezwungen, kann Dinge tun, die man in der Nachwelt
> vor Entsetzlichkeit nicht begreift. Der Gesichts-
> punkt der Gerechtigkeit ist hier für Sterbliche zu
> hoch. Wir aber sind allein auf unsere Vernunft
> angewiesen, auf unser Urteil von heute. Für wen
> und gegen wen? Das war noch immer die vernünftigste,
> die gerechteste aller Fragen.(131)

The critical 'epic' impact of such statements is, however,
negligible when so much of the underlying historical
fiction is transparently an attempt to justify the GDR as
it is today.
 The ending of Forster in Paris is correspondingly not
the Lenzian "so siechte er hin". This comes at the

beginning of Neutsch's final chapter, whereas Forster's
death scene is bathed in sentiment and symbolism. The
map he is studying slips from his hand, and his last sensation is that of absorbing all the suffering of this
world into his breast. He drifts into death with a vision
of an attainable Utopia, embarking on a journey towards a
world of socialist freedom in which he will find love and
be reunited with his children - a world not too far removed from Forster's day, as the factual "konnte" suggests:

> Das Land, das er ansteuern wollte, konnte so fern
> nicht mehr sein, das Land, in dem der Mensch
> glücklich und frei, denkend und tätig leben würde.(147)

The contrast could not be more pronounced between Neutsch's
implication that today's GDR is that promised land, and
the long-term perspective on Utopia in the work of' his
fellow-authors. The inescapable conclusion is that
Forster in Paris was deliberately conceived as a corrective
to the impression of a painfully slow transition from the
'deutsche Misere' given by the earlier variants on Lenz,
but that Neutsch can find nothing better to support his
argument than the clichés of a discredited Socialist
Realism.

Forster in Paris serves as a reminder of how easily
historical models can be manipulated, and thus underlines
the inherent weakness of this genre of 'epic prose', when
its basis is an historical narrative. Its value as literary realism is restricted because there is little scope
for a differentiated portrayal of contemporary experience
(whereas Unvollendete Geschichte is the exception which
points to the productive potential of adapting a model
like Lenz to an explicitly contemporary context). The
unlikelihood of anyone other than a literary specialist
being able to come close to a full appreciation of these
works considerably reduces their potential popular impact
in a society in which literature is still regarded as a
primary source of critical information, of 'Lebenshilfe' -
although the fault here lies more in the continuing
existence of some of the political taboos which Erich
Honecker claimed had been lifted in 1971, than in the
growing cultural sophistication of the authors. Nevertheless, the course of GDR literature has been decisively
modified through their recognition of the profound
relevance of Büchner's Lenz to contemporary experience
and their willingness to confront residual features of
the 'deutsche Misere' in the GDR.

CONCLUSION

"Ich bin ein spätbürgerlicher Schriftsteller - was könnte ich als Schriftsteller auch anderes sein?" Stephan Hermlin's rhetorical question during his speech to the Eighth Writers' Congress in May 1978 created virtually the only stir in a gathering designed - after the unprecedentedly solid protest of authors against the Politbüro's decision to expatriate Wolf Biermann - to show that the 'real' majority still viewed their writing as a collective activity neatly harmonised with SED cultural policy. Hermlin was, of course, not suggesting for a moment that he was not also a communist writer: describing the role of the latter as being a "Sohn aller nach vorn und rückwärts gewandten Utopien, ein Sohn von Ketzern und heiliggesprochenen Märtyrern", he made it clear that he saw no contradiction between the two categories. He also insisted on the creative writer's right to 'dream' outside the bounds of political expediency ("vernunftlos ... träumen").[1] In the light of the mainstream development of GDR fiction described above, it would have been quite absurd if this sense of the historical continuity of the writer's task and this moral acceptance of the inevitability of painful conflicts with society in the defence of creative perceptions had not been expressed at the 1978 Congress. Yet most of the other established authors who shared Hermlin's convictions - such as Wolf, de Bruyn, Fühmann and Braun - had chosen not to play (or had been prevented from playing) any active part in the proceedings, and their views might otherwise have been entirely ignored at the first major cultural forum to follow the controversy of 1976.

This does not mean, however, that in the aftermath of the 'Biermann crisis' there was another attempt to suppress dissent as extensively as in the period following the Eleventh Plenum in 1965. On the contrary, these authors - now internationally respected - have been treated with what appears to have been considerable tolerance since 1976. Apart from minor (if significant) exceptions such as Braun's essay "Büchners Briefe", their recent creative writing and essays have all been published in the GDR. There is undeniable literary quality and critical force in a list of recent prose works which includes Christa Wolf's <u>Kindheitsmuster</u> (1976) and <u>Kein Ort. Nirgends</u> (1979), Fühmann's later stories in his collected <u>Erzählungen</u> (1977) and his 'subjective' study of Trakl, <u>Vor Feuerschlünden</u> (1982), de Bruyn's <u>Märkische Forschungen</u> (1978) - intimately involved with the historical issues

treated in the previous chapter - Hermlin's <u>Abendlicht</u>
(1979) and Braun's expanded edition of <u>Das ungezwungne</u>
<u>Leben Kasts</u> (1979). Most of these works have been ex-
tensively discussed in the GDR's leading cultural journals
and in volumes of literary criticism which have fully
maintained the analytical depth displayed before 1976 by
commentators such as Dieter Schlenstedt and Hans Kaufmann.
[2]   Braun's <u>Kast</u> (containing a fourth part, "Die
Tribüne", not included in the original edition of 1972) is
the only one of the titles just mentioned not to have been
prominently assessed, for reasons which have never been
clarified but which highlight the inconsistencies still
inherent in a more permissive cultural policy. Its implications are at least as radical as those of <u>Unvollendete</u>
Geschichte [3], and there may even be a degree of compensation for the continuing refusal to publish the latter in
book form behind the decision to tolerate the challenging
new part of a work previously available. "Die Tribüne" ·
differs too from the other titles mentioned above in that
the fiction is entirely located in the political and
economic context of the GDR in the 1970s: whereas the
contemporary experience of the narrator may be a vital
element in <u>Kindheitsmuster</u> or <u>Abendlicht</u>, it is manifestly
not his exclusive concern. On the whole, it seems that
the cultural-political line has been fairly flexible in
relation to those established authors whose commitment to
the state is still deemed unambiguous, and who are general
ly willing to convey their criticisms unsystematically, in
an historical context, and at a culturally sophisticated
level.
    The fact that this important body of prose writing has
been published in the GDR in the years since 1976 has
tended to be obscured in the West. The widely-held perception of recent cultural life in the GDR - as a story of
polarisation, constant confrontation and an ignominious
retreat from the spirit of open debate heralded by
Honecker's earlier speeches - is less than the whole
truth. [4]   The list of authors who have left the GDR in
disillusionment, whether permanently or on long-term
visas, is indeed depressingly long: Jurek Becker, Günter
Kunert, Sarah Kirsch, Rolf Schneider and Karl-Heinz Jakobs
- to name just a handful - have all played significant
roles in the development of GDR literature. It would,
however, be an untenable simplification to view these
much discussed 'dissidents' as the sole keepers of the
GDR's socialist conscience. The differences between those
intellectuals who have physically distanced themselves
from the GDR, and others (such as Hermlin and his colleague
mentioned above) who have chosen to remain, often appear
insubstantial and dependent almost on matters of tempera-

ment. The two groups have evidently retained close personal ties and a sense of shared purpose. For those who
have left, the ostensible issue has frequently been
whether a new work is accepted for publication in the
GDR, but the disintegration of a fragile working relationship with SED authority has usually been well advanced
before this point has been reached. Works like Becker's
Schlaflose Tage (1978) or Schneider's November (1979) -
which have only appeared in the West - may not be
spectacularly more explicit about the GDR of the 1970s
than Braun's "Tribüne": indeed, they were undoubtedly
also conceived in the hope that they might contribute
positively to a revival of openly self-critical debate
after the crisis of 1976. Yet the SED judgment on the
continuing political reliability of Becker and Schneider
evidently went marginally against them, as it went,
equally marginally, in favour of Braun, and it is on an
accumulation of such conflicts with authority and border-
line decisions that the creative future of individual
authors may, almost arbitrarily, depend.
     The critically-minded authors who remain in the GDR
have shown no inclination in their writing to reach any
accommodation with the SED leadership, while the attitude
of those politicians - notably Honecker himself and Kurt
Hager - who pronounce at major conferences on the state
of cultural life now has some of the features of the
'repressive tolerance' displayed (in the view of critics
like Herbert Marcuse) by the media of the pluralist West
towards its radical intellectuals. The GDR's outstanding
authors are rarely singled out for praise in major cultural-
political speeches as they were in the earlier 1960s, when
the spirit of pragmatic cooperation was most evident:
Wolf's Kindheitsmuster or Hermlin's Abendlicht, for
example, may be included in lists of creative achievements
under the rubric 'Auseinandersetzung mit dem Faschismus',
which conveniently obscures their dimension of critical
reference to today's GDR; the 'epic' intentions of a work
like Kein Ort. Nirgends are also unlikely to be acknowledged
- the political irritation such works provoke may however
be betrayed in general criticism of unnamed authors for
failing to understand that "unsere realistischen Ideale
[werden] schrittweise verwirklicht", a criticism which
also suggests that their "utopische Vorstellungen" are
virtually synonymous with "Pessimismus".[5]   Yet neither
are these authors singled out for criticism from public
platforms in the way in which the more explicitly outspoken Schneider or Karl-Heinz Jakobs or Stefan Heym have
been.
     Another indicator of change in cultural-political stra-
tegy is that the SED leadership has been increasingly

willing to let the Writers' Union, under the presidency of Hermann Kant since 1978, try to resolve conflicting views of the writer's role in relation to Party authority, at a 'professional' level. Kant's success as a mediator has been mixed, to say the least, and his attacks on authors regarded as having betrayed the GDR have at times been no less harsh than those of political leaders; he has, however, on other occasions provided a speedy litera ry commendation for politically challenging works like Kindheitsmuster and Abendlicht, which might conceivably have defused potential non-literary controversy.[6]

The literary means of carrying on the moral debate on identity, with its undoubted political implications, have therefore not been withdrawn since 1976. In other words, the vital function of literature in the GDR as an open process of communication between the author and a wide readership, contributing to the goal of "kollektive Selbstverständigung"[7], is still acknowledged by politicians who appreciate that popular frustrations need to be articulated and prefer this essentially private level of exchange through the medium of the book to other, more threatening, public forms of debate. Thus an increasingly sophisticated dialogue continues, although the literary avant-garde - for its own good reasons of creative authenticity as well as on grounds of political discretion - no longer provides the depth of immediate response to specifi economic and political changes which it did in the aftermath of the 'Bitterfelder Weg'.

One obvious exception to this state of affairs, which exposes a possible contradiction in Hermlin's representative statement on the role of established GDR authors as late-bourgeois utopian dreamers uninvolved with short-terr political practicalities, has emerged in the early 1980s. The goal of a socialist community which will make a reali of the vision in the Communist Manifesto - "eine Assoziation, worin die freie Entwicklung eines jeden die Bedingung für die freie Entwicklung aller ist"[8] - has never been more at risk than under the conditions of the increasingly tense East-West nuclear confrontation of the present day, and the threat of the total destruction of Central Europe in a 'limited' nuclear exchange has galvanised these authors into a series of public initiatives, ever since Hermlin - to widespread surprise - was able to organise a 'Begegnung zur Friedensförderung' for writers (and scientists) from both German states in December 1981 the first writers' conference on this scale to be held since 1947.

Hermlin produced the most surprising quotation of the conference - Lenin's statement of 1917 that unilateral gestures are the way to overcome militarism - a sentiment

which accorded closely with the tone of moral exhortation
in the contributions of the other critical GDR intellectuals
who had been publicly reticent since 1976. De Bruyn,
drawing his inspiration from the Sermon on the Mount,
spoke of "Moral" as an "Überlebensstrategie", while
Fühmann pleaded for the preservation of a "Menschheit"
which has been prevented by the "Machtgebilde der Blöcke
und Lager" from developing its true potential. Pointing
to the shared responsibility of both power blocks for the
present crisis, they all stressed the desperate need for
confidence-building measures. Braun attacked the basic
notion of a "kleiner Frieden" dependent on fearsome
military strength as being, in the specific East European
context, an "Alibi für den schier unänderlichen Sozialismus" and saw the necessary connection between this situation and   institutionalised state repression - "die
für diesen Frieden notwendigen unterdrückerischen Strukturen, die für diesen Frieden notwendige Kommandogewalt,
das für diesen Frieden notwendige Informationsmonopol".
He identified a "kommunistische[n] Impuls" behind grass-
roots peace movements in the West and, like Fühmann and
de Bruyn, urged toleration of similar groups in the GDR
as a means of satisfying the popular "Hunger nach Mitent-
scheidungen". None of them went quite as far as Christa
Wolf in her wholesale rejection of "diese Zivilisation",
and of "Industriegesellschaften" which have arisen
historically because of the suppression of the feminine
principle - "dieses Wegdrängen des weiblichen Faktors".[9]
    In this atmosphere of crisis, the ultimate goals of
self-realisation, a communist society and international
peace are freed from conventional ideological qualifica-
tions and seen to be   interdependent. There is a sense,
too, of the special responsibilities these East German
authors share with their colleagues from the Federal
Republic, as children of the Third Reich, in attempting
to prevent what would be the ultimate European war. The
greatest problem for the East German authors, however,
remains that of finding politically acceptable ways of
translating this unambiguous opposition to the authoritarian structures of the GDR into progress towards these
ultimate goals. Indeed, the longing for a pre-industrial
state of innocence and the identification with Romantic
ideals, which is evident here in Christa Wolf's speech,
suggests that their idea of utopia is still partially
dependent on the historically regressive notions we first
observed in the exile projections of Becher. In the meantime, the SED leadership sticks rigidly to the general
policy line that the authors' primary duty is to contribute to the "Formung des sozialistischen National- und
Vaterlandsbewußtseins" and the "Vertiefung des sozialis-

tischen Heimatbewußtseins" while maintaining ideological
vigilance against the subversive machinations of the
"Klassengegner" in the cultural arena.[10]

The possibility of progress beyond this impasse is
clearly not dependent alone on developments within the
GDR. There is no doubt that a return to the spirit of
detente in seats of government in the West and a genuine
start to the process of nuclear disarmament would deprive
the GDR, to quote Braun again, of its "Alibi für den schier
unänderlichen Sozialismus". Whether this would show the
SED more able than in the relatively stable early 1970s
to bring about real popular participation in decision-
making remains an open question: it would certainly
demonstrate the achievement of a more stable identity as
a distinctive German state if it did.

There are few encouraging signs for the immediate
future. GDR literature, and not least in the prose works
discussed above, has succeeded, stage by stage, in exposing the untenability of propagandist simplifications
regarding the quality of individual and social experience
in the GDR, and has underlined the extent to which the
undeniable material achievements of the past three decades
have yet to be matched in terms of political progress
towards communist goals. The authors highlighted above
have proven their creative integrity and produced works
of lasting literary value, but they are still, in some
respects, constricted within the conceptual parameters
of the German cultural heritage with which they identify
so strongly. Their vision of self-perfection has survived
against intimidating odds, although the haunting doubt
which concludes the utopian deliberations of Kein Ort.
Nirgends is still no closer to a reassuring resolution:

> Man wird uns für rasend halten. Unser unausrottbarer
> Glaube, der Mensch sei bestimmt, sich zu
> vervollkommnen, der dem Geist aller Zeiten strikt
> zuwiderläuft. Ein Wahn?

NOTES

INTRODUCTION

1. This necessarily simplified presentation of aspects of the Marxist cultural debate of the 1930s which relate to the mainstream development of GDR literature is indebted to the many detailed accounts and documentations published over the 1970s, especially H. Gallas, Marxistische Literaturtheorie, Neuwied, 1971, W. Mittenzwei (Ed.), Dialog und Kontroverse mit Georg Lukács, Leipzig, 1975, M. Löwy, Georg Lukács: From Romanticism to Bolschevism, London, 1979, and Zur Tradition der deutschen sozialistischen Literatur, Berlin, 1979. The central importance of the identity issue to modern German literature generally is illuminated in the first chapter of R. Hinton Thomas and K. Bullivant, Literature in Upheaval: West German Writers and the Challenge of the 1960s, Manchester, 1974.

2. See the afterword of 1970 to his Essays über Realismus, (Werke, Vol. 4), Neuwied, 1971, p. 677.

3. Ibid., pp. 14, 47, 141, 182-4.

4. Ibid., pp. 31-2.

5. Ibid., p. 57.

6. Zur Tradition der deutschen sozialistischen Literatur, p. 432.

7. See, for example, his introduction to Skizze einer Geschichte der neueren deutschen Literatur, Darmstadt, 1975, pp. 16-22.

8. Deutsche Literatur in zwei Jahrhunderten, (Werke, Vol. 7), pp. 69-88.

9. The pressures throughout the Stalin era to reverse these priorities are memorably recorded by Stephan Hermlin in his Abendlicht, Berlin, 1979, pp. 20-22.

10. Deutsche Literatur, pp. 182-3.

11. Georg Lukács: From Romanticism to Bolschevism, p. 204

12. Deutsche Literatur, pp. 334-419 (pp. 392 ff.).

13. See Benjamin, Versuche über Brecht, Frankfurt, 1966, pp. 117-38; "Ein Briefwechsel zwischen Anna Seghers und Georg Lukács", in Essays über Realismus, pp. 345-76 (p. 348).

14. "Der Autor als Produzent", in Versuche über Brecht, pp. 95-116 (pp. 109-10).

15. Gesammelte Werke, Frankfurt, 1967, Vol. 19, pp. 314, 309, and Vol. 17, p. 1009.

16. "Ein Briefwechsel", pp. 345-8.

CHAPTER 1

1.   Bobrowski, Literarisches Klima, Berlin, 1977, p. 23;
     Becher, Auf andere Art so große Hoffnung, Berlin,
     1969, p. 480.
2.   Kleine Prosa, (Gesammelte Werke, Vol. 9), Berlin,
     1974, pp. 366, 371.
3.   Von der Größe unserer Literatur: Reden und Aufsätze,
     Leipzig, 1971, p. 26.
4.   See Lyrik, Prosa, Dokumente: Eine Auswahl, Wiesbaden,
     1965, pp. 57-8;   Von der Größe unserer Literatur,
     p. 26.
5.   Sinn und Form, (2. Sonderheft J.R. Becher), 1959,
     137.
6.   Levisite oder Der einzig gerechte Krieg, (Gesammelte
     Werke, Vol. 10), Berlin, 1969.
7.   Von der Größe, pp. 43, 32, 89.
8.   See "Kühnheit und Begeisterung" and "Das große Bünd-
     nis", ibid., pp. 110-30, 131-48 (p. 146).
9.   Ibid., pp. 171-2.
10. Ibid., p. 153.
11. Autobiographisches, (Werke, Vol. 19), Frankfurt, 1968,
     p. 106.
12. Design and Truth in Autobiography, London, 1960, p.59.
13. K. Pinthus (Ed.), Menschheitsdämmerung, Reinbek, 1966,
     p. 213.
14. Although there is still no satisfactory biography of
     Becher, the main details of his life can be found in
     N. Hopster, Das Frühwerk Johannes R. Bechers, Bonn,
     1969; P. Raabe (Ed.), Expressionismus: Aufzeichnungen
     und Erinnerungen der Zeitgenossen, Olten, 1965;
     H. Haase, Johannes R. Becher, (Schriftsteller der
     Gegenwart), Berlin, 1981.
15. "Größe und Verfall des Expressionismus", Essays über
     Realismus, pp. 109-49.
16. H. Huppert, "Im lyrischen Dezernat", Sinn und Form,
     (2. Sonderheft), 313.
17. All page references to Abschied. Wiederanders,
     (Gesammelte Werke, Vol. 11), Berlin, 1975, are in-
     cluded in the text in round brackets.
18. See R. Hinton Thomas, "Das Ich und die Welt: Ex-
     pressionismus und Gesellschaft", in W. Rothe (Ed.),
     Expressionismus als Literatur, Berne, 1969, pp. 19-36.
19. W. Herzfelde, "Wandelbar und Stetig", in Sinn und
     Form, (2. Sonderheft), 48.
20. "J.R. Bechers 'Abschied'", in Schicksalswende,
     Berlin, 1948, pp. 314-332 (p. 330).
21. Dieter Schiller argues in his important recent essays
     on Abschied that there is an "Erzähler-Medium"

responsible for the symbolical elucidation of Gastl's
exemplary experiences, as a deliberate structural
principle. The didactic anonymity of these 'narrator'
interventions conflicts so crassly, however, with the
vivid immediacy of the main narrative that a sense of
structural unity is never established. See Abschied.
Wiederanders, Nachwort, pp. 633-8; "Entwicklungsroman
als Bewußtseinsroman", in S. Bock und M. Hahn (Eds.),
Erfahrung Exil: Antifaschistische Romane 1933-45,
Berlin, 1979, pp. 277-8, 297-301.

22. "J.R. Bechers 'Abschied'", p. 210.
23. See M. Löwy, Georg Lukács, pp. 202-4, and Lukács' own
account in Gelebtes Denken: Eine Autobiographie im
Dialog, Frankfurt, 1981, pp. 157-84.
24. See R.A. Nisbet, The Sociological Tradition, London,
1971, pp. 71-78.
25. See L. Rubiner (Ed.), Kameraden der Menschheit,
Leipzig, 1971, pp. 64, 66; K. Pinthus (Ed.), Menschheitsdämmerung, pp. 42, 44.
26. Sinn und Form, (2. Sonderheft), 217, 203.
27. Menschheitsdämmerung, pp. 285-7.
28. Both documents are held in the Johannes R. Becher-
Archiv in Berlin: Fallada's commentary is undated,
the review in Der Morgen appeared on 22. December
1945.
29. Lyrik, Prosa, Dokumente, p. 147.
30. Ibid., p. 154.
31. Von der Größe, pp. 302-41.
32. Page references to Auf andere Art so große Hoffnung:
Tagebuch 1950, (Gesammelte Werke, Vol. 12), are included in the text.
33. "Bechers 'Tagebuch 1950'", in Deutsche Literatur und
Weltliteratur, Berlin, 1957, pp. 665-81.
34. "Rebellion und Revolution im expressionistischen
Gedicht: Bechers frühe Lyrik im Urteil seines Tage-
buches von 1950", in W. Mittenzwei (Ed.), Revolution
und Literatur, Leipzig, 1971, pp. 302-3.
35. Republished in the Gesammelte Werke, Vols. 13-14,
Berlin, 1972. See also Jürgen Rühle's essay,
"J.R. Bechers Poetische Konfession" in his Literatur
und Revolution, Munich, 1963, pp. 216-34.
36. Sinn und Form, (2. Sonderheft), 491-2.
37. Bemühungen II, pp. 137-8.
38. Bemühungen I, pp. 220-1, 360-1.
39. The most helpful account of Becher's role during the
'Thaw' is Hans Mayer's "DDR 1956: Tauwetter, das
keines war", Frankfurter Hefte, 11/1976, 15-23 and
12/1976, 29-38.
40. K. Jarmatz (Ed.), Kritik in der Zeit, Halle, 1970,
pp. 373-5. For a critical appraisal of the 'Aufbau-

roman' see Marc Silbermann, Literature of the Working
World: A Study of the Industrial Novel in East Germany,
Berne, 1976.

41. "Das Problem der Perspektive", in Essays über Realismus, pp. 651-7.

42. Gesammelte Werke, Vol. 11, pp. 435-607: subsequent
page refs. in the text are to this edition. See
D. Schiller, Nachwort, pp. 647-8, and "Entwicklungsroman als Bewußtseinsroman", p. 270. H. Küntzel, in
ignoring Wiederanders completely, misses the paradig-
matic significance of Becher's development as a prose
writer for GDR literature: "Von 'Abschied' bis
'Atemnot': Über die Poetik des Romans ... in der
DDR", in J. Hoogeveen and G. Labroisse (Eds.), DDR-
Roman und Literaturgesellschaft, Amsterdam, 1981,
pp. 1-32.

43. H.F. Bachmair, "Vorläufige Bemerkungen zu J.R. Bechers
Roman-Fragment 'Wiederanders'" (unpublished typescript, dated Sept. 1960, held in the Becher-Archiv).

CHAPTER 2

1. See Christa Wolf, "Die Literaturtheorie findet zur
literarischen Praxis", Neue Deutsche Literatur 11/
1955, 159ff.

2. GDR critics have been at pains ever since to deny
this ambiguity, e.g. Werner Neubert, "Franz Fühmann:
Zur Ideologie und Psychologie eines Werkes", NDL
4/1974, 44-70 (p.49).

3. Alexander Abusch, "Im ideologischen Kampf für eine
sozialistische Kultur", in E. Schubbe, (Ed.),
Dokumente zur Kunst-, Literatur-, und Kulturpolitik
der SED, Stuttgart, 1972, p. 490. The ideological
debate on war literature is well documented in Frank
Trommler's essay "Von Stalin zu Hölderlin: Über den
Entwicklungsroman in der DDR", Basis, Vol. 2, 1971,
141-90. The GDR's first comprehensive study of the
revival of the 'Entwicklungsroman' was Sigrid
Töpelmann's Autoren, Figuren, Entwicklungen, Berlin,
1975 (pp. 192-321).

4. For Kurella's speech see Marianne Lange, Beiträge
zur Gegenwartsliteratur, Heft 16, Berlin 1959, 23;
Hermann Kant und Frank Wagner, "Die große Abrechnung:
Probleme der Darstellung des Krieges in der deutschen
Gegenwartsliteratur", in K. Jarmatz, Kritik in der
Zeit, pp. 416-23 (p. 423).

5. First delivered as a lecture at the East Berlin Akademie der Künste in January 1956: see Essays über Realismus, (Werke, Vol. 4), Neuwied, 1971, pp. 551-603.
6. Ibid., pp. 574, 595.
7. Ibid., p. 575.
8. See Trommler, "Von Stalin zu Hölderlin", 183-5.
9. Reference will be made in the text to the following editions (indicated by the appropriate initial): de Bruyn, Der Hohlweg, Halle, 1963 (= H); Fühmann, Das Judenauto, Zurich, 1968 (= J); Noll, Die Abenteuer des Werner Holt, Vol. 1, Berlin, 1968, Vol. 2, Berlin, 1974 (= WH, WH 2); Schulz, Wir sind nicht Staub im Wind, Halle, 1968 (= S).
10. See H.J. Geerdts, "Die Schicksalsfrage Büchners neu gestellt: Bemerkungen zu Nolls Roman 'Die Abenteuer des Werner Holt'", Weimarer Beiträge 1/1965, 147-58.
11. See Trommler, "Von Stalin zu Hölderlin", 163-5.
12. Goethe's contrast (of Sept. 1823) between the richness of British history, which Walter Scott had been able to draw on for his novels, and the drabness of contemporary German society, is quoted by Roy Pascal in The German Novel, London, 1965, p. 29.
13. De Bruyn provides an important corrective, through his portrayal of Eckert, to the ideological assumption that qualities revealed in youth are a reliable pointer towards future development: the initially progressive Eckert falls prey to egotism in his pursuit of a journalistic career and shows little regard subsequently for Weichmantel.
14. "Erpreßte Versöhnung", in Noten zur Literatur, Vol. 2, Frankfurt, 1965, pp. 152-87 (pp. 185-87).
15. See Der russische Realismus in der Weltliteratur, (Werke, Vol. 5), Neuwied, 1964, pp. 545-65 (p. 551).
16. "Sechs Personen diskutieren einen Autor", NDL 4/1964, 105-19 (112).
17. See Stegreif und Sattel: Anmerkungen zur Literatur und zum Tage, Halle, 1967, p. 14.
18. "Der Holzweg", in G. Schneider (Ed.), Eröffnungen: Schriftsteller über ihr Erstlingswerk, Berlin, 1974, pp. 138-43.
19. The wish expressed by de Bruyn in "Der Holzweg" that he should have limited himself to the post-war months most vividly embedded in his consciousness was fulfilled by at least one GDR author, Günter Kunert, in the aftermath of these novels. His picaresque portrayal of the period, Im Namen der Hüte, although published in the Federal Republic in 1967, did not appear in the GDR until 1976.

238

CHAPTER 3

1. See the excerpts from the speeches by Walter Ulbricht
   and Alfred Kurella in E. Schubbe (Ed.), Dokumente,
   pp. 534-8.
2. Ingeborg Gerlach, Bitterfeld: Arbeiterliteratur und
   Literatur der Arbeitswelt in der DDR, Kronberg, 1974,
   p. 34.
3. See again the speeches referred to in note 1, as well
   as Alexander Abusch's attack on Lukács shortly before
   the Parteitag (reprinted in his Humanismus und Realismus in der Literatur, Leipzig, 1971, pp. 166-80).
4. The list of contributors to a representative volume
   of the annual anthology 'Ich schreibe': Arbeiter
   greifen zur Feder, Berlin und Halle, 1960ff., (i.e.
   Vol. 3, 1962) includes a factory librarian, the editor
   of a works newspaper, the organiser of a centre for
   'Volkskunst', an official of the 'Gesellschaft für
   deutsch-sowjetische Freundschaft', a trade union
   officer and a technologist. The manual workers are
   distinctly in a minority.
5. His close friendship with Brecht, which began with
   their collaboration on the Berliner Ensemble's production of Strittmatter's Katzgraben (1953), has often
   been the subject of his anecdotal short prose.
6. "An die Basis - gegen die Selbstzufriedenheit", in
   'Greif zur Feder Kumpel': Protokoll der Autorenkonferenz ... im Kulturpalast des Elektrochemischen
   Kombinats Bitterfeld, Halle, 1959, pp. 45-52 (p. 52).
7. "Unser Weg ist richtig", in V. Deutscher Schriftstellerkongreß: Referate und Diskussionsbeiträge,
   Berlin, 1961, pp. 112-28 (p. 118).
8. Neue Deutsche Literatur 10/1961, 129-33. See Jakobs'
   own revealing account of his industrial experience in
   J. Walther (Ed.), Meinetwegen Schmetterlinge: Gespräche mit Schriftstellern, Berlin, 1973, pp. 23-32.
9. See E. Deuerlein (Ed.), DDR: Geschichte und Bestands-
   aufnahme 1945-70, Munich, 1971, pp. 160-67, 236.
10. Wolf's literary debut was her Moskauer Novelle (1961)
    Kant's the collection of stories Ein bißchen Südsee
    (1962). The other novel fundamental to this literary
    breakthrough is Erwin Strittmatter's Ole Bienkopp
    (1963), which offers a more penetrating critique of
    the Stalin era than the four works analysed below,
    but has no narrative point of reference in the early
    1960s.
11. V. Deutscher Schriftstellerkongreß, pp. 32-66. Re-
    printed in her Glauben an Irdisches, Leipzig, 1974,
    pp. 231-69 (266-7, 261).

12. Reference will be made in the text to the following editions, with title initials as indicated: Reimann, Die Geschwister, Berlin, 1963 (= G); Wolf, Der geteilte Himmel, Halle, 1971 (= GH); Neutsch, Spur der Steine, Halle, 1968 (= SS); Kant, Die Aula, Berlin, 1966 (= A).

13. Kant's innovations were first highlighted in the essay by Silvia and Dieter Schlenstedt, "Modern erzählt: Zu Strukturen in Hermann Kants Roman 'Die Aula'", in NDL 12/1965, 5-34.

14. See David Childs, East Germany, London, 1969, pp. 24-35.

15. Uwe Johnson develops this idea as a central metaphor in Das dritte Buch über Achim (1961), which is, on one level, about the problems of writing a truthful biography of an East German cycling champion.

16. See above, note 10.

17. The story is included in Neutsch's Tage unseres Lebens, Leipzig, 1973.

18. "Notwendiges Streitgespräch", in NDL 3/1965, 88-97 (p. 88). As an indication of the popularity of these novels, Der geteilte Himmel had sales of well over 100,000 in the GDR in its first year, while 80,000 copies of Spur der Steine were published within a few months in 1964 (see NDL 3/1965, 192).

19. Martin Reso's 'Der geteilte Himmel' und seine Kritiker, Halle, 1965, gives a clear impression of the breadth of the debate and the quality of some of the contributions; the growth of interest in the Federal Republic is marked by works such as M. Reich-Ranicki's Deutsche Literatur in Ost und West, Munich, 1963.

20. Published separately as Über die Entwicklung einer volksverbundenen sozialistischen Nationalkultur, Berlin, 1964, (pp. 12-13, 9).

21. "Brief an den Minister für Kultur", in Erfahrungen und Widersprüche: Versuche über Literatur, Rostock, 1975, pp. 5-15 (pp. 7, 9).

22. See Protokoll der ... im Kulturpalast des Elektrochemischen Kombinats Bitterfeld abgehaltenen Konferenz, Berlin, 1964, pp. 224-33 (p. 229); E. Schubbe (Ed.), Dokumente, p. 1099.

23. First published in Sinn und Form 1-2/1965; reprinted in his Geschichten aus der Produktion, Vol. 1, Berlin (West), 1974, pp. 85-136 (p. 118).

24. Bericht des Politbüros an die 11. Tagung des Zentralkomitees der SED, Berlin, 1966, pp. 56-7. Schubbe offers extracts from the main contributions, Dokumente, pp. 1076-1117.

CHAPTER 4

1. Frankfurt, 1966, pp. 266-7, 287.
2. "Das Neue und das Bleibende in unserer Literatur", in
    Deutscher Schriftstellerverband (Ed.), VI. Deutscher
    Schriftstellerkongreß: Protokoll, Berlin, 1969, pp.
    44-5.
3. Halle, 1970, p. 17.
4. See R. Hinton Thomas and Keith Bullivant, Literature
    in Upheaval, Manchester, 1974, pp. 7-12.
5. For example Schriften zum Theater, Berlin, 1964 and
    Schriften zur Literatur und Kunst, Berlin, 1966,
    (both edited by W. Hecht). The first extensive selec-
    tion from Walter Benjamin's literary criticism, Lese-
    zeichen (Ed. G. Seidel), was not published until 1970
    (Leipzig), although it was prepared in 1965.
6. Gesammelte Werke, Frankfurt, 1967, Vol. 19, p. 527.
7. Lesen und Schreiben, Berlin, 1972, pp. 62-5.
8. See Strittmatter, Schulzenhofer Kramkalender (1966)
    and Ein Dienstag im September (1970); Kunert, Tag-
    träume in Berlin und andernorts (1972); de Bruyn,
    Maskeraden (1966).
9. Lesen und Schreiben, pp. 70-87.
10. "Die zumutbare Wahrheit" was omitted from the GDR
    edition of Lesen und Schreiben, but is included in
    Wolf's Fortgesetzter Versuch, Leipzig, 1979, pp. 245-
    57.
11. Included in Gesammelte Erzählungen, Darmstadt, 1980,
    pp. 41-64 (p. 47).
12. Erik Neutsch's Auf der Suche nach Gatt, Halle, 1973,
    is closely comparable in many respects to the other
    four novels, but is not considered here because it is
    largely derivative in its conception. Reference will
    be made in the text to the following editions, with
    title initials as indicated: de Bruyn, Buridans
    Esel, Halle, 1968 (= BE); Wolf, Nachdenken über
    Christa T., Frankfurt, 1971 (= CT); Kant, Das Im-
    pressum, Berlin, 1973 (= I); Reimann, Franziska
    Linkerhand, Berlin, 1974 (= FL).
13. See de Bruyn's interview with S. Töpelmann, Weimarer
    Beiträge 6/1968, 1171-83 (p. 1171).
14. Invaluable insights into the novel's progress are pro-
    vided by her correspondence with Annemarie Auer, much
    of which is included in W. Liersch (Ed.), Was zählt,
    ist die Wahrheit, Halle, 1975, pp. 288-330.
15. See H.P. Anderle (Ed.), Mitteldeutsche Erzähler,
    Cologne 1965, pp. 248-55.
16. Letter of 1.7.65, published in Sonntag 9/73, but
    curiously omitted from the Liersch anthology.

17. See her interview with Auer, <u>Sonntag</u> 7/68.
18. Interview with H. Plavius, <u>NDL</u> 6/68, 9-13.
19. "Selbstinterview" (1966), republished in <u>Fortgesetzter Versuch</u>, pp. 45-8.
20. Not published until 1972, as the title essay of the volume <u>Lesen und Schreiben</u>, pp. 176-224 (reference here is to the sections 'Weltbilder' and 'Realitäten', pp. 204-16).
21. In her interview of 1973 with Hans Kaufmann, republished in <u>Fortgesetzter Versuch</u>, pp. 77-104 (p. 83).
22. A. Grosse emphasises this weakness in her essay "Vom Wert der Geschichte", <u>WB</u> 8/72, 65-91 (pp. 84-5).
23. See his interview with Grosse, which precedes her essay: <u>WB</u> 8/72, 32-64 (pp. 57-8).
24. <u>Lesen und Schreiben</u>, pp. 209, 223.
25. Interview with H. Plavius, <u>NDL</u> 6/68, 12.
26. The most extensive critical portrayal of the events of 17. June 1953 by a GDR author is Stefan Heym's <u>Fünf Tage im Juni</u> (1974), which has not appeared in the GDR. See my review article, <u>Times Higher Educational Supplement</u>, 11.2.1977.
27. <u>Auf andere Art so große Hoffnung</u>, Berlin, 1969, p. 224. Wolf quotes the relevant passage in her essay of 1966, "Tagebuch - Arbeitsmittel und Gedächtnis", <u>Lesen und Schreiben</u>, p. 76.
28. "Selbstinterview", pp. 46, 48.
29. Chapter 13, pp. 420-49: see his interview with Grosse, <u>WB</u> 8/72, 58-59.
30. <u>Lesen und Schreiben</u>, pp. 218, 181.
31. "Produktive Sehnsucht: Struktur, Thematik und politische Relevanz von ...'Nachdenken über Christa T.'", in <u>Basis</u>, Vol. 2, 1971, 191-233 (p. 215).
32. See Roy Pascal, "Georg Lukács:The Concept of Totality", in his <u>Culture and the Division of Labour</u>, University of Warwick, 1974, pp. 63-100.

CHAPTER 5

1. See above, pp. 144-5, and the section 'Weltbilder' in Wolf's <u>Lesen und Schreiben</u>, Berlin, 1972, pp. 204-10. My findings in this chapter also formed the basis of the article "'Ewige deutsche Misere'? - GDR authors and Büchner's 'Lenz'", in G. Bartram and A. Waine (Eds.), <u>Culture and Society in the GDR</u>, Dundee, 1983.
2. See above, pp. 5-10. Lukács does accord high praise to Büchner, but as the author of <u>Dantons Tod</u> rather than <u>Lenz</u>: see "Der faschistisch verfälschte und der wirkliche Georg Büchner", in his <u>Deutsche Literatur</u>,

pp. 249-72.

3. The most accessible summary of Lukács' view of the cultural heritage is his Skizze einer Geschichte der neueren deutschen Literatur (both parts of which were published by the new Aufbau Verlag in 1945), Darmstadt, 1975 (p. 57).

4. The 'Misere' is broadly defined in the introduction to Skizze einer Geschichte, pp. 16-22.

5. See above, pp. 130-3.

6. See Glauben an Irdisches, pp. 272-3, 351 (cf. her speech of 1935, "Vaterlandsliebe", ibid., pp. 9-13).

7. With some justice, to the extent that they were dependent on "Literatenlegenden" as much as literary analysis of these authors' work: see Lukács, Essays über Realismus, p. 359.

8. Lesen und Schreiben, pp. 91-126 (pp. 100-2).

9. Werner Bräunig, another 'victim' of the Eleventh Plenum, reached remarkably similar conclusions to Wolf on the contemporary significance of Lenz in his essay of 1968, "Prosa schreiben", reprinted in Ein Kranich im Himmel, Halle, 1981, pp. 387-403, although he failed to apply his insights effectively to his subsequent creative writing.

   The broader interest in artists of the 'Goethe era' in recent GDR literature is indicated in essays such as Klaus Werner, "Zur Darstellung der Kunst- und Künstlerproblematik ...", in M. Diersch und W. Hartinger (Eds.), Literatur und Geschichtsbewußtsein, Berlin, 1976, pp. 150-83; Bernd Leistner, Unruhe um einen Klassiker: Zum Goethe-Bezug in der neueren DDR-Literatur, Halle, 1978; Hans Kaufmann, Versuch über das Erbe, Leipzig, 1980; Patricia Herminghouse, "Die Wiederentdeckung der Romantik ...", in J. Hoogeveen und G. Labroisse (Eds.), DDR-Roman und Literaturgesellschaft, Amsterdam, 1981, pp. 217-48.

10. Glauben an Irdisches, pp. 177, 187.

11. Büchner's narrative technique (and his historical importance in the development of German prose) has been illuminatingly analysed by Roy Pascal in The Dual Voice, Manchester, 1977, pp. 60-66, and his "Büchner's 'Lenz' - Style and Message", Oxford German Studies, Vol. 9, 1978, 68-83.

12. My emphasis: see Pascal, "Büchner's 'Lenz'", 74-76. Page references in the text are to Georg Büchner, Werke und Briefe, Munich, 1965.

13. References in the text are to Bobrowski, Die Erzählungen, Berlin, 1979.

14. In 1967 he was co-editor of Johannes Bobrowski: Selbstzeugnisse und Beiträge über sein Werk and

243

published a monograph on Bobrowski in the series
"Schriftsteller der Gegenwart" (cf. the latter volume,
pp. 95-99, 61-69).

15. Brecht's description of the play in his prologue,
Gesammelte Werke, Vol. 6, p. 2333.

16. Wetterzeichen, Berlin, 1967, p. 51.

17. See F. Hölderlin, Werke (Kleine Stuttgarter Ausgabe),
Vol. 6, p. 455. The curious origins of the story
are described by B. Jentzsch, "Schöne Erde Vaterland",
in Selbstzeugnisse, pp. 128-33, and a detailed analysis is provided by G. Hartung, "Bobrowskis
Boehlendorff", in G. Rostin (Ed.), Selbstzeugnisse
und neue Beiträge, Berlin, 1975, pp. 261-91.

18. Hölderlin, Werke, Vol. 4, pp. 309-11.

19. J. Walther (Ed.), Meinetwegen Schmetterlinge, p. 128.

20. With Hans Kaufmann, Weimarer Beiträge 6/1974, 112.
(Both interviews are reprinted in Wolf, Fortgesetzter
Versuch, pp. 59-104).

21. References in the text are to the Darmstadt, 1982,
edition.

22. See WB 7/1970, 10-26. The extensive interest in
Hölderlin in both German states is indicated by
B. Greiner, "Zersprungene Identität ...", in
K. Lamers (Ed.), Die deutsche Frage im Spiegel der
Literatur, Stuttgart, 1978, pp. 85-120.

23. Berlin (West), 1970.

24. Lektüre, Berlin, 1979, p. 112.

25. See Leistner's balanced assessment in Unruhe um einen
Klassiker, pp. 87-90.

26. Werke, Vol. 3, p. 160.

27. Johannes Bobrowski, p. 64.

28. Werke, Vol. 6, pp. 462-4; Vol. 2, pp. 196-8, 246-8.

29. Werke, Vol. 3, p. 32; Vol. 6, p. 362; Vol. 1, p. 304
and Vol. 6, p. 406.

30. Werke, Vol. 1, pp. 230-3. Leistner underlines the
untenability of Wolf's view of Goethe and Schiller
here, rather than seeking to appreciate his 'epic'
intentions: Unruhe um einen Klassiker, pp. 90-94.

31. See his interview with Silvia Schlenstedt (WB 10/1972)
and his speech to the Seventh Writers' Congress, both
reprinted in Es genügt nicht die einfache Wahrheit:
Notate, Leipzig, 1975, (pp. 118, 121, 135, 137).

32. See, for example, "Im Ilmtal" and Hinze und Kunze as
adaptations of Goethe's "An den Mond" and Faust (discussed by Leistner, pp. 49-55).

33. These developments are effectively summarised by
Wolfgang Emmerich, Kleine Literaturgeschichte der
DDR, Darmstadt, 1981, pp. 180-2.

34. "Tabus", in Es genügt nicht, pp. 102-4.

35. These invaluable volumes of interviews/correspondence, edited by J. Walther, G. Schneider and W. Liersch respectively, have all been referred to above.
36. See, for example, Günter de Bruyn, Das Leben des Jean Paul Friedrich Richter, Frankfurt, 1978; Franz Fühmann, Fräulein Veronika Paulmann ... oder Etwas über das Schauerliche bei ETA Hoffmann, Rostock, 1979; Christa Wolf, "Nun ja! Das nächste Leben geht aber heute an", Sinn und Form 2/1980, pp. 392-418; Gerhard Wolf, afterword to Und grüß mich nicht unter den Linden: Heine in Berlin, Berlin, 1980, pp. 275-99. De Bruyn argues specifically that Jean Paul, in 1790, narrowly avoided Lenz's fate (p. 98).
37. The point was originally made persuasively by GDR commentators such as Ernst Schumacher and Stephan Hermlin: see "Diskussion um Plenzdorf", SF 1/1973, 241, 244.
38. See Robert Weimann, "Goethe in der Figurenperspektive", SF 1/1973, 222-38; Peter Wapnewski, "Zweihundert Jahre Werthers Leiden oder: Dem war nicht zu helfen", in Zumutungen, Düsseldorf, 1979, pp. 44-65. References in the text are to the Rostock, 1973, edition.
39. The Werther originals can be found in Goethe, Werke (Hamburger Ausgabe), Vol. 6, pp. 11, 62, 71.
40. In a speech of 28. May 1973: see G. Rüß (Ed.), Dokumente zur Kunst-, Literatur- und Kulturpolitik der SED 1971-74, Stuttgart, 1976, p. 777. References in the text are to Unvollendete Geschichte, Frankfurt, 1977.
41. Braun's treatment of motifs and narrative features of Lenz has been perceptively analysed by Charlotte Koerner, "Volker Brauns 'Unvollendete Geschichte': Erinnerung an Büchners 'Lenz'", in Basis, Vol. 9, 1979, 149-68.
42. See Koerner, 153-5.
43. According to Braun's verbal account, in a discussion during his British lecture tour in February 1980, it derives from an unpublished taped interview with the young couple he calls 'Karin' and 'Frank'.
44. P. 534: it is one of the few revealing poems in the "Nachlese" section of this volume.
45. Gedichte, Leipzig, 1976, p. 44.
46. Werke und Briefe, pp. 134, 162, 33.
47. Connaissance de la RDA, No. 7, (Nov. 1978), 8-17.
48. Published in SF 4/1976, reprinted in Fortgesetzter Versuch, pp. 105-36 (134-5).
49. These three stories make up the volume Unter den Linden, Berlin, 1974.
50. See Emmerich, Kleine Literaturgeschichte, pp. 187-9, and Karl-Heinz Jakobs' subjective account in

Der Spiegel, 48/1981, 86-108.

51. Published in <u>NDL</u> 2/1978, reprinted in <u>Fortgesetzter</u>
     <u>Versuch</u>, pp. 280-90 (284-6).

52. See P. Goldammer (Ed.), <u>Schriftsteller über Kleist</u>,
     Berlin, 1976. Kunert's "Pamphlet für K." appeared
     with a postscript in <u>SF</u> 5/1975, 1091-7. The context
     is explained in detail by H. Küntzel, "Der andere
     Kleist: Wirkungsgeschichte und Wiederkehr Kleists in
     der DDR", in P.G. Klussman und H. Mohr (Eds.), <u>Jahr-</u>
     <u>buch zur Literatur in der DDR</u>, Vol. 1, Bonn, 1980,
     105-39.

53. Page references in the text to the Darmstadt, 1979,
     edition.

54. GDR critics such as Günter Hartung have attempted to
     deny the openness of these 'Wir' statements (see
     <u>Connaissance de la RDA</u>, No. 13, (Nov. 1981), 25-34),
     but the textual evidence of <u>Kein Ort</u>, as well as the
     wider context of 'epic prose' and Wolf's earlier work,
     suggests otherwise.

55. The paragraph on p. 87 beginning "Bei Struensee,
     ja ..." consists mainly of a paraphrase of statements
     made by Kleist in his letter of 25. November 1800
     (<u>Sämtliche Werke und Briefe</u>, Vol. 2, Munich, 1977,
     p. 602): this provides authentic motifs which can be
     fictionally elaborated later in the narrative. Wolf
     employs this technique extensively. By publishing an
     edition of Günderrode's work (<u>Der Schatten eines</u>
     <u>Traumes</u>, Darmstadt, 1979) to coincide with <u>Kein Ort</u>,
     Wolf was clearly encouraging careful comparison of
     the original writings and her own 'epic' elaboration
     of them.

56. "Der Bestand des Irdischen sichern helfen", <u>Neue</u>
     <u>Zürcher Zeitung</u>, 18-19. October, 1980.

57. In an interview, <u>NDL</u>, 5/1979, 80.

58. "Reise zu Büchner", in <u>Fast die Wahrheit</u>, Berlin,
     1979, pp. 187-92.

59. <u>Fast die Wahrheit</u>, pp. 237, 241, 257, 260.

60. References in the text are to the Halle, 1981, edition.

61. See above, pp. 210-11.

62. See Forster, <u>Im Anblick des großen Rades: Schriften</u>
     <u>zur Revolution</u>, Darmstadt, 1981, pp. 222-3.

CONCLUSION

1. Republished in Hermlin, Aufsätze, Reportagen, Reden,
    Interviews (Ed. U. Hahn), Munich, 1980, pp. 123-8.
2. See, for example, Schlenstedt's Wirkungsästhetische
    Analysen, Berlin, 1979, Kaufmann's Versuch über das
    Erbe, Leipzig, 1980, or the collection of essays
    edited by Kaufmann, Tendenzen und Beispiele: Zur DDR-
    Literatur in den siebziger Jahren, Leipzig, 1981.
3. The two works are revealingly compared by Ian Wallace
    in his invaluable essay, "The Pyramid and the Mountain
    Volker Braun in the 1970s", in I. Wallace (Ed.), The
    GDR under Honecker 1971-81, Dundee, 1981, pp. 43-62.
4. West Germans relying on journals like Der Spiegel,
    Die Zeit and Stern for their view of East German
    literature since 1976 would have had their attention
    directed predominantly towards the new generation of
    exile authors and their conflicts with SED authority.
5. See, for example, Kurt Hager's two major speeches of
    1981, "Antwort auf Fragen der Kulturpolitik" and "Der
    X. Parteitag und die Kulturpolitik", in his Beiträge
    zur Kulturpolitik, Berlin, 1981, pp. 175-225 (pp.
    198-9, 216-7).
6. Kant's essays and speeches of the period 1976-80 are
    included in his Zu den Unterlagen, Berlin, 1981.
7. The term is central to Schlenstedt's Wirkungsästhetisch
    Analysen (see pp. 35-45).
8. Hermlin's equally representative rediscovery of the
    priority inherent in the phrase is recounted in his
    Abendlicht, Berlin (West), 1979, pp. 20-2.
9. Berliner Begegnung zur Friedensförderung: Protokolle
    des Schriftstellertreffens, Darmstadt, 1982, esp.
    pp. 38, 80-2, 101-3, 116-9, 159-61.
10. Hager, Beiträge zur Kulturpolitik, pp. 202-3, 196.

SELECT BIBLIOGRAPHY

Primary Works

Becher, Johannes R., Kleine Prosa, Berlin, 1974 (Gesammelte Werke, Vol. 9)
----, 'Levisite' oder Der einzig gerechte Krieg, Berlin, 1969 (Gesammelte Werke, Vol. 10)
----, Abschied/Wiederanders, Berlin, 1975 (Gesammelte Werke, Vol. 11)
----, Auf andere Art so große Hoffnung: Tagebuch 1950, Berlin, 1969 (Gesammelte Werke, Vol. 12)
----, Bemühungen, Berlin, 1973 (Gesammelte Werke, Vols. 13-14)
----, Von der Größe unserer Literatur: Reden und Aufsätze, Leipzig, 1971

Bobrowski, Johannes, "Boehlendorff", in Die Erzählungen, Berlin, 1979
----, Selbstzeugnisse und Beiträge über sein Werk, Berlin, 1967
----, Selbstzeugnisse und neue Beiträge über sein Werk, (ed. G. Rostin), Berlin, 1975

Braun, Volker, Unvollendete Geschichte, Frankfurt, 1977
----, Das ungezwungne Leben Kasts, Frankfurt, 1979
----, Es genügt nicht die einfache Wahrheit: Notate, Leipzig, 1975

Bräunig, Werner, Ein Kranich am Himmel: Unbekanntes und Bekanntes (ed. H. Sachs), Halle, 1981

Brecht, Bertolt, Gesammelte Werke, Frankfurt, 1967

Bruyn, Günter de, Der Hohlweg, Halle, 1963
----, Maskeraden, Halle, 1966
----, Buridans Esel, Halle, 1968
----, Preisverleihung, Halle, 1972
----, Das Leben des Jean Paul Friedrich Richter, Frankfurt, 1978
----, Märkische Forschungen, Halle, 1978

Claudius, Eduard, Menschen an unsrer Seite, Leipzig, 1971

Fries, Fritz Rudolf, Der Weg nach Oobliadooh, Frankfurt, 1966

248

Fühmann, Franz, "Kameraden", in Erzählungen 1955-1975,
    Rostock, 1977
----, Kabelkran und Blauer Peter, Rostock, 1961
----, Das Judenauto: Vierzehn Tage aus zwei Jahrzehnten,
    Zurich, 1968
----, 22 Tage oder Die Hälfte des Lebens, Frankfurt, 1973
----, Erfahrungen und Widersprüche: Versuche über Litera-
    tur, Rostock, 1975
----, Fräulein Veronika Paulmann ... oder Etwas über das
    Schauerliche bei ETA Hoffmann, Rostock, 1979
----, Vor Feuerschlünden: Erfahrung mit Georg Trakls
    Gedicht, Rostock, 1982

Hastedt, Regina, Die Tage mit Sepp Zach, Berlin, 1959

Hermlin, Stephan, Scardanelli, Berlin (West), 1970
----, Lektüre 1960-71, Berlin, 1979
----, Abendlicht, Berlin (West), 1979
----, Aufsätze, Reportagen, Reden, Interviews (ed. U. Hahn),
    Munich, 1980

Heym, Stefan, Fünf Tage im Juni, Munich, 1974

Jakobs, Karl-Heinz, Beschreibung eines Sommers, Berlin,
    1969

Kant, Hermann, Die Aula, Berlin, 1966
----, Das Impressum, Berlin, 1973
----, Der Aufenthalt, Berlin, 1977
----, Zu den Unterlagen: Publizistik 1957-1980, Berlin,
    1981

Kunert, Günter, Im Namen der Hüte, Munich, 1970
----, Tagträume in Berlin und andernorts: Kleine Prosa,
    Erzählungen, Aufsätze, Munich, 1972
----, Warum schreiben? Notizen zur Literatur, Munich, 1976

Marchwitza, Hans, Roheisen, Berlin, 1955

Müller, Heiner, "Der Bau", in Geschichten aus der Pro-
    duktion, Vol. 1, Berlin (West), 1974

Mundstock, Karl, "Bis zum letzten Mann", in H. Korall and
    W. Liersch (eds.), Erfahrungen: Erzähler der DDR,
    Halle, 1969

Neutsch, Erik, Spur der Steine, Halle, 1968
----, Die anderen und ich: Erzählungen, Halle, 1970
----, Tage unseres Lebens: Geschichten, Leipzig, 1973
----, Auf der Suche nach Gatt, Halle, 1973

Neutsch, Erik, Forster in Paris, Halle, 1981
----, Fast die Wahrheit: Ansichten zu Kunst und Literatur, Berlin, 1979

Noll, Dieter, Die Abenteuer des Werner Holt, Part I ("Roman einer Jugend"), Berlin, 1968
----, Die Abenteuer des Werner Holt, Part II ("Roman einer Heimkehr"), Berlin, 1974

Plenzdorf, Ulrich, Die neuen Leiden des jungen W., Rostock, 1973

Reimann, Brigitte, Ankunft im Alltag, Berlin, 1961
----, Die Geschwister, Berlin, 1963
----, Franziska Linkerhand, Berlin, 1974

Schulz, Max Walter, Wir sind nicht Staub im Wind, Halle, 1968
----, Triptychon mit sieben Brücken, Halle, 1974
----, Stegreif und Sattel: Anmerkungen zur Literatur und zum Tage, Halle, 1967

Seghers, Anna, Glauben an Irdisches: Essays aus vier Jahrzehnten, Leipzig, 1974

Strittmatter, Erwin, Der Wundertäter, Part I, Berlin, 1969
----, Ole Bienkopp, Berlin, 1968
----, Schulzenhofer Kramkalender, Berlin, 1969
----, Ein Dienstag im September: 16 Romane im Stenogramm, Berlin, 1970

Thürk, Harry, Die Stunde der toten Augen, Berlin, 1971

Wolf, Christa, Der geteilte Himmel, Halle, 1971
----, "Juninachmittag", in Gesammelte Erzählungen, Darmstadt, 1980
----, Nachdenken über Christa T., Neuwied, 1969
----, Unter den Linden: Drei unwahrscheinliche Geschichten, Berlin, 1974
----, Kindheitsmuster, Berlin, 1976
----, Kein Ort. Nirgends, Darmstadt, 1979
----, Lesen und Schreiben: Aufsätze, Berlin, 1972
----, Fortgesetzter Versuch: Aufsätze, Gespräche, Essays, Leipzig, 1979
----, (ed.), Karoline von Günderrode, Der Schatten eines Traumes: Gedichte, Prosa, Briefe, Zeugnisse von Zeitgenossen, Darmstadt, 1979

Wolf, Gerhard, Der arme Hölderlin, Darmstadt, 1982
----, Johannes Bobrowski (Schriftsteller der Gegenwart),

250

Berlin, 1967
Wolf, Gerhard, Beschreibung eines Zimmers: 15 Kapitel über Johannes Bobrowski, Berlin, 1973

Reference and Documentation

Behn, Manfred (ed.), Wirkungsgeschichte von Christa Wolfs 'Nachdenken über Christa T.', Königstein, 1978

Berliner Begegnung zur Friedensförderung: Protokoll des Schriftstellertreffens am 13./14. Dezember 1981, Darmstadt, 1982

Böttcher, Kurt et al. (eds.), Schriftsteller der DDR, (Meyers Taschenlexikon), Leipzig, 1975

Brenner, P.J. (ed.), Plenzdorfs 'Die neuen Leiden des jungen W.': Materialien, Frankfurt, 1982

Bundesministerium für innerdeutsche Beziehungen (ed.), DDR-Handbuch, Bonn, 1979

Deutscher Schriftstellerverband (ed.), IV. Deutscher Schriftstellerkongreß, Januar 1956: Protokoll, (2 vols.), Berlin, [1956]

----, V. Deutscher Schriftstellerkongreß vom 25. bis 27. Mai 1961: Referate und Diskussionsbeiträge, Berlin, [1961]

----, VI. Deutscher Schriftstellerkongreß vom 28. bis 30. Mai 1969: Protokoll, Berlin, [1969]

[renamed Schriftstellerverband der DDR], VII. Schriftstellerkongreß - 14. bis 16. November 1973: Protokoll, (2 vols.), Berlin, [1974]

----, Die Verantwortung des Schriftstellers in den Kämpfen unserer Zeit: Materialien zum VIII. Schriftstellerkongreß der DDR (Berlin 29.-31. Mai 1978), Munich, 1978

Greif zur Feder, Kumpel: Protokoll der Autorenkonferenz ... am 24.4.1959 im Kulturpalast des Elektrochemischen Kombinats Bitterfeld, Halle, 1959

Jarmatz, Klaus (ed.), Kritik in der Zeit: Der Sozialismus - seine Literatur - ihre Entwicklung: Dokumentation, Halle, 1970

Liersch, Werner (ed.), Was zählt, ist die Wahrheit: Briefe von Schriftstellern der DDR, Halle, 1975

Löffler, Anneliese (ed.), Auskünfte: Werkstattgespräche
mit DDR-Autoren, Berlin, 1974

Raabe, Paul (ed.), Expressionismus: Der Kampf um eine
literarische Bewegung, Munich, 1965

Raddatz, Fritz J. (ed.), Marxismus und Literatur: Eine
Dokumentation (3 vols.), Reinbek, 1969

Reso, Martin (ed.), 'Der geteilte Himmel' und seine
Kritiker: Dokumentation, Halle, 1965

Rüß, Gisela (ed.), Dokumente zur Kunst-, Literatur- und
Kulturpolitik der SED, Vol. 2 (1971-74), Stuttgart,
1976

Schmitt, Hans-Jürgen (ed.), Die Expressionismusdebatte:
Materialien zu einer marxistischen Realismuskon-
zeption, Frankfurt, 1973

Schneider, Gerhard (ed.), Eröffnungen: Schriftsteller über
ihr Erstlingswerk, Berlin, 1974

Schubbe, Elimar (ed.), Dokumente zur Kunst-, Literatur-
und Kulturpolitik der SED, Vol. 1 (1949-70),
Stuttgart, 1972

Walther, Joachim (ed.), Meinetwegen Schmetterlinge: Gespräche mit Schriftstellern, Berlin, 1973

Zur Tradition der deutschen sozialistischen Literatur:
Eine Auswahl von Dokumenten, (4 vols.), Berlin, 1979

Zweite Bitterfelder Konferenz: Protokoll der ... am 24.
und 25. April [1964] im Kulturpalast des Elektrochemischen Kombinats Bitterfeld abgehaltenen
Konferenz, Berlin, 1964

Periodicals

Basis: Jahrbuch für deutsche Gegenwartsliteratur, (ed.
R. Grimm and J. Hermand), Frankfurt, 1970-

Connaissance de la RDA, (ed. University of Paris VIII,
Vincennes), Paris, 1976-

Deutschland-Archiv: Zeitschrift für Fragen der DDR und der
Deutschlandpolitik, Cologne, 1968-

GDR Bulletin: Newsletter for Literature and Culture in the
GDR, (ed. P. Herminghouse), Washington University,
St. Louis, 1974-

GDR Monitor, (ed. I. Wallace), Dundee, 1979-

Jahrbuch zur Literatur in der DDR, (ed. P.G. Klussmann and
    H. Mohr), Bonn, 1980-

Die Linkskurve: Berlin 1929-32 (reprint), Glashütten im
    Taunus, 1970

Neue Deutsche Literatur (NDL), (ed. Schriftstellerverband
    der DDR), Berlin, 1953-

New German Critique, (ed. D. Bathrick et al.), Milwaukee,
    1973-

Sinn und Form (SF), (ed. Akademie der Künste der DDR),
    Berlin, 1949-

Sonntag: Die kulturpolitische Wochenzeitung, (ed. Kultur-
    bund zur demokratischen Erneuerung Deutschlands),
    Berlin, 1946-

Das Wort: Literarische Monatsschrift 1936-39 (reprint),
    Hilversum/Zurich, 1969

Weimarer Beiträge: Zeitschrift für Literaturwissenschaft,
    Ästhetik und Kulturtheorie (WB), Berlin/Weimar, 1955-

Secondary Literature

Abusch, Alexander, Humanismus und Realismus in der Litera-
    tur: Aufsätze, Leipzig, 1971

Adorno, Theodor W., Noten zur Literatur (3 vols.),
    Frankfurt, 1961

Bahro, Rudolf, Die Alternative: Zur Kritik des real
    existierenden Sozialismus, Cologne, 1977

Bartram, Graham, and Anthony Waine (eds.), Culture and
    Society in the GDR (GDR Monitor Special Series
    No. 2), Dundee, 1984

Batt, Kurt, Widerspruch und Übereinkunft: Aufsätze zur
    Literatur, Leipzig, 1978

Benjamin, Walter, Versuche über Brecht, Frankfurt, 1966
----, Lesezeichen: Schriften zur deutschsprachigen Litera-
    tur, (ed. G. Seidel), Leipzig, 1970

Bock, Sigrid, and M. Hahn (eds.), Erfahrung Exil: Anti-
    faschistische Romane 1933-45, Berlin, 1979

Brettschneider, Werner, Zwischen literarischer Autonomie
    und Staatsdienst: Die Literatur der DDR, Berlin
    (West), 1972

Deutsche Akademie der Künste (ed.), Sinn und Form: Zweites Sonderheft Johannes R. Becher, Berlin, [1959]

Diersch, M., and W. Hartinger (eds.), Literatur und Geschichtsbewußtsein: Entwicklungstendenzen der DDR-Literatur in den sechziger und siebziger Jahren, Berlin, 1976

Eifler, Margret, Dialektische Dynamik: Kulturpolitik und Ästhetik im Gegenwartsroman der DDR, Bonn, 1976

Einhorn, Barbara, Der Roman in der DDR 1949-69, Kronberg, 1978

Emmerich, Wolfgang, Kleine Literaturgeschichte der DDR, Darmstadt, 1981

Feitknecht, Thomas, Die sozialistische Heimat: Zum Selbstverständnis neuerer DDR-Romane, Berne, 1971

Fischer, Ernst, Kunst und Koexistenz: Beitrag zu einer modernen marxistischen Ästhetik, Reinbek, 1966

Franke, Konrad, Die Literatur der DDR, Munich, 1971

Gallas, Helga, Marxistische Literaturtheorie: Kontroversen im Bund proletarisch-revolutionärer Schriftsteller, Neuwied, 1971

Geerdts, Hans-Jürgen (ed.), Literatur der DDR in Einzeldarstellungen, Stuttgart, 1972

Gerlach, Ingeborg, Bitterfeld: Arbeiterliteratur und Literatur der Arbeitswelt in der DDR, Kronberg, 1974

Greiner, Bernhard, Von der Allegorie zur Idylle: Die Literatur der Arbeitswelt in der DDR, Heidelberg, 1974

Haase, Horst, et al. (eds.), Geschichte der Literatur der DDR, Berlin, 1976

Haase, Horst, Johannes R. Becher (Schriftsteller der Gegenwart), Berlin, 1981

Hager, Kurt, Beiträge zur Kulturpolitik: Reden und Aufsätze 1972 bis 1981, Berlin, 1981

Havemann, Robert, Dialektik ohne Dogma? Naturwissenschaft und Weltanschauung, Reinbek, 1971
----, Fragen, Antworten, Fragen: Aus der Biographie eines deutschen Marxisten, Reinbek, 1972

Hohendahl, Peter-Uwe, and Patricia Herminghouse (eds.), Literatur und Literaturtheorie in der DDR, Frankfurt, 1976

Honecker, Erich, Bericht des Politbüros an die 11. Tagung des Zentralkomitees der SED, Berlin, 1966

Honecker, Erich, Die Kulturpolitik unserer Partei wird erfolgreich verwirklicht, Berlin, 1982

Hoogeveen, Jos, and Gerd Labroisse (eds.), DDR-Roman und Literaturgesellschaft, Amsterdam, 1981

Hutchinson, Peter, Literary Presentations of Divided Germany: The Development of a Central Theme in East German Fiction 1945-70, Cambridge, 1977

Jäckel, Günter, and Ursula Roisch, Große Form in kleiner Form: Zur sozialistischen Kurzgeschichte, Halle, 1974

Jäger, Manfred, Sozialliteraten: Funktion und Selbstverständnis der Schriftsteller in der DDR, Düsseldorf, 1973

Kaufmann, Eva, and Hans Kaufmann (eds.), Erwartung und Angebot: Studien zum gegenwärtigen Verhältnis von Literatur und Gesellschaft in der DDR, Berlin, 1975

Kaufmann, Hans, Versuch über das Erbe, Leipzig, 1980
----, (ed.), Tendenzen und Beispiele: DDR-Literatur in den siebziger Jahren, Leipzig, 1981

Lamers, K. (ed.), Die deutsche Frage im Spiegel der Literatur, Stuttgart, 1978

Leistner, Bernd, Unruhe um einen Klassiker: Zum Goethe-Bezug in der neueren DDR-Literatur, Halle, 1978

Löwy, Michael, Georg Lukács: From Romanticism to Bolschevism, London, 1979

Lukács, Georg, Schicksalswende: Beiträge zu einer neuen deutschen Ideologie, Berlin, 1948
----, Essays über Realismus (Werke, Vol. 4), Neuwied, 1971
----, Der russische Realismus in der Weltliteratur (Werke, Vol. 5), Neuwied, 1964
----, Deutsche Literatur in zwei Jahrhunderten (Werke, Vol. 7), Neuwied, 1964
----, Skizze zu einer Geschichte der neueren deutschen Literatur, Darmstadt, 1975
----, Gelebtes Denken: Eine Autobiographie im Dialog, Frankfurt, 1981

Mayer, Hans, Deutsche Literatur und Weltliteratur: Reden und Aufsätze, Berlin, 1957
----, Zur deutschen Literatur der Zeit: Zusammenhänge, Schriftsteller, Bücher, Reinbek, 1967
----, "DDR 1956: Tauwetter, das keines war", Frankfurter Hefte 11-12, 1976

Mittenzwei, Werner and Reinhard Weisbach (eds.), Revolution und Literatur, Leipzig, 1972

Mittenzwei, Werner (ed.), Dialog und Kontroverse mit
    Georg Lukács: Der Methodenstreit deutscher
    sozialistischer Schriftsteller, Leipzig, 1975
----, Der Realismus-Streit um Brecht, Berlin, 1978

Nalewski, Horst, and Klaus Schuhmann (eds.), Selbster-
    fahrung als Welterfahrung: DDR-Literatur in den
    siebziger Jahren, Berlin, 1981

Pascal, Roy, The German Novel, London, 1965
----, Design and Truth in Autobiography, London, 1960
----, From Naturalism to Expressionism: German Literature
    and Society 1880-1918, London, 1973
----, Culture and the Division of Labour (Occasional
    Papers in German Studies, No. 5), University of
    Warwick, 1974
----, The Dual Voice: Free indirect Speech and its Func-
    tioning in the nineteenth century European Novel,
    Manchester, 1977
----, "Büchner's 'Lenz' - Style and Message", Oxford
    German Studies, Vol. 9, 1978

Pracht, Erwin, and Werner Neubert, Sozialistischer Realis-
    mus: Positionen, Probleme, Perspektiven, Berlin,
    1970

Raddatz, Fritz J., Traditionen und Tendenzen: Materialien
    zur Literatur der DDR, Frankfurt, 1972

Reich-Ranicki, Marcel, Deutsche Literatur in West und Ost:
    Prosa seit 1945, Munich, 1963
----, Zur Literatur der DDR, Munich, 1974

Rühle, Jürgen, Literatur und Revolution: Der Schriftsteller
    und der Kommunismus, Munich, 1963

Sauer, Klaus (ed.), Christa Wolf: Materialienbuch,
    Darmstadt, 1979

Schlenstedt, Dieter, "Ankunft und Anspruch: Zum neueren
    Roman in der DDR", Sinn und Form 3/1966
----, Wirkungsästhetische Analysen: Poetologie und Prosa
    in der neueren DDR-Literatur, Berlin, 1979

Schmitt, Hans-Jürgen (ed.), Einführung in Theorie,
    Geschichte und Funktion der DDR-Literatur, Stuttgart,
    1975
Silbermann, Marc, Literature of the Working World: A Study
    of the Industrial Novel in East Germany, Berne, 1976

Stephan, Alexander, Christa Wolf, Munich, 1979

Thomas, R. Hinton, and Wilfried van der Will, The German
    Novel and the Affluent Society, Manchester, 1968

Thomas, R, Hinton, "Das Ich und die Welt: Expressionismus und Gesellschaft", in W. Rothe (ed.), Expressionismus als Literatur, Berne, 1969

---- and Keith Bullivant, Literature in Upheaval: West German Writers and the Challenge of the 1960s, Manchester, 1974

Töpelmann, Sigrid, Autoren, Figuren, Entwicklungen: Zur erzählenden Literatur in der DDR, Berlin, 1975

Trommler, Frank, "Von Stalin zu Hölderlin: Über den Entwicklungsroman in der DDR", in Basis, Vol. 2, 1971

----, Sozialistische Literatur in Deutschland: Ein historischer Überblick, Stuttgart, 1976

Wallace, Ian (ed.), The GDR under Honecker 1971-1981 (GDR Monitor Special Series No. 1), Dundee, 1981

Weimann, Robert, Kunstensemble und Öffentlichkeit, Halle, 1982

Williams, Raymond, The Country and the City, London, 1973

CHRONOLOGY

1933	Hitler's rise to power: mass emigration of German intellectuals - Lukács and leading KPD authors (including Becher) to USSR, the majority (including Brecht and Seghers) elsewhere in Europe.
1934	First Soviet Writers' Congress (Zhdanov codifies Socialist Realism, Becher's speech "Das große Bündnis"). Lukács: "Größe und Verfall des Expressionismus".
1935	Comintern adopts Popular Front strategy. Congress for the Defence of Culture in Paris (Becher, Seghers, Brecht amongst speakers). Lukács: "Hölderlins 'Hyperion'".
1936	(-38) Height of Stalin's purges in USSR. Lukács: "Wilhelm Meisters Lehrjahre".
1937	(-38) 'Expressionism Debate'.
1938	Brecht's critical essays on Lukács (published 1967). Becher completes Abschied (published Moscow 1940).
1939	(-41) Soviet-German non-aggression pact. Outbreak of Second World War. Lukács/Seghers correspondence published. Lukács: "Gottfried Keller".
1941	Seghers in Mexico, Brecht in USA; Lukács imprisoned for two months. Lukács: "J.R. Bechers 'Abschied'".
1942	(-45) Soviet Union and USA fully involved in the World War; opportunities for publications (except of a propagandist nature) by German exiles very restricted.
1945	End of Second World War: division of Germany includes establishment of Soviet Zone of Occupation. Becher made president of 'Kulturbund zur demokratischen Erneuerung Deutschlands'. Lukács: Skizze einer Geschichte der neueren deutschen Literatur (in two parts, Aufbau Verlag). Becher: Abschied (Aufbau).
1946	Creation of SED (Ulbricht deputy chairman, from 1950 general secretary).
1947	First German Writers' Congress. Seghers returns to Soviet Zone.

1948	Height of 'Cold War'. Brecht returns to Soviet Zone.
1949	Establishment of German Democratic Republic. 'Goethe Year' celebrations. Brecht's 'Berliner Ensemble' created.
1950	Second Writers' Congress (formation of Writers' Union, with Seghers as president - until 1978). Ideological emphasis on 'socialist reportage'.
1951	SED campaign against 'formalism'. First 'Aufbauroman' - Claudius: Menschen an unsrer Seite. Becher: Auf andere Art so große Hoffnung.
1952	Third Writers' Congress. Socialist Realism deemed obligatory. (-57) Becher: Bemühungen (in 4 vols.).
1953	Death of Stalin. 'Workers' Rising' of 17. June.
1954	Becher made Minister of Culture .
1955	Cultural 'Thaw'. Crisis of 'Aufbauroman' following Marchwitza's Roheisen. New 'war literature' initiated by Fühmann's Kameraden.
1956	Twentieth Congress of Soviet CP (Khrushchev reveals crimes of Stalin era). Fourth Writers' Congress (Becher's speech: "Von der Größe unserer Literatur"). Lukács' lectures: Die Gegenwartsbedeutung des kritischen Realismus (published in West 1958). Death of Brecht. Suppression of 'revisionist' regime in Hungary (Lukács officially discredited). (-57) Becher working at Wiederanders (fragment published 1975).
1957	SED Cultural Conference reimposes rigid control. Kurella's dominant position as secretary to Politbüro's 'Cultural Commission' (until 1963); endorses idea of 'Entwicklungsroman' based on war-experience.
1958	SED Party Conference proclaims 'sozialistische Kulturrevolution'. Death of Becher.
1959	First Bitterfeld Conference (exodus of young writers into industrial world).

259

1960   Noll: <u>Die Abenteuer des Werner Holt</u> (Part 1)

1961   Fifth Writers' Congress (Seghers' speech "Die
       Tiefe und Breite in der Literatur").
       First wave of 'Bitterfelder Weg' fiction (Jakobs,
       Fühmann, Neutsch, Reimann).
       Erection of Berlin Wall.

1962   Fühmann: <u>Das Judenauto</u> .
       Schulz: <u>Wir sind nicht Staub im Wind</u>.

1963   SED Party Conference introduces 'New Economic
       System'.
       Hager responsible for cultural policy in Polit-
       büro (as head of 'Ideological Commission').
       De Bruyn: <u>Der Hohlweg</u>.
       Noll: <u>Die Abenteuer des Werner Holt</u> (Part 2).
       Reimann: <u>Die Geschwister</u>.
       Wolf: <u>Der geteilte Himmel</u>.

1964   Second Bitterfeld Conference (background of
       public debate on <u>Der geteilte Himmel</u> and
       Strittmatter's <u>Ole Bienkopp</u>).
       Neutsch: <u>Spur der Steine</u>.
       Kant: <u>Die Aula</u> serialised (book published 1965).

1965   Seghers emphasises 'anti-classical' cultural
       heritage.
       Bobrowski: <u>Boehlendorff und Mäusefest</u> (stories).
       Eleventh Plenum of SED Central Committee condemns
       'Popularisierung von Schwierigkeiten'.
       (-68) Experimentation with 'shorter prose forms'
       (Kunert, Strittmatter, de Bruyn, Wolf).

1967   Brecht: <u>Gesammelte Werke</u> published in 20 vols.
       Wolf: <u>Juninachmittag</u>.

1968   'Prague Spring'.
       Wolf's essays "Lesen und Schreiben" (published
       1972) and "Glauben an Irdisches".
       De Bruyn: <u>Buridans Esel</u>
       Wolf: <u>Nachdenken über Christa T</u>. (provokes
       intense controversy).

1969   Sixth Writers' Congress (main speech by Schulz).
       Kant: <u>Das Impressum</u> partly serialised (published
       1972).

1970   (-72) 'Normalisation' of relations between GDR
       and FRG.
       Hermlin: <u>Scardanelli</u>.

1971   Honecker replaces Ulbricht as first secretary
       of SED.
       Fourth Plenum of Central Committee (Honecker's

'no taboos' speech).
Death of Lukács.

1972   Plenzdorf: <u>Die neuen Leiden des jungen W.</u> (in <u>Sinn und Form</u>) - stage version performed throughout GDR (book edition and major public debate 1973).
G. Wolf: <u>Der arme Hölderlin</u>.

1973   Seventh Writers' Congress (main speech by Kant; official abandonment of 'Bitterfelder Weg'). Spirit of open, self-critical discussion.

1974   Reimann: <u>Franziska Linkerhand</u> published posthumously.

1975   Braun: <u>Unvollendete Geschichte</u> (in <u>Sinn und Form</u>).

1976   Authors' protest against expatriation of Biermann. Wolf: <u>Kindheitsmuster</u>.

1977   (-81) Beginnings of 'new exile' period: many authors in West on long-term visas (Kunert, Becker, Schneider, Jakobs).

1978   Eighth Writers' Congress (main speech by Kant, who succeeds Seghers as president of Writers' Union; most significant authors not present).

1979   Wolf: <u>Kein Ort. Nirgends</u>.
Hermlin: <u>Abendlicht</u>.

1980   (-81) Political and cultural liberalisation in Poland

1981   Neutsch: <u>Forster in Paris</u>
'Begegnung zur Friedensförderung' organised by Hermlin.

INDEX